# Rethinking School Health

# Rethinking School Health

*A Key Component of Education for All*

Donald Bundy

**THE WORLD BANK**
**Washington, D.C.**

ISBN: 978-0-8213-7907-3
eISBN: 978-0-8213-8397-1
DOI: 10.1596/978-0-8213-7907-3

Library of Congress Cataloging-in-Publication Data
Rethinking school health : a key component of education for all / Donald Bundy, editor.
    p. cm. — (Directions in development)
  Includes bibliographical references.
  ISBN 978-0-8213-7907-3 (alk. paper) — ISBN 978-0-8213-8397-1
  1. School health services—United States—Evaluation. 2. School health services—United
States—Planning. 3. School children—Health and hygiene—United States. 4. School
hygiene—United States. I. Bundy, Donald. II. World Bank.
  LB3409.U5S355 2011
  371.7'1—dc22

                                                                              2010044310

Cover photo: Lesley Drake/Deworm the World
Cover design: Quantum Think

# Contents

## Figures

## Maps

## Tables

# Foreword

Education is one of the most important drivers of the development of individuals and societies. It not only has powerful implications for the creation of human capacity, but also helps people realize their full potential and expand their connections with the world. Economic analyses repeatedly demonstrate that education gives a high economic return within the life-span of an individual and is a key factor underlying the economic growth of nations. Viewed from these perspectives, the decision at the turn of the millennium of governments and development partners to pursue the goal of Education for All (EFA) was not only an important contribution to one sector, but the launch of an endeavor with major implications for the future of humanity.

The early perception of the goal of Education for All was that all children should have access to education—every child should be able to exercise the right to go to school. This limited goal soon broadened to address the quality of the education that a child received at school and the factors that ensured the child was able to stay in school long enough to learn enough. These additional objectives have expanded the goal of EFA, so that it now aims to ensure that every child has the opportunity to complete an education of good quality, although definitions of quality and completeness remain under discussion.

This book, aptly entitled *Rethinking School Health: A Key Component of Education for All*, takes the goal of EFA further. It pursues modern good practice in education by exploring a child-centered approach to education, asking the question, given equal opportunities to access education, does every child have an equal chance to learn? The evidence shows that the answer is a resounding no—poor children, because they suffer most from ill health and malnutrition, are less able to attend and complete school, and to learn while there. But the positive experience of school health and school feeding programs in low-income countries over the past decade shows that carefully designed programs can provide a cost-effective solution to this problem. Moreover, these programs are intrinsically pro-poor, as their greatest benefits are for the poor, the sick, and the hungry.

The question now is not whether school health and school feeding programs are necessary to EFA, but how they can be implemented at meaningful scale in the poorest countries, which need them the most. This is the challenge that we now face, and this book provides an important resource for identifying the correct responses to it.

Elizabeth King
Director, Education
The World Bank

Qian Tang
Assistant Director-
    General for Education
UNESCO

Susan Durston
Associate Director
Education Programmes
UNICEF

# About the Book

## The 9th Meeting of the High Level Group for Education for All, Addis Ababa, Ethiopia, February 22, 2010

This book was written in response to a request from the International Advisory Panel (IAP) of Education for All (EFA). It was submitted in draft form to the 9th Meeting of the High Level Group for Education for All, held at the African Union Headquarters in Addis Ababa on February 22, 2010.

The High Level Group for EFA was established at the Global Education Forum in Dakar in April 2000 to provide continuing oversight of global progress toward EFA goals by 2015. The Group has met every year since 2000. The cosponsoring organizations of the High Level Group are the United Nations Educational, Scientific and Cultural Organization (UNESCO), United Nations Children's Fund (UNICEF), United Nations Population Fund (UNFPA), United Nations Development Program (UNDP), and the World Bank. The IAP comprises representatives of developing countries, donors, multilateral agencies, civil society, and the private sector. It was created in 2007 to advise UNESCO on achieving maximum coherence and political momentum within the EFA movement. Membership of the panel has recently been expanded to ensure greater representation from counties of the South.

The conference version of this book was presented to the High Level Group during the School Health and Nutrition theme of the 9th Meeting. It was explained with the help of a short documentary entitled "Health, Equity, and Education for All: How School Health and School Feeding Programs Are Leveling the Playing Field."[1] The issues raised by the report were discussed during the subsequent two days of the 9th Meeting, and the conclusions and recommendations of the group were included in the formal Communique.

The following paragraphs on school health and nutrition are excerpts from the Communique of the 9th Meeting of February 24, 2010:

- Barriers of cost, distance, and discrimination continue to deter millions of poor and marginalized children from attending school.
- In addition, poor health, malnutrition and diseases . . . affecting hundreds of millions of poor children . . . reduce enrollment, increase absenteeism and diminish cognitive development and learning.
- More and more countries are implementing cost-effective, evidence-based policies and interventions to achieve EFA . . . including school fee abolition, ECD programs, targeted school health and feeding programs.
- Action Point No 1: We call upon Education for All Partners to intensify efforts to support initiatives targeted at the most marginalized, such as cash transfers, school health and school feeding, scholarships, and gender-specific-interventions.
- Action Point No 2: We recommend governments to ensure that their education policies, strategic planning, and practice . . . include all children in education . . . enable all marginalized populations to enter, complete, and benefit from meaningful learning.

## Note

1. See the film on the YouTube website: http://www.youtube.com/watch?v=RcIss0w_50c (accessed August 2010).

# Acknowledgments

This document was prepared for the School Health and Nutrition theme of the Education for All (EFA) High Level Meeting in Addis Ababa, Ethiopia, in February 2010. Preparation of the document was led by the World Bank in response to a request from the International Advisory Panel (IAP) of EFA. The cosponsoring organizations of the EFA High Level Meetings are the United Nations Educational, Scientific and Cultural Organization (UNESCO), the United Nations Children's Fund (UNICEF), the United Nations Population Fund (UNFPA), the United Nations Development Programme (UNDP), and the World Bank. The IAP comprises representatives of developing countries, donors, multilateral agencies, civil society, and the private sector. It was created in 2007 to advise UNESCO on achieving maximum coherence and political momentum within the EFA movement. Membership of the panel has recently been expanded to ensure greater representation from counties of the South.

This document was conceived and edited by Donald Bundy (World Bank), with logistical support from Kristie Neeser (Partnership for Child Development) during the writing phase, and from Veronica Grigera, Fahma Nur, and Tara O'Connell (World Bank) during production. Technical contributions were requested and received from 63 contributors, representing

25 country school health teams, development partners, and civil society organizations (see list of contributors).

The peer reviewers for the document were Harold Alderman, Luis Benveniste, and Damien de Walque of the World Bank; Robert Prouty of the Education For All–Fast Track Initiative Secretariat; and Daniel Gilligan of the International Food Policy Research Institute.

Guidance for the preparation of the document, to be published as part of the Directions in Development Series, was led by the Chief Economist of the Human Development Network of the World Bank, Ariel Fiszbein, with the Education Director of the World Bank, Elizabeth King, and the Education Sector Manager, Robin Horn. The document also benefited from specific guidance from the World Bank Human Development team for the Africa Region; especially the Health, Nutrition, and Population Sector Manager, Eva Jarawan; and the Education Sector Manager, Christopher Thomas.

# Contributors

Dan Abbott, Specialist for School Health and Nutrition, International Programs, Save the Children USA, Washington, DC, United States

Emmanuelle Abrioux, Life Skills Based Education, UNICEF East Asia and the Pacific, Bangkok, Thailand

Amrita Ahuja, Giorgio Ruffolo Postdoctoral Fellow in Sustainability Science, Kennedy School of Government, Harvard, Massachusetts, United States

Rina Arlianti, Education and Training Consultant, Jakarta, Indonesia

Jenelle Babb, UNESCO Regional Office of the Caribbean, Kingston, Jamaica

Simon Baker, Regional HIV/AIDS Adviser, UNESCO Asia-Pacific Regional Bureau for Education, Bangkok, Thailand

Koli Banik, Education Specialist, Education for All–Fast Track Initiative Secretariat, Washington, DC, United States

Michael Beasley, Director, Partnership for Child Development, Imperial College, London, United Kingdom

Habib Benzian, Founding Director, The Health Bureau, Berlin, Germany

Jeff Berens, East Africa Director, Rural Water Project, Innovations for Poverty Action, Busia, Kenya

Carla Bertoncino, Human Development Economist, Africa Education Sector, The World Bank, Washington, DC, United States

Simon Brooker, KEMRI-Wellcome Trust Research Programme, Nairobi, Kenya

Donald Bundy, Lead Health and Education Specialist, Human Development Network, The World Bank, Washington, DC, United States

Carmen Burbano, Edward S. Mason Fellow, Mid-career Master in Public Administration Candidate, John F. Kennedy School of Government, Harvard University, Massachusetts, United States

Simon Bush, Director, African Alliances and Advocacy, Sightsavers International, Accra, Ghana

Balla Camara, Ministry of Education, Conakry, Guinea

Christopher Castle, HIV Team, UNESCO, Paris, France

Christophe Cornu, EDUCAIDS and Country Implementation Team Leader, Section on HIV and AIDS, Division for the Coordination of UN Priorities in Education, UNESCO, Paris, France

David Crosby, Centre for Vision in the Developing World, St. Catherine's College, Oxford, United Kingdom

Nilanthi de Silva, Professor of Medical Parasitology, Faculty of Medicine, University of Kelaniya, Ragama, Sri Lanka

Joy Del Rosso, Senior Nutrition Adviser, The Manoff Group, Washington, DC, United States

Angela Demas, Senior Education Specialist, Latin America and the Caribbean Region, The World Bank, Washington, DC, United States

Ruth Dixon, Programme Manager, Partnership for Child Development, Imperial College, London, United Kingdom

Lesley Drake, Executive Director, Deworm the World, Washington, DC, United States

Roshini Ebenezer, Monitoring and Evaluation Consultant, Harvard University, Massachusetts, United States

Maria-Luisa Escobar, Lead Health Economist and Program Leader, Health Systems, World Bank Institute, The World Bank, Washington, DC, United States

Meenakshi Fernandes, Associate Policy Analyst, RAND, Washington, DC, United States

Alissa Fishbane, Deputy Director, Deworm the World, Washington, DC, United States

Nora Fyles, Strategic Policy and Performance Branch, Canadian International Development Agency, Gatineau, Canada

Marito Garcia, Lead Social Protection Specialist, Africa Social Protection Sector, The World Bank, Washington, DC, United States

Aulo Gelli, Partnership for Child Development, Imperial College, London, United Kingdom

Rachel Glennerster, Executive Director, Abdul Latif Jameel Poverty Action Lab, Department of Economics, Massachusetts Institute of Technology, Massachusetts, United States

Natasha Graham, Education for All–Fast Track Initiative Secretariat, Washington, DC, United States

Dominic Haslam, Head, Government Relations, Sightsavers International, London, United Kingdom

Anna Maria Hoffmann, Education Specialist, HIV/AIDS and Life Skills Education, Education Section, UNICEF, New York, United States

Arlene Husbands, Caribbean Program Coordinator, Education Development Center, Bridgetown, Barbados

Ziauddin Hyder, Senior Nutrition Specialist, Africa Health, Nutrition, and Population, The World Bank, Washington, DC, United States

Matthew Jukes, Assistant Professor, Comparative Education, Harvard University, Massachusetts, United States

Aggrey Kibenge, Ministry of Education and Sports, Kampala, Uganda

Michael Kremer, Gates Professor of Developing Societies, Department of Economics, Harvard University, Massachusetts, United States

Seunghee F. Lee, Senior Director for School Health and Nutrition, International Programs, Save the Children USA, Washington, DC, United States

Karen Levy, Regional Director, Africa, Deworm the World, Nairobi, Kenya

Graeme MacKenzie, Adlens Ltd., Oxford, United Kingdom

Venkatesh Mannar, President, The Micronutrient Initiative, Ottawa, Canada

Amicoleh Mbeye, Ministry of Education and Sports, Banjul, The Gambia

Michael Mills, Lead Economist, Africa Health, Nutrition, and Population, The World Bank, Nairobi, Kenya

Hasan Minto, Senior Adviser, Refractive Error, Sightsavers International, Islamabad, Pakistan

Bella Monse, CEO, Fit for School, Manila, Philippines

Antonio Montresor, Preventive Chemotherapy and Transmission Control, Department of Control of Neglected Tropical Diseases, WHO, Geneva, Switzerland

Aynsley Morris, Communications Manager, The Micronutrient Initiative, Ottawa, Canada

Sophie Naudeau, Senior Education Specialist, Africa Education Sector, The World Bank, Washington, DC, United States

Kristie Neeser, Home Grown School Feeding Programme Coordinator, Partnership for Child Development, Imperial College, London, United Kingdom

Lynnette Neufeld, Chief Technical Adviser, The Micronutrient Initiative, Ottawa, Canada

Michelle Neuman, Human Development Specialist, Africa Education Sector, The World Bank, Washington, DC, United States

Tara O'Connell, Operations Officer, School Health, Nutrition, School Feeding, and HIV, The World Bank, Washington, DC, United States

Karen Peffley, Operations Analyst, The World Bank, Washington, DC, United States

Isabel Rocha Pimenta, Health Sector Specialist, The World Bank, Washington, DC, United States

Aleksandra Posarac, Lead Human Development Economist, The World Bank, Washington, DC, United States

Robert Prouty, Head, Education for All–Fast Track Initiative Secretariat, Washington, DC, United States

Hnin Hnin Pyne, Senior Health Specialist, Water and Sanitation Program, The World Bank, Washington, DC, United States

Claire Risley, Research Associate/Manager, Partnership for Child Development, Imperial College, London, United Kingdom

Natalie Roschnik, Adviser for School Health and Nutrition, International Programs, Save the Children USA, Washington, DC, United States

Delphine Sanglan, Senior Professional Assistant, Solidarity and Development Unit, Education International, Brussels, Belgium

Justine Sass, UNESCO, Paris, France

Malick Sembene, Ministry of Education, Dakar, Senegal

Katri Tala, Prevention, Treatment and Rehabilitation Unit, UNODC, Vienna, Austria

Kwok-Cho Tang, Department of Chronic Diseases and Health Promotion, WHO, Geneva, Switzerland

Andy Tembon, Regional Coordinator, Africa Health, Nutrition, and Population, The World Bank, Washington, DC, United States

Alexandria Valerio, Lead Education Specialist, Education Sector, Human Development Network, The World Bank, Washington, DC, United States

Mohini Venkatesh, Specialist for School Health and Nutrition, International Programs, Save the Children USA, Washington, DC, United States

Nancy Walters, Chief, School Feeding Policy Unit, World Food Programme, Rome, Italy

Annie S. Wesley, Senior Program Specialist, The Micronutrient Initiative, Ottawa, Canada

Ekua Yankah, Education Sector, Division for the Coordination of UN Priorities in Education, UNESCO, Paris, France

Stephanie Simmons Zuilkowski, Doctoral Candidate, Graduate School of Education, Harvard University, Massachusetts, United States

# Abbreviations

| | |
|---|---|
| ACT | artemisinin-based combination therapy |
| ACU | AIDS Control Unit, Ministry of Education, Kenya |
| ADEA | Association for the Development of Education in Africa |
| AIDS | acquired immune deficiency syndrome |
| ARC | Arab Resource Collective |
| ARI | acute respiratory infection |
| ART | antiretroviral therapy |
| BIAS | *Bulan Imunisasi Anak Sekolah*, Indonesia |
| BMI | body mass index |
| BOS | *Bantuan Operasional Sekolah*, Indonesia |
| CARICOM | Caribbean Community |
| CBO | community-based organization |
| CCT | conditional cash transfer |
| CF | Catalytic Fund |
| CFS | Child Friendly School |
| CSHS | Clean, Safe, and Healthy Schools, Peru |
| CIDA | Canadian International Development Agency |
| CRC | Convention on the Rights of the Child |
| DAC | Development Assistance Committee |
| DALYs | disability-adjusted life years |

| | |
|---|---|
| DFID | Department for International Development, United Kingdom |
| DFS | double-fortified salt |
| DtW | Deworm the World |
| ECD | early child development |
| ECOWAS | Economic Community of West African States |
| EDC | Education Development Center |
| EDUCAIDS | Global Initiative on Education and HIV&AIDS (led by UNESCO) |
| EduCan | Education Sector School Health and HIV/AIDS Coordinator Network of the Caribbean |
| EFA | Education for All |
| EFA-FTI | Education for All–Fast Track Initiative |
| EI | Education International |
| EMIS | education management information system |
| EPDF | Education Program Development Fund, EFA-FTI |
| ESACIPAC | Eastern and Southern Africa Centre of International Parasite Control, Kenya Medical Research Institute |
| ESP | education sector plan |
| FAO | Food and Agriculture Organization of the United Nations |
| FBO | faith-based organization |
| FCI | Food Corporation of India |
| FFS | Fit for School Program, Philippines |
| FHB | Family Health Bureau, Ministry of Health, Sri Lanka |
| FRESH | Focusing Resources on Effective School Health |
| FTI | Fast Track Initiative |
| GMSR | Greater Mekong Subregion |
| GSHS | Global School-Based Student Health Survey |
| GTZ | Gesellschaft für Technische Zusammenarbeit |
| HAS | Health Action Schools |
| Hb | hemoglobin |
| HGSF | home-grown school feeding |
| HIV | human immunodeficiency virus |
| HIV/AIDS | human immunodeficiency virus/acquired immune deficiency syndrome |
| HPS | Health Promoting Schools |
| HW | hand washing |
| IAP | International Advisory Panel |
| IATT | Inter-Agency Task Team for HIV and Education |

| | |
|---|---|
| INGO | international nongovernmental organization |
| IOTF | International Obesity Taskforce |
| IP | investment program |
| IPA | Innovations for Poverty Action |
| IPT | intermittent preventive treatment |
| IQ | intelligence quotient |
| JCSH | (Pan-Canadian) Joint Consortium for School Health |
| JICA | Japan International Cooperation Agency |
| KEMRI | Kenya Medical Research Institute |
| KESSP | Kenya Education Sector Support Programme |
| LEG | local education group, EFA-FTI |
| LLIN | long-lasting insecticide-treated net |
| M&E | monitoring and evaluation |
| MCH | maternal and child health |
| MICS | Multi Indicator Cluster Survey |
| MDG | Millennium Development Goal |
| MINEDU | Ministry of Education, Peru |
| MoE | ministry of education |
| MoH | ministry of health |
| MONE | Ministry of National Education, Indonesia |
| MOU | memorandum of understanding |
| NAC | National AIDS Council |
| NCD | noncommunicable disease |
| NGO | nongovernmental organization |
| OECD | Organisation for Economic Co-operation and Development |
| PCD | Partnership for Child Development |
| PNCS | National School Feeding Program, Haiti |
| PPP | public-private partnership |
| PSABH | Primary School Action for Better Health Program, Kenya |
| PTA | parent-teacher association |
| PTR | pupil-teacher ratio |
| SD | standard deviation |
| SFP | school feeding program |
| SHN | school health and nutrition |
| SHPP | School Health Promotion Program, Sri Lanka |
| SISWA | System Improvement through Sector Wide Approaches |
| SPM | *Standar Pelayanan Minimal*, Indonesia |
| STH | soil-transmitted helminth |

| | |
|---|---|
| STI | sexually transmitted infection |
| SWAp | sectorwide approach |
| TB | tuberculosis |
| TQSI | Ten Question Screening Instrument |
| UKS | *Usaha Kesehatan Sekolah*, Indonesia |
| UN | United Nations |
| UNAIDS | Joint United Nations Programme on HIV/AIDS |
| UNDP | United Nations Development Programme |
| UNESCO | United Nations Educational, Scientific and Cultural Organization |
| UNFPA | United Nations Population Fund |
| UNGEI | United Nations Girls' Education Initiative |
| UNICEF | United Nations Children's Fund |
| UNODC | United Nations Office on Drugs and Crime |
| USAID | U.S. Agency for International Development |
| WFP | World Food Programme |
| WHO | World Health Organization |
| WIFS | weekly iron–folic acid supplementation |

*All dollar amounts are U.S. dollars unless otherwise indicated.*

# Executive Summary

The provision of quality schools, textbooks, and teachers can result in effective education only if a child is in school and ready and able to learn. The child is at the center of efforts to achieve Education for All (EFA) by 2015 and to address the Millennium Development Goals (MDGs) of universal basic education and gender equality in educational access. A child who is hungry or sick will not be able to complete a basic education of good quality. In order to achieve EFA, it is essential that the poorest children, who suffer most from ill health and hunger, are able to attend school and learn while there.

School health and nutrition programs can contribute to EFA and have become a part of national development policy worldwide. They have a long history in rich countries, where they were among the first social protection programs to emerge at the beginning of the 20th century. In middle- and low-income countries, school health programs were viewed primarily as having health sector-specific objectives until the World Education Forum in Dakar in 2000. Since then, there has been increasing recognition of the role of good school health and nutrition programs in achieving the goal of Education for All.

## A Strong Education Rationale for Ensuring Good Health and Avoiding Hunger at School Age

Some of the most common health conditions of school-age children affect their education. Malaria and worm infections can reduce enrollment and increase absenteeism, while hunger and anemia can affect cognition and learning, thus exacerbating the problems of even those children who do go to school. The pain associated with tooth decay, and the diarrhea and respiratory disease associated with poor hygiene, may also affect both attendance and learning.

These are not rare problems. The major health conditions that affect children's education are highly prevalent among poor schoolchildren. It is estimated that in low-income countries, worms infect some 169 million school-age children, each of whom loses some 3.75 IQ points as a consequence. Some 300 million schoolchildren have iron-deficiency anemia, causing them to lose some 6 IQ points per child. Hunger affects learning and attention: some 66 million schoolchildren go to school hungry. All of these conditions translate into the equivalent of between 200 million and 500 million days of school lost to ill health in low-income countries each year. The potential scale of benefit from school health programs is therefore exceptionally great, particularly among the poorest children. This pro-poor outcome is relatively unusual among education interventions, the majority of which offer greater benefit to the more capable children who can better take advantage of the opportunities on offer.

A pervasive school system provides a platform for delivering simple health interventions to schoolchildren. This approach may be more cost-effective than the health system, as there are typically more teachers than nurses and more schools than clinics, often by an order of magnitude. In cost-benefit analyses, school health programs often compare well with many other education interventions and have the additional advantage of optimizing the benefits of the education already being offered to poor children. These programs are often remarkably low in cost; for example, deworming and iron supplements cost less than a dollar per child per year. In the complex set of conditions required for a child to learn well, improved health can be one of the simplest and cheapest to achieve.

## Education Sector Benefits from a Life-Cycle Approach to Child Development

Child development interventions require a life-cycle approach to intervention, starting *in utero* and continuing throughout childhood. This implies a sequence of programs to promote maternal and child health (MCH), followed by early child development (ECD) programs to ensure good health, nutrition, and stimulation in preparation for going to school. MCH and ECD are important contributors to education outcomes and might be promoted by the education sector as part of an overall national strategy for child development, helping ensure that children arrive at school at the appropriate age and ready to learn.

Programs at school age are thus part of a continuum of supportive programs, from MCH during fetal development and infancy, through ECD in early childhood, and finally to school health and nutrition programs as a component of EFA. The World Bank Education Strategy identifies three key objectives for intervention that can help improve the education outcomes for schoolchildren: (i) ensuring children are ready to learn and enroll on time (MCH, ECD); (ii) keeping children in school and learning by enhancing attendance and reducing dropout rates (ECD, school health, school feeding); and (iii) improving learning at school by enhancing cognition and educational achievement (school health, school feeding).

One implication of this approach is that it is in the interest of the education sector to encourage and promote the general sequence of MCH, ECD, and school health and nutrition programs. However, education may have direct responsibility only for the last of these components, as MCH is typically implemented by the health sector and ECD often by a combination of sectors, including civil society and the private sector. All of these programs may be supported by social protection mechanisms.

## Health and Nutrition Interventions that Promote Gender Equity and Equality and Contribute to MDG3

School health and nutrition programs can play an important role in contributing to the gender dimension, not least because some of the most common health conditions affecting education are more prevalent in girls, and because gender-based vulnerability and exclusion can place girls at greater risk of ill health, neglect, and hunger.

There are many different ways in which school health and nutrition interventions can help address gender imbalances in education. Women and girls are, for physiological reasons, more likely to experience higher rates of iron-deficiency anemia, with well-documented consequences for cognition. Two of the most common school-based interventions, deworming and iron supplementation, each address anemia directly and therefore offer particular benefits to girls. Iron-fortified food also can contribute to reducing anemia; there is evidence that such school feeding interventions can additionally have a disproportionate benefit in enhancing girls' enrollment. The scale of effect can be large. Avoiding malaria infection in early life, for example, results in increased participation by girls in education at school age; in The Gambia, this difference was the equivalent of an extra year of schooling.

This book tries to highlight gender issues where possible, but in practice, many studies need to make a greater effort to ensure disaggregation of data by sex so that the role of school health and nutrition in addressing gender concerns can be better understood. Nevertheless, the evidence suggests that many of the most common school health and nutrition interventions have potentially important consequences for gender issues, and that these programs should be a recognized component of efforts to achieve MDG3 and the EFA gender goals.

## Schools that Effectively Deliver School Health and Nutrition Interventions

School health and nutrition programs for children of school age are usually delivered through the school system, often supported by a formal policy between the health and education sectors. There are safe, simple, and effective school-based options by which the education sector, typically with oversight from the health sector, can address the most common health and nutrition conditions that affect school-age children, options that have been shown to affect educational outcomes. Some of the most commonly used interventions, and the respective conditions they seek to avoid or prevent, include deworming and worm infection, bed nets and malaria, hand washing and bacterial infections, toothbrushing and dental caries, eye glasses and refractive error, physical exercise and/or healthy diet and weight concerns, micronutrients and micronutrient deficiency, and food and hunger.

There are effective school-based options for addressing many of the most common health and nutrition conditions, but there is a need to make informed choices. There is considerable variation in cost: only a few U.S. cents per child per annum for iodization of salt, deworming, chlorine water treatment, and iron supplements; several dollars for eye glasses, bed nets, toothbrushing, and hand washing; and $40–$50 for school feeding and some medical referrals.

Some of these activities can be addressed by teachers or other education staff with a minimum of training and with oversight from the health sector (for example, deworming, bed net distribution, toothbrushing, hand washing), while others require the direct involvement of often rare specialists (for example, vision correction and dentistry). Some activities require a single annual activity or an even less frequent intervention (for example, deworming, malaria treatment, distribution of bed nets, dispensing eyeglasses); some, a weekly action (for example, iron supplementation, chlorine water treatment); and some, a daily or more frequent intervention (for example, toothbrushing, hand washing, school feeding, physical exercise).

Schools are a particularly effective platform for delivering these interventions because the effects can be optimized by exploiting the role of the school as a teaching and learning institution. For some interventions, learning is the main component (for example, addressing the stigma associated with HIV), while in others, learning is a means to promote access to a service (for example, deworming). Effective delivery relies on the school providing children with age-appropriate, actionable knowledge; serving as a conduit for knowledge on health and nutrition for the community; demystifying health and nutrition; and reinforcing positive behavioral messages and addressing stigma. These diverse roles are a particularly strong reason why schools provide an effective platform for health and nutrition interventions.

Since the inclusion of school health in the strategic thinking around the World Education Forum in Dakar in 2000, some of these interventions have been implemented by an increasing number of low-income countries as part of a systematic approach to school health and nutrition. In Sub-Saharan Africa, for example, the percentage of countries implementing comprehensive school health programs rose from 4 percent in 2000 to nearly 50 percent by 2008, while in South and East Asia, coverage nearly doubled over the same period.

## The Substantial Experience of School Health and Nutrition Programs in Practice

For most countries the challenge is to optimize existing programs. Most countries are not starting from scratch; instead, they already have school health and nutrition programs, often including school feeding programs, that need to be modified to address new priorities or needs. In most cases the aim is to expand the geographical coverage of an existing program so that it reaches poor and marginalized children. For example, Sri Lanka has changed its modality from being primarily health-system based to an education sector model so that it can use the network of schools as a more extensive delivery platform. Guyana has complemented an existing, largely urban, school health program with a new rural model to reach additional areas of the country. The Philippines has supplemented an existing comprehensive model that proved reluctant to go to scale with a simplified model that can rapidly be rolled out nationally.

There are compelling arguments for public investment in school health and nutrition programs, including their contribution to economic growth, high rates of return, and large externalities. Conversely, there is evidence of market failure that might argue against private provision of programs. Although public resources may play the major role, contributions from other sectors can be important. Nongovernmental organizations (NGOs) have proven particularly effective in supporting school health and school feeding programs, particularly at the local level, and there are examples (for example, Japan, the Republic of Korea, Indonesia) of successful contributions by the private sector, particularly among dense urban populations and in middle-income countries.

Targeting often lies at the heart of practical success. Targeting reduces costs, facilitates management, and may optimize outcomes. The deworming program in Kenya, for example, reached more than 70 percent of needy children by operating in less than one-third of the country. The school feeding program in Guyana reached its entire target population by working in 4 of the 11 regions of the country. In Sri Lanka, a deliberate decision to precede the School Health Promotion Program with a national mapping exercise led program components to be matched with local needs—the difference perhaps most starkly demonstrated in nutrition, with malnutrition the target in the north and obesity the issue in the capital.

Education sector planners are increasingly recognizing the relevance of school health and nutrition to their education goals and beginning to take responsibility for implementing these programs as part of the sectoral response. Increasingly planners are locating these programs in the education service administration and including them in education sector plans. Since the funding channels for some aspects of the programs are often unfamiliar to the education sector, such as those for procuring drugs and food, one solution is to embed the various components within an overall sectorwide approach. This tactic has the added advantage of allowing access to pooled funding from multiple sectors, potentially including the health sector.

## Important Technical Challenges Remain

For some of the most prevalent health conditions of schoolchildren, there are important knowledge gaps, indicating an unfinished research agenda. There is a need for better evidence of the impact on education of some simple but very common ailments. For both diarrhea and tooth decay (and toothache), for example, the evidence of impact on education is only inferred; similarly, the growing importance of noncommunicable diseases among schoolchildren in middle- and low-income countries has not been matched by education sector analysis of the effects of these diseases on education.

In some areas there is a need for operational guidance. In many countries in Africa, malaria is most prevalent among schoolchildren because of the successful efforts to control infection in other age groups, yet there is a lack of formal guidance on how to address malaria in schools. Vision correction is also a priority from an education perspective, an area that would benefit from a comparative cost analysis of available approaches, including a formal assessment of the efficacy and safety of self-refracting eye glasses.

In addition, there is a need for more comparative analysis of the cost-benefits of school health and nutrition programs versus other education and social safety net interventions, as well as for operational research to help define the determinants of the transition of such programs to national ownership. Furthermore, school health can play a very important role not only in preventing disabilities, but also in removing the barriers to education for children with disabilities. Education and health policy makers and practitioners need to have good, practical examples and empirical evidence of cost-effective school health interventions in developing countries.

## The Importance of Partnerships to the Development of School Health and Nutrition Programs

This review shows that school health programs are characterized by effective partnerships and networks at the international, regional, and national levels. The World Education Forum at Dakar launched a multiagency partnership, "Focusing Resources on Effective School Health" (FRESH), which set out a broad planning framework for school health programming. When linked with operational guidance such as the United Nations Children's Fund (UNICEF) Child Friendly Schools approach, FRESH has contributed to the recognition that school health programs require several elements to achieve successful outcomes. Reviews of country and development partner policies show that this concept of multiple elements—for example, linking good health education with good health services—has been widely accepted, promoted, and implemented.

The area of HIV and education has shown particularly strong development. In 2002, the UNAIDS (Joint United Nations Programme on HIV/AIDS) Inter-Agency Task Team for Education was established by the cosponsoring agencies; it has since catalyzed partnership efforts, including the working group to accelerate the education sector response to HIV in Sub-Saharan Africa. The UNESCO Global Initiative on Education and HIV&AIDS (EDUCAIDS) and Education International's EFAIDS[1] initiative both make direct connections between HIV responses and EFA. Most recently, the World Food Programme and the World Bank have begun working jointly with countries to enhance the quality and efficiency of school feeding programs that also include school health and education objectives.

## Evolving Roles for Development Partners

Although the World Education Forum in Dakar in 2000 represented a dialogue involving countries, development agencies, and civil society organizations, it appears that governments have made the greatest changes to their internal policies and thinking to promote the cross-sectoral work that underlies effective school health and nutrition programs. In general, agencies remain focused either on health or on education; where they address both, they face administrative issues in working across the boundaries. The growing interest in school health on the part of the Fast Track Initiative (FTI) partnership is helping change this approach. Another change that might help agencies work more easily across sectors would be to develop Development Assistance Committee (DAC)[2] purpose codes to report on cross-sectoral school health programs.

The absence of one focal point for cross-sectoral tasks between the education and health sectors has perhaps had an important positive benefit: encouraging the creation of partnerships across traditional sectoral boundaries. Instead of having a single coordination point, the school health and nutrition area is characterized by an exceptionally large number of partnerships and networks, many of which have proven effective in promoting knowledge sharing and coordination. These networks and partnerships should perhaps receive more direct and specific support from development partners as a way to help countries help themselves. There is nevertheless a tendency to coalesce around single issues—most notably HIV—which may contribute to fragmentation of partner efforts and distract them from the broader goals of school health and nutrition programs. Perhaps an important next step in the evolution of these partnerships would be for development partners to seek the kind of harmonization and alignment across sectors that are already perceptible within some country programs.

## Benefits of Simplification and Consolidation of Program within Education Sector Plans

There is a growing tendency for fragmentation of efforts in the field of school health, with separate and different administrative structures developing around different health issues. This is perhaps most notable around HIV, but it is also recognizable in the areas of hand washing and vision promotion, program areas that are most often led by the health sector. Paradoxically, fragmentation is happening at a time when the health sector globally is giving greater focus to a health-systems approach. School health programs are entirely consistent with this view of health delivery, representing a well-proven means of improving the health and education of a subset of the population that is often poorly served by traditional health systems. Now is the time for the health and education sectors to mainstream and consolidate their joint school health activities, and for ministries of health and education to agree formally on their responsibilities and strengths within national school health programs.

One strong feature of school health and school feeding programs is that they benefit poor children most, but only if the programs reach them. Today, far more countries have policies and plans to implement school health programs than those that are actually doing so. The analysis in this study suggests that there is one central issue: efforts to provide comprehensive programs can result in programs that are too complex or demanding to go to scale—the classic challenge of the best driving out the good. There may be a particular message here for development partners: to advocate for scale and simplicity rather than comprehensiveness. And there are indeed good examples of how doing one or a few simple, yet important, interventions is well within the scope of education systems. For example, the Kenya deworming program reached 3.5 million needy children in one year and the Philippines Fit for School Program is going to scale with deworming, hand washing, and toothbrushing.

This book describes how the school has been used as a platform for delivering familiar, safe, and simple health and nutrition interventions to even hard-to-reach children in low-income countries. This has often been achieved by reducing the school health program to its simple essentials and targeting delivery at the communities most in need. The watchwords for pro-poor school health programs may thus become safe, simple, and scalable.

## Enough Known to Act Now

School health and nutrition programs are near universal in rich and middle-income countries, where they are often viewed as essential to the longer-term development of children, especially because they contribute to the establishment of lifelong healthy behaviors and diet. Low-income countries, too, are seeking to implement effective school health and nutrition programs, especially since Dakar 2000, but in these countries the focus is rather different. Ill health and hunger remain common, especially among the poor, and have important consequences for education. An increasing number of low-income countries now use their schools as a platform for delivering simple, safe, and cost-effective health and nutrition interventions with the specific aims of achieving the education MDGs and the goals of EFA.

There are necessary caveats in moving toward wider implementation of school health and nutrition programs. The use of a school as a delivery platform should not detract from the school's primary role as a center for teaching and learning—in other words, the delivery of health and nutrition interventions should not serve as a tax on the education system that it is trying to help. Similarly, the potentially large increase in demand for education created by school health and nutrition interventions must be matched by a concomitant increase in supply of quality education—school health and nutrition should be mainstreamed within a systematic education sector plan. There are good examples of countries that have recognized these issues and rolled out effective programs which avoided these potential pitfalls.

Enough is known now to recognize the importance of school health and nutrition programs as contributors to education achievement in low-income countries. School health and nutrition programs should be viewed alongside more traditional interventions—such as abolishing school fees, providing cash transfers, and offering incentives or subsidies—as important components of the battery of responses that can contribute to increasing participation in education. These interventions may not be relevant everywhere, but in many communities and countries, using schools to promote good health and avoid hunger may make a crucial contribution to Education for All.

## Notes

1. A contraction of Education for All and HIV and AIDS.
2. Part of the Organisation for Economic Co-operation and Development.

CHAPTER 1

# Context and Rationale

Schoolchildren are rarely mentioned in education sector plans. Typically, these plans focus on the familiar components of quality education: adequate classrooms staffed with well-trained teachers using appropriate learning materials. This book argues that these investments, essential for delivering quality education, will not result in effective educational outcomes if children are sick or hungry. Achieving Education for All (EFA) requires that all children, especially poor children and girls, are healthy enough both to attend school and to learn while there. Furthermore, the book makes the case that, especially in low-income countries, the health sector alone cannot respond effectively to these needs, and the education system itself has an important and often remarkably cost-effective role to play. Finally, although this book will focus on helping school-age children, it recognizes that schoolchildren can realize their full potential only by building on a foundation of good early development. This book is written primarily for the education sector, although the issues of hunger, ill health, and social safety nets are also relevant to social protection.

## How This Book Is Organized

The overall theme of this book is that schools offer a delivery platform for a range of interventions, including those that can address ill health and hunger, and that these interventions can contribute to educational out-comes, including the goals of EFA.

The book is organized into six chapters. This first chapter sets the scene, describing the historical context and setting out the issues of today. Chapter 2 presents the evidence for the impact of a range of health and nutrition interventions on measures of educational outcomes. Chapter 3 begins by emphasizing the importance of a life-cycle approach to child development, with a sequence of interventions that help ensure readiness for education—especially maternal and child health (MCH) and early child development (ECD)—before exploring a number of common health and nutrition conditions of school-age children that have demon-strated consequences for education, and for which school-based interven-tions exist. Chapter 4 examines practical examples of how these interventions have been used as components of actual school health and nutrition programs. Chapter 5 describes the partnerships that have devel-oped to provide guidance and support on designing and implementing school health and nutrition programs. Finally, chapter 6 seeks to draw some overall conclusions.

There are at least two important caveats here. First, the anticipated educational benefits depend on increasing the demand for education by helping make children healthy enough to enroll on time and attend school, and on the enhanced ability of healthy children to learn when in school. But these educational benefits can accrue only if this increase in demand is met by a concomitant supply of education of adequate qual-ity; school health and nutrition programs should therefore be intrinsic to an integrated education strategy. Second, and linked to the first caveat, the main business of schools is education, and the use of the schools to deliver other interventions has the potential to adversely affect this pri-mary role. It is important to obtain the correct balance; school health and nutrition programs can offer major benefits for education, but will achieve perverse outcomes if they act as a tax on education.

An underlying theme throughout the book is the importance of a life-cycle approach to child development, recognizing that child development is a process and that early development may have profound positive or negative consequences for later outcomes (see, for example, Glewwe, Jacoby, and King 2001; Behrman and Hoddinott 2005; Martorell et al. 2009; Nores and Barnett 2009).

A settled terminology for describing noneducation interventions in schools has yet to be established. Here the book follows traditional practice in using the term "school health and nutrition" to include the whole gamut of interventions that can be delivered from a school platform— which variously aim to improve health, enhance nutrition, alleviate hunger, or prevent disease—while recognizing that any individual intervention may address only one of these aims. "School health" is used to refer to school-based interventions that address health conditions specifically, reserving the use of "nutrition" for when a specific nutrition outcome is sought, such as correcting a micronutrient deficiency. When an intervention involves the supply of food specifically, the term "school feeding" is used. The author apologizes in advance for the sometimes clumsy construction that attends this usage, and for any confusion caused by these potentially overlapping terminologies.

## 100 Years of School Health and School Feeding Programs in Rich Countries

There is nothing new about recognizing the connection between ill health, hunger, and education. When, at the beginning of the 20th century, the reforming Liberal government sought to create a welfare state in Britain, its first actions were to pass the Education (Provision of Meals) Act of 1906 and the Education (Administrative Provisions) Act of 1907, which together established free meals and medical inspections in state schools (Atkins 2007). By the 1920s, these policies were fully implemented and the government was conducting trials to assess the benefits of the interventions for educational outcomes (Pollock 2006; Atkins 2005). At around the same time, the creation of the Rockefeller Foundation in the United States was spurred by the realization that hookworm infection in schoolchildren and the resulting anemia were major contributors to underdevelopment in the southern states. There was accordingly a concomitant need for school-based deworming programs (Ettling 1981).

Modern analysis of the data from these early school health programs shows long-run benefits, due largely to the returns to education (Bleakley 2007). And when Japan in 1948 faced similar challenges, a national school-based deworming program was established, which at its peak examined and treated 12 million children, had an annual turnover of nearly $9 million in today's prices, and reduced infection in schoolchildren from 73 percent to less than 0.01 percent by 1985 (Bundy et al. 2006).

## Movement of School Health and Nutrition Programs to a Pro-Poor and Education-Outcomes Focus

The focus of school health and nutrition programs in low-income countries began to shift in the 1980s, moving away from a medical approach that favored elite schools in urban centers toward school-based programs that sought to improve education access and completion, particularly for poor students, by improving health and tackling hunger.

In an effort to reconceptualize the relationship between health and education, the United Nations Educational, Scientific and Cultural Organization (UNESCO) hosted a series of workshops on this topic in the 1980s (Bundy 1989; Halloran, Bundy, and Pollitt 1989) and supported one of the first authoritative reviews of the topic (Pollitt 1990). Similarly, the United Nations Development Programme (UNDP), in conjunction with the Rockefeller, Edna McConnell Clark, and J. S. McDonnell foundations, supported the creation of a research network. Managed by the Partnership for Child Development, the network aims to strengthen and disseminate the evidence base across the education and health sectors (Berkley and Jamison 1990; Bundy and Guyatt 1996). This paradigm shift coincided with the world conference on Education for All in Jomtien, Thailand, in 1990, and led to renewed efforts by countries and agencies to develop more effective programmatic approaches to school health and nutrition.

In the 1990s there was also increasing emphasis by development partners on the role of school health and nutrition programs. Yet often the primary focus of these programs was enhancing health rather than improving education outcomes. The United Nations Population Fund (UNFPA) pioneered programs on population and family life education (PopEd) as an intrinsic part of school curricula, with a specific emphasis on reproductive and sexual health. The World Health Organization (WHO) launched its Global School Health Initiative to foster the development of health-promoting schools (WHO 1996), based on the Ottawa Charter of Health Promotion, which sought to foster healthy lifestyles and develop environments conducive to health (WHO 1986; European Commission, World Health Organization Regional Office for Europe, and Council of Europe 1996).

The United Nations Children's Fund (UNICEF) promoted Child Friendly Schools as a holistic way to promote children's rights, as expressed in the *Convention on the Rights of the Child* (UNICEF 1990), and children's access to education, as stated in the "World Declaration on Education for All" (UNESCO 1990). This approach included a gender component, which was further strengthened when girls' education became the first priority of UNICEF's Medium Term Strategic Plan, 2002–2005. It also used skills-based health education, including life skills to promote health and learning (UNICEF et al. 2003). Also during the 1990s, the World Bank Human Development Network sought to support countries in implementing school health and nutrition programs (Del Rosso and Marek 1996; World Bank 1993) and launched an International School Health Initiative with the aim of raising awareness of the importance of health and nutrition among decision makers in the education sector.

## Greater Harmonization of School Health and Nutrition Programs around a Common Framework

The proliferation of development-agency initiatives in school health had the potential to cause confusion. Fortunately, although these new school health programs had different stated priorities—such as public health, quality education, and child rights—their content when implemented at the country level was rather similar in practice (see table 1.1). This consistency provided an opportunity for the agencies to harmonize around a common implementation framework, while at the same time retaining the policy differences that reflected their differing priorities.

A step forward in international coordination and cohesion was achieved when the Focusing Resources on Effective School Health (FRESH) framework was launched at the World Education Forum in Dakar in April 2000. The concept was developed and launched jointly by UNESCO, UNICEF, the WHO, and the World Bank, with early partners including the Education Development Center, Education International, the Partnership for Child Development, and the World Food Programme (WFP). In order to emphasize similarities rather than differences, the FRESH partnership agreed on a common position that recognized "that the goal of universal education cannot be achieved while the health needs of children and adolescents remain unmet and that a core group of cost-effective activities can and must be implemented across the board to meet those needs and to deliver on the promise of EFA" (World Bank 2000, 2).

This statement reflects an expanded commentary on the "Dakar Framework for Action" (UNESCO 2000), which defines three ways in which health relates to EFA: as an input and condition necessary for learning, as an outcome of effective quality education, and as a sector that must collaborate with education to achieve the goal of EFA.

**Table 1.1 Characteristics of Agency-Specific School Health and Nutrition Programs within the FRESH Framework**

| FRESH framework | Health Promoting Schools (WHO) | Child Friendly Schools (UNICEF) | PopEd (UNFPA) | Global School Feeding Campaign (WFP) |
|---|---|---|---|---|
| Policy | Respects an individual's well-being and dignity<br>Provides multiple opportunities for success<br>Acknowledges good efforts and inventions, as well as personal achievements | Respects and realizes the rights of every child<br>Acts to ensure inclusion, respect, and equality of opportunity for all children<br>Is gender sensitive and girl friendly<br>Is flexible and responds to diversity<br>Sees and understands the whole child in a broad context<br>Enhances teacher capacity, morale, commitment, and status | Creates a supportive and enabling policy environment for reproductive health and HIV prevention for young people | Focuses on the poorest and most food-insecure communities<br>Gives priority to girls and AIDS-affected children |
| School environment | Is healthy<br>Provides opportunities for physical education and recreation | Is healthy, safe, and secure<br>Is protective emotionally and psychologically | Protects young people from early and unwanted pregnancy, sexually transmitted diseases, sexual abuse, and violence | Serves as a platform for an essential package approach that includes water, sanitation, and environmental measures |

| | | | | |
|---|---|---|---|---|
| Education | Provides skills-based health education<br>Fosters health and learning | Promotes quality learning outcomes<br>Provides education that is affordable and accessible<br>Provides skills-based health education, including life skills relevant to children's lives | Strengthens HIV/AIDS and sexual and reproductive health education programs | Supports learning through good nutrition<br>Promotes access to education |
| Services | Provides school health services<br>Provides nutrition and food-safety programs<br>Provides programs for counseling, social support, and mental health promotion<br>Provides health promotion programs for staff<br>Includes school and community projects and outreach | Promotes physical health<br>Promotes mental hea th | Ensures access to youth-friendly sexual and reproductive health services | Provides food<br>Promotes and supports deworming |
| Supportive partnerships | Engages health and education officials, teachers, teachers' unions, students, parents, health providers, and community leaders in efforts to make the school a place of health | Is child oriented<br>Is family focused<br>Is community based | Targets young people in school and out of school<br>Ensures active participation of parents, youth, community leaders, and organizations | Promotes community and school partnerships |

*Source:* Bundy et al. 2006.

The FRESH framework proposes that four core components should be considered when designing an effective school health and nutrition program. It also suggests that the program will be most equitable and cost-effective if all of these components are made available together in all schools. The FRESH framework further proposes that these four core components can be implemented effectively only if they are supported by strategic partnerships between the health and education sectors, especially teachers and health workers; schools and the community; and children and those responsible for implementation. In the follow-up to the Dakar Forum, UNESCO designated FRESH as an interagency flagship program, both to receive international support and as a strategy to achieve EFA.

## Growth in School Health Programs in Low-Income Countries since Dakar 2000

Since 2000, there has been a significant change in the way in which development agencies and organizations have addressed school health and nutrition programming (see figure 1.1). A survey of agency policy in 2000 showed that a majority of agencies that described themselves as active in school health and nutrition in practice confined their activities to health education. By 2007, a survey of the same agencies showed that most had adopted a more comprehensive approach that included health services, health policies, and the school environment, essentially following the FRESH framework.

This change was also mirrored in the decisions made by countries. A survey of 36 countries in Sub-Saharan Africa in 2000 suggested that only 8 percent implemented a school health and nutrition program that met the new criteria for equity and effectiveness (see figure 1.2). By 2007, some 44 percent of these countries had fully compliant programs and many of the remainder were well on their way to achieving a comprehensive approach. In 11 countries in Asia a similar picture emerged, albeit starting from a higher base in 2000 (see figure 1.2).

## Emergence of HIV as a Programmatic Issue for the Education Sector

Although HIV has been recognized as a major health issue since the 1980s, few countries had addressed the epidemic from an education sector perspective. Section 27 of the "Dakar Framework for Action"

**Figure 1.1    Support for School Health Activities by Education Sector Development Partners, 2000–07**

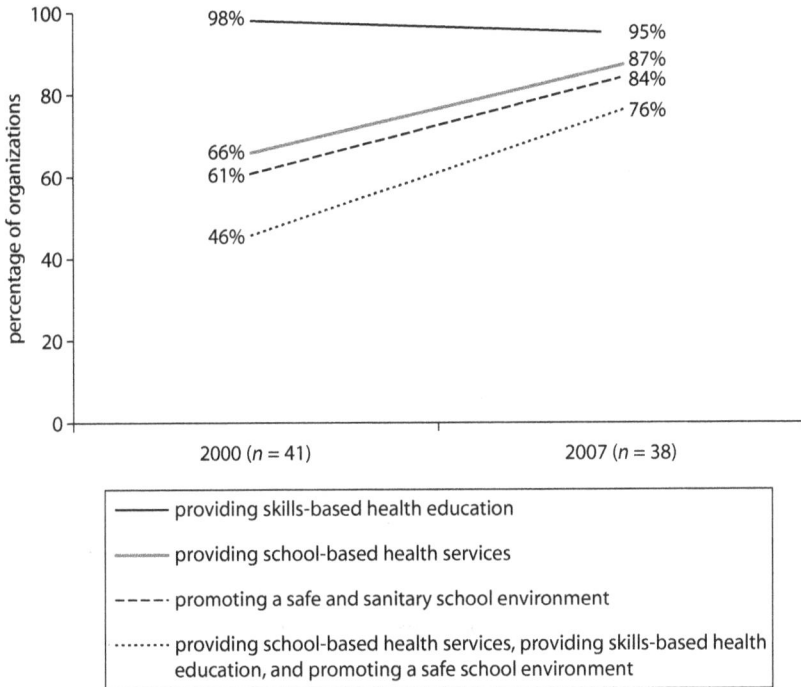

*Source:* Partnership for Child Development 2007.

(UNESCO 2000, 14) is forthright about identifying "the terrifying impact of HIV/AIDS on education" and calling for "maximum use of education's potential to transmit messages on prevention and to change attitudes and behaviours."

Soon after 2000, a number of agencies included education in broader HIV policies (see, for example, UNAIDS 2001; ILO 2001) or launched specific education sector policies with respect to HIV (see, for example, UNESCO 2002, 2004; World Bank 2002; UNICEF 2004). The latter generally emphasize the potential impact of HIV on both education supply and teachers—an important labor issue because teachers often represent some 50–60 percent of the national public sector work force. These policies also stress the potential value of the education sector as a prevention tool that could potentially reach some 40 percent of the population of many countries, including nearly all children and youth. At around the

**Figure 1.2    Support for School Health Programs in Sub-Saharan Africa and South and East Asia since 2000**

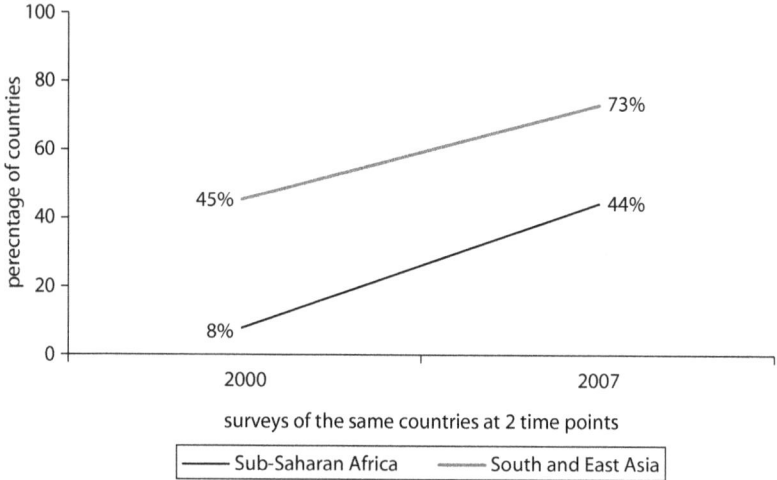

*Source:* Partnership for Child Development 2007.

same time, countries themselves began to launch national HIV policies, for example, Botswana in 1998, Jamaica in 2001, Rwanda in 2002, and Kenya in 2004.

Just as occurred with general school health programming a decade earlier, a proliferation of HIV-specific program approaches were adopted by development agencies. There was also a concomitant increase in national programs. In 2002, the Joint United Nations Programme on HIV/AIDS (UNAIDS) created the Inter-Agency Task Team for HIV and Education (IATT) as a more formal evolution of the Inter-Agency Working Group, which had been in existence since 2000. UNAIDS launched the Global Initiative on Education and HIV&AIDS (EDUCAIDS) program in 2004 and Education International—the world's largest federation of teachers' unions—launched EFAIDS in 2006.

The IATT established a working group to Accelerate the Education Sector Response to HIV in Sub-Saharan Africa in 2002; by 2005, this group had helped spawn ministry of education HIV networks within some of the major regional economic communities (for example, ECOWAS and CARICOM).[1] By 2007, it was estimated that the education sectors of some 27 countries in Sub-Saharan Africa had established mechanisms to include at least some aspects of HIV responses in school health programming.

The vision of the importance of HIV in today's world is very different from that at the beginning of the decade (UNAIDS 2008). For a majority of countries worldwide, the impact of HIV is declining and the availability of effective therapy has transformed the prospects of people, including teachers and students, who are living with HIV. In such areas, the primary role of education may be to ensure access to care and treatment of teachers and students, reduce stigma, and promote understanding of the need to focus control efforts on high-risk groups. In the southern cone of Africa, however, HIV remains a major constraint on development and the education sector there still has a vigorous role to play.

## Growing Recognition of the Importance of School Feeding for Education

As described at the beginning of this chapter, the provision of meals in schools was one of the earliest public welfare programs and among the first introduced through the education sector. School meals as an educational intervention in low-income countries have experienced major swings in popularity and the perception of their value has strongly polarized opinions among development practitioners (compare, for example, Del Rosso and Marek 1996 with Bundy and Strickland 2000). More recent analyses, however, provide a more consistent picture (Kristjansson et al. 2007). A joint study by the World Food Programme and the World Bank (Bundy et al. 2009), which compares the provision of school feeding programs globally with estimates of global patterns of hunger, poverty, and educational achievement, shows that, perhaps for the first time in history, every country for which information is available is seeking to provide food, in some way and at some scale, to its schoolchildren (see maps 1.1–1.4).

Analysis suggests that in some circumstances, school feeding programs can offer important benefits to the education sector by enhancing enrollment and reducing absenteeism; by reducing hunger, such programs can also improve cognition and educational outcomes (Adelman, Alderman, et al. 2008; Bundy et al. 2009). But perhaps the strongest evidence points to the benefits of school feeding programs, when appropriately designed and targeted, as social safety nets (Grosh et al. 2008). This evidence helps explain why the food, fuel, and financial crises that emerged in 2008 led to a substantial increase in demand from low-income countries for school feeding programs.

School meal programs are near ubiquitous in rich and middle-income countries, perhaps reflecting the recognition by governments of their

**Map 1.1    Poverty: Percentage of Population Living in Households with Per Capita Consumption or Income below the Poverty Line**

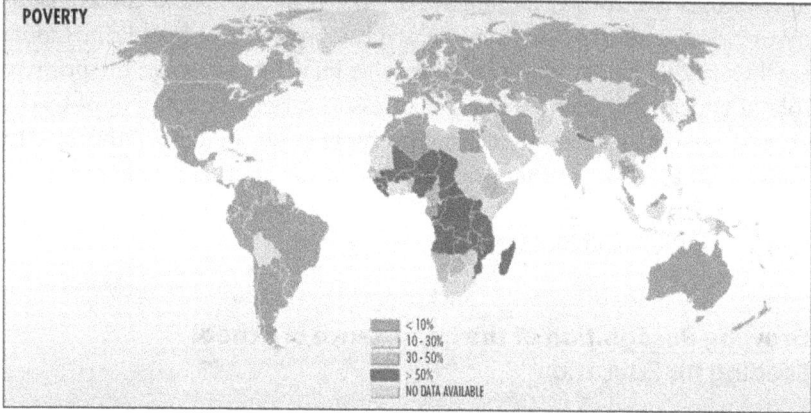

*Source:* Bundy et al. 2009.
*Note:* The poverty line estimates use purchasing power parity exchange rates for latest available year. A color version of the map appears at the end of the book.

**Map 1.2    Hunger: Percentage of Population below the Minimum Level of Dietary Energy Consumption, 2002–05**

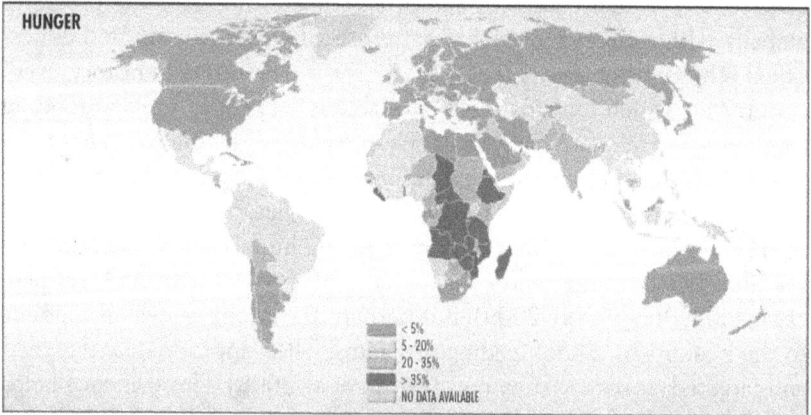

*Source:* Bundy et al. 2009.
*Note:* The proportion of the population below the minimum level of dietary energy consumption, referred to as the prevalence of undernourishment, is the percentage of the population that is undernourished or food deprived. Figures are from latest available year. Standards derived from an FAO/WHO/UNU Expert Consultation (FAO, WHO, and UN University 2004). A color version of the map appears at the end of the book.

## Map 1.3    Primary School Completion Rate, 2000–06

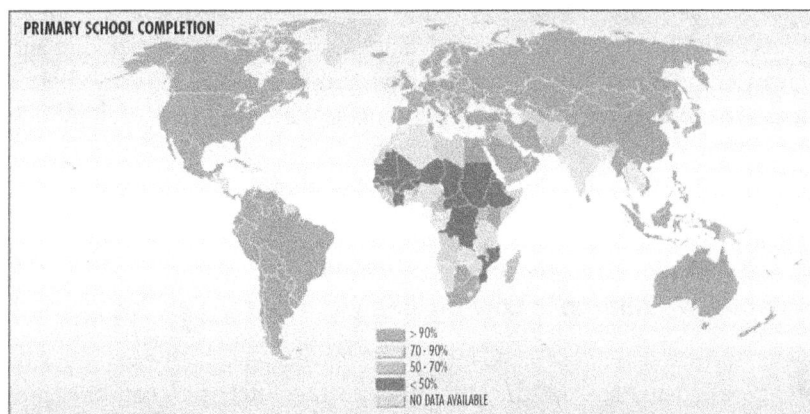

*Source:* Bundy et al. 2009.
*Note:* Primary completion rate is the total number of students in grade 6 (excluding repeaters) divided by the to-tal number of children of grade age. Figures are from latest available year. All data are from the UNESCO Institute for Statistics except for Australia, Canada, China, Japan, New Zealand, Sweden, Thailand, and the United Kingdom, which are from national data. A color version of the map appears at the end of the book.

## Map 1.4    School Feeding: Country Programs, 2006–08

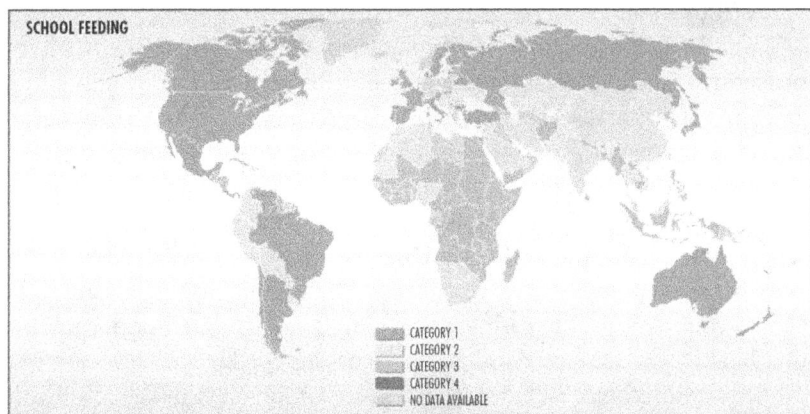

*Source:* Bundy et al. 2009.
*Note:* Category 1 = countries where school feeding is available in most schools, sometimes or always; category 2 = countries where school feeding is available in some way and at some scale; category 3 = countries where school feeding is available primarily in the most food-insecure regions; category 4 = countries where there is no school feeding. The sources are World Food Programme data for low-income and lower-middle-income countries and national data for the remaining countries. Because this is a work in progress, comments and any further information on school feeding programs are welcomed. A color version of the map appears at the end of the book.

social protection and education sector benefits. In recent years, these countries have increasingly focused on improving the quality of school meals, reflecting the growing understanding of the importance of diet and nutrition for education, as seen, for example, in the U.K. Feed Me Better campaign (Belot and James 2009). Eating habits established in childhood are an important determinant of the longer-term health and development of children, especially with respect to noncommunicable diseases.

## Rising Prevalence of Noncommunicable Diseases in School-Age Children in Low-Income Countries

Noncommunicable diseases—including cancers, heart disease, obesity, and type 2 diabetes—are the main diseases that affect rich countries and have been described as diseases of affluence. For poor communities, greater emphasis tends to be given to infectious diseases, such as malaria, HIV, tuberculosis (TB), and worms. Today, epidemiological analysis shows that noncommunicable diseases are growing in importance for the populations of middle- and low-income countries (Bloom et al. 2006). Obesity, often associated with type 2 diabetes, is increasingly prevalent in school-children—see, for example, surveys of schools in Sri Lanka and the Caribbean (Wickramasinghe et al. 2008; O'Connell, Venkatesh, and Bundy 2009)—and is likely to track into adulthood.

Similarly, behaviors that are established during school age, such as tobacco use and dietary preferences, contribute to the development of noncommunicable diseases later in life (Freedman et al. 2009). Studies—only in rich countries to date—associate obesity with lower test scores and psychosocial costs during school age, as well as compromised participation and productivity in the labor market as adults (Pagan and Davila 1997; Dietz 1998; Taras and Potts-Datema 2005). In order to address the roots of noncommunicable diseases in childhood, low- and middle-income countries are increasingly providing schoolchildren opportunities for a healthy diet and physical activity, and supporting the development of habits and informed choice, as intrinsic components of school health and school feeding programs.

## Ensuring Support for the Most Marginalized Out-of-School Children

School health and nutrition programs contribute to the completion and educational quality goals of EFA, but they also have a very important impact beyond school by drawing children—especially girls—into schools and encouraging them to stay.

Despite EFA efforts, more than 72 million primary school-age children are out of school; most of these children are poor and marginalized and 54 percent are girls (UNESCO 2010). School health programs, such as those in Guinea and Madagascar, have consistently demonstrated that many of these children will take advantage of simple services, for example deworming, provided in schools (Del Rosso and Marek 1996) and can benefit from school feeding programs (Bundy et al. 2009). In these cases the school acts essentially as a community center. It has also been demonstrated that deworming programs in schools benefit out-of-school children by reducing disease transmission in the community as a whole (Bundy et al. 1990), which has the important consequence for EFA of more children attending school (Miguel and Kremer 2004).

Thus school health and nutrition programs, including school feeding programs, can increase enrollment and reduce absenteeism[2] and contribute to the EFA goals. This suggests that school health and nutrition programs should be considered alongside other approaches to promote enrollment and attendance, such as abolition of school fees and provision of quality education.

Nevertheless, it is apparent that children who remain out of school cannot benefit from many of the important components of school-based programs. Thus, there remains a need for more flexible approaches that combine the best of nonformal, informal, and community-based interventions to ensure that the most disadvantaged out-of-school children still have access to the most important health messages, such as skill-based health education and life-skills development programs to prevent HIV (see, for example, UNICEF 2009).

## School Health and Nutrition Programs Today

This chapter has sought to provide a context for school health and nutrition programs. In the context of richer countries, it has shown that such programs are almost universal in high- and middle-income countries, where they have traditionally been viewed as contributing to social safety nets or welfare packages. Today these programs are seen as having a role that goes beyond social protection, since they are also implemented in countries such as Brazil and Mexico, alongside high-quality, high-coverage, and well-evaluated conditional cash transfer programs, which are an effective tool for social protection (Fiszbein et al. 2009). The perceived role of school health and nutrition programs in these countries is in promoting health and a healthier diet and, as is increasingly recognized in recent political statements in the United States and Europe, the quality of learning and education outcomes.

In low-income countries too, school health and nutrition programs are becoming universal, reflecting the considerable growth in these programs over the past decade in particular (see figures 1.1 and 1.2). The coverage of such programs, however, is often limited, and in many cases is socially regressive, providing most benefit to the urban elite. Policy analysis suggests that the objectives of these programs are rarely defined, and where they are, tend to emphasize health and nutrition outcomes that the programs are often ill-designed to deliver, rather than the education and social protection roles that they may be able to fulfill.

The current global financial crisis is forcing a reprioritization of the objectives of school health and nutrition programs, especially in low-income countries. There is growing recognition of the potential value of these programs as social safety nets (Grosh et al. 2008) and increasing demand for them following the social shocks associated with the current crisis (Bundy et al. 2009). There is also growing recognition that these school-based interventions can encourage school participation and learning. This book will explore the evidence for these benefits and the practical experiences of middle- and low-income countries in implementing programs, as well as seek to identify the factors that contribute to cost-effective school health and nutrition programs.

## Notes

1. Economic Community of West African States (ECOWAS) and the Caribbean Community (CARICOM).
2. For reviews of the evidence, see Pollitt, Cueto, and Jacoby (1998); Miguel and Kremer (2004); Adelman, Gilligan, and Lehrer (2008); and Bundy et al. (2009).

## References

Adelman, S. W., H. Alderman, D. O. Gilligan, and K. Lehrer. 2008. "The Impact of Alternative Food for Education Programs on Learning Achievement and Cognitive Development in Northern Uganda." International Food Policy Research Institute, Washington, DC.

Adelman, S. W., D. O. Gilligan, and K. Lehrer. 2008. *How Effective Are Food for Education Programs? A Critical Assessment of the Evidence from Developing Countries.* Food Policy Review 9. Washington, DC: International Food Policy Research Institute.

Atkins, P. 2005. "Fattening Children or Fattening Farmers? School Milk in Britain, 1921–1941." *Economic History Review* 58 (1): 57–78.

———. 2007. "School Milk in Britain, 1900–1934." *Journal of Policy History* 19 (4): 395–427.

Behrman, J. R., and J. Hoddinott. 2005. "Programme Evaluation with Unobserved Heterogeneity and Selective Implementation: The Mexican PROGRESA Impact on Child Nutrition." *Oxford Bulletin on Economics and Statistics* 67 (4): 547–69.

Belot, M., and J. James. 2009. "Healthy School Meals and Educational Outcomes." ISER Working Paper 2009-01, Institute for Social and Economic Research, Essex, U.K.

Berkley, S., and D. Jamison. 1990. *A Conference on the Health of School-Age Children.* New York: United Nations Development Programme and Rockefeller Foundation.

Bleakley, H. 2007. "Disease and Development: Evidence from Hookworm Eradication in the American South." *Quarterly Journal of Economics* 122 (1): 73–117.

Bloom, B. R., C. M. Michaud, J. R. La Montagne, and L. Simonsen. 2006. "Priorities for Global Research and Development Interventions." In *Disease Control Priorities in Developing Countries*, 2nd ed., ed. D. Jamison, J. G. Breman, A. R. Measham, G. Alleyne, M. Claeson, D. Evans, P. Jha, A. Mills, and P. Musgrove, 103–18. New York: World Bank and Oxford University Press.

Bundy, D. A. P. 1989. "New UNESCO International Project." *Parasitology Today* 5 (6): 168.

Bundy, D. A. P., C. Burbano, M. Grosh, A. Gelli, M. Jukes, and L. Drake. 2009. *Rethinking School Feeding: Social Safety Nets, Child Development, and the Education Sector.* Washington, DC: World Bank.

Bundy, D. A. P., and H. L. Guyatt. 1996. "Schools for Health: Focus on Health, Education, and the School-Age Child." *Parasitology Today* 12 (8): 1–16.

Bundy, D. A. P., S. Shaeffer, M. Jukes, K. Beegle, A. Gillespie, L. Drake, S.-H. F. Lee, A.-M. Hoffmann, J. Jones, A. Mitchell, C. Wright, D. Barcelona, B. Camara, C. Golmar, L. Savioli, T. Takeuchi, and M. Sembene. 2006. "School-Based Health and Nutrition Programs." In *Disease Control Priorities in Developing Countries*, 2nd ed., ed. D. Jamison, J. G. Breman, A. R. Measham, G. Alleyne, M. Claeson, D. Evans, P. Jha, A. Mills, and P. Musgrove, 1091–108. New York: World Bank and Oxford University Press.

Bundy, D. A. P., and B. Strickland. 2000. "School Feeding/Food for Education Stakeholders' Meeting." USAID Africa Bureau Office of Sustainable Development, Washington, DC. http://www.schoolsandhealth.org/pages/schoolfeeding.aspx.

Bundy, D. A. P., M. S. Wong, L. L. Lewis, and J. Horton. 1990. "Control of Geohelminths by Delivery of Targeted Chemotherapy through Schools." *Transactions of the Royal Society of Tropical Medicine and Hygiene* 84 (1): 115–20.

Del Rosso, J. M., and T. Marek. 1996. *Class Action: Improving School Performance in the Developing World through Better Health and Nutrition.* Washington, DC: World Bank.

Dietz, W. 1998. "Health Consequences of Obesity in Youth: Childhood Predictors of Adult Disease." *Pediatrics* 101 (suppl.): 518–25.

Ettling, J. 1981. *The Germ of Laziness: Rockefeller Philanthropy and Public Health in the New South.* Cambridge, MA: Harvard University Press.

European Commission, World Health Organization Regional Office for Europe, and Council of Europe. 1996. "Facts about the European Network of Health-Promoting Schools." European Commission, Brussels.

FAO (Food and Agriculture Organization), WHO (World Health Organization), and UN University. 2004. "Human Energy Requirements: Report of a Joint FAO/WHO/UNU Expert Consultation." FAO Food and Nutrition Technical Report 1, FAO, Rome.

Fiszbein, A., N. Schady, F. H. G. Ferreira, M. Grosh, N. Kelleher, P. Olinto, and E. Skoufias. 2009. *Conditional Cash Transfers: Reducing Present and Future Poverty.* Washington, DC: World Bank.

Freedman, D. S., W. H. Dietz, S. R. Srinivasan, and G. S. Berenson. 2009. "Risk Factors and Adult Body Mass Index among Overweight Children: The Bogalusa Heart Study." *Pediatrics* 123 (3): 750–57.

Glewwe, P., H. G. Jacoby, and E. M. King. 2001. "Early Childhood Nutrition and Academic Achievement: A Longitudinal Analysis." *Journal of Public Economics* 81 (3): 345–68.

Grosh, M., C. del Ninno, E. Tesliuc, and A. Ouerghi. 2008. *For Protection and Promotion: The Design and Implementation of Effective Safety Nets.* Washington, DC: World Bank.

Halloran, M. E., D. A. P. Bundy, and E. Pollitt. 1989. "Infectious Disease and the UNESCO Basic Education Initiative." *Parasitology Today* 5 (11): 359–62.

ILO (International Labour Organization). 2001. "An ILO Code of Practice on HIV/AIDS and the World of Work." ILO, Geneva.

Kristjansson, E., V. Robinson, M. Petticrew, B. MacDonald, J. Krasevec, L. Janzen, T. Greenhalgh, G. A. Wells, J. MacGowan, A. P. Farmer, B. Shea, A. Mayhew,

P. Tugwell, and V. Welch. 2007. "School Feeding for Improving the Physical and Psychosocial Health of Disadvantaged Elementary School Children." *Cochrane Database of Systematic Reviews* 1.

Martorell, R., B. L. Horta, L. S. Adair, A. D. Stein, L. Richter, C. H. D. Fall, S. K. Bhargava, et al. 2009. "Weight Gain in the First Two Years of Life Is an Important Predictor of Schooling Outcomes in Pooled Analyses from Five Birth Cohorts from Low- and Middle-Income Countries." *Journal of Nutrition* 140 (2): 348–54.

Miguel, E., and M. Kremer. 2004. "Worms: Identifying Impacts on Education and Health in the Presence of Treatment Externalities." *Econometrica* 72 (1): 159–217.

Nores, M., and W. S. Barnett. 2009. "Benefits of Early Childhood Interventions across the World: (Under) Investing in the Very Young." *Economics of Education Review* 29 (2): 271–82.

O'Connell, T., M. Venkatesh, and D. Bundy. 2009. "Strengthening the Education Sector Response to School Health, Nutrition, and HIV/AIDS in the Caribbean Region: A Rapid Survey of 13 Countries." World Bank, Washington, DC.

Pagan, J. A., and A. Davila. 1997. "Obesity, Occupational Attainment, and Earnings: Consequences of Obesity." *Social Science Quarterly* 78 (3): 756–70.

Partnership for Child Development. 2007. *Directory of Support to School-Based Health and Nutrition Programmes.* London: Partnership for Child Development.

Pollitt, E. 1990. *Malnutrition and Infection in the Classroom.* Paris: United Nations Educational, Scientific, and Cultural Organization.

Pollitt, E., S. Cueto, and E. R. Jacoby. 1998. "Fasting and Cognition in Well- and Undernourished Schoolchildren: A Review of Three Experimental Studies." *American Journal of Clinical Nutrition* 67 (4): 779s–84s.

Pollock, J. 2006. "Two Controlled Trials of Supplementary Feeding of British Schoolchildren in the 1920s." *Journal of the Royal Society of Medicine* 99 (6): 323–27.

Taras, H., and W. Potts-Datema. 2005. "Obesity and Student Performance at School." *Journal of School Health* 75 (8): 291–95.

UNAIDS (Joint United Nations Programme on HIV/AIDS). 2001. *The Global Strategy Framework on HIV/AIDS.* Geneva: UNAIDS.

———. 2008. *Report on the Global AIDS Epidemic 2008.* Geneva: UNAIDS.

UNESCO (United Nations Educational, Scientific and Cultural Organization). 1990. "World Declaration on Education for All: Meeting Basic Learning Needs." Presented at the World Conference on Education for All, Jomtien, Thailand, March 5–9.

———. 2000. "The Dakar Framework for Action: Education for All—Meeting Our Collective Commitments." Presented at the World Education Forum, Dakar, April 26–28.

———. 2002. *Towards an African Response: UNESCO's Strategy for HIV/AIDS Education in Sub-Saharan Africa.* Dakar, Senegal: UNESCO.

———. 2004. *UNESCO's Strategy for HIV/AIDS Prevention Education.* Paris: UNESCO International Institute for Educational Planning.

———. 2010. *EFA Global Monitoring Report 2010: Reaching the Marginalized.* Paris: UNESCO.

UNICEF (United Nations Children's Fund). 1990. *Convention on the Rights of the Child.* New York: UNICEF.

———. 2004. *Girls, HIV/AIDS, and Education.* New York: UNICEF.

———. 2009. *Promoting Quality Education for Orphans and Vulnerable Children: A Sourcebook of Programme Experiences in Eastern and Southern Africa.* New York: UNICEF.

UNICEF (United Nations Children's Fund), WHO (World Health Organization), World Bank, UNFPA (United Nations Population Fund), and UNESCO (United Nations Educational, Scientific, and Cultural Organization). 2003. *Skills for Health: Skills-Based Health Education, Including Life Skills: An Important Component of a Child-Friendly/Health-Promoting School.* World Health Organization's Information Series on School Health Document 9. New York: WHO Press.

WHO (World Health Organization). 1986. *Ottawa Charter.* Geneva: WHO.

———. 1996. "Global School Health Initiative." WHO/HPR/98.4, WHO, Geneva.

Wickramasinghe, V. P., S. P. Lamabadusuriya, G. J. Cleghorn, and P. S. W. Davies. 2008. "Assessment of Body Composition in Sri Lankan Children: Validation of a Bioelectrical Impedance Prediction Equation." *European Journal of Clinical Nutrition* 62 (10): 1170–77.

World Bank. 1993. *World Development Report: Investing in Health.* New York: Oxford University Press.

———. 2000. "The FRESH Framework: A Toolkit for Task Managers." Human Development Network, World Bank, Washington, DC.

———. 2002. *Education and HIV/AIDS: A Window of Hope.* Washington, DC: World Bank.

# CHAPTER 2

# Evidence of the Importance of Health and Nutrition for Education for All

The previous chapter provided background on the development of school health and nutrition programs in the context of Education for All (EFA). This chapter examines the evidence base that justifies these programs, exploring first the evidence for the interaction between health and education and then why they are particularly relevant to educational efforts to achieve EFA. Much of the content for this chapter is derived from three earlier analyses (Jukes, Drake, and Bundy 2008; Bundy et al. 2006, 2009).

## Impact on Education of Health and Nutrition Interventions at Different Stages in the Life Cycle of the Child

There is evidence that improving children's health and nutrition contributes to reaching the EFA goals of access, completion, and achievement in primary schools. As such, this chapter is most concerned with EFA goals 2, 5 and 6, which address issues of access, gender equity, and the quality of basic education, which map to the two education-related Millennium Development Goals (MDGs) of universal primary education completion and gender equality.

---

This chapter was written with Matthew Jukes.

Figure 2.1 helps frame the analysis. The figure shows schematically how the age-specific patterns of education are related to the age-specific patterns of disease and programmatic intervention. The figure is based on the main elements of the World Bank education strategy for basic education, which identifies three key objectives for intervention at sequential stages in the life cycle of a child: (i) ensuring children are ready to learn

**Figure 2.1    Health and Nutrition Interventions throughout Childhood Contribute to Education Outcomes**

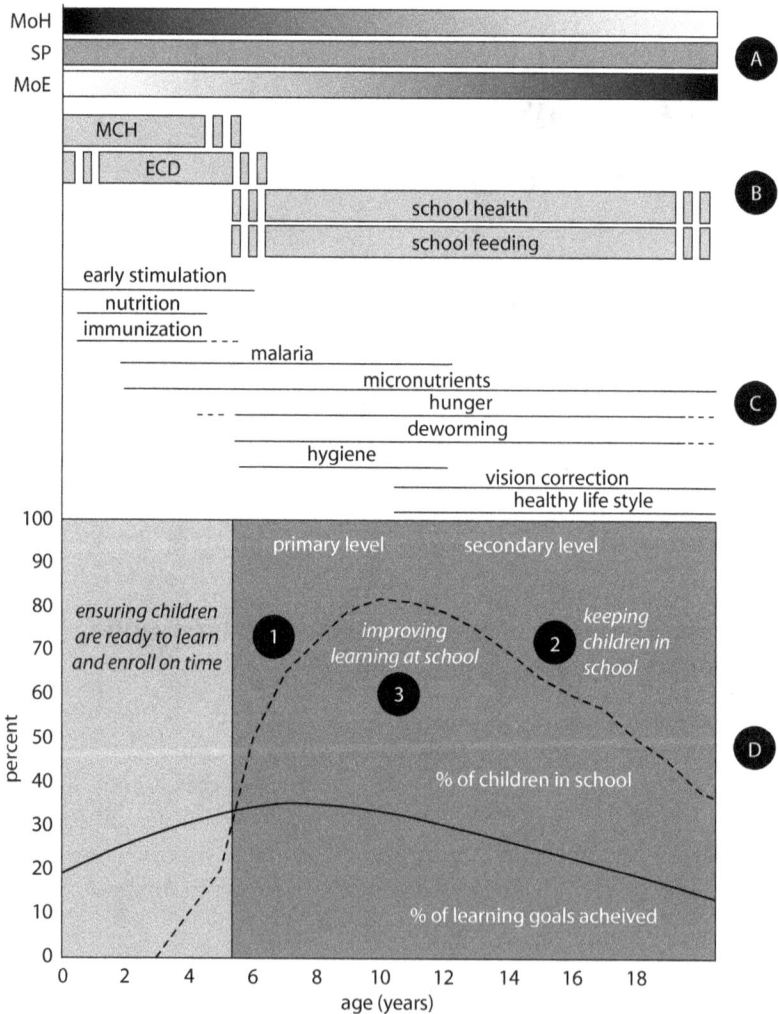

(continued next page)

and enroll on time; (ii) keeping children in school by enhancing atten-dance and reducing dropout rates; and (iii) improving learning at school by enhancing cognition and educational achievement. This chapter explores the evidence that interventions to improve health and nutrition and avoid hunger can contribute to these three objectives.

The figure emphasizes a sequence of different types of programs, often targeting different conditions, that together help ensure child development throughout the life cycle. By looking at this issue as a sequence, it is clear that the later (downstream) interventions build on the early (upstream) interventions, emphasizing the importance of starting early. This is especially the case where early deficits cannot be rectified subsequently.

The figure also shows that the sectoral responsibility for these inter-ventions is to some extent age dependent. The health sector typically takes the lead in delivering the maternal and child health programs that

---

*Source:* Adapted from Bundy and Guyatt 1996 and World Bank Education Sector Strategy 2010.

*Note:* The figure focuses on basic education only, the main focus of EFA. This figure focuses on interventions targeting improvements in health and nutrition. The x axis shows the age of the child. Note that for maternal and child health interventions it is common practice to view these as benefiting children from −9 months of age (that is, maternal health interventions that benefit the developing fetus), but this detail is omitted here as a simplification. The ordinate of the figure seeks to illustrate four different aspects of education, health, and nutrition at different stages in the life cycle of the child. The lowest window (D) provides an illustrative example of a typical education pattern in a low-income country. Some children enroll in school early, but most enroll much later than the official age. Attendance and enrollment peak around age 10 and then decline, often rapidly, as attendance becomes erratic and children drop out of school. These trends are most marked for girls. This part of the figure also shows an illustrative line for learning, as assessed in comparison with normative, age-specific standards. Learning is shown to start before school age and increase slightly with early schooling, but often deteriorates thereafter. This part of the figure emphasizes the three objectives of the World Bank education strategy and shows approximately how they relate to the age distribution.

Window C uses some examples of interventions to illustrate age specificity. For example, early immunization against diseases of childhood is important because both the risk of disease and the likelihood of infection are greater in young children. Similarly, early nutrition during the window of opportunity (typically described as from −9 to 24 months) is essential for physical and mental growth and development. Early mental stimulation is essential to cognitive development, not just during the early years but throughout preschool development. Other interventions, such as malaria control and micronutrients, may be viewed as relevant throughout the intersection between early life and school age, while some, such as deworming, are especially important at school age because the infection is most prevalent and intense in this age group. Refractive error and thus vision correction becomes more common in early adolescence, as does the relevance of behavioral-change interventions related to sexuality. These again are broad generalizations and will vary among countries, but are intended to illustrate the age dependency of health and nutrition interventions. Window B translates this age-dependency into the age-specificity of some possible programmatic responses, following the general sequence of maternal and child health programs (including early nutrition and integrated management of childhood illness), early child development programs (including early stimulation), and school health and nutrition programs (including school feeding). Window A attempts to show that there are at least three main sectors that are involved throughout this age range, with the strongest role usually played by health in early life, education during school age, and social protection throughout.

ECD = early child development, MCH = maternal and child health, MoE = ministry of education, MoH = ministry of health, SP = social protection.

are so important to children in the age range covering fetal development and the first two years of life—a range often called the window of opportunity and identified by the shorthand –9 to 24 months. There is then a mix of sectors, including education, that contribute to the period covered by early child development programs, usually taken to be two to six years of age. Thereafter, school health and nutrition programs seek to support children of school age. Thus there is a shifting of the center of gravity of responsibility from the health to the education sectors as children age, with social protection playing a potentially important role throughout. As we shall see in later chapters, however, this is a generalization, as approaches vary considerably among countries.

This figure is used to guide the analysis of the evidence base in this chapter. In the next sections the evidence is presented in relation to the three key objectives of the World Bank education strategy. Note that the evidence in this area is limited by the need for cross-sectoral investigation teams that have expertise in both the health and nutrition interventions and measures of cognitive and educational outcomes. In reporting these results the authors have specifically sought to identify the gender dimension of study findings, but in a majority of cases, data were not disaggregated by sex.

## Evidence for Strategic Objective 1: Ensuring that Children Are Ready to Learn and Enroll on Time

Health and nutrition interventions before school age (see figure 2.1) aim to ensure that children are ready to learn, usually assessed in terms of cognitive development, and that they enroll at the appropriate age, which is country specific but typically in the range of four to six years of age.[1]

### Ensuring that Children Enroll on Time

Many diseases have effects on school enrollment. Short stature due to poor nutritional status can lead parents to delay children's enrollment. Studies across Asia and Africa have found that stunted children (those with low height for age) enroll in school later than other children (Jamison 1986; Moock and Leslie 1986; Glewwe and Jacoby 1995; Partnership for Child Development 1999). The causality of the relationship is not yet fully understood, but it is notable that in the Philippines, the main effect is delayed enrollment, with no strong connection between early child nutrition and subsequent learning effort (Glewwe, Jacoby, and King 2001).

The relationship with enrollment is illustrated in figure 2.2. Children are grouped according to the number of years that they lag behind their peers at school. Children who are the appropriate age for their grade have an age-for-grade score of zero. Those who are a year older than the appropriate age for their grade have an age-for-grade z-score of –1, and so on. Children with a negative age-for-grade score most likely enrolled late in school. The figure shows that more children are stunted (low height for age) among children who are too old for their grade.

**Figure 2.2    Relationship between Stunting and Late Enrollment in Schoolchildren from Ghana and Tanzania**

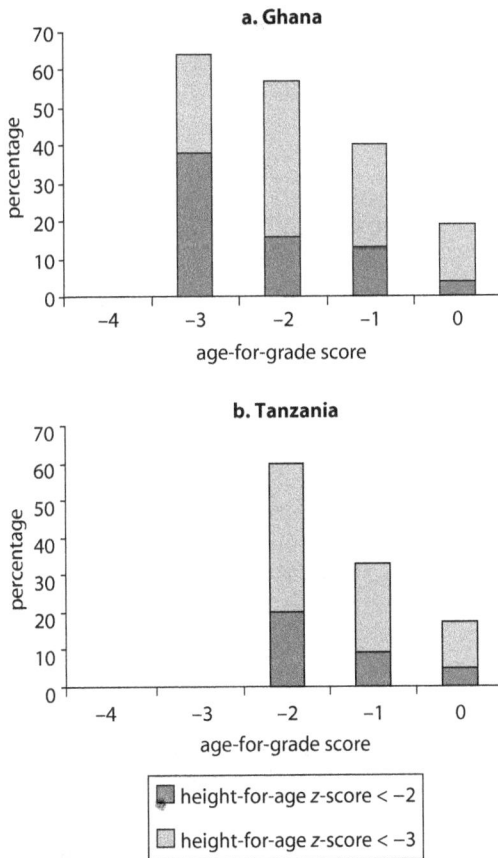

*Source:* Partnership for Child Development 1999.
*Note:* Age-for-grade score = number of years behind in schooling.

### *Ensuring that Children Are Ready to Learn: The Long-Term Benefits for Cognition and Educational Achievement of Early Health and Nutrition Interventions*

Illness and malnutrition in early childhood can result in long-term effects on educational achievement that are measurable at school age. There are many ways in which these long-term effects can occur. For example, poorly nourished young children are less sociable, more apathetic, and generally less likely to interact with their environment. Responding to their apathy, mothers are less likely to interact with these poorly nourished children. This lack of stimulation from the environment can affect children's mental development. In addition, malaria, iron deficiency, and undernutrition have direct effects on the brain. Suffering from these diseases in early childhood has a long-term impact on cognitive development through adolescence.

Table 2.1 presents some of the evidence for the effect of health and nutrition interventions in early life on subsequent cognitive and educational outcomes. The benefits of early nutrition and early stimulation are perhaps best known, and are well illustrated in the table. It is also apparent that early health interventions can have long-term benefits for education. This effect is illustrated by a study from The Gambia, which found that children who were protected from malaria for three consecutive transmission seasons before age 5 had improved cognitive performance at ages 17 to 21 (Jukes et al. 2006). For children who received the longest protection from malaria, the improvement in cognitive function was around 0.4 of a standard deviation (SD).

A recently pooled analysis of five birth cohort studies from low- and middle-income countries shows that weight gain in the first two years of life is an important predictor of schooling outcomes (Martorell et al. 2009). The authors suggest that it is not child size or growth per se that determines these outcomes, but rather that "growth failure in early childhood should be viewed as a marker of lack of nutrients at the cellular level that has systemic effects on growth and development in general." A recent meta-analysis of 30 early childhood interventions in infants through the pre-kindergarten age group found that stimulation and education are also important to cognitive outcomes and that educational interventions, or those interventions that included educational components, had greater effects than nutritional interventions alone (Nores and Barnett 2009).

**Table 2.1  Long-Term Impact of Health Interventions in Early Childhood on Cognitive and Educational Outcomes**

| Study | Country | Intervention | Age (years) | Sample characteristics | Effect size (SD) | Outcomes |
|---|---|---|---|---|---|---|
| Grantham-McGregor et al. 1994 | Jamaica | Stimulation | 14 | Severely malnourished | 0.68 | IQ |
| Walker et al. 2000 | Jamaica | Stimulation | 11–12 | Stunted | 0.38 | IQ |
| Walker et al. 2000 | Jamaica | Nutritional supplements | 11–12 | Stunted | No effect | IQ |
| Chang et al. 2002 | Jamaica | Stimulation or supplements | 11–12 | Stunted | No effect | Education tests |
| Pollitt, Watkins, and Husaini 1997 | Indonesia | Nutritional supplements | 8 | Initially > 18 months | Positive | Working memory |
| Jukes et al. 2006 | Gambia, The | Malaria prevention | 14–19 | Community cohort | 0.25–0.4 | Cognitive function |

*Source:* Jukes, Drake, and Bundy 2008.
*Note:* SD = standard deviation; IQ = intelligence quotient.

**Figure 2.3    Impact of Early Childhood Malaria Chemoprophylaxis on Educational Attainment in The Gambia**

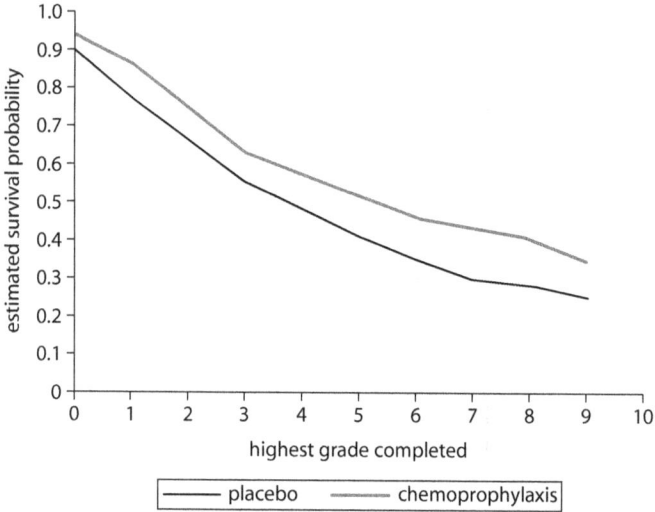

*Source:* Jukes et al. 2006.

### Ensuring that Children Are Ready to Learn: The Long-Term Effects of Poor Early Health on Subsequent Dropout Rates

A less commonly investigated phenomenon is the impact of early intervention on subsequent participation in education. This effect was investigated during a study in The Gambia described previously (Jukes et al. 2006). As figure 2.3 shows, children who were protected from malaria for three consecutive transmission seasons before age five were more likely to persist in school to higher grades. On average, children protected from malaria in the first few years of life stayed at school more than one year longer than those who had not been protected, and the effect was larger for girls. This is a potentially important area that deserves further investigation in terms of other early interventions.

## Evidence for Strategic Objective 2: Keeping Children in School by Enhancing Attendance and Reducing Dropout Rates

Even if early interventions have helped children enroll in school at the appropriate age, it is commonly reported that illness can cause children to miss school. Malaria in some areas of Africa has been cited as the source of more than 50 percent of preventable absenteeism (Brooker 2009). Worm infection in Kenya is also associated with absenteeism; schoolchildren who were given treatment against worms (hookworm and bilharzia) recorded improvements in school participation in a combined measure of enrollment and attendance (Miguel and Kremer 2004). In the first year of treatment, participation increased by 7 percentage points (from a baseline of around 75 percent participation).

Table 2.2 provides other examples of interventions that have improved school attendance, especially food, and table 2.3 explores the quality of the evidence that interventions improve attendance and enrollment. Note

**Table 2.2    Effectiveness of Interventions on Improving School Attendance**

| Study | Country | Intervention | Age (years) | Sample characteristics | Increase in % attendance |
|---|---|---|---|---|---|
| **Feeding** | | | | | |
| Powell et al. 1998 | Jamaica | Daily breakfast for 1 year | M = 9 | | 2.3 |
| van Stuijvenberg et al. 1999 | South Africa | Fortified biscuits | 6–11 | | 15.0 |
| **Deworming** | | | | | |
| Simeon et al. 1995 | Jamaica | Deworming | 7–10 | Mild–moderate whipworm | 6.7[a] |
| Miguel and Kremer 2004 | Kenya | Deworming | 6–18 | | 7.0 |
| **Malaria prevention** | | | | | |
| Fernando et al. 2006 | Sri Lanka | Antimalaria pills (chloroquine) | 6–12 | | 3.4 |

*Source:* Jukes, Drake, and Bundy 2008.
*Note:* M = mean.
a. For children with poor nutritional status only.

**Table 2.3    Qualitative Assessment of the Effect of School Feeding and Complementary Actions on Education Outcomes and Cognition**

| Intervention | Enrollment | Attendance | Educational achievement | Cognition |
|---|---|---|---|---|
| In-school meals | + (♀ effect) | +++ | +++ | +++ |
| Take-home rations | + (♀ effect) | + | ++ | ++ |
| Fortified biscuits | + | + | + | ++ |
| Micronutrient supplementation | + | +++ | +++ | +++ |
| Deworming | Not assessed | +++ | ++ | ++ |

*Source:* Bundy et al. 2009.
*Note:* + = evidence from quasi-experimental evaluation; ++ = evidence from at least one randomized controlled trial (RCT); +++ = evidence from more than one RCT; ♀ effect = enhances enrollment of girls.

that gender is an important factor, with school feeding programs having particularly strong effects on the attendance of girls.

Surprisingly, the authors identified no studies that explored the role of ill health and hunger at school age on dropout specifically, although it is recognized in nonhealth contexts that persistent absenteeism is a precursor of permanent dropout. In this context it is perhaps relevant to emphasize the long-term benefits of early intervention against malaria in reducing dropout rates, as discussed previously.

### Evidence for Strategic Objective 3: Improving Learning at School by Enhancing Cognition and Educational Achievement

Children's learning continues to suffer from poor health and nutrition while they are at school. Figure 2.4 illustrates the age-dependency of some common conditions, and shows how some are actually more common among school-age children. Cognitive abilities in this age group are poorer among children who, for example, are hungry and have malaria, worm infections, or iron deficiency. Treating children for these diseases and conditions can improve their potential to learn. Table 2.4 shows some examples of how health and nutrition interventions affect the cognitive function and educational achievement of school-age children. The table illustrates that, perhaps surprisingly, the quality of evidence tends to be stronger in this area than for more simple metrics, such as enrollment, perhaps reflecting the relative sophistication of the experimental designs needed to measure cognitive outcomes.

In interpreting these results, it is important to recognize that improving health may improve cognition, but quality education is then needed to help children exploit this potential. One study from Tanzania illustrates how, for most children, treatment alone cannot eradicate the cumulative effects of lifelong infection, nor compensate for years of missed learning opportunities. Deworming does not lead inevitably to improved cognitive development, but it does provide children with the potential to learn. Children in Tanzania who were given deworming treatment did not improve their performance on various cognitive tests, but did benefit from a teaching session in which they were shown how to perform the tests (Grigorenko et al. 2006). Performance on a reasoning task at the end of the study was around 0.25 SD higher in treated children than in those who still carried worm infections. The treated children's performance was similar to that of

**Figure 2.4    Age Distribution of Infection-Specific Morbidity**

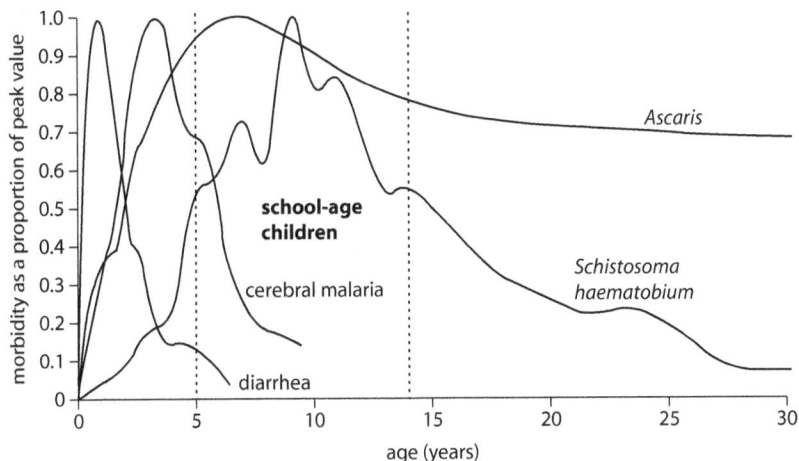

*Source:* Bundy and Guyatt 1996.

children who began the study without infection. This suggests that children are more ready to learn after treatment for worm infections and that they may be able to catch up with uninfected peers if their improved learning potential is then exploited effectively in the classroom (see figure 2.5).

In general, improving health and nutrition brings the greatest educational benefits to the poorest and most vulnerable schoolchildren. In some cases, greater benefits are seen for children suffering from several conditions of ill health. For example, the greatest benefits of deworming are seen for children with heavy worm loads who also have poor nutritional status (Simeon et al. 1995). In many countries, girls are disadvantaged in educational access, but malaria prevention helps reduce the enrollment gap between girls and boys (Jukes et al. 2006). Health and nutrition interventions also help the most economically disadvantaged children. Early childhood nutritional supplements also have a greater long-term effect on children from poor families.

A number of studies (Simeon and Grantham-McGregor 1989; Pollitt, Cueto, and Jacoby 1998; Simeon 1998) have found that missing breakfast impairs educational performance to a greater extent among children with poor nutritional status. In one study in Jamaica, eating breakfast improved the scores of malnourished children by 0.25 SD more than adequately nourished children in three cognitive

**Table 2.4  Impact of Health Interventions on Cognitive Function and Educational Achievement of School-Age Children**

| Study | Country | Intervention | Age (years) | Sample characteristics | Effect size (SD) | Outcomes |
|---|---|---|---|---|---|---|
| **Iron** | | | | | | |
| Pollitt et al. 1989 | Thailand | Iron supplementation | 9–11 | Iron deficient | No effect | Raven's Progressive Matrices |
| | | | | | | Education tests |
| Soemantri, Pollitt, and Kim 1985 | Indonesia | Iron supplementation | 10–11 | Iron deficient | 0.42 | Education tests |
| | | | | | 0.51 | Concentration |
| Seshadri and Gopaldas 1989 | India | Iron supplementation | 8–15 | Iron deficient | Positive[a] | 4 cognitive tests |
| **Feeding** | | | | | | |
| Powell et al. 1998 | Jamaica | Daily breakfast for 1 year | M = 9 | | 0.11[b] | Arithmetic |
| | | | | | No effect | Reading |
| | | | | | No effect | Spelling |
| Whaley et al. 2003 | Kenya | Meat/energy[c] supplement for 2 years | M = 7.6 | | 0.16[d] | Raven's Progressive Matrices |
| | | | | | No effect | Verbal comp |
| | | | | | 0.11–0.15 | Arithmetic |
| **Micronutrients** | | | | | | |
| Vazir et al. 2006 | India | Multiple micronutrients for 1 year | 6–15 | | Positive | Attention test |
| | | | | | No effect | 2 cognitive tests |
| | | | | | No effect | IQ |
| | | | | | No effect | 4 education tests |
| **Malaria prevention** | | | | | | |
| Fernando et al. 2006 | Sri Lanka | Antimalaria pills (chloroquine) | 6–12 | | 0.65 | Mathematics |
| | | | | | 0.59 | Language |

44

| Clarke et al. 2008 | Kenya | IPT (amodiaquine and sulfadoxine-pyrime-thamine) | 10–18 | | 0.20–0.55 | Sustained attention |
|---|---|---|---|---|---|---|
| **Deworming** | | | | | | |
| Nokes et al. 1992 | Jamaica | Deworming | 9–12 | Moderate–high whipworm infection | 0.16–0.26 | 3 cognitive tests |
| | | | | | No effect | 5 cognitive tests |
| Simeon, Grantham-McGregor, and Wong 1995 | Jamaica | | 7–10 | Mild–moderate whipworm | ~0.15[e] | Verbal fluency |
| | | | | | No effect | 6 cognitive tests |
| Simeon et al. 1995 | Jamaica | | 6–12 | Whipworm infection | 0.16[f] | Spelling |
| | | | | | No effect | Reading |
| | | | | | No effect | Arithmetic |
| | | | | | No effect | 7 cognitive tests |
| Sternberg et al. 1997 | Jamaica | | M = 10.3 | Mild–moderate whipworm | No effect | 7 cognitive tests |
| Nokes et al. 1999 | China | Deworming | 5–16 | S. japonicum infection | 0.59[g] | Verbal fluency |
| | | | | | No effect | 4 cognitive tests |
| Grigorenko et al. 2006 | Tanzania | Deworming | 11–13 | Heavy S. haematobium | 0.08–0.32 | 3 "dynamic" cognitive tests |
| | | | | Moderate hookworm infection | 0.09 | 1 cognitive test |
| | | | | | No effect | 7 cognitive tests |

*Source:* Jukes, Drake, and Bundy 2008.

*Note:* SD = standard deviation; M = mean; IPT = intermittent preventive treatment.

a. Effect is positive in 2/4 cognitive tests for girls given 60 mg of iron daily and boys given 30 mg of iron and in all tests for boys given 40 mg of iron.

b. Effect only for youngest children.

c. A milk supplement had no effect.

d. No effects from energy supplement.

e. Effect only for children with poor nutritional status.

f. Effect only for children with heaviest worm loads.

g. Effect only for youngest children.

**Figure 2.5    Effect of Treating Children for Worm Infections on Syllogisms Test Scores over Time**

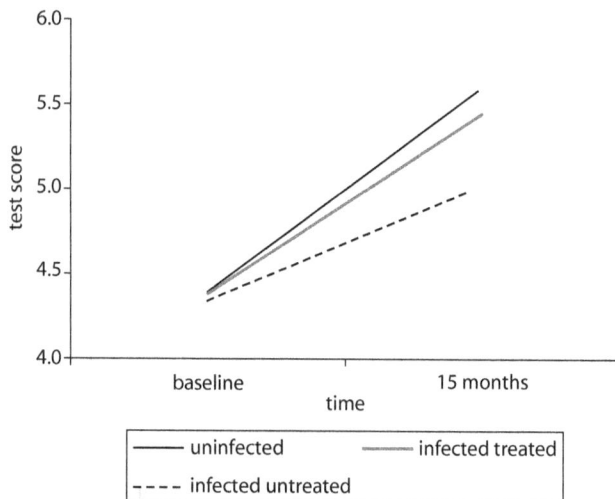

*Source:* Grigorenko et al. 2006.

tests of memory and processing speed and one test of arithmetic (see figure 2.6) (Simeon and Grantham-McGregor 1989). This finding echoes those of several other sections of this book: the effects of various health and nutritional problems on children's education interact with one another. Invariably, the children who are initially worst off benefit the most.

These studies show that the greatest benefits of intervention accrue to the children who are worst off at the outset—the poor, the sick, and the malnourished—which suggests that school health and school feeding programs can be pro-poor.

This indicates that a major advantage of school health and nutrition programs is that they do something that few other education interventions do: they offer the greatest benefit to the poorest children. To understand why that is the case, the concepts of "double jeopardy" and "capability theory" need to be invoked. The concept of double jeopardy was originally applied to at-risk children in the United States (Parker, Greer, and Zuckerman 1988) and refers to the way in which the poorest people in society suffer twice at the hands of disease and poor nutrition. First, poor people are in jeopardy by being more likely to suffer from poor health and poor nutrition. With few exceptions, the diseases that affect

**Figure 2.6    Differential Impact of Missing Breakfast on Cognitive Function of Malnourished and Well-Nourished Children in Jamaica**

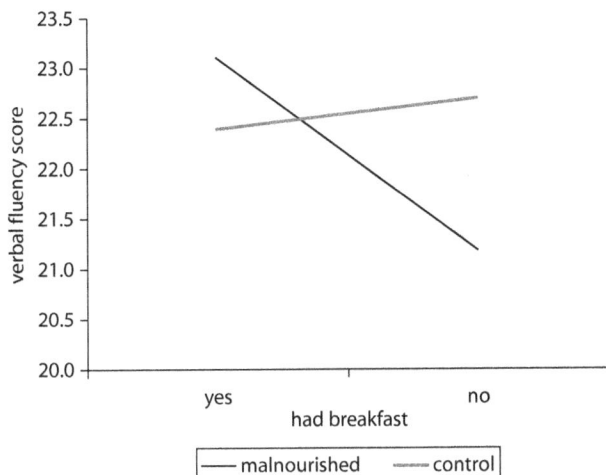

*Source:* Simeon and Grantham-McGregor 1989.

children and their education are most prevalent in poor countries and the poorest communities within those countries. Second, as the evidence shows, these conditions of poor health and nutrition have the biggest educational impact on the poor and, even when a disease reaches rich and poor alike, the poor are most likely to experience disruption to their learning as a result.

Another way of understanding how school health and nutrition programs promote equity is through capability theory. In his influential account of this theory, Amartya Sen (1999) argues that development should be a process of expanding people's capabilities to pursue a life that they have reason to value. This contrasts with resource-based views of development, which promote the expansion of available resources, such as income. One of the arguments for a focus on capabilities rather than resources is based on equity: the more capable students—that is, the richer, smarter, healthier children—are able to benefit most from resources with the result that inequalities are widened. This theoretical position is borne out by evidence. From textbook provision (Kremer 2003) to teacher incentives (Muralidharan and Sundararaman 2009), many educational interventions bring the greatest benefits to the highest-achieving children. But with school health and nutrition programs, the capabilities of the poorest—and usually least capable—students are improved to the greatest extent, thereby promoting equity in the classroom. Note also that when a more equal distribution of capabilities is achieved, further investments in resources, such as the provision of new textbooks, will benefit children more equally. Capability theory helps explain why school health and nutrition programs can help level the playing field for education for all.

## Estimating the Scale of Impact of Health and Nutrition on Educational Outcomes

Thus far the chapter has discussed evidence that ill health, hunger, and malnutrition have negative consequences for educational outcomes. This section tries to quantify the scale of these effects. One way to think about the long-term benefits of improved cognitive abilities resulting from better health is to assess the implications for increased educational attainment—often synonymous with the number of years spent at school. Three different approaches, described in more detail elsewhere (Jukes, Drake, and Bundy 2008), are used to estimate the relationship between improved cognitive abilities and equivalent years of schooling.

### Estimating the Scale of Impact at the Individual Level
The first approach is to consider improvements in cognitive abilities and educational achievement in the early years of schooling and estimate the long-term impact that they may have on time spent at school. In countries with high dropout rates, a small improvement in achievement in the early grades may be enough to ensure promotion to the next grade level and renewed motivation and ability to succeed. In this way, a small improvement in scores in the early years can have a large cumulative impact over the long term.

One study in South Africa assessed the direct impact of test scores in grade 2 on students' progression through primary school (Liddell and Rae 2001). They found that children who score 0.25 SD above the average in grade 2 exams were approximately 1.5 times more likely to complete grade 7.[2] Figure 2.7 shows how the dropout pattern is different for children who scored 0.25 SD higher than the mean on their grade 2 exams. If a school health and nutrition intervention raised exams scores by 0.25 SD and had a similar impact on dropout rates, the extra cumulative years

**Figure 2.7    Estimating School Dropout Rates with and without School Health and Nutrition Interventions in South Africa**

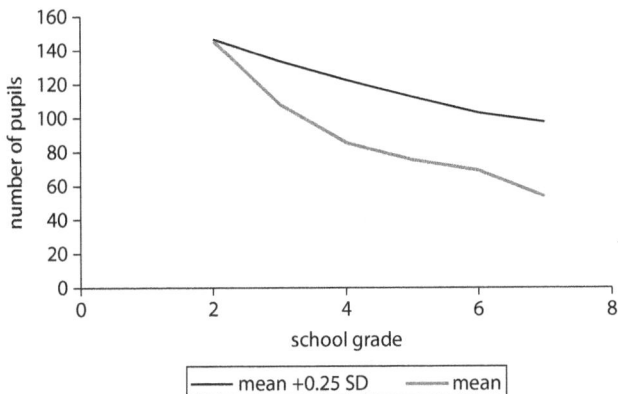

*Source:* Liddell and Rae 2001.

of schooling would average 1.19 years per pupil over the course of primary school.

The second approach is to estimate the number of years of schooling required for sick children to catch up with healthy children. For example, in Tanzania heavy schistosomiasis (a worm infection) was associated with a decrease in arithmetic scores of 1.4 marks (0.25 SD) (Jukes et al. 2002). An extra year's schooling was associated with an increase in arithmetic scores of 2.2 marks (0.42 SD). Thus, the negative effect of heavy schistosomiasis was equivalent to that of missing just over half a year of schooling.

Finally, the cognitive gains from an extra year of schooling can be estimated retrospectively. In a study of adults in South Africa, each additional year of primary schooling was associated with a more modest 0.1 SD increase in cognitive test scores (Moll 1998). According to these estimates, a typical increase of 0.25 SD associated with a school health and nutrition intervention is equivalent to an additional 2.5 years of schooling.

These three different methods for estimating the effect of school health and nutrition interventions on educational attainment suggest that the typical scale of benefit from these interventions would increase educational attainment by between 0.5 and 2.5 years. That is, children would stay at school for between 0.5 and 2.5 years longer as a result of a school health and nutrition intervention. This estimate is consistent with the few observations from the field that have measured educational outcomes directly. For example, a study in The Gambia found that preventing malaria in early childhood resulted in children staying in school about one year longer (Jukes et al. 2006).

### Estimating the Scale of Impact at the Global Level

So far, the discussion in this chapter has focused on the individual. But a key argument for school health and nutrition programs is that diseases affecting education are highly prevalent. Thus, school health and nutrition programs have the potential to bring the benefits discussed previously to vast numbers of children. This section tries to quantify this potential global impact.

Table 2.5 examines three common diseases in terms of their impact on the cognitive ability of the estimated 575 million school-age children in low-income countries (UNESCO 2008). Empirical deficits in test scores attributable to these diseases are converted into an equivalent loss in IQ points. Clearly, conditions of poor health and nutrition have more complex effects on cognitive functioning than are implied by the conversion into IQ points. However, IQ provides a widely understood scale with which to illustrate the global impact of cognitive impairments resulting from disease.

The table also estimates the additional number of cases of children with IQs less than 70 (a measure that is part of the definition of mild mental retardation; American Psychiatric Association 1994), which are attributable to each disease. It also estimates the lost years of schooling attributable to impaired cognitive function (as estimated in the previous section).

The estimates suggest that these three common diseases may result in an additional 15 million to 45 million cases of mild mental retardation in

**Table 2.5    Estimates of the Global Cognitive Impact of Common Diseases of School-Age Children in Poor Countries**

| Common diseases | Prevalence (%) | Total cases (millions) | IQ points lost per child | Additional cases of < 70 (millions) | Lost years of schooling (millions) |
|---|---|---|---|---|---|
| Worms | 30 | 169 | 3.75 | 15.8 | 201 |
| Stunting | 52 | 292 | 3 | 21.6 | 284 |
| Anemia | 53 | 298 | 6 | 45.6 | 524 |

*Source:* Jukes, Drake, and Bundy 2008.

primary schoolchildren and a loss of the equivalent of between 200 million and 524 million years of primary schooling worldwide. While the precision of these striking figures may be open to debate, they clearly show that even minor cognitive deficits resulting from ubiquitous diseases can result in extraordinarily large-scale effects.

## Estimating the Scale of Benefit of Health and Nutrition Interventions

The analysis above shows that some common conditions, each of which may have a relatively small effect in itself, are so prevalent that they add up to a major burden. This section addresses the long-run impact of these conditions on individuals and then relates this impact to the cost of the interventions. Because the interventions offer benefits for both health and education, data are presented on both outcomes.

### Improving Children's Health

The impact of poor health and nutrition is typically expressed as a "global burden of disease estimate" that focuses on the mortality and physical morbidity attributable to disease (Murray and Lopez 1996). In these estimates, schoolchildren are often perceived as healthy if they are not suffering from any clear physical symptoms of a disease. Prevalent chronic conditions that have insidious effects are often invisible in public health statistics and, as a result, the apparent benefits of school health and nutrition programs may be underestimated.

For health outcomes, the concept of disability-adjusted life years (DALYs) has proved valuable in capturing the burden of often invisible ill health. This measure not only includes the number of years of life lost by premature death due to a disease, but also estimates the equivalent fraction of a year lost through suffering an illness. The advantage of such a method is that it permits the estimation and quantification of the total impact of a disease over a lifetime. This metric has been used to estimate the cost of simple school health services—deworming, micronutrient supplements, and chlorination of water—at around $20–$34 per DALY. Table 2.6 compares this value with estimates for some other public health interventions.

The comparison suggests that simple school health services are in the same range as those public health services considered to be good value, or "best buys." The school health services considered in this analysis are among those with the lowest cost; it does not follow that other, more

**Table 2.6    Cost (US$) per DALY Gained of School Health and Nutrition Programs Relative to Other Common Public Health Interventions**

| Health intervention | Cost per DALY gained |
|---|---|
| Expanded program on immunization plus | 12–30 |
| School health services | 20–34 |
| Family planning services | 20–150 |
| Integrated management of childhood illness | 30–100 |
| Prenatal and delivery care | 30–100 |
| Tobacco and alcohol prevention programs | 35–55 |

*Source:* Jukes, Drake, and Bundy 2008.

expensive, school health interventions are similarly of good value. This is an area where estimates for more interventions would be helpful.

### Improving Education

Table 2.6 addresses the benefits of school health and nutrition programs in terms of improvements in children's health, but the benefits extend beyond physical health to include improved education outcomes. Measures of mortality or health-related disability do not capture the impact of ill health on cognitive development or educational outcomes— potential benefits that are particularly relevant at an age when the foundations are laid for lifelong learning and productivity in adulthood.

Including education in burden of disease estimates is difficult because simple metrics have not been developed to quantify the lifelong impact of diseases on children's learning. An equivalent measure is needed to estimate the impact of improved education throughout people's lives. One way to calculate the lifelong benefits of education is to consider its impact on economic productivity. This approach has the advantage of quantifying the effect in a way that can be compared with other interventions and summing up the effect over a lifetime. The most common approach to assessing the economic benefits of education has been to calculate the increase in wages resulting from an increase in years of education.

The following sections consider the cost-effectiveness of school health and nutrition programs for improving children's education.

### Economic Benefits of Increased School Participation

Evidence suggests that an additional year spent at school increases productivity. Increased years of schooling are associated with higher

worker productivity in waged employment and other economically productive activities, such as farming (Jamison and Lau 1982;
Psacharopoulos and Woodhall 1985; Strauss and Thomas 1995). The
impact of education on productivity is quantified in calculations of rates
of return to education. These rates of return can be thought of as the
percentage increase in annual wages resulting from an additional year
spent at school. Overall, studies find that the returns to years of schooling in wages are higher in poor countries than in rich countries. For Sub-
Saharan Africa, for example, studies have documented a 12 percent rate
of return to one additional year in school, compared to 10 percent in
Asian countries, 7.5 percent for Organisation for Economic Co-operation
and Development (OECD) countries, and 12 percent in Latin American
and Caribbean countries. These returns are very high, even allowing for
a portion of this return to be attributed to ability and other factors that
are not the product of schooling itself (Card 2001).

Where improved health results in children spending more time at
school, the rates of return calculations discussed previously can be used
to estimate the benefits of school health interventions. For example, a
study in Kenya found deworming treatment improved primary school
participation by 9.3 percent, with an estimated 0.14 additional years of
education per pupil treated over the course of their schooling (Miguel
and Kremer 2004). The study used information on rates of return to education in Kenya to estimate that treating one child increased lifetime
wages by $30 at a cost of only $0.49 for the deworming treatment.[3] This
investment seems a little more costly when the costs of potential additional teacher resources, which may be needed to cope with increased
attendance, are added. Even taking this into account, however, the benefit of $30 can be gained from an investment of under $10—a high return
on a small investment.

## Economic Benefits of Long-Term Improvements in Cognitive Abilities

A number of school health and nutrition interventions are associated with
increases in cognitive abilities (see table 2.7 for examples). If these short-
term benefits are roughly maintained over the course of children's schooling, the cognitive abilities of children when they leave school would be
improved, on average, by around 0.25 SD.

In the United States (Zax and Rees 2002), an increase in IQ of one SD
is associated with an increase in wages of over 11 percent. Similar estimates have been made for the relationship between cognitive abilities

**Table 2.7    Cognitive Impact of Selected School Health and Nutrition Interventions**

| Study | Intervention and duration | Age | Sample characteristics | Effect size (SD) | Outcomes |
|---|---|---|---|---|---|
| Simeon and Grantham-McGregor 1989 | Breakfast (1 day) | 9–10 | Malnourished | 0.25 | Memory, speed of processing, arithmetic |
| Soemantri, Pollitt, and Kim 1985 | Iron supplementation (2 months) | 10–11 | Iron deficient | 0.40 | Education |
| Nokes et al. 1992 | Deworming (3 months) | 9–12 | Moderate–heavy whipworm | 0.25 | Memory |
| Grigorenko et al. 2006 | Deworming (18 months) | 11–13 | Heavy hook-worm/bilharzia | 0.25 | Learning |

*Source:* Jukes, Drake, and Bundy 2008.

and wages in Ghana, Kenya, Pakistan, South Africa, and Tanzania (Hanushek and Woessmann 2007). The estimated increase in wages associated with a SD increase in cognitive abilities ranges from 5 to 48 percent, with typical values around 20 percent. Extrapolating this result, a 0.25 SD increase in cognitive abilities—which is an approximate estimate of the range of benefits resulting from those school health and nutrition interventions that have been studied—would lead to roughly a 5 percent increase in wages. For most of the countries listed above (excluding South Africa), this represents around a $25 increase in yearly earnings due to a school health and nutrition intervention.[4]

Estimated additional earnings help us think about the impact of school health and nutrition interventions on economic productivity after school. An additional year of primary schooling leads to around a 10 percent increase in wages in poor countries. For countries such as Ghana, Kenya, Pakistan, and Tanzania, this represents an increase in wages of around $50 per year. The cost-benefit analysis would be more complex in these cases, however, as the additional year of schooling would come with additional costs. Thus the increase in wages of $50 per year cannot be viewed as the return solely on the small investment in improved health. Nevertheless, it appears that an additional year of primary school is a good investment, particularly in poor countries. In this situation, improved health can be seen as the catalyst—the facilitating factor—that makes the investment in education possible.

The estimates presented in this section are necessarily speculative; more precise estimates are required. However, they appear to suggest that the long-run returns are substantial in comparison with the cost of simple school health services, which may be less than $1 per child. In this case the resulting improvements in education lead to economic returns many times the value of the investment. For more expensive interventions this may not be the case, further studies are needed to assess this conjecture.

### Comparing School Health and Nutrition Programs with Other Programs to Improve Education Outcomes

An important question is how school health and nutrition programs compare with other interventions to improve education. This is an area of study that is underdeveloped generally but particularly so for interventions that offer benefits across sectors; it is also an area that is particularly open to misinterpretation. Figure 2.8 compares different types of interventions in terms of the number of extra years of schooling that can be bought for a $100 investment. School-based deworming, school-based micronutrient supplements, and school feeding all seem to be particularly good investments, although one has to take care not to apply a simplistic interpretation. Not only are the interventions very different, but so too are the range of outcomes and political economies of the countries in which the studies were conducted.

The results of studies on conditional cash transfers (CCTs) in Mexico help illustrate the difficulties of interpretation. Although CCT interventions have, relatively, the smallest return, this rate of return (in the context of Mexico) has long-run benefits that make the CCT program, Comunidades, a particularly good investment. This is even truer because CCTs offer substantial additional benefits, especially for health and social protection (see Fiszbein et al. 2009). CCT programs are thus a potentially very cost-effective method to increase school enrollment (Morley and Coady 2003; Fiszbein et al. 2009). The Comunidades Program is estimated to have increased enrollment by 3.4 percent and increased schooling by 0.66 years, with an average cash transfer for grades 3–8 of about $136 per child per school year (Schultz 2004). Gains from a similar program in Nicaragua were estimated at 0.45 years of school at a cost of $77 per year (Maluccio and Flores 2005).

Experience with CCTs has now been documented in some 30 countries and similarly encouraging results obtained. Yet it is still unclear to

**Figure 2.8    Additional Years of Schooling per $100 Invested in a Program**

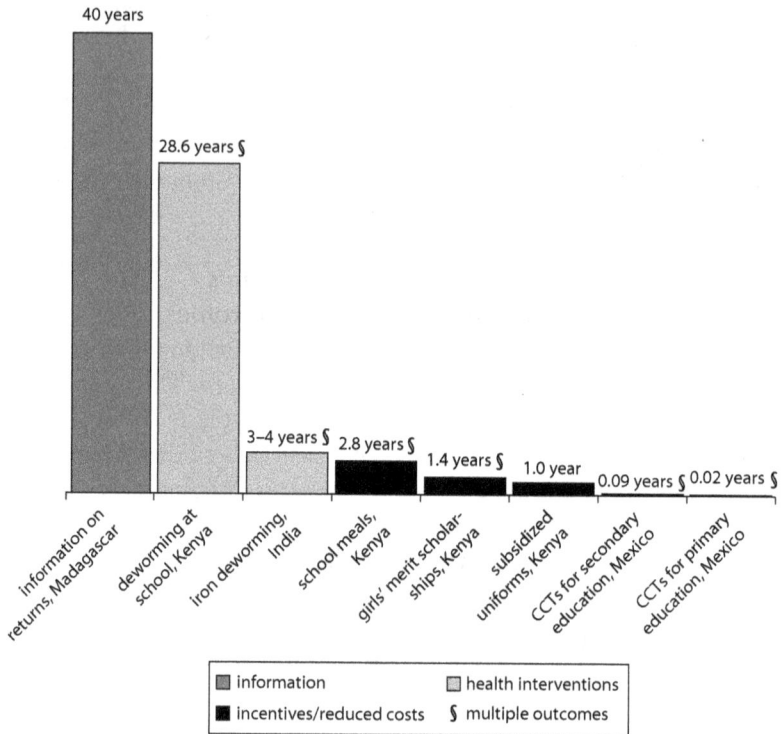

40 years

28.6 years §

3–4 years §  2.8 years §  1.4 years §  1.0 year  0.09 years § 0.02 years §

information on returns, Madagascar

deworming at school, Kenya

iron deworming, India

school meals, Kenya

girls' merit scholar-ships, Kenya

subsidized uniforms, Kenya

CCTs for secondary education, Mexico

CCTs for primary education, Mexico

☐ information         ☐ health interventions
■ incentives/reduced costs   § multiple outcomes

Source: http://www.povertyactionlab.org/policy-lessons/education/student-attendance.
Note: Graph includes interventions on deworming and iron, school feeding, incentives and subsidies, as well as actionable knowledge.

what extent the CCT approach is applicable generally. In Cambodia a CCT program resulted in a 20 percent increase in enrollment, an effect that is even more impressive because it was achieved with an income transfer of around 2 percent, rather than the 20 percent of Comunidades (Filmer and Schady 2010). However, in Morocco and the Republic of Yemen, efforts to introduce similar programs have foundered on logistical issues.

The way in which benefits are achieved introduces another important distinction in interpreting comparative studies. CCTs and other incentive and subsidy interventions have their main education effects on attendance and have little measurable benefit on learning outcomes. Health and nutrition programs also benefit attendance and can have additional effects on cognition and learning. From the school health perspective, CCTs resemble the benefits of a take-home ration rather than the physiological benefits of the delivery of health services and food. It is perhaps for this reason that most middle-income countries offer school health services and, often, school feeding programs alongside their CCT programs.

It is also perhaps worth noting the very different scale of investment required. Successful CCT programs are generally very large in scope, representing a commitment of between 0.1 and 0.2 percent of gross national income. This is much greater than the cost of school feeding, and several orders of magnitude greater than the cost of basic school health services such as deworming.

The educational gains of school health and nutrition programs should also be considered in the context of alternative educational inputs, such as improving teacher salaries and qualifications, reducing class size, improving school infrastructure, or providing additional instructional materials. This consideration is addressed in figure 2.9. There are many studies that relate student outcomes to school characteristics, but few provide information on the relative or actual costs of the educational inputs (Pritchett and Filmer 1999). The evidence from the few randomized evaluations that have been conducted suggests that the scale of impact of additional education inputs is typically of a similar or lower magnitude compared to that of school health and nutrition programs (Kremer 2003). In Brazil and India, instructional materials (such as additional textbooks) had the highest productivity, raising student test scores significantly more than other inputs for each dollar spent. However, even these interventions only had an impact of between 0.06 SD and 0.4 SD (Lockheed and Verspoor 1999). In Kenya, textbook provision had no impact on the lowest-achieving 60 percent of the students and raised test scores by 0.2 SD for the highest-achieving 40 percent. The data in this chapter suggest that school health and nutrition interventions improve educational achievement by a similar amount (0.25–0.4 SD).

Unfortunately there are no meta-analyses that specifically compare outcomes for a range of school health and nutrition interventions in low-income countries. The nearest analysis is a recent study of the cognitive impact of ECD interventions in 23 countries, only 9 of which could be classified as low income. This analysis showed that the six studies that used cash transfers as the intervention had the smallest average effect on cognition and the six using nutrition interventions achieved an intermediate effect, while the largest effect was achieved by the majority of

**Figure 2.9   Comparative Cost and Effectiveness of Education Interventions in Terms of Outcomes**

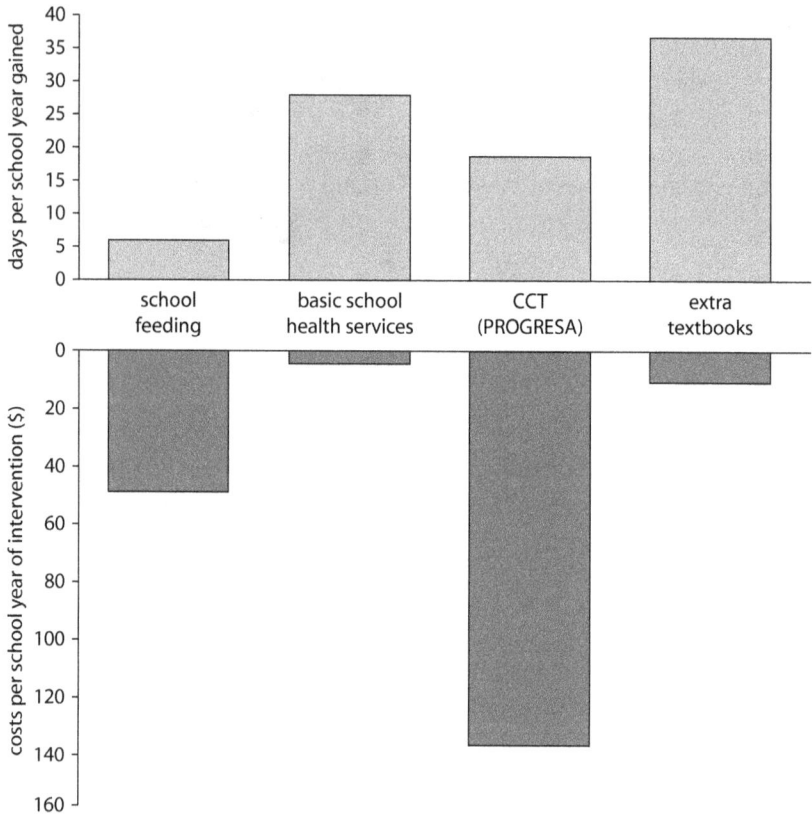

*Source:* JPAL 2005; Jukes, Drake, and Bundy 2008.

studies (*n* = 26) that used education alone or in combination with other interventions (Nores and Barnett 2009). This effect may of course be age specific, since the importance of early stimulation is well documented.

It is misleading to view school health and nutrition programs as competitive with education investments. The evidence shows that improving health can increase participation and learning—that is, increase demand—but this will result in improvements in education outcomes only if there is concomitant improvement in education supply. Similarly, improving the quality of education supply will not benefit those children who are too sick or hungry to attend school or learn while there. There is a clear argument for including school health and nutrition programs among the list of interventions known to enhance education demand. These include abolishing school fees and offering incentives or subsidies, such as providing uniforms or stipends. But the overall message is that there needs to be a balance between supply and demand.

## Conclusions: Evidence of the Importance of Health and Nutrition for Education for All

The importance of health and nutrition interventions for education is a function of the patterns of ill health and disease in school-age children. School health and nutrition programs owe their effectiveness to the confluence of certain aspects of disease in school-age children:

- Diseases that affect education are highly prevalent.
- Poor health and malnutrition are more common in poor children.
- Many of the prevalent diseases that affect education are preventable and treatable.
- School-age children bear the greatest burden of some of the most common diseases that affect education.
- Improving children's health and nutrition can bring substantial benefits for cognitive development and education.

Health and nutrition interventions, starting early and continuing throughout childhood, can contribute to MDG2 and the goals of EFA. The life-cycle sequence of MCH (–9 to 24 months), ECD (0–6 years), and school health and nutrition programs (6–15 years) can make an important contribution to educational outcomes and to EFA. Each programmatic approach contributes to one or more of the following key objectives of a basic EFA strategy:

- Ensuring that children are ready to learn and enroll in school on time: MCH and ECD interventions are associated with these outcomes.
- Keeping children in school by enhancing attendance and reducing dropout rates: school health and nutrition, school feeding, and MCH interventions are associated with these outcomes.
- Improving learning at school by enhancing cognition and educational achievement: school health and nutrition and school feeding programs are associated with these outcomes.

These results suggest that a life-cycle approach is necessary, involving a sequence of age-appropriate interventions that include MCH, ECD, and school health and nutrition programs.

**Health and nutrition interventions can promote gender equity and equality, as well as contribute to MDG3.** Gender is a particularly central issue in education, as recognized in MDG3, which specifically addresses gender equality and equity in education. It is apparent that school health and nutrition programs can play an important gender role in promoting EFA, since there is a gender dimension to the management of some of the most common conditions and their associated and widely used interventions, for example:

- Deworming and iron supplementation both offer particular benefits to girls because women and girls are, for physiological reasons, more likely to experience high rates of anemia.
- School feeding has a strong impact on the enrollment of girls.
- Avoiding malaria infection in early life results in increased participation by girls in education at school age; in The Gambia, this difference was the equivalent of an extra year of schooling.

Given the demonstrated importance of gender in relation to these conditions, it is clearly essential that all future studies of other school health and nutrition interventions ensure that data are disaggregated by sex, and that the presence or absence of a gender role is clearly defined.

**School health and nutrition programs can contribute to equity in education.** The greatest educational (and health) benefits of intervention accrue to the children who are worst off to begin with—the poor, the sick, and the malnourished. This has the effect of "leveling the playing field"—that is, helping the worst-off children achieve their potential and catch up with the better-off children. There are two important ways in which school health and nutrition programs help to achieve this outcome:

- They help address the issue of double jeopardy: poor children who suffer disproportionately from ill health also benefit disproportionately from the interventions.
- They help address the inequities intrinsic to capacity theory: the capabilities of the poorest, and usually least capable, students are improved to the greatest extent.

**The potential scale of the education benefit from school health and nutrition interventions is large.** Using three different methods, it is estimated that effective school health and nutrition programs in primary schools in low-income countries could potentially

- Help children stay in school for between 0.5 and 2.5 years longer—an estimate consistent with the few observations from the field that have measured educational outcomes directly.
- Enhance IQ per child by some 3.75–6 IQ points.
- Prevent the loss of the equivalent of between 200 million and 524 million years of primary schooling.

While the precision of these striking figures may be open to debate, they show that even minor cognitive deficits resulting from ubiquitous diseases can result in large-scale effects.

**School-based health and nutrition interventions should be considered alongside more traditional education interventions in seeking to achieve EFA.** It is apparent that school health and nutrition interventions can play a similar role to more traditional interventions—for example, abolishing school fees, instituting cash transfers, and offering incentives or subsidies such as providing uniforms or stipends—in increasing participation in education. Their value will be context specific, as will the appropriateness of specific components. One universal, however, is that the delivery of these interventions must not be so burdensome as to serve as a tax on the very education that they seek to promote.

## Notes

1. For further discussion of these issues in the contexts of Bolivia, Indonesia, Mexico, and the Philippines, see, respectively, Glewwe, Jacoby, and King (2001); Behrman, Cheng, and Todd (2004); Behrman and Hoddinott (2005); and Frankenberg, Suriastini, and Thomas (2005).
2. Authors' calculations are based on reported results from Liddell and Rae (2001).
3. The figure of $30 reflects the fact that people value future earnings less than current earnings. (A bird in the hand is worth two in the bush.) Future earnings are "discounted to the present" in the jargon.
4. This figure is based on gross national income per capita, which ranges from $400 to $700 in the listed countries, with a median around $500.

## References

American Psychiatric Association. 1994. *Diagnostic and Statistical Manual of Mental Disorders*. 4th ed. Washington, DC: American Psychiatric Association.

Behrman, J. R., Y. Cheng, and P. E. Todd. 2004. "Evaluating Preschool Programs When Length of Exposure to the Program Varies: A Nonparametric Approach." *Review of Economics and Statistics* 86 (1): 108–32.

Behrman, J. R., and J. Hoddinott. 2005. "Programme Evaluation with Unobserved Heterogeneity and Selective Implementation: The Mexican PROGRESA Impact on Child Nutrition." *Oxford Bulletin on Economics and Statistics* 67 (4): 547–69.

Brooker, S. 2009. *Malaria Control in Schools: A Toolkit on Effective Education Sector Responses to Malaria in Africa*. Washington, DC: World Bank; London: Partnership for Child Development.

Bundy, D. A. P., C. Burbano, M. Grosh, A. Gelli, M. Jukes, and L. Drake. 2009. *Rethinking School Feeding: Social Safety Nets, Child Development, and the Education Sector*. Washington, DC: World Bank.

Bundy, D. A. P., and H. L. Guyatt. 1996. "Schools for Health: Focus on Health, Education, and the School-Age Child." *Parasitology Today* 12 (8): 1–16.

Bundy, D. A. P., S. Shaeffer, M. Jukes, K. Beegle, A. Gillespie, L. Drake, S.-H. F. Lee, A.-M. Hoffmann, J. Jones, A. Mitchell, C. Wright, D. Barcelona, B. Camara, C. Golmar, L. Savioli, T. Takeuchi, and M. Sembene. 2006. "School-Based Health and Nutrition Programs." In *Disease Control Priorities in Developing Countries*, 2nd ed., ed. D. Jamison, J. G. Breman, A. R. Measham, G. Alleyne, M. Claeson, D. Evans, P. Jha, A. Mills, and P. Musgrove, 1091–108. New York: World Bank and Oxford University Press.

Card, D. 2001. "Estimating the Return to Schooling: Progress on Some Persistent Econometric Problems." *Econometrica* 69 (5): 1127–60.

Chang, S. M., S. P. Walker, S. M. Grantham-McGregor, and C. A. Powell. 2002. "Early Childhood Stunting and Later Behaviour and School Achievement." *Journal of Child Psychology and Psychiatry and Allied Disciplines* 43 (6): 775–83.

Clarke, S. E., M. C. Jukes, J. K. Njagi, L. Khasakhala, B. Cundill, J. Otido, C. Crudder, B. B. Estambale, and S. Brooker. 2008. "Effect of Intermittent Preventive Treatment of Malaria on Health and Education in Schoolchildren: A Cluster-Randomised, Double-Blind, Placebo-Controlled Trial." *Lancet* 372 (9633): 127–38.

Fernando, D., D. de Silva, R. Carter, K. N. Mendis, and R. Wickremasinghe. 2006. "A Randomised, Double-Blind, Placebo-Controlled, Clinical Trial of the Impact of Malaria Prevention on the Educational Attainment of Schoolchildren." *American Journal of Tropical Medicine and Hygiene* 74 (3): 386–93.

Filmer, D., and N. Schady. 2010. "Promoting Schooling through Scholarships in Cambodia: Evidence from the Cambodia Education Sector Support Project." Impact Evaluation Brief, World Bank, Washington, DC.

Fiszbein, A., N. Schady, F. H. G. Ferreira, M. Grosh, N. Kelleher, P. Olinto, and E. Skoufias. 2009. *Conditional Cash Transfers: Reducing Present and Future Poverty*. Washington, DC: World Bank.

Frankenberg, E., W. Suriastini, and D. Thomas. 2005. "Can Expanding Access to Basic Healthcare Improve Children's Health Status? Lessons from Indonesia's 'Midwife in the Village' Programme." *Population Studies* 59 (1): 5–19.

Glewwe, P., and H. G. Jacoby. 1995. "An Economic Analysis of Delayed Primary School Enrollment in a Low-Income Country: The Role of Early Childhood Nutrition." *Review of Economics and Statistics* 77 (1): 156–69.

Glewwe, P., H. G. Jacoby, and E. M. King. 2001. "Early Childhood Nutrition and Academic Achievement: A Longitudinal Analysis." *Journal of Public Economics* 81 (3): 345–68.

Grantham-McGregor, Sally, Christine Powell, Susan Walker, Susan Chang, and Patricia Fletcher. 1994. "The Long-term Follow-up of Severely Malnourished Children Who Participated in an Intervention Program." *Child Development* 65 (2): 428–39.

Grigorenko, E. L., R. J. Sternberg, M. Jukes, K. Alcock, J. Lambo, D. Ngorosho, C. Nokes, and D. A. P. Bundy. 2006. "Effects of Antiparasitic Treatment on Dynamically and Statically Tested Cognitive Skills over Time." *Journal of Applied Developmental Psychology* 27 (6): 499–526.

Hanushek, E. A., and L. Woessmann. 2007. "The Role of Education Quality in Economic Growth." Policy Research Working Paper 4122, World Bank, Washington, DC.

Jamison, D. T. 1986. "Child Malnutrition and School Performance in China." *Journal of Development Economics* 20 (2): 299–309.

Jamison, D. T., and L. J. Lau. 1982. *Farmer Education and Farm Efficiency*. Baltimore, MD: Johns Hopkins University Press and World Bank.

JPAL (Jameel Poverty Action Lab). 2005. "Education: Meeting the Millennium Development Goals." *Fighting Poverty: What Works* 1: 1–4.

Jukes, M. C. H., L. J. Drake, and D. A. P. Bundy. 2008. *School Health, Nutrition and Education for All: Leveling the Playing Field*. Cambridge, MA: CABI Publishing.

Jukes, M. C. H., C. A. Nokes, K. J. Alcock, J. K. Lambo, C. Kihamia, N. Ngorosho, A. Mbise, W. Lorri, E. Yona, L. Mwanri, A. D. Baddeley, A. Hall, D. A. P. Bundy, and the Partnership for Child Development. 2002. "Heavy Schistosomiasis Associated with Poor Short-Term Memory and Slower Reaction Times in Tanzanian School Children." *Tropical Medicine and International Health* 7 (2): 104–17.

Jukes, M. C. H., M. Pinder, E. L. Grigorenko, H. B. Smith, G. Walraven, E. M. Bariau, R. J. Sternberg, L. J. Drake, P. Milligan, Y. B. Cheung, B. M. Greenwood, and D. A. P. Bundy. 2006. "Long-Term Impact of Malaria Chemoprophylaxis on Cognitive Abilities and Educational Attainment: Follow-up of a Controlled Trial." *PLoS Clinical Trials* 1 (4): e19.

Kremer, M. 2003. "Randomised Evaluations of Educational Programmes in Developing Countries: Some Lessons." *American Economic Review* 93 (2): 102–6.

Liddell, C., and G. Rae. 2001. "Predicting Early Grade Retention: A Longitudinal Investigation of Primary School Progress in a Sample of Rural South African Children." *British Journal of Educational Psychology* 71 (3): 413–28.

Lockheed, M. E., and A. M. Verspoor. 1999. *Improving Primary Education in Developing Countries*. Washington, DC: World Bank and Oxford University Press.

Maluccio, J., and R. Flores. 2005. "Impact Evaluation of a Conditional Cash Transfer Program: The Nicaragua *Red de Protección Social*." Research Report 141, International Food Policy Research Institute, Washington, DC.

Martorell, R., B. L. Horta, L. S. Adair, A. D. Stein, L. Richter, C. H. D. Fall, S. K. Bhargava, et al. 2009. "Weight Gain in the First Two Years of Life Is an Important Predictor of Schooling Outcomes in Pooled Analyses from Five Birth Cohorts from Low- and Middle-Income Countries." *Journal of Nutrition* 140 (2): 348–54.

Miguel, E., and M. Kremer. 2004. "Worms: Identifying Impacts on Education and Health in the Presence of Treatment Externalities." *Econometrica* 72 (1): 159–217.

Moll, P. G. 1998. "Primary Schooling, Cognitive Skills, and Wages in South Africa." *Economica* 65 (258): 263–84.

Moock, P. R., and J. Leslie. 1986. "Childhood Malnutrition and Schooling in the Terai Region of Nepal." *Journal of Development Economics* 20 (1): 33–52.

Morley, S., and D. Coady. 2003. *From Social Assistance to Social Development: Targeting Educational Subsidies in Developing Countries*. Washington, DC: Center for Global Development and International Food Policy Research Institute.

Muralidharan, K., and V. Sundararaman. 2009. "Teacher Performance Pay: Experimental Evidence from India." NBER Working Paper 15323. National Bureau of Economic Research, Cambridge, MA.

Murray, C., and A. Lopez, eds. 1996. *The Global Burden of Disease*. Global Burden of Disease and Injury Series. Vol. I. Boston: Harvard University Press.

Nokes, C., S. M. Grantham-McGregor, A. W. Sawyer, E. S. Cooper, B. A. Robinson, and D. A. P. Bundy. 1992. "Moderate to Heavy Infections of *Trichuris trichiura* Affect Cognitive Function in Jamaican School Children." *Parasitology* 104 (3): 539–47.

Nokes, C., S. T. McGarvey, L. Shiue, G. Wu, H. Wu, D. A. P. Bundy, and G. R. Olds. 1999. "Evidence for an Improvement in Cognitive Function Following Treatment of *Schistosoma japonicum* Infection in Chinese Primary Schoolchildren." *American Journal of Tropical Medicine and Hygiene* 60 (4): 556–65.

Nores, M., and W. S. Barnett. 2009. "Benefits of Early Childhood Interventions across the World: (Under) Investing in the Very Young." *Economics of Education Review* 29 (2): 271–82.

Parker, S., S. Greer, and B. Zuckerman. 1988. "Double Jeopardy: The Impact of Poverty on Early Child Development." *Pediatric Clinics of North America* 35 (6): 1227–40.

Partnership for Child Development. 1999. "Short Stature and the Age of Enrolment in Primary School: Studies in Two African Countries." *Social Science and Medicine* 48 (5): 675–82.

Pollitt, E., S. Cueto, and E. R. Jacoby. 1998. "Fasting and Cognition in Well- and Undernourished Schoolchildren: A Review of Three Experimental Studies." *American Journal of Clinical Nutrition* 67 (4): 779s–84s.

Pollitt, E., P. Hathirat, N. J. Kotchabhakdi, L. Missell, and A. Valyasevi. 1989. "Iron Deficiency and Educational Achievement in Thailand." *American Journal of Clinical Nutrition* 50 (3 suppl): 687–96.

Pollitt, E., W. E. Watkins, and M. A. Husaini. 1997 "Three-Month Nutritional Supplementation in Indonesian Infants and Toddlers Benefits Memory Function 8 Years Later." *American Journal of Clinical Nutrition* 66 (6): 1357–63.

Powell, C. A., S. P. Walker, S. M. Chang, and S. M. Grantham-McGregor. 1998. "Nutrition and Education: A Randomized Trial of the Effects of Breakfast in Rural Primary School Children." *American Journal of Clinical Nutrition* 68: 873–79.

Pritchett, L., and D. Filmer. 1999. "What Education Production Functions Really Show: A Positive Theory of Education Expenditures." *Economics of Education Review* 18 (2): 223–39.

Psacharopoulos, G., and M. Woodhall. 1985. *Education for Development: An Analysis of Investment Choices.* New York: Oxford University Press.

Schultz, T. P. 2004. "School Subsidies for the Poor: Evaluating the Mexican Progresa Poverty Program." *Journal of Development Economies* 74 (1): 199–250.

Sen, A. 1999. *Development as Freedom.* Oxford, U.K.: Oxford University Press.

Simeon, D. T. 1998. "School Feeding in Jamaica: A Review of Its Evaluation." *American Journal of Clinical Nutrition* 67 (4): 790s–94s.

Simeon, D. T., and S. M. Grantham-McGregor. 1989. "Effects of Missing Breakfast on the Cognitive Functions of School Children of Differing Nutritional Status." *American Journal of Clinical Nutrition* 49 (4): 646–53.

Simeon, D. T., S. M. Grantham-McGregor, J. E. Callender, and M. S. Wong. 1995. "Treatment of *Trichuris trichiura* Infections Improves Growth, Spelling Scores, and School Attendance in Some Children." *Journal of Nutrition* 125 (7): 1875–83.

Simeon, D. T., S. M. Grantham-McGregor, and M. S. Wong. 1995. "*Trichuris trichiura* Infection and Cognition in Children: Results of a Randomized Clinical Trial." *Parasitology* 110 (4): 457–64.

Soemantri, A. G., E. Pollitt, and I. Kim. 1985. "Iron Deficiency Anemia and Educational Achievement." *American Journal of Clinical Nutrition* 42 (6): 1221–28.

Sternberg, R. J., C. Powell, P. McGrane, and S. M. Grantham-McGregor. 1997. "Effects of a Parasitic Infection on Cognitive Functioning." *Journal of Experimental Psychology—Applied* 3 (1): 67–76.

Strauss, J., and D. Thomas. 1995. "Human Resources: Empirical Modeling of Household and Family Decisions." In *Handbook of Development Economics*, ed. J. Behrman and T. N. Srinivasan, 1885–2025. Amsterdam: Elsevier Science.

UNESCO (United Nations Educational, Scientific and Cultural Organization). 2008. "EDUCAIDS Overviews of Practical Resources." EDUCAIDS Web site. http://portal.unesco.org/en/ev.php-URL_ID=36412&URL_DO=DO_TOPIC&URL_SECTION=201.html.

van Stuijvenberg, M. E., J. D. Kvalsvig, M. Faber, M. Kruger, D. G. Kenoyer, and A. J. S. Benade. 1999. "Effect of Iron-, Iodine-, and Beta-Carotene-Fortified Biscuits on the Micronutrient Status of Primary Schoolchildren: A Randomized Controlled Trial." *American Journal of Clinical Nutrition* 69 (3): 497–503.

Vazir, S., B. Nagalla, V. Thangiah, V. Kamasamudram, and S. Bhattiprolu. 2006. "Effect of Micronutrient Supplement on Health and Nutritional Status of Schoolchildren: Mental Function." *Nutrition* 22 (1): S26–S32.

Walker, S. P., S. M. Grantham-McGregor, C. A. Powell, and S. M. Chang. 2000. "Effects of Growth Restriction in Early Childhood on Growth, IQ, and Cognition at Age 11 to 12 Years and the Benefits of Nutritional Supplementation and Psychosocial Stimulation." *Journal of Pediatrics* 137 (1): 36–41.

Whaley, S. E., M. Sigman, C. Neumann, N. Bwibo, D. Guthrie, R. E. Weiss, S. Alber, and S. P. Murphy. 2003. "The Impact of Dietary Intervention on the Cognitive Development of Kenyan Schoolchildren." *Journal of Nutrition* 133 (11): 3965S–71S.

World Bank. 2010. "Learning for All: Investing in People's Knowledge and Skills to Promote Development." World Bank Education Strategy 2020. Washington, DC.

Zax, J. S., and D. I. Rees. 2002. "IQ, Academic Performance, Environment, and Earnings." *Review of Economics and Statistics* 84 (4): 600–16.

# CHAPTER 3

# Education Sector Responses to the Health and Nutrition of Schoolchildren

In this chapter we take an education sector view of how health and nutrition interventions intended to benefit education work in practice. The previous chapter has shown that some of the most common health and nutrition conditions of childhood have consequences for education, and that a programmatic sequence of health and nutrition interventions is required to support children throughout the key stages of their development. This chapter takes these ideas a step further by exploring which of these conditions can be addressed by the education sector. Specifically, it examines what can be achieved before school age to prepare children for school and, once the children are at school, what schools themselves can do to support health and nutrition at school age.

## Interventions before School Age*

The analyses in the previous chapter concluded that a life-cycle approach is required to ensure that children are ready for schooling and fully able to take advantage of the education provided. In programmatic terms, this

---

\* Contributors to this section: Michelle Neuman, Ziauddin Hyder, Carla Bertoncino, Alexandria Valerio, Marito Garcia, and Sophie Naudeau.

implies the need for a sequence of maternal and child health (MCH), early child development (ECD), and school health and nutrition programs, each building on the foundation of its predecessor, and each targeting the priority conditions of the relevant age group.

Which sector takes the lead in implementing these interventions also shows an age-dependent trend. MCH programs are typically managed by the public sector and led by the health sector. ECD programs may involve a combination of roles for the health and education sectors, but are more often managed by the private sector and civil society. Schools are most commonly managed by the public sector, and school-based interventions for school-age children are most often implemented by the education sector, although typically with the oversight of the health sector. The social protection sector often has a role to play in all age groups. These are, of course, broad generalizations; the relative emphasis in practice is context specific.

### Maternal and Child Health

Early interventions (from –9 to 24 months) within MCH programs have a critically important role to play in the subsequent lives of children. It would be difficult to express this more clearly than Behrman and Hoddinott (2005, 548): "Physical growth lost in early years as a consequence of malnutrition is, at best, only partially regained during childhood and adolescence, particularly when children remain in poor environments. Malnutrition, particularly severe malnutrition in early childhood, often leads to deficits in cognitive development. Poorly nourished children tend to start school later, progress through school less rapidly, have poorer academic achievement and perform less well on cognitive achievement tests when older, including into adulthood." A recent pooled analysis of five cohort studies shows that weight gain during the first two years of life is an important predictor of schooling outcomes (Martorell et al. 2009).

The scale of the challenge addressed by MCH programs is considerable. It is estimated that 156 million children below the age of five are stunted (Grantham-McGregor et al. 2007), representing more than one-quarter of that age group in low-income countries, and more than half of all children under the age of five in Sub-Saharan Africa and South Asia. These stunted youngsters typically become stunted schoolchildren who are less likely to enroll in school at the right age and who, on average, have lower achievement levels.

To address these issues, proper nutrition is needed *in utero* and during the first few years of life for brain development to take place, as well as for certain areas of the brain to function normally in later life, making it possible for children to learn and eventually lead healthy, productive lives (Martorell et al. 2005; Alderman, Behrman, and Hoddinott 2005). Table 3.1 shows some examples of how some early interventions affect mental development in the early years. The long-run benefits are impressive: in Guatemala, nutritional supplementation during the first two years of life is associated with, on average, 46 percent higher wages as adults (Hoddinott et al. 2008).

MCH programs typically target the development of the fetus *in utero* (that is, maternal health) and children up to two years of age (that is, child health, including neonatal and infant health). The focus on children between the ages of –9 and 24 months involves a range of health and nutrition interventions that are almost entirely delivered as a public sector response through the health sector, often with a strong community component. It is rare for the education sector to play any direct role in the implementation of MCH programs, but the sector has an important role in encouraging and promoting the uptake of MCH interventions within the community generally, and especially among school-going adolescents who may soon become parents.

### Early Child Development Programs

The years after two years of age before a child goes to school (around six years of age) are also very important to development. ECD programs aim to provide interventions that bridge this gap and support development between two and six years of age. In practice, however, the period covered is usually much shorter.

The education rationale for investing in ECD is strong. Quality ECD activities can complement the care and education that children receive from their families and communities and promote children's school readiness—that is, their cognitive, social-emotional, physical, and language development (see Grantham-McGregor et al. 2007 for a review). Children who participate in quality ECD programs are more likely to enroll in primary school and to enroll on time. They also are less likely to drop out or repeat grades and more likely to perform better in school and complete the primary school cycle (see Arnold 2004 for a review). The costs of ECD programs are often partially or fully offset by these reduced inefficiencies in the education system.

Many of the ECD interventions address health and nutrition needs, but the human brain cannot develop to its full potential through good health and nutrition alone; early childhood behavioral stimulation also

Table 3.1 Impact of Health Interventions on Cognitive Development during Early Childhood

| Study | Country | Intervention | Age (months or years) | Sample characteristics | Effect size (SD) | Outcomes |
|---|---|---|---|---|---|---|
| Jukes et al. forthcoming | India | Iron (30 days) + deworming | 2–6 years | ECD pupils | 0.18 | Attention |
| Seshadri and Gopaldas 1989 (study 1) | India | Iron (60 days) | 5–8 years | Anemic vs. non-anemic | Positive | IQ |
| Seshadri and Gopaldas 1989 (study 2) | India | Iron (60 days) | 5–6 years | Anemic vs. non-anemic boys | 0.33<br>0.67 | Verbal IQ<br>Performance IQ |
| Soewondo, Husaini, and Pollitt 1989 | Indonesia | Iron (56 days) | 4 years | Anemic vs. non-anemic | Positive<br>No effect | Learning task<br>3 cognitive tests |
| Stoltzfus et al. 2001 | Zanzibar | 12 months iron + deworming | 6–59 months | Community | 0.14 | Language |
| McKay et al. 1978 | Colombia | Nutrition + education from 42 months | 84 months | Malnourished | 0.80 | Cognitive ability |
| Grantham-McGregor et al. 1991 | Jamaica | Psychosocial stimulation | 9–24 months | Malnourished | 0.79 | Mental development |
| Grantham-McGregor et al. 1991 | Jamaica | Nutritional supplementation | 9–24 months | Malnourished | 0.66 | Mental development |
| Vermeersch and Kremer 2004 | Kenya | School feeding | 4–6 years | ECD pupils | 0.40[a] | Educational achievement |

Source: Jukes, Drake, and Bundy 2008.
Notes: IQ = intelligence quotient; SD = standard deviation.
a. Effect only for pupils of most experienced teachers.

plays a critical role in the process of brain formation and development. Brain development is experience based and has long-lasting effects. ECD programs promoting behavioral stimulation that target the zero-to-six-year age group tap into both critical and sensitive windows of opportunity and periods of brain development (see table 3.1). It is worth stressing here that parents play the key role in providing stimulation during the early years.

Evidence from Jamaica shows that, for stunted children, the benefits of a combination of nutritional supplements and stimulation were additive and that children receiving both interventions caught up to nonstunted children in terms of IQ (Walker et al. 2005). A long-term follow-up at school age showed that children who had received early stimulation had better cognitive, educational, and psychosocial functioning over time. Stunted children who received stimulation had significant long-term benefits in terms of cognition, benefits that did not persist in stunted children who received nutrition without stimulation. Similarly, young Vietnamese children who received both nutrition and stimulation did significantly better on a cognitive test at age six than children who had received the nutrition intervention alone (Watanabe et al. 2005). The effect was greater among stunted children, suggesting that early stimulation can play a protective role against the negative effects of growth failure on cognition.

A recent meta-analysis of 30 different early child interventions in 23 different countries, including a mix of high- and low-income countries, concluded that "educational or mixed interventions (with educational, care, or stimulation components) have the largest cognitive effects compared to cash transfers or solely nutritional interventions" (Nores and Barnett, 2009, 272).

Children with more disadvantaged backgrounds enter school with lower levels of the knowledge and social competencies that are important for subsequent school success. Research has demonstrated that in the absence of programs to compensate for this early disadvantage, achievement gaps tend to widen over time, making the case for such programs even more compelling for poor countries as a way of leveling the playing field. The evidence indicates that the benefits of ECD programs extend beyond the dimensions of cognitive, behavioral, and emotional development, educational outcomes, child maltreatment, health, and crime. In fact, they generate longer-lasting gains in labor market outcomes, dependency, and prosocial behaviors, among other effects.

As with MCH, there are strong rates of return to ECD interventions compared with interventions later in the life cycle (Carneiro and

Heckman 2003). Studies in middle- and high-income countries suggest a potential return rate of 7–16 percent annually to high-quality ECD programs (Rolnick and Grunewald 2007). A comprehensive meta-analysis of ECD programs (Rand Corporation 2005), which analyzed 20 longitudinal studies, found benefit-cost ratios ranging from 1.26 to 17.07, depending on both the length of the studies and the number and/or intensity of dimensions included in a given program. The favorable economic returns from ECD were not limited to small demonstration programs or higher-cost intensive programs, and they increased with appropriate targeting. The longitudinal study of the Perry Preschool Program in the United States shows that some benefits from participation in ECD can persist through adulthood. Public savings from higher earnings and lower social costs (for example, lower incarceration rates) generated a benefit-cost ratio of 17.1 (Schweinhart et al. 2005). In low-income countries, analyses of nonexperimental evaluations of ECD have found smaller but still positive benefit-cost ratios in the range of 2.4 to 5.8.

Investing early also can reduce social inequalities. Though the most rigorous evaluation data come from wealthier countries, research from countries as diverse as Cape Verde, the Arab Republic of Egypt, Guinea, Jamaica, and Nepal has found that children from the most disadvantaged backgrounds benefit the most from ECD programs, although they are also often the ones with the least access and thus the least likelihood of participating.

Many of the ECD interventions address health and nutrition needs, and mirror those of earlier child health interventions. Such interventions are typically delivered by the health sector, but in many low-income countries, health services for children above two years of age are much more limited than the MCH services provided to younger children. One public sector solution is to expand access to MCH "health days" to include children up to six years, as has been tried in Uganda (Alderman et al. 2006).

Combining health care with behavioral stimulation requires a different approach, for example, the development with civil society of community-based programs, such as those in Mozambique and Cambodia. In India, the Integrated Child Development Scheme aims to provide child care centers for preschool children, offering early education and behavioral stimulation, as well as in some cases linking with the health system to deliver simple interventions (Awasthi et al. 2008). The education sector was a partner in these examples, but was not directly involved in implementation.

In middle- and high-income countries, and much more rarely in low-income countries (for example, Eritrea and Kenya), the education sector provides formal preschools that accept children one or two years imme-diately prior to enrollment in school. Apart from the limited coverage achieved in the communities most in need, this approach leaves a gap of several years between the end of MCH programs and the beginning of school or preschool access. Even in rich countries, ECD programs during the early, vulnerable years are usually outside the public sector and are commonly implemented by civil society organizations and the private sector (see Rand Corporation 2005).

The sectoral picture is therefore particularly complicated for ECD. Multiple sectors are engaged, often with different sectors contributing at different stages in the process, but the public sector is often least engaged during this phase of development. In considering the role of the educa-tion sector, the overall conclusion is that this sector has a key role in lead-ing the policy dialogue to promote, coordinate, and support national efforts to provide ECD interventions to preschool children, but is often a late and relatively small actor in implementation.

## Interventions at School Age

The remainder of this chapter focuses on the school years—in this case, taken to be the range 6–15 years of age—and what schools can do to address some common health and nutrition problems of school-age chil-dren that have demonstrated consequences for education. The focus is on conditions for which there are existing interventions that are sufficiently safe, simple, and well evaluated to be appropriate for implementation through schools by the education sector, typically with health sector supervision. In examining each of these interventions, the same format is followed. First, the condition is explored in terms of its impact on educa-tion. By focusing on the effects of specific interventions, the comments here are intended to complement the general exploration of the evidence on impact in chapter 2. Next, some of the responses to that condition which are appropriate for education sector implementation are described. Finally, descriptions of (or direction to source materials on) how an intervention is implemented in practice as part of a school health program are provided. Where possible, examples of large-scale programs with meaningful coverage have been chosen.

The interventions included here are those for which there is evidence of an effect on education, although the quality of the evidence varies. The inter-ventions were also selected on the basis of some practical experience of implementation at scale, though this, too, shows variation. In attempting to

compare interventions it should be recognized that there is also considerable variation in cost—deworming costs only a few U.S. cents per year per
child and school feeding costs some $40. In the anticipated time scale of the
outcome, moreover, micronutrient supplements and deworming might be
viewed as "quick wins," but promoting a healthy life style operates on a gen-
erational time scale.

## Deworming*

**Impact on education.** More than 400 million school-age children worldwide are infected with parasitic worms. These worms include the schistosomes (also known as bilharzia) and soil-transmitted helminths
(STHs), which include whipworms (*Trichuris*), roundworms (*Ascaris*),
and hookworms (*Necator* and *Ancylostoma*). In current terminology, the
schistosomes and STHs are often considered part of the complex of five
diseases that are targeted worldwide as the Neglected Tropical Diseases
(the other three diseases are riverblindness, lymphatic filariasis, and trachoma). Worm infections are chronic conditions that affect children's
health, nutrition, and development. As a consequence, they limit their
ability to access and benefit from education. In 2001, the World Health
Organization (WHO) set the goal of treating 75 percent of school-age
children at risk of infection by 2010.

School-age children tend to have the highest burden of worm (schistosomes and STHs) infection—in terms of both numbers infected and
intensity of infection—and consequently also experience the greatest
morbidity (see figure 3.1).

Worms can cause children to become anemic and malnourished and
can impair their mental and physical development (Hotez et al. 2006;
Stephenson 1987). Over the short term, children are often too sick or
too tired to concentrate in school, or to attend school at all. Worm
infections, like undernutrition, are associated with impaired cognitive
development and decreased educational achievement (Simeon and
Grantham-McGregor 1989; Mendez and Adair 1999). Some studies
suggest that infected schoolchildren perform poorly on cognitive function tests (Watkins and Pollitt 1997), have delayed reaction times, and
suffer from poor short-term memory (Jukes et al. 2002). As discussed

---

* This section was contributed by Lesley Drake, Simon Brooker, and Antonio
  Montresor.

**Figure 3.1    Age-Intensity Profile of Soil-Transmitted Worm Infections**

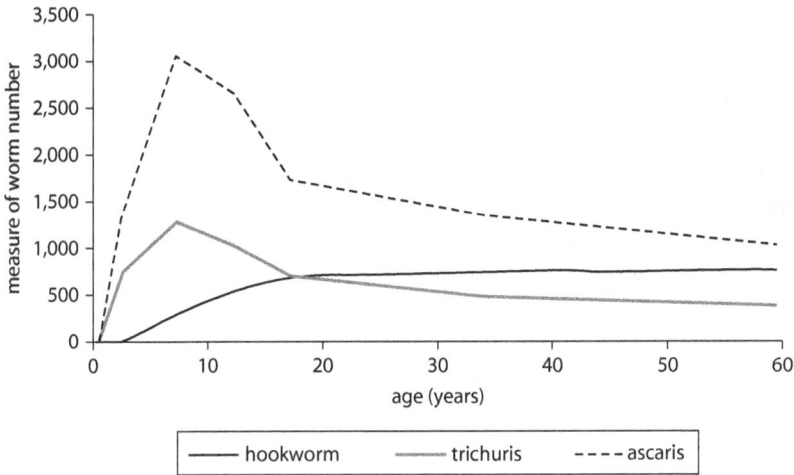

*Source:* Bundy et al. 1992.

in chapter 2, worms have a potentially important impact on education because they are so common; it is estimated that infection leads to an average intelligence quotient (IQ) loss of 3.75 points per child infected and 200 million years of lost schooling (Jukes, Drake, and Bundy 2008). Worm infections also have long-run negative effects on learning and income; children in the American South at the beginning of the 20th century who were persistently infected with hookworm were found 13 percent less likely to be literate and earned 43 percent less as adults compared to those who received treatment for their worms (Bleakley 2007).

*Options for school-based responses.* Treatment for worms is simple, safe, and inexpensive, and has beneficial effects on educational outcomes. In a randomized evaluation in Kenya, deworming in schools reduced school absenteeism by 25 percent (Miguel and Kremer 2004). Deworming may also increase the potential to learn while at school (Grigorenko et al. 2006)—treated children scored 0.25 SD higher on reasoning tasks than children who still had worms and had scores similar to children who were uninfected at the outset of the trial, suggesting that the effects of infection can be largely reversed. Importantly, deworming has been shown both to be pro-poor and to have the greatest impact on the most vulnerable children (Simeon et al. 1995); it is therefore a particularly relevant intervention for Education for All (EFA).

In areas of high worm prevalence, the WHO recommends regular (usually annual) treatment of all schoolchildren without the need for individual diagnosis (Montresor et al. 2002). Since the pills used to treat infections are effective, low in cost, and very safe—with few, minor side effects—they can be distributed without the need for expensive screening procedures or specialized personnel.

The most efficient way to reach the highest number of school-age children is through the existing and extensive infrastructure of schools. Teachers are in close contact with the community and, with minimal training and support from the local health system, can deliver drugs effectively and safely to students (World Bank 2003b). Since deworming is a proven education intervention, it should be a priority for the education sector in many low-income countries, whereas the health sector may prioritize the needs of younger children and pregnant women.

Schools are a cost-effective delivery mechanism for deworming. School-based deworming costs less than $0.50 per child per year, inclusive of all program costs, including the drugs, training, logistics, monitoring and evaluation, and advocacy materials. Deworming is most cost-effective when targeted at areas of high prevalence, as this ensures that resources are most efficiently focused, treating children who suffer the greatest morbidity and who therefore stand to gain the greatest benefits from the process. As discussed in chapter 5, a comparison of rigorously evaluated education interventions showed that school-based deworming is one of the most cost-effective ways to increase school attendance rates.

The use of mass treatment raises two issues. First, there is the need to use approaches that minimize the risk of the development of drug resistance, and the concomitant need to monitor drug efficacy. Second, it is sometimes argued that improvements in sanitation and access to clean water will contribute to reducing worm infection, and a trend toward lower prevalence of infection is indeed seen in some areas as low-income countries become more prosperous and facilities improve. However, the distribution of these benefits remains uneven, and this inequity is likely to become exaggerated by the current financial crisis. In the interim, deworming provides an immediate low-cost solution for the rural and urban poor.

***Practical experience of implementation.*** Building on the strong evidence for school-based deworming and its cost-effectiveness, there has been a recent groundswell of activity and advocacy encompassing the U.S. Agency for International Development (USAID), the World Bank, the Education for All–Fast Track Initiative (EFA-FTI), the World Food Programme (WFP), and the United Kingdom's Department for International Development (DFID), among others.

Education sector–led, school-based deworming programs have resulted in the deworming of millions of children in many countries, including Cambodia, The Gambia, Ghana, India, Kenya, Malawi, Mali, Nigeria, Tanzania, and Uganda. In 2004, Cambodia became the first country to reach the target of 75 percent of at-risk children via a school-based delivery model of deworming. Kenya achieved similar coverage in 2009 when the national program resulted in the deworming of more than 3.6 million children at a cost of only $0.36 per child. In India, deworming is occurring at the state level. Following the newly launched government program in the state of Andhra Pradesh, where more than 2 million children in 22,000 schools were dewormed for less than $0.20 per child, other state governments, including those of Bihar and Delhi, National Capital Territory, are beginning implementation using the same model.

An increasing number of countries are now recognizing the significant impact that school-based deworming can have on education as well as on the health and nutrition of school-age children, with programs increasingly taken to national scale.

### School Feeding*

*Impact on education.* In the past decade, access to primary education has improved significantly in many parts of the world. Yet 72 million children of primary school age, 48 percent of them in Sub-Saharan Africa, are not in school; 54 percent of these out-of-school children are girls (UNESCO 2010). Enrolling children in school, though, is only the first step. Once they are enrolled, vulnerable children are likely to require support throughout their schooling in order to minimize the risk of absenteeism and dropping out. The irregular school attendance of malnourished and unhealthy children can also be an important factor in their poor performance. Even short-term hunger, common in children who are not fed before going to school, can have an adverse effect on learning (Jacoby, Cueto, and Pollitt 1996). Children who are hungry have more difficulty

---

* This section was contributed by Carmen Burbano and Aulo Gelli.

concentrating and performing complex tasks (Grantham-McGregor, Chang, and Walker 1998).

Micronutrient malnutrition—particularly deficiencies of iron, iodine, and vitamin A—has also been shown to have a negative impact on the education of school-age children. An estimated 53 percent of school-age children suffer from iron-deficiency anemia. Iodine deficiency disorders affect an estimated 60 million school-age children—5 percent of the total. Vitamin A deficiency affects an estimated 85 million, or 7 percent of the total (Jukes, Drake, and Bundy 2008). The extra demands on school-age children to perform chores or walk long distances to school create a much greater need for energy than that needed by younger children. Survey data from WFP school feeding programs in 12 low-income food-deficit countries showed, for instance, that in newly assisted schools, over 60 percent of pupils, on average, did not have breakfast before going to school (WFP 2007).

This section is an abstract of analyses conducted jointly by the World Bank and the World Food Programme (Bundy et al. 2009b), and of three recent publications (Kristjansson et al. 2007; Adelman, Gilligan, and Lehrer 2008; and Jukes, Drake, and Bundy 2008).

### Options for school-based responses

**Rationale for school feeding.** School feeding programs, defined here as the provision of food to schoolchildren either through in-school meals or in the form of take-home rations, have been widely implemented as a strategy to reduce social vulnerability, increase school participation, and mitigate the effects of hunger on learning and educational achievement.

In terms of social vulnerability, school feeding programs are relatively easy to scale up in a crisis and can provide a benefit per household of more than 10 percent of household expenditures, with a larger benefit in the case of take-home rations. In many contexts, well-designed school feeding programs can be targeted with moderate accuracy. Where school enrollment is low, school feeding may not reach the poorest children, but in these settings, alternative safety net options are often quite limited and geographically targeted expansion of school feeding may still provide the best option for a rapid scale-up of safety nets. Targeted take-home rations may provide somewhat more progressive outcomes. Further research is required to assess the longer-term relative merits of school feeding versus other social safety net instruments in these situations. Table 3.2 reviews the key criteria used to assess safety net policy and applies them to school feeding.

**Table 3.2 School Feeding as a Safety Net**

| Criteria | Definition | School feeding modalities (meals, snacks, take-home rations) |
|---|---|---|
| Appropriate | The program responds to the particular needs of a country and is customized to the context. | • All three modalities can respond to the particular needs of a country and be used to customize the program to the context. |
| Adequate | The program should provide full coverage and meaningful benefits to the population that it is trying to assist. | • Meals benefit schoolchildren directly. The size of the transfer can be on the order of 10 percent of base household income or more, which is in line with common practice. There may be additional benefits from educational achievement that are not costed. Household benefits would increase with the number of children in school who are receiving meals.<br>• Snacks and biscuits give benefits similar to those of meals, with some differences. The size of the transfer may be less than that of meals, and it may have less of an effect on enrollment and attendance.<br>• Take-home rations benefit the child and the household that receives the rations. While meals and biscuits are capped in value, the size of take-home rations may be expanded. |
| Equitable | The program should provide benefits to individuals or households that are equal in all important respects (horizontal equity) and may provide more benefits to the poorest children and households (vertical equity). | • Meals and snacks are difficult to target on an individual basis, but can be targeted geographically at poor schools.<br>• Take-home rations may be targeted individually to reach certain vulnerable groups or households. |
| Cost-effective | The program should run efficiently with the minimum resources required to achieve the desired impact, but with sufficient resources to carry out all program functions well. | • Meals programs have high nontransfer costs—around 30 percent of total costs, representing preparation and transport costs.<br>• Snacks and biscuits may have lower nontransfer costs than meals—around 20 percent.<br>• Take-home rations appear to have surprisingly high nontransfer costs of around 35 percent. |

*Source:* Bundy et al. 2009b.

In terms of school participation, food incentives offered to students (for example, school meals) and food incentives offered to families (for example, take-home rations, especially for girls, orphans, and vulnerable children) compensate parents for direct educational costs and opportunity costs from the loss of child labor when children go to school. Evidence from randomized controlled trials and quasi-experimental evaluations suggests that implementation of school feeding programs is associated with increased enrollment, particularly of girls.

Additionally, students in school feeding programs have the potential for improved educational achievement. Analyses show that school feeding can alleviate short-term hunger and increase children's ability to concentrate, learn, and perform specific tasks. These effects are greater among children who are also chronically undernourished. If the food is fortified and combined with deworming, there may be additional benefits for children's cognitive abilities and educational achievement. A qualitative assessment of the relative effects of school feeding and complementary interventions is shown in table 2.3.

Well-designed school feeding programs, which include micronutrient fortification and deworming, can provide nutritional benefits and should complement and not compete with nutrition programs for younger children, which remain a clear priority for addressing malnutrition overall.

**School feeding modalities and trade-offs.** There are three main modalities for school feeding, which have distinct benefits and trade-offs that need to be considered during the design of a program. In-school meals (average per capita cost of $40 per year) tend to be less finely targeted and capped at the value of the transfer. They also have potentially large opportunity costs for education and incur higher administrative costs, yet they have the potential not only to increase attendance but to act more directly on learning, especially if fortified and combined with deworming. In-school snacks and biscuits (average per capita cost of $13 per year) have lower administrative costs, but also lower transfer and incentive values, though the scale of benefit relative to meals needs to be better quantified.

Take-home rations (average per capita cost of $50 per year) can be more finely targeted and can provide higher-value transfers than school meals, but have significant administrative costs—although this finding is based on a very limited data set. Rations have a strong safety net potential and appear to result in increases in attendance, and perhaps educational achievement, on a similar scale to in-school meal programs. Thus, from a social protection point of view, they may be preferred to in-school meal programs.

**Costs, sustainability, and implementation.** Coverage of school feeding is most complete in rich and middle-income countries (see map 1.4 in chapter 1). Yet where the need is greatest—in terms of hunger, poverty, and poor social indicators—the programs tend to be the smallest. Such programs are usually targeted to the most food-insecure regions and tend to be most dependent on external assistance.

Concerns about cost-effectiveness, the costs of food versus education, and the long-term viability of donor-supported programs pervade policy discussions of school feeding. A recent analysis that compared the cost of school feeding relative to the cost of education focused on two main findings (Bundy et al. 2009b). First, as figure 3.2

**Figure 3.2    Relative Cost of School Feeding and Education**

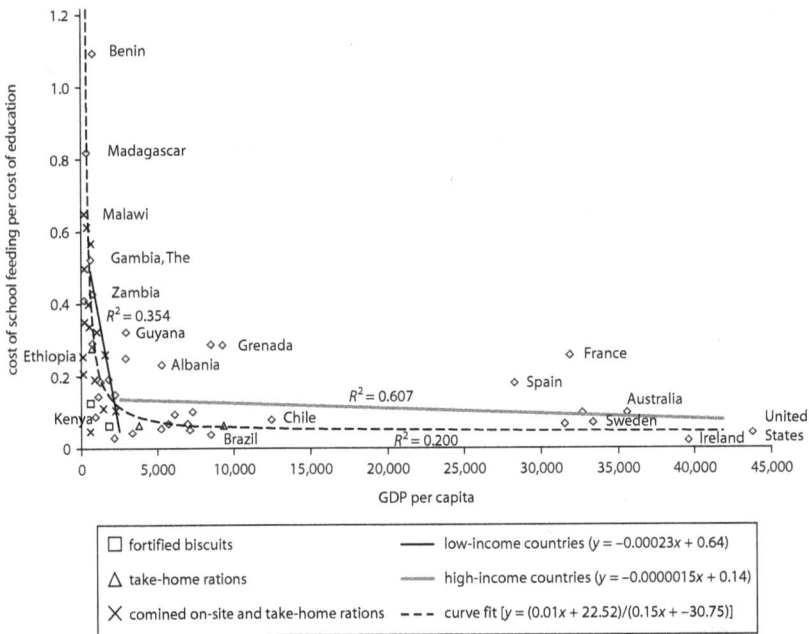

*Source:* Bundy et al. 2009b.

shows, school feeding programs in low-income countries exhibit large variations in cost, with concomitant opportunities for cost containment. Second, as countries become richer, school feeding costs become a much smaller proportion of their investment in education. For example, in Zambia, the cost of school feeding is about 50 percent of the annual per capita costs of primary education; in Ireland it is only 10 percent. This presents a strong case for focused support to help low-income countries move through the transition to sustainable national programs.

An assessment of 28 countries that have transitioned from external support to sustainable national school feeding programs suggests a multistage process in which countries begin largely dependent on external resources and implementation and move through a transitional stage of mixed government and external financing (with external technical and implementation support), finally becoming responsible for a government-run and -budgeted program. The main preconditions for a transition to sustainable national programs are mainstreaming school feeding in national policies and plans (especially education sector plans), national financing, and national implementation capacity. Countries that have made this transition have all become less dependent on external sources of food by linking the programs with local agricultural production. Figure 3.3 illustrates how programs change as countries evolve through the transition process.

These conclusions suggest that further benefits might accrue from better aligning development partner support for school feeding with processes already established to harmonize development cooperation in the education sector, notably EFA-FTI. A key element of such alignment is ensuring that all new programs are designed within the policy framework of the education sector and that existing programs are revisited so that they also conform to the framework. Findings also point to the fact that countries may benefit from having a clear understanding of the duration of donor assistance and a concrete plan for transition to national ownership, complete with time frames and milestones for the process. Additionally, local procurement is being actively evaluated as a means for achieving sustainable school feeding programs and, at the same time, using the purchasing power of the program as a stimulus for the local agricultural economy.

As noted earlier, with costs on average of about $50 per child per year, school feeding in low-income countries is a relatively expensive education intervention. However, the evidence base on school feeding includes a

**Figure 3.3    The School Feeding Transition**

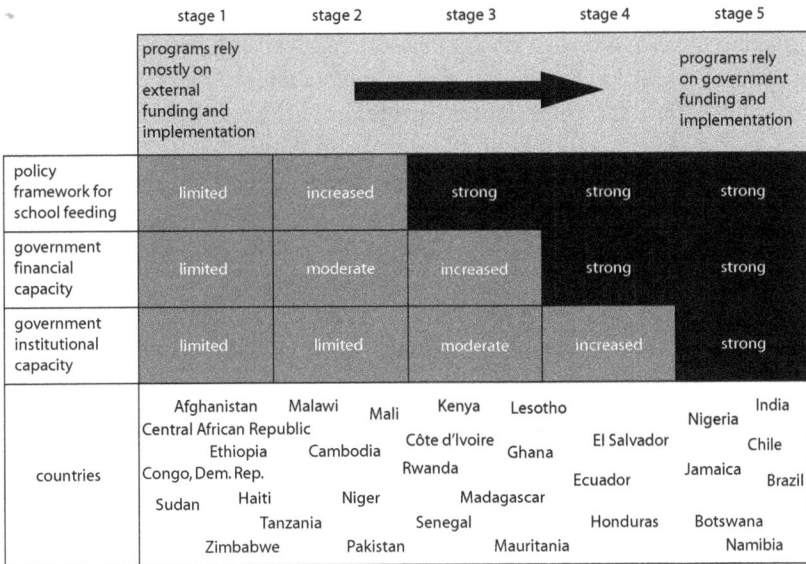

|  | stage 1 | stage 2 | stage 3 | stage 4 | stage 5 |
|---|---|---|---|---|---|
|  | programs rely mostly on external funding and implementation | | | | programs rely on government funding and implementation |
| policy framework for school feeding | limited | increased | strong | strong | strong |
| government financial capacity | limited | moderate | increased | strong | strong |
| government institutional capacity | limited | limited | moderate | increased | strong |
| countries | Afghanistan  Malawi  Mali<br>Central African Republic<br>Ethiopia  Cambodia<br>Congo, Dem. Rep.<br>Sudan  Haiti  Niger<br>Tanzania<br>Zimbabwe  Pakistan | | Kenya  Lesotho<br>Côte d'Ivoire  Ghana<br>Rwanda<br>Madagascar<br>Senegal<br>Mauritania | El Salvador<br>Ecuador<br>Honduras | India<br>Nigeria<br>Chile<br>Jamaica  Brazil<br>Botswana<br>Namibia |

*Source:* Bundy et al. 2009b.

broad range of benefits that can be delivered to vulnerable school-age chil-dren simultaneously across education, health, and nutrition dimensions. As yet, however, there is no single metric that captures the cost-effectiveness of school feeding and combines its different benefits—namely enrollment, attendance, dropout rate, learning, and cognition—making comparisons with other interventions incomplete. In addition, field-level experiences from middle- and high-income countries suggest that school feeding may also benefit agriculture and community development. Building the evi-dence base on the agricultural benefits of school feeding, as well as tack-ling the issue of cost-effectiveness metrics, are two important areas of ongoing research.

***Practical experience of implementation.*** While the rationale for school feeding, particularly as an education and social safety net intervention, is clear, the current challenge is implementation. Ensuring that every child gets a meal in school every day, while not creating a tax on the educational role of the school, is not easy. Implementing school feeding means dealing with many of the intractable problems of service deliv-ery in low-income countries, such as lack of financial resources, low capacity for management and implementation, inadequate and unsustainable models of service delivery, inappropriate accountability mechanisms, and lack of space for innovation and learning. Thus, a successful transition toward national ownership and sustainability depends on the extent to which all these factors are taken into consideration throughout the multiple stages of implementation and whether they are systematically tackled. Doing so ensures convergence between the policy intention of the government and its actual capability to deliver. This section presents brief descriptions of the implementation of several school feeding programs and how these issues are being handled in practice. See also box 3.1.

**School feeding as a key program in the plans of the government of Haiti.** School feeding is a top priority for Haiti. Several years ago, the program

**Box 3.1**

## Home-Grown School Feeding

School feeding programs run for a fixed number of days a year and normally have a predetermined food basket, thus providing an opportunity for local farmers and producers to benefit by generating a stable, structured, and predictable demand for their products, thereby building the agricultural market and the enabling systems around it. This is the concept behind home-grown school feeding (HGSF), an intervention identified by the Millennium Hunger Task Force as a "quick win" in the fight against poverty and hunger. Despite recent efforts, there is still a need to strengthen the evidence base on the optimal implementation and effectiveness of HGSF to improve policy and program support. One such operational research investment, supported in part by a new $12 million grant from the Bill & Melinda Gates Foundation and led by the Partnership for Child Development (PCD), is supporting government action to deliver cost-effective school feeding programs sourced from smallholder farmers in Sub-Saharan Africa. PCD program activities include generating and disseminating the evidence base on HGSF, delivering technical support to government policies and programs, and developing partnerships and networks. In the short term, the program is supporting the learning and knowledge exchange processes across different countries, with technical assistance under way in Côte d'Ivoire, Ghana, Kenya, Mali, and Nigeria.

was identified by the government as a safety net that could be quickly and efficiently scaled up to reach all children enrolled in school, which is why it created the Programme National des Cantines Scolaires (PNCS, the National School Feeding Programme) and started allocating funds for school feeding. More recently, the need and importance of the program increased after the earthquake that struck the country in January 2010. In April, school feeding was included as a crucial program in the National Plan for Reconstruction of Haiti and is one of the seven recommendations of the Presidential Commission on Education.

Under the leadership of the PNCS—the national institution in charge of school feeding—several stakeholders are currently providing support for the program. Partners include the WFP, World Bank, government of Brazil, USAID, and at least 25 national and international nongovernmental organizations (NGOs) that support the implementation. Together, they are reaching approximately 1 million schoolchildren in the country. Although the program is currently targeted, the government hopes to reach all the schoolchildren in the country.

The sustainability, quality, and cost-effectiveness of school feeding in Haiti will depend on the consolidation of all efforts and harmonization of strategies and approaches, oriented toward a planned, systematic transition to national ownership over a number of years. With this in mind, the government, together with the WFP and World Bank, among other partners, has initiated preparations for a long-term transition strategy that will put the milestones in place for a successful transition to sustainability. The strategy serves as a compact between the government and its partners. It includes actions aimed at strengthening the legal and policy framework for school feeding, the institutional framework and national capacity for implementation, and a specific effort to link school feeding with local agricultural production (another key aspect of reconstruction of Haiti).

**Innovation in Kenya.** The government of Kenya has been implementing two different home-grown school feeding programs in its efforts to provide sustainable, nationally owned school feeding to vulnerable children in the country. Since 2006, the Njaa Marafuku Kenya (Eradicate Hunger in Kenya) Program, led by the Ministry of Agriculture, has aimed to improve the health and nutrition of vulnerable people and schoolchildren by integrating school meals with nutrition education, mother and child health, and the adoption of agricultural technologies for increased productivity. As such, Njaa Marafuku is a collaborative initiative by the agriculture sector ministries together with the Ministry of Education and the Ministry of Public Health.

The program targets areas that have high levels of poverty (including high school dropout rates, poor primary school performance, and high levels of child malnutrition) *and* the potential to increase smallholder agricultural production. Currently, 31,720 children in 48 schools are being targeted across six provinces. The program provides cash grants to schools for food procurement alongside transfers to support smallholder farmer production. The grants for food purchases are scaled down yearly as the program is handed over to the community by year three, and as farmers progressively repay their initial transfers in the form of food for schools.

More recently, the government launched a second initiative, the Home-Grown School Feeding Programme, in 2009. The program aims to feed 550,000 schoolchildren previously fed through a WFP operation. The new program uses the existing financial mechanisms of the Ministry of Education (including the Kenya Education Sector Support Programme, or KESSP—see chapter 4) to send financial resources directly to more than 2,000 schools, which then use their school management committees to procure food locally. The program aims to contribute to poverty reduction and provide a social safety net, while at the same time enhancing access to and participation in education. The school feeding program also has economic and social goals, since the hope is that local procurement will provide predictable and sustainable demand for local food production—thus increasing access to markets by local smallholder farmers, 80 percent of whom are women—and boost long-term economic development in program communities.

The costs, benefits, and trade-offs of the two different government programs in Kenya will be evaluated during the next four years to provide inputs to support the transition process.

**India and the world's largest school feeding program.** India has a long tradition of school feeding programs (some date to the 1920s), largely funded by state governments. In 2001, India's Supreme Court directed state governments to introduce school feeding programs in all government-assisted primary schools as a right of all children. This was the result of a petition from the People's Union for Civil Liberties, a large coalition of organizations and individuals that led a Right to Food Campaign.

The Mid-Day Meal Program operates through the Food Corporation of India (FCI), which procures food domestically and distributes it to a network of FCI stores, where it is transported to individual schools and villages. The program is largely decentralized, with operations varying throughout the country. The central government supports the states by providing free food grains (for example, rice or wheat) to implementing state agencies and reimbursing the costs of transportation to district authorities. States pay for any additional food items required, as well as for food preparation. States can choose from providing cooked meals at school or dry rations. Currently, the program has near universal coverage, reaching 130 million schoolchildren throughout India.

**Transitioning to national ownership in El Salvador.** In 2008, the school feeding program in El Salvador was fully taken over by the government after 24 years of partnership with the WFP. The program started during the country's internal crisis in 1984, when it reached 300,000 students, or 90 percent of school-age children in rural areas. In 1997, six years after the signing of the peace accords, the government began to take over program management responsibilities, while the WFP withdrew from areas of the country not classified among the most food insecure.

To start the transition, most of the financing for the government program came from a trust fund generated by a national privatization initiative. As the program developed, the national school feeding program was financed increasingly through regular government budget allocations. The program was included within the broader National School Health Program, which is at the center of the country's social safety net system. By 2006, government allocations totaled $10 million and the program was reaching 651,260 children in 3,500 schools.

Coverage at the national level reached 88 percent of rural primary schools and poor urban schools in 2006. The government achieved 100 percent coverage in 2008, coinciding with the planned date for the complete transition of responsibilities to national institutions (WFP 2006). Currently, the government receives external support for technical assistance, logistics, and procurement through a trust fund that was established in 2008. Through this agreement, the WFP is piloting procurement innovations under its corporate Purchase for Progress initiative, which aims to link local procurement with the school feeding program.

### Micronutrients*

*Impact on education.* Micronutrients—or vitamins and minerals—are vital components of good nutrition, improving human health, and advancing physical and intellectual development in many important ways. Needed in small quantities, these nutrients are essential for physiological processes throughout the life cycle; they are not produced by the body and must be consumed as part of a healthy diet or, if a diet is insufficient, through fortified foods or supplements. All vitamins and minerals are important, but particular emphasis is given to vitamin A, iodine, iron, zinc, and folic acid, both because the prevalence of deficiency in these micronutrients is high in many populations and because they play pivotal roles in maintaining health and productivity.

Gestation and the first years of life are a critical period; micronutrient deficiency during this time has severe and irreversible consequences for child growth and development. The importance of prevention, timely detection, and treatment of micronutrient deficiency during this period, combined with other interventions—such as the promotion of breast-feeding and early childhood stimulation to ensure that children reach their intellectual potential as they enter school age—has been well documented (Micronutrient Initiative 2009a).

Ensuring the adequate micronutrient status of school-age children and adolescents can enhance their learning and school performance. As a result, the cost-effectiveness of investments in education is increased. Some nutrition interventions also improve school attendance, supporting the realization of Millennium Development Goal 2: achieving universal primary education.

Overt severe malnutrition (low weight for age) has devastating effects on a child. Programs to increase total food intake, such as school feeding programs in populations with a high prevalence of malnutrition, can improve diverse aspects of cognitive functioning, including verbal fluency, attention, and memory, among others (Chandler et al. 1995; Grantham-McGregor, Chang, and Walker 1998; Pollitt, Cueto, and Jacoby 1998). Such programs have also been shown to help keep children in school and improve on-time attendance, even among the nonmalnourished (Fernald, Ani, and Grantham-McGregor 1997; see "School Feeding" in this chapter for more information).

---

* This section was contributed by Annie S. Wesley, Lynnette Neufeld, Venkatesh Mannar, and Aynsley Morris.

The majority of children of school age, even in economically disadvantaged populations, do not suffer from observable forms of malnutrition. However, "hidden hunger," or nonobserved micronutrient deficiencies, also affects school performance. Evidence suggests that a number of school-based interventions can alleviate deficiencies and improve children's educational performance. School-based programs to improve children's daily intake of key micronutrients have been shown to have positive effects on many aspects of cognitive functioning; some of these programs may have lasting benefits for the individual and, in the case of adolescent girls, for future generations.

Educating schoolchildren about good nutrition in general and micronutrients in particular is an important part of curriculum development. It is equally important to use schools and other educational facilities, such as early learning centers, as a base from which to reach parents and other community members with information about micronutrient health. The following section focuses on micronutrients that (i) school-age children are likely to be deficient in, (ii) are important for educational outcomes, and (iii) have existing sufficiently safe and simple interventions that have been well evaluated and are appropriate for implementation by the education sector.

### Evidence for the importance and impact of specific micronutrients

Iodine. It is estimated that iodine deficiency affects 60 million school-age children (Bundy et al. 2006) and that iodine deficiency is associated with a 13.5 point reduction in IQ (Bleichrodt and Born 1994). By the time children are of school age, any iodine deficiency disorders they suffer may have already caused irreversible damage to the brain (Zimmermann 2009; see also "Interventions before School Age" in this chapter). Nonetheless, iodine is an essential nutrient throughout life and the adequate provision of iodine to school-age children through cost-effective interventions that can be practically implemented at scale, specifically the use of iodized salt in any foods prepared for a school, is essential.

According to Tiwari and others (1996), iodine-deficient children are slow learners with a concurrent low "motivation to achieve." A study conducted in Benin examined whether an improvement in iodine status during primary school years could have an effect on mental and psychomotor performance of children. Study findings suggested a "catch-up" effect in terms of mental performance among children whose iodine status, as measured by increased urinary iodine concentration, was improved. Children with improved iodine status might also have had better attention or concentration, as indicated by improvements in the level and speed of task performance in tests with a time limit (van den Briel et al. 2000).

In addition, recent studies have clearly shown that a reversal of mild to moderate iodine deficiency in school-age children results in improved cognitive functioning and a partial reversal of the adverse effects of iodine deficiency (Zimmermann et al. 2006; Gordon et al. 2009). In Albania, a randomized placebo-controlled trial conducted by Zimmermann and colleagues (2006) found that a single oral dose of iodized oil (containing 400 mg iodine) corrected iodine deficiency and resulted in significantly improved performance on tests measuring information processing rates and ability to reason and solve problems, compared to the control group. Improvements ranged from 8 to 28 percent of the baseline score. Gordon and colleagues (2009) also used a randomized placebo-controlled trial, showing that the intervention group (which received 150 mg iodine daily for 28 weeks) improved significantly more than the control group on two tests of perceptual reasoning (by 9 percent and 6 percent, respectively), as well as on overall cognitive functioning (effect size of 0.19 SD). The authors of both papers stated that these interventions resulted in "small but significant" improvements in cognition.

In the above-mentioned controlled studies, iodine deficiency was corrected with iodine supplements, an appropriate intervention where salt iodization is not in effect or not well implemented and for controlled trials where effects are sought over short time periods. However, the accepted strategy of universal salt iodization to meet the iodine needs of all people, especially women prior to conception (UNICEF and WHO 1994) remains the intervention of choice for cost, simplicity, and sustainability reasons. Iodized salt has also been shown to correct even severe iodine deficiency among school-age children (Zimmermann et al. 2003) and therefore may result in similar cognitive benefits. School feeding programs should ensure that salt used in any foods is iodized.

**Iron.** More than half of school-age children in low-income countries are estimated to suffer from iron-deficiency anemia (Hall et al. 2001). As with iodine, children who suffer from iron deficiency in the early years may have irreversible deficits in many aspects of development (Pollitt 1997; Lozoff 2007). Interventions to prevent, diagnose, and treat iron deficiency in early life are essential. In addition to its key role during the prenatal and preschool period, iron deficiency and anemia during school years have a direct negative effect on cognition. Studies have shown that infants with anemia caused by iron deficiency have lower mental scores and lower motor scores than infants without anemia (Walker et al. 2007). However, unlike younger children, several studies (reviewed by Taras 2005) demonstrated that schoolchildren treated for iron deficiency had improved comprehension and improved verbal and cognitive performance.

Improvements in school performance and achievement as a result of correcting iron deficiency during school age are attributed to improved attention and reduced lethargy, rather than to improved brain function and/or intelligence. Iron also contributes to the health of older female children as they reach puberty, preparing them for future motherhood and improving the nutrition of the next generation of learners. A large-scale, school-based iron and folic acid supplementation trial in India concluded that weekly iron–folic acid supplementation (WIFS), combined with monthly education sessions and deworming every six months, is cost-effective in reducing the prevalence of anemia in adolescent girls (Vir et al. 2008). In recognition of this vital nutrient, the WHO has developed policy guidelines for WIFS programs for women of reproductive age (WHO 2009) and will soon release guidelines for the implementation of school-based WIFS programs in Asia, where the high prevalence of iron deficiency has devastating effects on girls, women, and their offspring.

Although ensuring adherence to WIFS likely poses a greater challenge than the less-frequent deworming component, the use of the school system as a delivery mechanism for WIFS will likely result in fewer adherence issues than those experienced by programs that provide supplements to individuals through the health care system. The above-mentioned effectiveness trial demonstrated high (greater than 85 percent) adherence due to counseling on the benefits of WIFS, despite the "real-world" setting of low supervision (Vir et al. 2008). To be effective, this intervention would require the full cooperation of all relevant ministries and stakeholders at all levels and ideally be integrated into existing supplementation programs for pregnant and lactating women so that women are adequately covered over the life cycle.

There is some evidence to suggest that iron supplementation of non-iron-deficient preschool-age children living in malaria-endemic areas results in increased morbidity and mortality (Sazawal et al. 2006). In response to these findings, the WHO (2007a) suggested that caution be exercised in iron supplementation of young children where malaria and infectious disease is highly prevalent. It is recommended that until further research can provide alternative solutions, iron supplementation in malaria-endemic areas be implemented only if screening for anemia is feasible and malaria prevention and control strategies are in place. These findings and recommendations are, however, limited to young children; to the authors' knowledge, no concerns have been raised regarding iron supplementation among school-age children.

Evidence exists that the preparation of school meals using different fortified staples, such as wheat flour, maize meal (Andang'o et al. 2007), or rice (Moretti et al. 2006), can improve the iron status of schoolchildren. An emerging vehicle for the delivery of both iron and iodine is double-fortified salt (DFS). Fortified with iodine and iron, this salt works complementarily with other approaches that seek to alleviate deficiencies of these two minerals. DFS trials in Karnataka, India, showed that after a 10-month intervention period using the salt, iron status improved significantly and the prevalence of anemia was reduced (Andersson et al. 2008). In Tamil Nadu, India, in response to a government mandate that double-fortified salt be used in school meals, millions of children are meeting up to one-third of their daily iron requirements (Micronutrient Initiative 2009b).

A recent analysis of school feeding programs by the WFP and the World Bank recommends fortified foods as a routine part of school-based programs. As noted previously, fortified school meals, take-home rations, and other feeding programs can increase attendance and facilitate learning (Bundy, Burbano et al. 2009). As with any intervention, food fortification programs must overcome administrative and logistical challenges to ensure that objectives are being met. (See the "School Feeding" section earlier in this chapter for information on home-grown school feeding strategies).

**Multiple micronutrients.** Micronutrient deficiency is caused by the low consumption of foods rich in micronutrients, typically fruits, vegetables, and foods of animal origin. Given that these foods are the main sources for many micronutrients, it is not uncommon for children, especially the poorest children, to simultaneously suffer from multiple micronutrient deficiencies. One response to this situation has been the use of products that provide two or more micronutrients. Commonly used products for this purpose include syrups, tablets, fortified foods (for example, biscuits) (Nga et al. 2009), beverages (Ash et al. 2003), and micronutrient powders that can be added to servings of foods in individual doses before they are consumed by a person; bulk food that is prepared and consumed in schools is also used (Osei et al. 2008).

The composition of micronutrient-rich foods and supplements varies and their use should be based on knowledge of the specific deficiencies in a given population. These products commonly contain a combination of iron, vitamin A, folic acid, zinc, and, sometimes, vitamin C. A recent review of the provision of multiple micronutrients to school-age children to enhance cognitive performance (Eilander et al. 2010) provided evidence that supplementation with multiple micronutrients can result in small but significant improvements in fluid intelligence and academic performance in otherwise healthy children. The authors emphasize that further research is still needed to fully understand the relationship between deficiencies, correction of deficiencies, and cognition. Provision of micronutrients through fortified foods has also been shown to enhance the efficacy of other health interventions, including deworming treatment (Nga et al. 2009).

***Options for school-based responses.*** The previous section gave several options for school-based responses to the prevention and treatment of iron, iodine, and multiple micronutrient deficiencies, all of which are related to cognitive functioning or educational outcomes. These include the use of iodized salt or DFS in the preparation of school meals, WIFS for adolescent girls, food fortification, and "point-of-use" fortification of school foods with multiple micronutrient powders. The use of any of these interventions should be based on knowledge of the deficiency in the target population.

In addition, schools are an important place for children and their families to learn about the importance and benefits of good nutrition, micronutrients, and the foods that contain them. For example, in several countries (for example, India), children are asked to bring salt samples from home to be tested in school for the presence of iodine. Children are then taught about the importance of using iodized salt and provided with take-home messages, including how their family can ensure purchased salt is iodized. Families are being educated about the importance of using iodized salt, including women of childbearing age, to prevent iodine-deficiency disorders in the next generation. Some countries (for example, Pakistan) are required by development assistance agencies to increase adequate iodized salt consumption as a prerequisite for the release of funding for education programs. Although not a school-level education activity, the requirement provides a clear message to governments at all levels of the importance of micronutrients for educational success.

Ensuring adequate micronutrients from conception through the growth years, including via school-based interventions, is an ideal way to prevent the devastating effects of "hidden hunger" in current and future generations of children so that they can better realize their full potential for lifelong learning and productivity.

### Malaria Control*

Malaria is an important cause of mortality and morbidity in school-children in Sub-Saharan Africa and may have profound consequences for their learning and educational achievement (Brooker et al. 2000; Bundy et al. 2000; Lalloo, Olukoya, and Olliaro 2006). The traditional focus of malaria control is on the young, who are most at risk of mortality, but this approach has the unintended consequence that young people may not acquire immunity to infection—since the acquisition of immunity is dependent on early exposure—and may be at increased risk at school age and above (Snow and Marsh 2002). Yet school-age children have the lowest insecticide-treated net use, and thus the least protection, of any age group in the community (Noor et al. 2009). Paradoxically, in many countries in Africa today, it is school-age children who have the highest prevalence of infection and who pose a threat to universal coverage targets and the ability to reduce local transmission. Adding malaria control interventions to existing school health programs offers a potentially cost-effective approach to controlling malaria in the school-age population (Bundy et al. 2006; Brooker et al. 2008; Brooker 2009).

*Impact on education.* Some 20–50 percent of African schoolchildren living in areas of stable high transmission experience clinical malaria attacks each year (Clarke et al. 2004). The risk of malaria attack is lower in areas of unstable malaria transmission, but attacks in those areas are more severe, as children have not acquired any significant level of immunity. Malaria accounts for up to 50 percent of all deaths among African school-age children: an estimated 214,000 deaths per year (Snow et al. 2003).

Malaria is also an important contributor to the complex factors, including diet and worm infection, that cause anemia. Control of malaria among school-age children can dramatically improve hemoglobin (Hb) levels

---

* This section was contributed by Simon Brooker.

(Geerligs, Brabin, and Eggelte 2003). In Africa, up to a quarter of girls give birth before the age of 18; malaria in pregnancy is therefore important when considering malaria in schoolchildren. Pregnancy-associated malaria is a major cause of low birth weight and maternal anemia in areas of stable transmission (Guyatt and Snow 2001), with severe anemia during pregnancy being a major risk factor for maternal death.

In Africa, malaria contributes between 5 and 8 percent of all causes of absenteeism from school, which is equivalent to 50 percent of all preventable absenteeism, or around 4 million to 10 million school days lost per year (Brooker et al. 2000). Absenteeism is a particular concern during a malaria epidemic in areas of unstable transmission. Conversely, preventing malaria in early life is associated with longer schooling (Jukes et al. 2006).

Malaria impairs cognition, learning, and educational achievement. These effects appear to be mediated through two pathways: the anemia associated with both asymptomatic and clinical malaria, and the neurological consequences of cerebral malaria (Holding and Snow 2001; Kihara, Carter, and Newton 2006). Recent evidence suggests that nonsevere malaria can adversely affect cognition, attention, and, ultimately, school performance (Fernando et al. 2006; Clarke et al. 2008). Malaria can also impact the education supply through the deaths and absenteeism of teachers. In areas of unstable transmission, the absenteeism of teachers can lead to the closure of schools during the malaria transmission season.

***Options for school-based responses.*** There is a clear policy context for the educational response to malaria. Previous experience has shown that stand-alone school malaria programs are not always effective or sustainable. Rather, it is important to see malaria in schools as part of a broader school health program. There are four main approaches to malaria control that can be incorporated into existing school health programs (Brooker 2009):

1. *Health education to promote appropriate behavior.* This is a natural, traditional activity by which schools contribute to malaria prevention. Skills-based malaria health education should promote the following:
   - *Attitudes,* such as responsibility for personal, family, and community health, as well as building the confidence to change unhealthy habits.
   - *Knowledge,* such as knowledge of symptoms of malaria and the importance of seeking appropriate treatment, as well as the importance of personal prevention, especially the use of long-lasting insecticide-treated nets (LLINs).

- *Skills,* such as avoiding behaviors likely to cause malaria, encouraging others to change unhealthy habits, and communicating messages about malaria and its prevention and control to families, peers, and members of the community.

2. *Distribution of insecticide-treated nets.* WHO now recommends that LLINs be used by everyone, including schoolchildren. For this to happen, there would have to be a dramatic increase in coverage from the current very low levels of LLIN use by schoolchildren—the lowest of any age group (Noor et al. 2009). This fact implies a need to provide free LLINs to schoolchildren, encourage residential (boarding) schools to provide nets in dormitories, and support this strategy with skills-based health education, as detailed previously.

3. *Preventive treatment.* There is currently a lack of specific policy guidance on whether antimalarial treatment services should be provided through schools. In Kenya, the mass administration of a full therapeutic course of antimalarial drugs to schoolchildren once a term, irrespective of infection status, dramatically reduced malaria parasitemia (the number of parasites in the blood of infected children), almost halved the rates of anemia, and significantly improved cognitive ability (Clarke et al. 2008). However, it is still necessary to evaluate the effectiveness of the approach in a wider range of infrastructures and malaria transmission settings in Africa.

4. *Presumptive treatment.* Prompt recognition and effective treatment of malaria among schoolchildren is essential. At present, this imperative implies the need for detection of cases and their referral to health clinics for treatment. A large-scale program of presumptive treatment by teachers in Malawi was shown to reduce the death rate of school-age children (Pasha et al. 2003; see also the Malawi case study in the following subsection). However, as is the case with preventive treatment, there is no specific policy guidance and presumptive treatment by teachers is not currently recommended. Instead, teachers should be trained to recognize the danger signs of malaria and the need for prompt referral to a health facility; schools should also have a policy for referral. These approaches are discussed in more detail in a recently published school malaria toolkit (Brooker 2009).

## *Practical experience of implementation*

**Effective malaria treatment in Malawi schools reduces deaths of school-children.** Malawi has a long tradition of school health programs. One such program introduced the presumptive treatment for malaria in 101 schools in the Mangochi District. Launched in 2000 with support from Save the Children USA, the project trained teachers to treat malaria in schools using a "pupil treatment kit," which included the antimalarial drug, sulfadoxine-pyrimethamine. In each school, three teachers received training, including recognition of the signs and symptoms used to diagnose malaria and safe administration of antimalarial treatment. Sick children were reported to teachers, suspected malaria cases were treated according to national guidelines, and pills to reduce fever (antipyretics) were provided to the sick children to take home. Sick children whose health did not improve were referred to a health facility.

An evaluation compared the death rates of schoolchildren three years before and two years after the program was introduced. Deaths from all causes declined from 2.20 to 1.44 deaths per 1,000 student-years, and deaths due to malaria specifically declined from 1.28 to 0.44 deaths per 1,000 student-years. The estimated cost of providing each child with access to a treatment kit was $0.38 per child per year, and the cost of a child receiving a malaria treatment was $2.30. Parents and communities initially contributed 10 percent toward the cost of replacing the kits; by 2007, communities were paying 80 percent of the drug costs.

In 2008, the Malawi government followed international best practice by introducing artemisinin-based combination therapies (ACTs), which aim to reduce the rate of development of drug-resistant strains of malaria. Current practice requires that these therapies be administered by medical personnel and not teachers. As a result, despite the program's success, antimalarial treatment was withdrawn from the pupil treatment kits. It remains to be determined whether teachers can provide ACT treatment.

**Developing a national school malaria strategy in Kenya.** The commitment of the Kenyan government to helping schoolchildren stay healthy and do well at school is indicated by its national school health program, jointly implemented by the education and health sectors. Despite the coordinated policy framework, malaria in schools remains an important issue, with research indicating that malaria accounts for 10–20 percent of all causes of death of schoolchildren in the country, as well as for 4 million to 10 million school days lost per year. Studies in Kenya show that this burden could be effectively addressed with currently available tools. For instance, as noted earlier, mass administration of a full therapeutic course of an antimalarial drug to schoolchildren once a term, irrespective of infection status, dramatically reduced malaria parasitemia, almost halved the rates of anemia, and significantly improved cognitive ability (Clarke et al. 2008).

To help formulate a national plan of action, the government held a stakeholder workshop in 2007 to review existing policies and guidelines and see what lessons could be learned from previous implementations of school-based malaria control. This workshop helped guide the integration of malaria control into the joint education and health sector national school health, nutrition, and meals program, which is supported through the Kenya Education Sector Support Programme (KESSP, see chapter 4). The workshop also helped catalyze the health sector's Malaria-free Schools Initiative, which was launched in 2009 as a key component of the National Malaria Strategy (2009–17) of the Ministry of Public Health and Sanitation. The emphasis on malaria control in schools by both education and health sector constituencies in Kenya reflects a focus on cross-sectoral approaches to policy and planning, supported by a strong evidence base of what works in the national context.

### HIV Prevention and Care*

HIV is not only a communicable viral disease; it is also a social disease. The worst effects of infection with the virus can be managed using daily antiretroviral therapy, but the infection cannot currently be cured. It is unlikely that a vaccine or cure will be developed on a time scale relevant to the current generation of children and adolescents. Key drivers in the spread of HIV are poverty, lack of information, and lack of hope for the future. The education sector has a role to play in addressing these factors. Schools can provide critical information about the disease, dispel rumors, and reduce stigma. Education gives young people skills that make them more economically self-reliant and less vulnerable, for example, less likely to trade sex for food or money for survival. And perhaps most critically, education can allow young people to imagine independent, successful adult lives for themselves. Having hope for the future

---

* This section was contributed by Matthew Jukes, Stephanie Simmons Zuilkowski, and Claire Risley.

empowers young people to make healthy decisions about their relationships and sexual health.

Section 27 of the 2000 "Dakar Framework for Action" (under "Achievements and Challenges") states that "the terrifying impact of HIV/AIDS on educational demand, supply, and quality requires explicit and immediate attention in national policy making and planning. Programmes to control and reduce the spread of the virus must make maximum use of education's potential to transmit messages on prevention and to change attitudes and behaviours" (UNESCO 2000, 14–15). Considering the negative effect of HIV/AIDS on the education system as a whole, the section in the Dakar Framework dealing with "meeting our collective commitments" (section 8(vii)) proposes to "[i]mplement as a matter of urgency education programmes and actions to combat the HIV/AIDS pandemic." In the years since then, much has been done by countries to respond to the challenges that HIV poses for the education sector. Much, however, still needs to be done, as evidenced by the results of two Fast Track Initiative (FTI) assessments of endorsed Education Sector Plans (Clarke and Bundy 2004, 2008).

The vision of the importance of HIV in today's world is very different from that at the beginning of the decade (UNAIDS 2008). For a majority of countries worldwide, the impact is declining, and the availability of effective therapy has transformed the prospects of those, including teachers and students, who are living with HIV. In such areas, the primary role of education may be to ensure access to care and treatment for teachers and students, reduce stigma, and promote understanding of the need to focus control efforts on high-risk groups. But in other areas, particularly the southern cone of Africa, HIV remains a major constraint on development. Though the population of Eastern and Southern Africa currently includes only about 6 percent of the world's population, about one-third of all new HIV infections take place in the region. HIV control there remains a major priority and the education sector still has a vigorous role to play. In reading the section that follows, it is important to keep in mind that very different programmatic responses will be required by different epidemiological situations.

***Impact on education.*** A child's access to education is likely to be reduced if his or her family is affected by HIV. Financial pressures increase when a family member is infected with HIV (Bachmann and Booysen 2004). When parents are ill, they may not be able to work or they may lose jobs due to absenteeism or stigma. The costs of medical treatments and care may stress family finances. Children may need to leave school and begin working to help support their families, or they may become caregivers. In addition, children in families affected by HIV/AIDS face stigma and discrimination by community members (UNICEF 2006; Pridmore 2008). Discrimination in schools may lead them to drop out (Robson and Sylvester 2007).

Well-designed school health programs can reduce the impact of these challenges on individual students by, for example, reducing peer discrimination against those with HIV. The consequences of HIV occur in both high- and low-prevalence situations, but the impact, in general, will scale with the level of the epidemic. One exception to this trend is stigma, which is universally high and, paradoxically, may be greatest in areas of low prevalence, where the reality of the disease remains a fearful enigma.

The number of orphans due to AIDS continues to rise, even while its prevalence may be steadying or falling (see table 3.3). This reflects the epidemiological progression of HIV and AIDS in populations through infection to disease to orphanhood, with a decade or more of lag time between each stage. Studies have reached different conclusions about the impact of orphanhood on the likelihood of children having access to education (compare, for example, UNICEF 2008 with Ainsworth, Beegle, and Koda 2001). It appears that in some countries, orphan-specific support programs adequately protect orphaned children, while in other countries they do not. In all cases the key determinant is the socioeconomic status of the child.

The impact of HIV on the supply side of education operates largely through teacher deaths and absenteeism. Although both of these impacts are mitigated by antiretroviral therapy (ART), this therapy remains unavailable for most people who require it (42 percent in 2008; see UNAIDS 2008). Absenteeism results from teachers living with HIV and from teachers caring for infected family members (Kelly 2000). Both HIV infection itself, and the consequent caregiving responsibilities, tend to affect females disproportionately; in many countries,

**Table 3.3    Number of Orphans Due to AIDS and the Prevalence of HIV among Adults, Worldwide**

|  | 2001 | 2007 |
|---|---|---|
| Currently living orphans (0–17 years) due to AIDS | 8,000,000 | 15,000,000 |
| Adult (15–49 years) prevalence of HIV (%) | 0.8 | 0.8 |

*Source:* UNAIDS 2008.

the relative predominance of women teachers in basic education compared to other professions makes education provision more of a concern than the impacts of HIV on other workforces. Even where teachers living with HIV can anticipate a long and healthy future due to timely and reliable provision of ART, teachers in particular face profound challenges due to the stigma of carrying the virus (see interviews in Bundy, Aduda, et al. 2009).

A cross-country comparison of quantitative impacts of HIV teacher mortality in some of the worst-affected countries is presented in figure 3.4. These estimates of current teacher mortality, carried out using the Ed-SIDA model (Grassly et al. 2003; Risley and Bundy 2007), suggest the scale of the impact in these countries and show that some of the countries with the worst teacher shortages (as indicated by high pupil-teacher ratios, for example, Zimbabwe) are among those with the highest mortality from AIDS.

Education is particularly important in regions that are facing a feminization of the epidemic. In South Asia, for example, an estimated one-third of people infected with HIV are women, and the proportion is growing. This is a result not only of the physiological vulnerability of women, but of the fact that girls are often more socially and economically vulnerable due to their status in society. Providing young people, especially girls, with the "social vaccine" of education offers them a real chance at a productive life (World Bank 2002). Young people, particularly girls, who fail to complete a basic education, are more than twice as likely to become infected with HIV. The Global Campaign for Education (2004) has estimated that some 7 million cases of HIV could be avoided in a decade by the achievement of Education for All.

**Options for school-based responses.** School-age children have the lowest prevalence of HIV infection of any age group. In countries with generalized epidemics, school health programs should have the primary goals of keeping children HIV-free as they grow up and reducing stigma toward those living with the infection. Where the epidemic is concentrated, the priority goal is usually to reduce the stigma associated with high-risk groups among the general population and thus facilitate targeted control efforts.

Schools are promising sites for HIV prevention education programs for several reasons. First, in most countries the vast majority of children enter and complete at least some primary education. Thus, schools are one of the few societal institutions that reach nearly everyone. Second, children who participate in HIV prevention programs at an early age may be more likely to delay sexual activity or adopt safer sex practices

102

**Figure 3.4    AIDS Mortality among Teachers Using Ed-SIDA Projections in Countries with Generalized Epidemics**

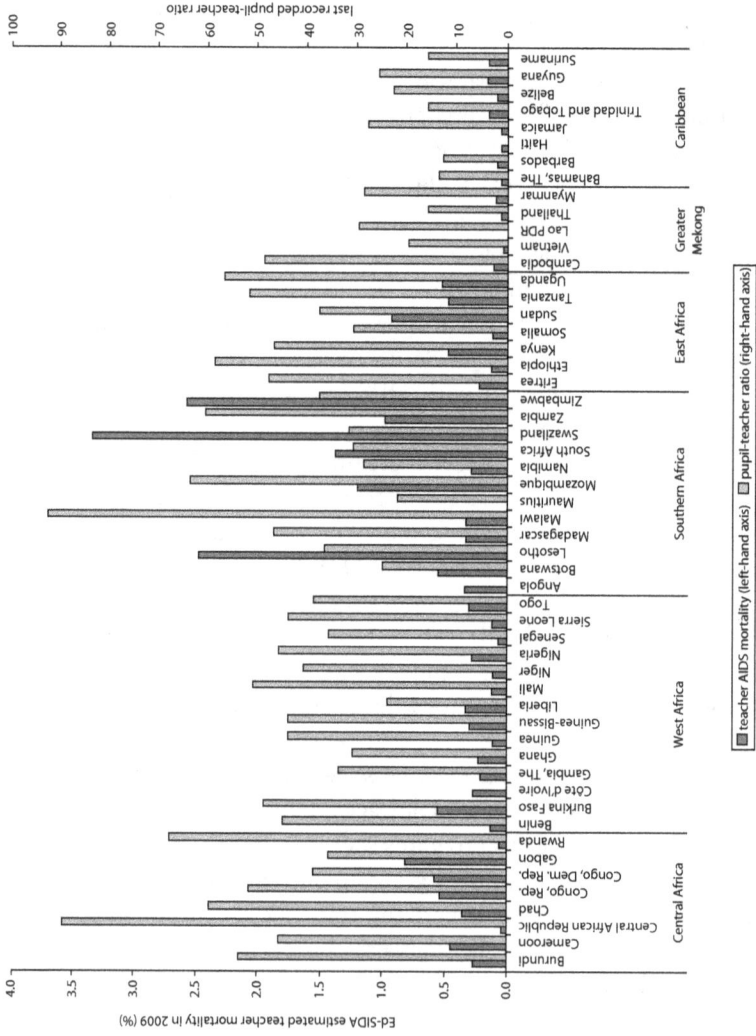

last recorded pupil-teacher ratio

Ed-SIDA estimated teacher mortality in 2009 (%)

teacher AIDS mortality (left-hand axis)    pupil-teacher ratio (right-hand axis)

*Source:* Original figure prepared by Claire Risley and Donald Bundy.

*Note:* Teacher AIDS mortality in high-prevalence countries is shown according to Ed-SIDA projections (see the "Schools and Health" website maintained by the Partnership for Child Development, http://www.schoolsandhealth.org/Pages/Ed-SidaModel.aspx, accessed January 2010). Countries with the highest mortality are Swaziland, Lesotho, South Africa, and Mozambique. The pattern of mortality does not always follow that of prevalence, largely because of ART. Botswana has relatively low mortality for its prevalence rate because of successes in rolling out ART. Sudan has relatively high mortality for its prevalence rate because of difficulties in ART provision. Pupil-teacher ratios in each country are according to UNESCO (see the website of the UNESCO Institute for Statistics, Montreal, http://www.uis.unesco.org, accessed January 2010). The countries where education is most at risk from HIV are those with both high mortality and a teacher shortage, as indicated by high national pupil-teacher ratios (PTRs). Countries scoring high on each of these measures are Zimbabwe, Lesotho, and Mozambique. High PTRs in Burkina Faso and the Democratic Republic of Congo could potentially be reduced by lowering the moderate teacher AIDS mortality in these countries.

than older adolescents and adults who are already sexually active (Gallant and Maticka-Tyndale 2004). Third, teachers are generally respected members of the community and therefore well placed to lead prevention efforts, if they are inclined to do so.

Schools may influence HIV risk in two ways: through specific, focused HIV prevention education and through general education. Specific HIV prevention education programs have a number of advantages. They are inexpensive compared to providing extra years of general education and when well designed and tightly focused, programs may have measurable impacts on children's risk behaviors. Kirby and others conducted a useful review of 83 studies that focus on preventing sexually transmitted infections, HIV/AIDS, and/or pregnancy in 22 countries (Kirby, Laris, and Rolleri 2006).

In addition to consolidating the findings of the studies, their review identifies 17 common traits of successful school sexual health programs associated with curriculum development, content, and implementation. Programs that successfully changed behaviors were based on theory, adapted to local values and resources, and tailored to fit participants' ages. They had clear, specific goals and were direct about the behaviors they intended to change. Successful programs used participatory methods, received buy-in from local officials, and followed through with the program as designed, rather than picking and choosing activities. School health program managers who incorporate these guidelines into their work may be more successful in reducing risk behaviors among youth.

While specific HIV prevention education programs are critical, general education may be protective as well. More educated people are more likely to be exposed to prevention information as part of formal schooling and also through the media (Gregson et al. 1998). Greater levels of education may also provide a framework of biological knowledge and an understanding of causality within which HIV prevention messages can be assimilated. Thus education helps individuals understand the connection between a risk behavior and its potential outcomes. More broadly, educational attainment can provide skills that lead to economic independence and a more hopeful view of the future, both of which may decrease risky behaviors in adolescence and adulthood.

Teachers living with HIV have an important role to play, since they are uniquely placed to communicate the HIV prevention and mitigation message, both in terms of conveying accurate messages and addressing stigma directly. This role may be important both for children and in encouraging the uptake of testing and treatment by other teachers.

*Practical experience of implementation.* A wide range of models of HIV prevention education are used in schools (see examples in box 3.2). A recent study in Kenya demonstrates the potential power of a brief, concentrated behavioral-change intervention. Dupas conducted a randomized controlled trial in primary schools in western Kenya to evaluate an education campaign focusing on the risks of cross-generational sex

---

**Box 3.2**

## Effective Sexuality Education*

Effective sexuality education can provide young people with age-appropriate, culturally relevant, and scientifically accurate information and offers a platform for HIV prevention in school and out of school (UNESCO 2009). Research shows that programs sharing certain key characteristics can help schoolchildren to abstain from or delay the debut of sexual relations, reduce the frequency of unprotected sexual activity, reduce the number of sexual partners, and increase the use of protection against unintended pregnancy and sexually transmitted infections (STIs) during sexual intercourse. UNESCO's latest review of 87 studies in 2008–2009 also highlighted the following findings, which have implications for policy-level decision makers and program developers as well as managers in education and the health sector.

Curriculum-based programs implemented in schools or communities should be viewed as an important component that can often (but not necessarily always) reduce risky sexual behavior. However, isolated from broader programs in the community, these programs do not always have a significant impact in terms of reducing HIV, STIs, or pregnancy rates.

There is evidence that programs did not have harmful effects; in particular, they did not hasten the initiation or increase sexual activity. The studies also demonstrate that it is possible, with the same programs, to delay sexual intercourse and increase the use of condoms or other forms of contraception. In other words, a dual emphasis on abstinence, together with use of protection for those who are sexually active, is not confusing to young people. Rather, it can be both realistic and effective.

Nearly all studies of sexuality education programs demonstrate increased knowledge.

*(continued next page)*

**Box 3.2** *(continued)*

About two-thirds of the studies demonstrate positive results on behavior among either the entire sample or an important subsample.

More than one-fourth of the programs improved two or more sexual behaviors among young people. Encouragingly, programs with positive behavioral results include those with strong evaluation designs and those that replicated similar programs, with consistent results.

Comparative analysis of effective and ineffective programs provides strong evidence that those incorporating the characteristics of effective programs can change the behaviors that put young people at risk of STIs and pregnancy.

Even if sexuality education programs improve knowledge, skills, and intentions to avoid sexual risk or use clinical services, reducing risk may be challenging to young people if social norms do not support risk reduction and/or clinical services are not available.

The sexuality education programs studied had one big gap in common: none of them appeared to address the behaviors that cause significant HIV infection among adolescents in large parts of the world (that is, Europe, Latin America and the Caribbean, and Asia). Those behaviors are unsafe injecting drug use, unsafe sexual activity in the context of sex work, and unprotected (mainly anal) sexual intercourse between men.

\* Contributed by Christopher Castle.

(Dupas 2006). The campaign involved a 40-minute talk, a 10-minute video, and a survey. The program was successful in reducing cross-generational sex: there was a 65 percent decrease in the number of pregnancies with adult fathers in the experimental group and no increase in pregnancies by same-age partners. These findings indicate that when a program has a clear goal and offers specific behavioral alternatives, even a brief information campaign may lead to significant changes in sexual behavior.

Lengthier, more integrated programs can be effective as well. Further evidence comes from a matched pairs evaluation of the Primary School Action for Better Health (PSABH) program in Kenya. PSABH was designed to incorporate HIV prevention information into classroom lessons, as well as extracurricular activities for upper-primary school students (Maticka-Tyndale, Wildish, and Gichuru 2007). The impact of the program differed by gender. Boys in program schools who had been highly exposed to the program were significantly more likely to report condom use at last sex, but there were no significant effects of the program on girls' reported condom use, even at the high exposure level. Both males and females in program schools who were virgins at baseline were significantly less likely to begin sexual activity during the program.

Evidence on school health programs designed to prevent HIV in Sub-Saharan Africa was examined in a review of 11 peer-reviewed studies with quantitative evaluation data that were published between 1990 and 2002 (Gallant and Miticka-Tyndale 2004). The majority of reviewed programs were successful in increasing knowledge—10 of 11 programs—and in changing student attitudes—7 of 7 programs. Programs were less successful overall in changing behaviors. Only one of the three studies focusing on sexual behavior found an impact on sexual debut and the number of partners (Shuey et al. 1999). Of four studies aimed at condom use, only one increased reported rates of condom usage (Harvey, Stuart, and Swan 2000).

Though sexual behaviors may be difficult to impact directly, related behaviors seem to be more malleable. Several studies were able to increase communication between students and their parents, friends, and sexual partners about sexual issues and HIV (Kuhn, Steinberg, and Matthews 1994; Klepp et al. 1997; Stanton et al. 1998; Shuey et al. 1999). The review also called attention to the importance of teacher commitment and comfort with the material; if teachers are reluctant to discuss sex or condoms, a school health program is unlikely to be a success.

With respect to evidence on the effects of general education on HIV risk, a clear consensus has not yet been reached on the statistical relationship between educational attainment and HIV infection. Some studies have found that education is protective, while others have identified higher education levels as a risk factor. Hargreaves and others (2007) have suggested one explanation for the conflicting results, concluding that studies conducted after 1997 were more likely to find a protective effect of education than earlier studies. One interpretation of these results is that education has become a protective factor over time, as populations have become more aware of both the risk of HIV transmission and the steps they can take to protect themselves. This leads to the conclusion that equitable expansion of primary and secondary schooling, particularly for girls, will help reduce their vulnerability to HIV.

To the authors' knowledge, no evidence exists that identifies increased educational attainment as the causal factor in an individual's sexual behavior. Much evidence suggests, however, that sexual behavior is associated with education level. Being enrolled in school, for example, has been associated with having fewer sexual partners (Magnani et al. 2002; Hargreaves et al. 2008; Clark, Poulin, and Kohler 2009) and a lower likelihood of having had sex (Meekers and Ahmed 2000; Magnani et al. 2002; Anderson, Beutel, and Maughan-Brown 2007; Hallett et al. 2007; Clark, Poulin, and Kohler 2009). Education level has also been associated with greater likelihood of condom use in a number of countries and contexts (Lugoe, Klepp, and Skutle 1996; Fylkesnes et al. 2001; Lagarde et al. 2001; Magnani et al. 2002; Zellner 2003; Maharaj 2005; Prata, Vahidnia, and Fraser 2005; de Walque et al. 2005; Hargreaves et al. 2007; Sandøy et al. 2007; Wouhabe 2007; Lurie et al. 2008; Trinitapoli (2009). These findings indicate that general education, alongside specific HIV prevention programs, is valuable in reducing the spread of HIV through unsafe sexual behavior.

Although this book is focused on EFA and basic education, it is worth noting that a recent study (Gupta and Mahy 2003) examined demographic and health survey data in eight countries using logistic regression models and found that secondary education was the *only* variable that was consistently and statistically significantly associated with lower probability of first intercourse before age 18 in all countries considered. It may be that the upward pressure on secondary level enrollment resulting from EFA is a potentially important factor in HIV prevention.

***Taking action.*** In countries with generalized or severe epidemics, the education sector response should include HIV prevention and mitigation of the impact of HIV on the education system itself, including on education supply and demand. The education sector has an additional important role to play in providing access to education to children who are orphaned or made vulnerable by AIDS, as well as ensuring that teachers and staff have access to care, treatment, and support.

In low-prevalence countries, which today include most countries in South Asia, East Asia, and the Caribbean, as well as in parts of Africa, education must tackle HIV-related stigma and discrimination in both educational institutions and society. Education has a powerful role to play in addressing harmful discriminatory attitudes in general, and those against people living with HIV in particular. Studies have shown that education increases understanding and tolerance, dramatically reducing levels of stigma and discrimination against vulnerable and marginalized communities and people living with HIV (World Bank 2002; UNESCO 2007).

The World Bank has published two sourcebooks that provide systematic, detailed descriptions of education sector programs that address HIV.

The first (World Bank 2003a) describes early government programs, typically implemented with the support of civil society organizations, in seven countries: Mozambique, Senegal, South Africa, Tanzania, Uganda, Zambia, and Zimbabwe. The second (World Bank 2008) describes 10 education sectorwide programs implemented as national programs by governments in eight countries: the Dominican Republic, Eritrea, The Gambia, Ghana, Israel, Kenya, Namibia, and Nigeria.

UNICEF and the World Bank together have published a sourcebook (UNICEF 2009) that describes 12 initiatives in 6 countries (Kenya, Rwanda, Swaziland, Uganda, Tanzania, and Zambia) that represent a wide range of approaches designed to address the educational rights and needs of orphans and vulnerable children.

### Hygiene, Water, and Sanitation*

Hygienic practices, access to sanitation, and the provision of clean water are all important contributors to children's health. Sanitation refers to the infrastructure and service provision required for the safe management of human excreta, including latrines, sewers, and wastewater treatment. Sanitation is clearly relevant to school health and, along with water supply and water quality, is typically managed as part of overall school infrastructure. While school health units of an education system may have an important role in advocating for better sanitation and clean water—often also monitoring water quality and reporting on access to water—school health programs do not have a mandate over these components.[1] Hygiene and hygiene promotion refer to human behaviors related to sanitation, such as hand washing. It is with respect to hygiene that school health education and school health services have a direct role to play.

*Impact on education.* Hygiene promotion is among the most cost-effective child survival interventions. Some of the conditions prevented by hygiene promotion, such as diarrhea and acute respiratory infection, are reported to be important causes of school absenteeism. According to a recent study cited by the Global Public-Private Partnership on Handwashing, hand washing with soap at critical times could help reduce school absenteeism by around 42 percent. To achieve this result, children must have access to water and soap in schools. A study by UNICEF and the International Red

---

* Contributors to this section: Hnin Hnin Pyne, Maria-Luisa Escobar, and Isabel Rocha Pimenta.

Cross in six low-income countries in 2006, however, documented low rates of soap availability in schools.

*Practical experience of implementation.* Using reductions in cases of diarrhea as a metric, it can be shown that hygiene, water (both quantity and quality), and sanitation each contribute to the improved health of children (see figure 3.5). Importantly, hand washing with soap has proven to be a particularly effective intervention; it is also significantly simpler and cheaper than the other water and sanitation options, as well as a ready candidate for inclusion in school health programs.

Hand washing with soap also reduces the risk of acute respiratory infections (ARIs), such as pneumonia and influenza, in young children by an average of 24 percent, with reductions ranging from 6 to 44 percent, depending on the study (see Rabie and Curtis 2006). This simple practice reduces the incidence of pneumonia alone by more than half (Luby et al. 2005).

The aforementioned Global Public-Private Partnership for Hand-washing with Soap, a coalition of international stakeholders that includes

**Figure 3.5    Reduction in Diarrhea Morbidity as a Result of Various Interventions**

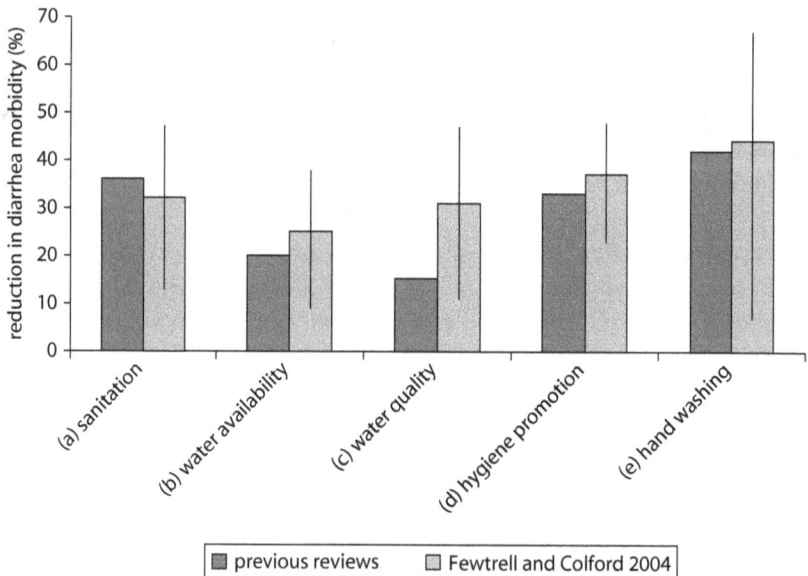

Sources: Cairncross 2004; a–d: Esrey et al. 1991; e: Curtis and Cairncross 2003.
Note: Vertical lines indicate the range of standard errors.

the Water and Sanitation Program,[2] the World Bank, United Nations Children's Fund (UNICEF), and UNILEVER, is a major programmatic actor in this area. Established in 2001, the partnership aims to give families, schools, and communities in developing countries the power to prevent diarrhea and respiratory infections by supporting the universal practice of proper hand washing with soap at critical times.[3] Hand washing and children's health are the stated focus of the partnership, which mentions schools, but does not consider EFA an objective.

At present, large-scale hand washing with soap programs, several of which are supported by the Water and Sanitation Program with funding from the Bill & Melinda Gates Foundation, promote hand washing as an intervention in multiple sectors—health, education, and water—but focus mainly on health outcomes. This focus may explain the low awareness of this program within the overall education community. However, in certain countries, such as Peru, the education sector is taking the lead in the implementation of hand washing with soap (see box 3.3). At the same time, school health programs often promote hand washing with soap since it is cheap and involves a familiar hygiene promotion intervention of proven effectiveness. (See, for example, the description of the Fit for School Program in the Philippines in chapter 4.) Additionally, chlorine dispensers are being explored in Kenya as a creative means of providing safe drinking water to schoolchildren (see box 3.4).

### Promoting Oral Health*

*Impact on education.* Dental decay (or dental caries) affects more than half of all school-age children worldwide and has been estimated to be the most prevalent noncommunicable disease of childhood (Beaglehole et al. 2009). In low- and middle-income countries, most decay remains untreated, with significant consequences for the individual and society at large. Pain resulting from untreated oral diseases leads to a complex sequence of related effects: infection impacting general health and well-being, the need to pay for treatment, loss of productivity and days at school, and a downward cycle of consequential health problems, poverty, and deprivation (Monse et al. 2010). In addition, gingivitis and bad breath impact the social interactions and self-esteem of children as much as they affect those of adults.

---

* This section was contributed by Habib Benzian and Bella Monse.

**Box 3.3**

## Promoting Hand Washing with Soap in Schools: The Institutionalizing of Hygiene in the Education Sector in Peru

The national Handwashing (HW) Initiative in Peru, managed by the Water and Sanitation Program and the Ministry of Education (MINEDU), developed a hygiene component to be inserted in the curricula of an ongoing national environmental program in the school system. Under the leadership of MINEDU, a policy was developed at national and regional levels in 2008 and 2009, and budgets were accordingly allocated for the implementation of specific activities.

*During 2009:*
- 1,846 schools became part of the Clean, Safe, and Healthy Schools Program
- 10,300 teachers were trained and given materials
- 74,728 children were reached in schools
- 29,000 hand-washing stations came into use at schools

The relationship among education authorities at all levels of the country has proven fundamental to the inclusion of hand washing in the activities and plans of MINEDU. In 2007, the vice-minister of education signed a resolution that paved the way for the smooth implementation of a social mobilization program called Clean, Safe, and Healthy Schools (CSHS). The program formalizes the Handwashing Initiative at the regional level through the use of a methodology for behavioral change. So far, most of the 24 regions of Peru have adopted CSHS, which uses hand washing promotion as a stand-alone indicator.

The goal of the Division of Environmental Education is to promote, train, and inform community education, environmental education, risk management, and disaster prevention. As part of its partnership with this division, MINEDU officials travel to intervention areas to promote the hand washing with soap package, which includes designation of a focal point and certification of trained teachers. Program methodology aims to introduce hygiene habits and promote behavioral change among children in schools. A person or committee becomes the focal point that will be responsible for environmental and sustainable education in a given school. The certification process for teachers takes into consideration a teacher's efforts to promote hygiene practices; this performance is then linked to career advancement bonuses. When the certification process was implemented in the Lambayeque region, the first group of 45 teachers received a "congratulations" resolution. Regional authorities are now working to implement certification throughout the region.

**Box 3.4**

# Kenya's Innovative Way to Provide Safe Drinking Water to Schoolchildren*

In November 2009, the Ministry of Education (MoE) of Kenya launched an innovative program to cost-effectively bring safe water to 33 primary schools in western Kenya.

Contaminated water can spread a range of diseases, including cholera. Treating water with a small amount of dilute chlorine solution kills most diarrhea-causing organisms. Kenya's Ministry of Public Health and Sanitation typically distributes free chlorine in response to cholera outbreaks, but there is no regular distribution. Chlorine products are available commercially (for example, Water-Guard), but such products are purchased by fewer than 10 percent of households in the region and by very few schools in Kenya. The products are expensive because the low cost of chlorine is greatly exceeded by the costs of packaging and distributing it for individual sale.

The new MoE program provides dilute chlorine in bulk, via a convenient valve-controlled dispenser next to a school-based water source. Using the school-based management system, the MoE has provided funding for drinking water stations (comprising a water storage container, spigot, and stand) so that students can drink treated water from these containers, rather than untreated water directly from the source. The cost of providing chlorine in this way is expected to be only one-quarter to one-half the cost of chlorine sold via more traditional retail distribution systems.

The MoE has selected schools with water sources that are used by both the school and members of the surrounding community, and has accordingly promoted dispenser use by the student population and nearby households. The dispensers now installed at 33 schools are expected to serve more than 24,000 students and more than 2,200 households. At scale, costs of manufacturing and delivering dispensers and chlorine refills could be as low as $0.15 per person per year. The estimated cost per disability-adjusted life year (DALY) saved is under $20, comparable to vaccines. The program was implemented with technical assistance from Innovations for Poverty Action (IPA), the NGO that developed the dispenser.

* Contributed by Michael Kremer, Amrita Ahuja, and Jeff Berens.

In many countries oral pain from untreated dental decay is reported by more than half of all schoolchildren and is among the most common reasons for absenteeism. The 2006 National Oral Health Survey in the Philippines reported results that may be typical for middle- and low-income countries: 97 percent of six-year-old children had tooth decay, which was associated with pain, anemia, a lower body mass index (BMI), and lower educational achievement (Department of Education 2008; Thammasat University 2003). Yet no child in the sample of more than 4,000 children surveyed in the study showed any signs of having received dental treatment.

School health programs in high-income countries traditionally address oral health, including both prevention and treatment, and have led to substantial oral health improvements. In low- and middle-income countries, however, the typical focus of such programs is on curative approaches that are often regressive (that is, available only to the urban elite). The WHO estimates that oral diseases are the fourth most expensive disease group in terms of treatment, even though most oral diseases, including dental decay, are preventable with simple, evidence-based, cost-effective interventions.

***Options for school-based responses.*** The focus of oral hygiene interventions in low- and middle-income countries should be on prevention. At the 60th World Health Assembly in 2007, the WHO urged governments "to promote oral health in schools, aiming at developing healthy lifestyles and self-care practices in children" (WHO 2007b, 3). Together with the World Dental Federation, the WHO announced that (i) prevention of tooth decay by using fluoride is the most realistic way of reducing the burden of tooth decay in populations, (ii) fluoride toothpaste remains the most widespread and significant form of fluoride used globally and the most rigorously evaluated vehicle for fluoride use, (iii) fluoride toothpaste is safe to use, and (iv) promoting the use of effective fluoride toothpaste twice a day is strongly recommended (WHO et al. 2007).

School health programs are well suited for oral health promotion. Although insufficient evidence exists to support education programs without behavioral intervention, the training of lifelong skills has recently been emphasized as an essential element of successful school health programs (Kay and Locker 1998; Hopkins et al. 2007; Peters et al. 2009). In addition to providing a hygienic and sanitary environment, an appropriate education sector response to the oral health needs of the school population in low- and middle-income countries should include the following specific elements:

- *Prevention, especially ensuring access to appropriate fluoride.* There are many ways to ensure access to appropriate fluoride in the school context, the most efficient and low-cost of which is daily toothbrushing with fluoride toothpaste as a routine school activity.

- *Sustained behavioral change.* Integrating good oral hygiene behavior—that is, brushing twice a day with fluoride toothpaste—into the daily routine of a school can promote the development of lifelong healthy habits. It is important that this behavior is reinforced at school and not left to the child at home; one of the most common (yet debatable) oral health interventions—distribution of information leaflets, toothbrush, and toothpaste to be used at home—will be effective only if this intervention is part of a systematic and sustained response at school.

- *Linking to the formal healthcare system.* Schools can provide basic oral care, such as pain relief and emergency care, and can initiate referral to health system practitioners, often through referral or permission slips that parents need to sign. Teachers can support the screening process by selecting those children who report themselves with dental problems. The issue here, however, is the lack and cost of curative services in most low-income settings.

### Practical experience of implementation
**Hong Kong SAR, China.** In the special administrative area of Hong Kong SAR, China, all primary school children in grades 1 through 6 have access to a free school dental service provided by the Department of Health. The service includes oral health education in school, a yearly examination, provision of sealants if needed, restorative care (fillings), root canal treatments, and tooth extractions. The comprehensive service is carried out in school dental clinics by qualified dental therapists under the supervision of dental surgeons. Transport to the clinic, appointments for treatment, and all follow-up visits are organized by the school system without the active involvement of the parents. If parents want their children to be treated by a private dentist, they must sign a waiver to exclude

their children from the public service. The costs of the program are estimated at close to $200 per year per child.

**The Philippines.** The Philippine Department of Education employs a workforce of 710 school dentists and 560 dental aides. On average, one dentist is responsible for about 20,000 students. Due to limited resources and the overwhelming treatment needs of the children, the school dental service is limited to dental education prior to an annual examination, provision of a referral slip, and advice to visit a private dentist. The National Oral Health Survey in 2006, however, provided evidence that the care index (percentage of decay lesions provided with treatment) was effectively zero.

In response to the disappointing outcome of the referral process, the national government piloted several concepts to introduce oral hygiene self-care in elementary schools. In 2008, the Department of Education launched the Fit for School Program, which is targeted at 1 million children in selected provinces. The oral health intervention (daily fluoride toothbrushing) is incorporated into a school health program that promotes a general concept of personal hygiene (see chapter 4 for details).

### Childhood Disability, Education, and School Health*
*Educational exclusion of children with disabilities.* As stated in the *EFA Global Monitoring Report 2010: Reaching the Marginalized,* "Disability is one of the least visible but most potent factors in educational marginalization. Beyond the immediate health-related effects, physical and mental impairment carries a stigma that is often a basis for exclusion from society and school" (UNESCO 2010, 181). School health programs can help not only address the prevention and rehabilitation of disability, but also create enabling environments to redress attitudinal and physical barriers that further marginalize children with disabilities.

*The prevalence of childhood disability.* Reliable data on childhood disability are scarce, and in many countries this remains a major challenge to developing effective education sector policy and responses to disability. Reported disability prevalence rates among children vary significantly, depending on the study and assessment tools used, and on disability

---

* This section was contributed by Aleksandra Posarac and Karen Peffley.

definition and measurement. Based on Global Burden of Disease data, the WHO estimated the average global prevalence of moderate and severe disability in children ages 0–14 years at 5 percent (WHO 2008). UNESCO estimates the number of children with disabilities under the age of 18 at between 120 million and 150 million (UNESCO 2003), implying a prevalence rate between 6.0 and 7.5 percent.

In the recent round of UNICEF's Multiple Indicator Cluster Survey (MICS), conducted at the beginning of the 2000s in 50 countries, an optional Child Disability Module was included in 26 countries. The results for 20 countries, including Albania, Bangladesh, Georgia, Ghana, India, Serbia, Sierra Leone, Thailand, and Uzbekistan, suggest that the percentage of children 2–9 years old who were found to be at the "increased risk of childhood disability" was between 14.0 and 35.0 percent in 15 of the 20 participating countries, and ranged across countries from 3.0 percent in Uzbekistan to 48.0 percent in the Central African Republic[4] (UNICEF and University of Wisconsin 2008). Reflecting the global distribution of the world's population, most of the children with disabilities live in developing countries.

**Children with disabilities and education.** A growing body of empirical research shows that children with disabilities tend to be disproportionately excluded from education. An analysis of 14 household surveys from 13 developing countries, including Bolivia, Chad, Indonesia, Mongolia, Mozambique, and South Africa, found that in all countries under study, disabled children 6–17 years of age were significantly less likely to start school or be enrolled at the time of the survey. "The order of magnitude of the school participation deficit associated with disability—which is as high as 50 percentage points in 3 of the 13 countries—is often larger than deficits related to other characteristics, such as gender, rural residence, or economic status differentials. The results suggest a worrisome vicious cycle of low schooling attainment and subsequent poverty among persons with disabilities" (Filmer 2008, 141).

According the *EFA Global Monitoring Report 2010*, which focuses on marginalized children, "the link between disability and marginalization in education is evident in countries at different ends of the spectrum for primary school enrolment and completion" (UNESCO 2010, 182). In Malawi and Tanzania, having disabilities doubles the probability of children never having attended school, and in Burkina Faso it increases the risk of children being out of school by two and a half times (Kobiané and Bougma 2009; Loeb and Eide 2004; United Republic of Tanzania

Government 2008). In some countries that are closer to achieving that goal, children with disabilities represent the majority of those left behind. In Bulgaria and Romania, net enrollment ratios for children ages 7–15 were over 90 percent in 2002 but only 58 percent for children with disabilities (Mete 2008; UNESCO 2010). In India, a nationwide survey of 87,874 households undertaken in 2005 found that approximately 4.3 percent of all out-of-school children were disabled. Of all disabled children, 38.1 percent were not attending school (Social and Rural Research Institute 2005).

Factors contributing to the marginalization of children with disabilities in education are complex. They may originate with the family of the disabled child, the school, and/or the community. These factors constitute barriers to the education inclusion of disabled children and include negative attitudes and low expectations; an inaccessible environment; an education system unprepared to include children with disabilities; lack of assistive devices, such as spectacles or hearing aids; and inadequate health and rehabilitation support.

Ensuring the inclusion of children with disabilities in education requires both systemic and school-level change. The former includes clear institutional frameworks and adequate national strategies and policies and their effective implementation. Changes at the school level include the removal of physical, information, and attitudinal barriers; development of adequate curricula; provision of school materials; teacher education and training; provision of assistive devices and support services; and school-level, health-related support.

***Childhood disability and school health.*** There is growing recognition of the connection between education and health for children with disabilities. In an expert exercise to establish research priorities in health regarding people with disabilities, access for children with disabilities to health-related rehabilitation and support services within the school system surfaces as one of the top 10 priorities worldwide (Tomlinson et al. 2009).

Specifically addressing learning and developmental disabilities, Durkin and colleagues (1994) note that quantifying the impact of disabilities and interventions is complicated. Part of this complication rests on the nature of disability, as persons with disabilities are not a homogeneous group. The wide variety of disabilities and their severity indicate that numerous interventions may be necessary (see Jamison et al. 2006). Furthermore, disability is not just a medical phenomenon; there are also important social and physical considerations (WHO 2001).

Thus disability is the result not only of a medical condition, but additionally an interaction between the functional limitation of that condition and the environment in which a person lives. There are significant opportunities for school health and education interventions to address the physical and attitudinal barriers that children with disabilities face. Such interventions intersect with disability in three ways:

- *Primary intervention*—the initial cause of the disabling health condition can be removed or mitigated. For example, a school health program could offer bicycle helmets and street-safety training to students.
- *Secondary prevention*—mitigate an existing functional limitation to prevent it from becoming a long-term disability. An example of a school health program addressing secondary prevention is the provision of micronutrients to compensate for lack of adequate food.
- *Tertiary prevention*—mitigate the existing disabilities through rehabilitative services. This involves, for instance, the provision of behavioral, physical, mobility, or speech therapies to address the rehabilitative needs of students with a wide range of disabilities.

In addition to preventive and curative health interventions, which all too often address only a medical condition, there are significant opportunities for school health and education interventions to address the physical and attitudinal barriers faced by children with disabilities.

*Implications for operations.* School health programs can address certain specific issues of disability. For example, at the simplest level, teachers can provide first-line screening for some conditions. This implies, of course, that other systems are in place to take over the subsequent follow-up processes. School health interventions on sanitation could ensure that toilet and hand washing facilities can be used by persons with disabilities (see Jones and Reed 2005). School interventions can also facilitate the removal of attitudinal barriers to children with disabilities. For example, field tests of the book "Just Like Other Kids" indicated that subsequent to reading the book, nearly 98 percent of children believed that students similar to the three characters with disabilities in the book could attend their school (World Bank 2001).

Mental disabilities are particularly stigmatizing, and there is a general dearth of mental health practitioners and services in developing countries (WHO 2001; Davidson and McFarlane 2006). There are numerous studies specific to conflict and natural disasters indicating that children's mental health is particularly important to address due to the wide-scale impact of these events (Math et al. 2008; Eapen et al. 1998; IASC 2007). The involvement of teachers in early detection of post-traumatic stress disorder and provision of basic psychosocial support could play an important role in overcoming the lack of mental health practitioners.

The design of schools can both prevent disabilities and enable children with mobility impairments to participate in education. For instance, in earthquake-prone geographies, constructing schools using readily available construction techniques can limit the number of deaths and injuries—and therefore disabilities—that result from earthquakes (OECD 2004). According to UNICEF, the resumption and/or continuation of education during emergencies is effective in assisting the delivery of health and nutrition (UNICEF 2008).

See box 3.5 for information about the EFA Fast Track Initiative and the Assessment of Childhood Disability.

### Vision: Correcting Refractive Error*

This section provides an example of how school-based health systems can provide screening and referral for correction of refractive error, one of the most common forms of physical disability in school-age children.

*Impact on education.* Good vision is necessary for education and is inextricably linked to quality of life and economic productivity. The WHO estimates that 153 million people worldwide are visually impaired as a result of uncorrected refractive errors—that is, they need glasses but do not have them (Resnikoff et al. 2008). Some 6.4 million of these people are in Africa and a further 21 million in Southeast Asia and the Western Pacific (based on WHO geographical regions, excluding India and China).

It is estimated that 12 million school-age children (ages 5–15) need glasses and do not have them. In this age group, 90–95 percent of visual impairment is due to myopia, or shortsightedness (Resnikoff et al. 2008). A randomized trial of more than 19,000 schoolchildren in 165 schools in Gansu province, western China, showed that the provision of eyeglasses increased test scores by 0.15–0.30 SD (Glewwe, Park, and Zhao 2006).

*Options for school-based responses.* To be effective and sustainable, refractive error programs must be integrated into the health system,

---

* This section was contributed by Simon Bush, Hasan Minto, and Dominic Haslam.

**Box 3.5**

# EFA–Fast Track Initiative and the Assessment of Childhood Disability*

*"There were 72 million children out of school in 2007. Seven out of every ten out of school children live in South and West Asia and Sub-Saharan Africa. These numbers are declining, but an estimated 56 million children could still be out of school by 2015. Measuring and overcoming marginalization must be at the heart of the Education for All agenda."*

*EFA Global Monitoring Report 2010: Reaching the Marginalized (UNESCO 2010)*

Seven of the world's top 12 countries in terms of out-of-school population size are current Fast Track Initiative (FTI) countries (Burkina Faso, Ethiopia, Ghana, Kenya, Mozambique, Niger, and the Republic of Yemen). Although the overall world's population of out-of-school children is declining, statistics for many countries are often only approximations.

Understanding and measuring marginalization are the two essential steps in the process of developing inclusive policies and strategies. *Who are the children out of school? Why are they out of school? And what can be done to bring them to school?* These are the questions that many FTI countries and their donors are trying to answer. Collecting, analyzing, and using data on who is out of school lies at the core of not only measuring the magnitude of the problem, but also understanding the needs of educational systems in terms of access and quality.

The elements of exclusion are complex. Children may be out of school and marginalized for a variety of reasons: poverty, disabilities, gender inequalities, child labor, poor health and nutrition, status as an ethnic minority, geographic and cultural disadvantages and related factors, orphanhood due to AIDS, living in conflict areas, and being dropouts from the existing educational system. These factors are not mutually exclusive; indeed, one of the most important elements in addressing exclusion is to better understand the many interactions among these elements.

As stated in "Education's Missing Millions," a report published in 2007 by World Vision and the Global Partnership for Disability and Development, while each category of out-of-school children deserves attention in research and support, the plight of children with disabilities who are out of school requires particular consideration. The United Nations has estimated that there are 650 million disabled

*(continued next page)*

**Box 3.5** *(continued)*

people worldwide, the majority of whom live in developing countries and one-third of whom are children. While this estimate is based on data that are often unreliable and with wide variations depending on the definitions used, there is little controversy that children in developing countries are disproportionately affected, with limited access to basic services, including schooling.

It has been estimated that one-third of the children (or about 24 million) out of school in the world are children with disabilities (UNESCO 2007). Again, the reliability of this estimate is uncertain because existing datasets are fragmentary and the methodologies used to gather such data are often weak and of unknown validity, with varying definitions by country and little basis for meaningful international comparisons.

**Priorities with Respect to Disability in EFA-FTI**

Most of the more than 40 countries receiving support through the FTI partnership mention children with disabilities in their education sector plans either as a specific target group or in the context of educating children with special needs, the disadvantaged, vulnerable or marginalized groups, or children. Half of these countries presented mainstreaming or inclusion as a policy option for the provision of education to children with disabilities.

The creation of databases on children with disabilities and special needs through surveys and screening was among the strategies most frequently mentioned in the education sector plans of the 43 countries whose plans have been endorsed to date. Countries express the need to develop screening methodologies and systems at school, regional, and national levels, as well as through specific studies to identify the causes of low school participation.

The Kenyan education sector plan, for example, listed specific issues and constraints in relation to access, equity, and quality in the provision of education for children with special needs: "lack of clear guidelines on the implementation of an all-inclusive education policy, lack of reliable data on children with special needs, inadequate tools and skills in identification and assessment, and curriculum that is not tailored to learners with special needs" (Republic of Kenya 2005, 43). In the education sector plan of the Lao People's Democratic Republic, it is stated that the lack of reliable and relevant disability data prevent the Ministry of Education from making rational decisions on education development, planning, budgeting, and management.

*(continued next page)*

**Box 3.5** *(continued)*

## Methodology for Surveying Childhood Disabilities in Developing Countries

Census and other regular data collection practices do not produce good-quality data on children with disabilities in developing countries because childhood disabilities are often easily mistaken, unrecognized, or require additional screening by a health professional. For the purpose of producing good-quality disability data that could be used for planning purposes, identification alone does not work, as it does not provide the necessary information about the nature of the disability and/or impairment. A health screening component is an essential part of data collection, particularly for children with disabilities.

The Ten Question Screening Instrument (TQSI) is a widely used approach for identifying children with disabilities. In low-income countries, the TQSI has been used either as a *single-phase TQSI*, which aims to identify the prevalence of disability based on maternal recall, or a *two-phase TQSI*, which follows up reported cases with professional medical and psychological examinations.

The initial experience of UNICEF in some 70 countries that have used the *single-phase TQSI*—which is administered at the household level and relies on parental recall—validated that the instrument can be used in populations where professional resources are extremely limited. However, in order to calculate disability prevalence rates, a second phase—medical screening—is increasingly recommended. The *two-phase TQSI* approach of epidemiological surveys that involve screening and clinical assessments (trialed in pilot projects in Bangladesh, Ethiopia, Jamaica, and Pakistan) is inevitably more expensive than the *single-phase TQSI*, yet within a cost range that makes it an attractive instrument both for sample-based and population-based surveys. Initial results using this instrument suggest levels of disability in school-age children of around 10–12 percent, which are similar to, but slightly higher than, levels in countries of the Organisation for Co-operation and Development, due in part to the relative absence of early intervention.

### Out-of-School and Disability Data Collection Model: The Cambodian Experience

To respond to the demand for actionable disability data, the FTI Secretariat is supporting the testing of an operational model for disability data collection that expands to include all out-of-school or marginalized and/or vulnerable children.

*(continued next page)*

**Box 3.5** *(continued)*

A simplified method using a *two-phase TQSI* approach will be implemented in Cambodia in late 2010. This model, with a focus on education participation (as opposed to an earlier medical-focused model) can then be scaled up and replicated at the global level, making it possible for low-income countries to collect data both on children with disabilities and marginalized or vulnerable children more broadly, and to link the data collection process directly with the provision of services, including access to primary education.

Cambodia's project for identification and service provision for out-of-school children (including screening children for disabilities), funded by FTI, will be administered at the household level using a sample of 20,000 children. This data collection exercise uses an existing school-mapping infrastructure, and is managed by three departments at the Ministry of Education (Primary, Special Needs, and Planning). The TQSI will be used to prescreen children for disabilities, with a follow-up medical assessment enabling the ministry to calculate both the out-of-school and disability prevalence rates.

The calculated prevalence rates will be used to plan programs and services for children out of school, including the provision of referrals and assistive devices for children with disabilities. In addition to addressing the needs of the out-of-school children, specific programs targeting high dropout rates at the primary level will be planned for in-school children who are at risk for dropping out.

In Cambodia, school feeding and school health programs, both at the ECD and primary levels, have been identified as one of the top strategies for addressing poverty and high levels of malnutrition among children in and out of school, including children with disabilities. These programs can be implemented as part of the inclusive education framework in combination with other EFA programs and initiatives, such as inclusive teacher training, a scholarship program designed to target the most disadvantaged and vulnerable children, and construction of accessible school buildings. While the initial exercise targets regions where vulnerability is believed to be greatest, this is intended as the first step in a national population-based effort.

* Contributed by Natasha Graham.

particularly into school health programs. Required services include screening and referral at the primary level, refraction and optical dispensing at the district level, and supported advanced care, including pediatric and contact lens services, at the tertiary level. In most low-income countries, however, this range of services is not available.

It is essential that these services be linked not only to the health system, but also horizontally to education and social development services. A recent analysis indicated that programs for the detection and treatment of refractive errors among schoolchildren would be highly cost-effective in all regions of the world (Baltussen, Naus, and Limburg 2009).

The key to successful services for correcting refractive error is adequate, well-trained, and motivated people with clearly defined job descriptions and career pathways in the public health system. Ideally, refractive services at the district level should be delivered by trained optometrists and dispensing opticians with the necessary competencies and knowledge. In countries where these cadres are not available, refractive services can be delivered by trained refractionists or optical technicians. The development of appropriate human resources requires both training new personnel and strengthening the skills of existing personnel in the areas of refraction, spectacle dispensing, spectacle manufacture, spectacle supply and distribution, visual health promotion, and program management.

School health programs also have a role to play in other issues of eye health, particularly vitamin A deficiency and trachoma, both of which affect the poorest, most vulnerable children. School health programs can also prevent or contain epidemics of viral conjunctivitis, warn children of the dangers of traditional eye remedies, and support children who have poor vision.

*Practical experience of implementation.* School health programs, such as those in Kenya and Eritrea, have demonstrated that appropriately trained teachers can identify children whose vision is impaired by refractive error. Providing these children glasses, however, remains a major challenge in low-income countries in Africa in particular, especially outside of urban centers.

There is an acute paucity of human resources to deliver refractive services in Africa. A consortium of organizations is presently supporting a regional optometry training program for Southern Africa, based at the Malawi School of Optometry. The program is innovative in its approach; it follows a multi-entry/multi-exit model, with exit points after two and four years, respectively. Candidates are drawn from within existing health services, which helps ensure smooth integration of services within health systems.

A regional initiative led by Sightsavers International in West Africa (Cameroon, The Gambia, Ghana, Guinea, Guinea-Bissau, Mali, Nigeria, Senegal, and Sierra Leone) has demonstrated that with the right support, government ministries can successfully integrate refractive, low vision, and optical services into the health system, leading to improved access and affordability of these services. Coverage, however, remains an issue.

The gold standard for correction of most refractive errors is the use of properly prescribed and dispensed spectacles, but in many low-income countries, especially in Sub-Saharan Africa, there are insufficient numbers of trained staff to meet demand, especially in rural areas (see box 3.6). Self-adjusting spectacles have recently become available that can be used by individuals themselves to alter the refractive power of the lenses. As yet, there is insufficient research to confirm the quality and accuracy of the refraction obtained for school-age children using this approach.[5]

### Prevention of Noncommunicable Diseases*

While much of the historic emphasis of health programs in middle- and low-income countries has been on infectious diseases—especially malaria, HIV, and tuberculosis—epidemiological analysis today shows that non-communicable diseases are growing in importance (Bloom et al. 2006). Many of these diseases are related to lifestyle, and school health programs have the potential to support the development of health and well-being over a child's life cycle. School programs can, for example, address poor diet and physical inactivity, two well-recognized health risk behaviors that can accelerate the development of noncommunicable diseases, such as obesity, Type 2 diabetes, and hypertension, which represent a growing fraction of the global burden of disease (WHO 2008).

Studies suggest that poor diet and physical inactivity can alter a child's physical development and track into adulthood, while other behaviors established during school age, such as tobacco use and unhealthy dietary preferences, contribute to the development of noncommunicable diseases later in life (Kemper, Post, and van Mechelen 1999; Yang et al. 2006; Freedman et al. 2009).

Compared with the evidence on the effectiveness of school health programs for communicable disease, there is compelling, but less consistent, evidence on the effectiveness of school health programs that address noncommunicable diseases and risk factors. This evidence has been reviewed for some of the major risk factors, including

- Unhealthy diets (Gortmaker et al. 1999; Campbell et al. 2001; Sahota et al. 2001)

---

* This section was contributed by Meenakshi Fernandes.

**Box 3.6**

# New Approaches: Bridging the Gap and Lowering the Barrier to Refractive Services*

The burden of uncorrected refractive error in developing countries is considerable. Despite various efforts to tackle the issue, coverage remains poor in many areas. Whereas there is one eye care professional for every 6,700 people in the United Kingdom (NHS Information Centre 2008), in parts of Sub-Saharan Africa, the ratio is closer to 1:1,000,000 (Mathenge et al. 2007; Carlson 2008). As such, the principal barrier to the provision of corrective eyewear to people in low- and middle-income countries remains that of limited access to eye care providers. With existing approaches, access to eye care services is likely to remain poor for many years to come.

For most children struggling with poor vision due to uncorrected refractive error, the solution is simple—a pair of eyeglasses. Ignoring their current refractive needs in favor of a comprehensive future eye care model is not an adequate healthcare response. This raises the question of whether corrective eyewear could be provided to children through existing infrastructure and human resources in the education sector.

Adjustable glasses could be part of a promising solution (Douali and Silver 2004; Smith, Weissberg, and Travison 2010). By allowing users to vary the correction provided by a pair of adjustable glasses to suit their own eyes, it is possible to overcome the lack of eye care professionals and infrastructure normally required to deliver glasses. To date, more than 35,000 adjustable eyeglasses have been delivered, including some 11,000 to adult learners enrolled in Ghana's National Functional Literacy Programme (MacKenzie, Dannhauser, and Spijkerman 2006).

Studies performed to date have demonstrated that good correction may be achieved in most adults with adjustable glasses (Douali and Silver 2004; MacKenzie, Dannhauser, and Spijkerman 2006; Smith, Weissberg, and Travison 2010). The preferred approach has been for a subject to follow a well-defined protocol under the supervision of an appropriately trained teacher or health worker.

The Centre for Vision in the Developing World, with support from the Partnership for Child Development at Imperial College, is undertaking studies to assess the use of adjustable glasses among school-going children. In collaboration with partners at the New England College of Optometry (Boston, Massachusetts), the National Eye Institute (Bethesda, Maryland), and the Sun Yat Sen University

*(continued next page)*

**Box 3.6** *(continued)*

(Guangzhou, China), around 1,800 children ages 13–16 are being assessed at locations in China (Guangzhou and Shantou) and the United States (Boston). The objective of this work is to compare the outcomes achieved with adjustable glasses with both autorefraction and the gold standard of subjective refraction. It is anticipated that results will be reported over the coming year. A successful outcome will justify further work to determine the acceptability and overall efficacy of using adjustable glasses within the education sector. The ultimate goal is the potential creation of a new way of providing refractive correction to the very many children who need it.

For more information on "Vision for Children in the Developing World," visit http://www.schoolsandhealth.org.

* Contributed by David Crosby and Graeme MacKenzie.

- Physical inactivity (Dobbins et al. 2001; Timperio, Salmon, and Ball 2004);
- Harmful use of alcohol and drugs (Tobler and Stratton 1997; Lloyd et al. 2000; Midford, Lenton, and Hancock 2000; National Drug Research Institute 2002)
- Violence and mental health (Wells, Barlow, and Stewart-Brown 2003; Browne et al. 2004; Green et al. 2005; American Counseling Association 2006; Stewart-Brown 2006)

Even when positive behavioral outcomes are achieved as a result of school health programs, however, these outcomes are not always sustained over time or broadened in impact through dissemination.

While many noncommunicable diseases associated with school age have major impacts on health, this section focuses on obesity since there is evidence—albeit to date, only from rich countries—that associates obesity with lower test scores and psychosocial costs at school age (Taras and Potts-Datema 2005; Dietz 1998). Management of obesity is based on the promotion of healthy lifestyles and hence provides a useful proxy for health promotion more generally.

**A new challenge for low-income countries and the education sector.**
While the incidence of noncommunicable disease has historically been

concentrated among adult populations in high-income countries, its prevalence among children in low- and middle-income countries is growing. It is argued that the underlying driving forces behind the latter prevalence are economic development, industrialization, and the nutrition transition—the process by which the prices of energy-dense foods, such as processed foods and meat, decrease relative to less energy-dense foods, such as fruits and vegetables.

Among the youth population, childhood obesity has become a major public health concern in high-income countries and an emerging concern in low- and middle-income countries. In recent years, increasing numbers of cases of adult-onset diabetes (Type 2 diabetes) have been identified in children in high-income countries; this trend is also emerging in low- and middle-income countries (Lipton et al. 2005; Saaddine et al. 2002). Other conditions that accompany obesity in adults and may soon accompany obesity in children are hyperlipidemia (elevated cholesterol and other fats in the blood) and hypertension (Dietz 1998). Obese children, moreover, are considerably more likely to be obese as adults and to suffer from other noncommunicable diseases (Must et al. 1999; Singh et al. 2008).

Studies find that obese children have lower math and verbal test scores, with the postulated reason for these scores being absenteeism. Accounting for the child's sociodemographic characteristics, however, weakens the relationship considerably (Taras and Potts-Datema 2005; Datar, Sturm, and Magnabosco 2004). Although studies in low- and middle-income countries are limited, those conducted in high-income countries suggest that the most immediate costs of childhood obesity are psychosocial (Dietz 1998). Children who are obese are more likely to be discriminated against and bullied by their peers, have lower self-esteem, and exhibit internalizing and externalizing problem behaviors (Dietz 1998; Datar and Sturm 2006). The psychosocial costs, as opposed to physical health consequences, of childhood obesity are likely to be a function of societal norms.

***Assessing the scale of the problem in school-age children.*** The most commonly used measure of childhood obesity is body mass index (BMI), a value produced by dividing an individual's height in meters by his or her weight in kilograms squared. The thresholds at which a child is considered to be obese vary by gender, age, and the classification system used. The International Obesity Taskforce (IOTF) definition is most widely used for cross-country comparisons (Lobstein, Baur, and Uauy 2004). However, as children from high-income countries are the reference population for this definition, the thresholds that denote whether or not a child is obese may not be appropriate for some populations.

In the United States and many other rich countries, childhood obesity prevalence began increasing around 1980 and has attained a level of about 20 percent, according to the latest estimates (Ogden, Carroll, and Flegal 2008). Obesity prevalence among adults is higher. While adults of lower socioeconomic status are more likely to be obese, rates of increase have been comparable across population groups, suggesting the causes are environmental (Truong and Sturm 2005).

Statistics on obesity prevalence in low- and middle-income countries are less reliable, especially among children. However, similar trends of childhood obesity preceding adult obesity, and of growing obesity prevalence in both rural and urban areas, are expected (Popkin 2006). Obesity prevalence has been found to be high, for example, in China, Egypt, Mexico, and South Africa—especially among women (Popkin et al. 2006). Several middle-income countries are also showing an annual increase in obesity or overweight status of more than 1 percent, including China, Indonesia, Mexico, and Thailand (Popkin 2006). Child obesity prevalence is, moreover, approaching levels exhibited by adults in Brazil, China, the United Kingdom, and the United States (Popkin et al. 2006).

In contrast to the pattern in the rich countries, obesity in low- and middle-income countries affects primarily people of higher socioeconomic status, although over time it has become more visible among people of lower socioeconomic status as well. In 1989, for example, a study found that obesity prevalence was higher among people of higher socioeconomic status than among people of lower socioeconomic status; by 1999, however, the relative levels had switched (Monteiro, Conde, and Popkin 2004). In addition, countries where stunting is common that are also experiencing rapid economic development are at greater risk for higher prevalence of childhood obesity (Popkin et al. 2006).

Current estimates from the IOTF find that 2–3 percent of children worldwide are obese (Lobstein, Baur, and Uauy 2004). In absolute numbers, this translates to approximately 30 million to 45 million children. Some studies find that obesity prevalence has increased substantially in certain countries. For example, obesity prevalence among children ages 10–18 in Brazil increased from 3.7 percent in 1980 to 12.6 percent by 1997. In China, obesity prevalence among the same age group increased from 4.8 percent in 1991 to 11.4 percent in 2004 (Popkin 2006).

Figure 3.6 presents country-specific statistics for children ages 13–15. These estimates were calculated from the Global School-Based Student Health Surveys (GSHS) conducted by the WHO and the U.S. Centers for Disease Control and Prevention between 2003 and 2007.

*Practical experience of implementation.* One of the greatest challenges of addressing childhood obesity is the limited recognition of the condition as a disease. Especially in low- and middle-income countries, obesity may be associated with power and affluence, rather than a form of malnutrition. Conditions that are most commonly associated with malnutrition in low- and middle-income countries include stunting (low height for age, an indicator of chronic malnutrition), being underweight (low weight for age, an indicator of chronic and acute malnutrition), and micronutrient deficiencies (for example, of iron, iodine, or vitamin A). Several studies from Africa suggest that the preferred body image is larger, especially for women (Holdsworth et al. 2004; Siervo et al. 2006). In countries with a high prevalence of HIV/AIDS, there may also be a preference for being overweight rather than thin (Kruger et al. 2005).

Schools can address the factors implicit in the development of noncommunicable diseases in two ways: by providing children opportunities to have a healthy diet and physical activity and by supporting the development of healthy habits and informed choice. The types of policies that a school incorporates to address these goals are contingent on the country, geographic region, school characteristics, and characteristics of the student population. Within a school, it may also be important to tailor policies to the age and gender of the target population.

As children spend a substantial amount of time at school, school meals can help children meet recommended dietary intake. With regard to animal products, schools could provide red meat, which offers important health benefits that cannot be derived from a vegetarian diet, rather than processed meats, which may contain high levels of preservatives, sodium, and saturated fat (Popkin 2009). In Brazil, a reform that occurred in 2000 mandated that 70 percent of a school's lunch budget be reserved for purchasing produce and minimally processed foods. The reform also stated a preference for arrangements with local, small producers (Coitinho, Monteiro, and Popkin 2002). Several studies have found that healthier school options have led to improved school performance. In response to Celebrity Chef Jamie Oliver's "Feed Me Better" campaign in London, children in primary schools who were affected by the campaign experienced higher achievement in English and science (Belot and James 2009).

**Figure 3.6    Obesity and Overweight Estimates by Country for Children Ages 13–15**

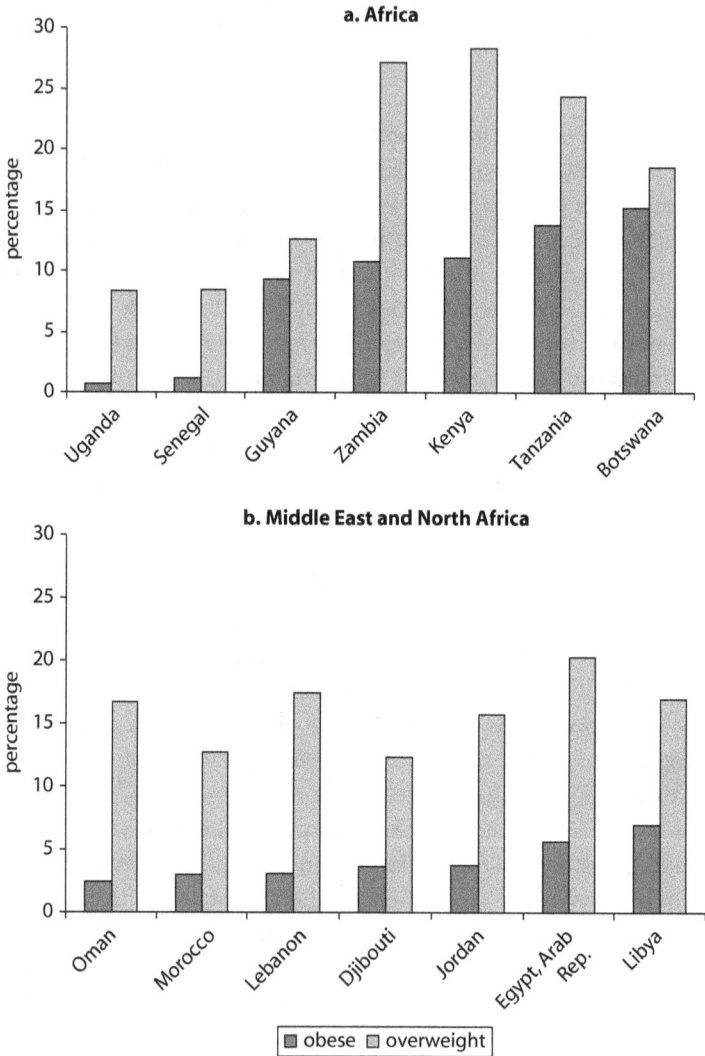

**a. Africa**

**b. Middle East and North Africa**

◼ obese  ◻ overweight

*Source:* Data from WHO and the U.S. Centers for Disease Control and Prevention.
*Note:* Weight and height are self-reported. Obesity status determined according to International Obesity Taskforce (IOTF) definition. The GSHS samples are almost always national, with very few exceptions (China, the República Bolivariana de Venezuela, Zimbabwe, and possibly one or two others). A two-stage sample selection process is used, which could be described as multistage cluster sampling, using probability proportional to size sampling during the first stage. Schools are first selected proportional to size, then a random selection of classes is made, then all children in the class selected. This robust sample selection is done centrally at the U.S. Centers for Disease Control and Prevention using a version of c-sample software especially developed for this purpose.

Another study in Kenya found that the provision of meat in schools had an impact on academic achievement (Whaley et al. 2003).

The provision of meals may also serve to mitigate food security, which has been found to be associated with childhood obesity in high-income countries (Alaimo, Olson, and Frongillo 2001; Casey et al. 2006; Rose and Bodor 2006). Children who have an uncertain food supply may consume more, or consume food items that are cheaper and more energy-dense. Others hypothesize that the body adapts to the condition by storing calories as fat. School meal programs can serve to mitigate the fluctuations in food supply that children may experience at home.

With regard to physical activity, short structured programs may be more feasible for schools to incorporate than longer periods of free play. Schools can provide short activity breaks of structured dance or calisthenics between lessons. Alternatively, physical activity could be incorporated into lessons. Studies in the United States have found that classroom-based activity breaks as short as 10 minutes can assist cognitive development. More specifically, they are associated with less disruptiveness, better focus, and better academic performance among children (Mahar et al. 2006; Donnelly et al. 2009). These programs may also promote a positive image of physical activity and address barriers faced by certain population subgroups who are at greater risk for physical inactivity, such as girls (Sallis, Prochaska, and Wendell 2000).

Supporting physical activity among children is also important because studies indicate that such activity declines as children age into adolescents and adults (Kohl and Hobbs 1998; Gordon-Larsen, Nelson, and Popkin 2004). In low- to middle-income countries undergoing rapid development, this trend may be compounded by a shift from labor-intensive to sedentary occupations characteristic of high-income countries.

Schools can also support physical activity by designating areas around the school that can be accessed by children. Facility structures in these areas may also encourage physical activity, particularly among older children (Sallis et al. 2001; Romero 2005; Davison and Lawson 2006; Gordon-Larsen et al. 2006; Ferreira et al. 2007). Access to facilities may be more important for urban children, who may have fewer safe areas in which to be physically active. However, facilities and space alone may not be sufficient. Other factors, such as supervision and safety, may be needed (Sallis et al. 2001).

Perhaps the most critical area in which schools can support the prevention of noncommunicable diseases is health education. By increasing knowledge, shaping attitudes, and providing children with decision-making tools related to nutrition and physical activity, these programs could support the development of healthy habits at school and home. For example, health education programs may be effective in shaping the purchase of food items at school canteens, as well as outside of school. The introduction of such programs would require training programs and materials for teachers. In Brazil, a television channel was developed for the specific purpose of educating teachers and providing videos for the classroom (Coitinho, Monteiro, and Popkin 2002). Evidence from the United States suggests that restrictions on the availability of for-purchase food items at school may not affect overall intake (Fernandes 2008). If not available at school, children may purchase the desired food items at other outlets.

Numerous policy interventions to prevent obesity have been developed in high-income countries, but most studies are based on small samples with relatively short periods of follow-up (Lobstein, Baur, and Uauy 2004; Sharma 2006). It is likely that, as with most behavioral-change interventions, the benefits will be slow to appear and difficult to attribute. In high-income countries, school health education interventions have focused on reducing the intake of certain food items (for example, items high in saturated fat), increasing fruit and vegetable consumption, reducing hours of television watched, and increasing physical activity (Lobstein, Baur, and Uauy 2004). These courses could also address food advertising and support children in advising their families about food purchase decisions. Consistency between education programs and school meals could also reinforce the message sent to children.

School health programs remain promising due to their low cost relative to treating and managing the chronic, often lifelong, consequences of noncommunicable diseases. As with other behavioral-change interventions, programs that are comprehensive, long-term, and implemented when children are young have the greatest potential to mitigate the development of such diseases.

## Conclusions: Education Sector Responses to the Health and Nutrition of Schoolchildren

MCH programs as a foundation. Maternal and child health programs lay the foundation for subsequent education outcomes. Although MCH programs are typically the responsibility of the health sector, early interventions within MCH programs have a critically important role to play in the subsequent lives of children, and in their performance and participation in education in particular. Stunted and malnourished children tend to start school later, progress through school less rapidly, have poorer academic achievement, and perform less well on cognitive achievement tests. It is rare for the education sector to play any direct role in the implementation of MCH programs, but the sector has an important role in encouraging and promoting the uptake of MCH interventions within communities in general, and among school-going adolescents who may soon become parents in particular.

**Contribution of ECD programs.** Early child development programs can contribute to education outcomes. Quality ECD activities can complement the care and education that children receive from their families and communities and can promote cognitive, socioemotional, physical, and language development, such that children are more likely to enroll, less likely to drop out, and more likely to complete the primary school cycle. ECD interventions that address health and nutrition needs are typically delivered by the health sector, but in many low-income countries, they are much more limited than the MCH services provided to younger children. Combining health care with behavioral stimulation is usually addressed by community approaches. The education sector can provide formal preschools that accept children one or two years immediately prior to enrollment, but this leaves a gap of several years between the end of MCH programs and the beginning of school or preschool.

Even in rich countries, the major vehicles for implementing ECD programs throughout the vulnerable years are civil society organizations and the private sector. The picture is therefore a complicated one in which multiple sectors are engaged, often with different sectors contributing at different stages of the process. Given the importance of ECD in preparing children for school, the overall conclusion is that the education sector has a key role in leading the policy dialogue to promote, coordinate, and support national efforts to provide ECD interventions to preschool children.

**Important role of the education sector.** The education sector can play a lead role in implementing health and nutrition interventions that improve the education of schoolchildren. There are safe, simple, and effective school-based options by which the education sector, typically with oversight from the health sector, can address the most common health and nutrition conditions that affect school-age children and that have been shown to affect educational outcomes. These interventions and the respective conditions they seek to avoid or prevent include deworming and worm infection; bed nets and malaria; hand washing and bacterial infections; toothbrushing and dental caries; eyeglasses and refractive error; physical exercise, healthy diet, and weight concerns; micronutrients and micronutrient deficiency; and food and hunger.

**Schools as a platform for health and nutrition.** Schools are a particularly effective platform for health and nutrition because the effects of school-based interventions can be optimized by exploiting the role of the school as a teaching and learning institution. All of the interventions considered in this chapter have some critical component that is dependent upon teaching and learning. In some, learning is the main intervention (for example, addressing the stigma associated with HIV), while in others, learning is a means to promote access to a service (for example, deworming). Effective delivery of this component relies on the school performing its main role as a teaching and learning institution to

- Provide children with age-appropriate, actionable knowledge;
- Serve as a conduit for knowledge on health and nutrition for the community;
- Demystify health and nutrition; and
- Reinforce positive behavioral messages and address stigma.

Viable delivery is a particularly strong reason why schools provide an effective platform for health and nutrition interventions.

**Varying requirements of interventions.** Common school-based health and nutrition interventions vary in cost and in simplicity of implementation. There are effective school-based options for addressing many of the most common health and nutrition conditions, but there is a need to make informed choices among the basic components of a school health and nutrition program. Notably, components vary in their requirements:

- The interventions considered here are a preselected subset of all options. One important criterion for inclusion was that the typical cost per child per year was under $50. Nevertheless, there is considerable range in cost: only a few U.S. cents per child per year for iodization of salt, deworming, chlorine water treatment, and iron supplements; a few

U.S. dollars for eyeglasses, bed nets, toothbrushing, and hand washing; and $40–$50 for school feeding and some medical referrals.

- Some activities described in this chapter can be addressed by teachers or other education staff with a minimum of training and with oversight from the health sector (for example, deworming, bed net distribution, toothbrushing, and hand washing), while others require the direct involvement of often rare specialists (for example, vision correction and dentistry).

- Some activities require a single annual activity or even less frequent intervention (for example, deworming, malaria treatment, distribution of bednets, dispensing eyeglasses), some a weekly action (for example, iron supplementation, chlorine water treatment), and some require a daily or more frequent intervention (for example, toothbrushing, hand washing, school feeding, physical exercise).

**Knowledge gaps that need to be addressed.** For some of the most prevalent health conditions and disabilities of schoolchildren there are important knowledge gaps:

- There is a need for better evidence of impact on education: for both diarrhea and tooth decay (and toothache), for example, the evidence of impact on education is inferred, but is based largely on association rather than on impact studies. The growing importance of noncommunicable diseases among schoolchildren in middle- and low-income countries has similarly not been matched by education sector analysis of the effects of these diseases on education.

- There is a need for operations research. For correction of refractory errors of vision there are solutions, but these depend on technical expertise that is rare in low-income countries, whereas alternative solutions—such as self-refraction—have yet to be adequately tested. For malaria control, distribution of insecticide-treated bed nets is an important response and it appears that school-based treatment approaches are cost-effective. However, such approaches are not currently being implemented due to a lack of policy endorsement.

- There is a need for better data on childhood disability and education. While many countries, particularly developed countries, collect data on childhood disability and education, more systematic, robust, and internationally comparable statistics to inform policies to include children with disabilities in developing countries are needed.

**Opportunities to address childhood disability.** There are significant opportunities for school health and education interventions to address childhood disability.

- School health interventions intersect with disability through primary, secondary, and tertiary prevention. For example, school health programs could offer bicycle helmets and street-safety training to students; micronutrients supplements could be provided to compensate for a lack of adequate food; and the rehabilitative needs of students with disabilities could be met through behavioral, physical, mobility, speech, and related therapies.

- There are also significant opportunities for school health and education interventions. School health interventions could address not only the specific medical causes and impairments, but also the physical and attitudinal barriers that exclude children with disabilities from educational opportunities.

## Notes

1. For more information about how sanitation issues relate to schools, see the joint publication of the World Bank, UNICEF, and the Water and Sanitation Program (2005), "Toolkit on Hygiene, Water, and Sanitation in Schools." Also see the resources listed in appendix A.
2. A multidonor partnership administered by the World Bank.
3. For more information, see the organization's website: http://www.globalhand washing.org (accessed January 2010). The site also provides access to Curtis, Cardosi, and Scott (2000), "The Handwashing Handbook."
4. To collect data on childhood disability the first phase of the Ten Question Screening Instrument (TQSI) was used. In this phase, data collection is based on maternal recall and the results are interpreted as indicating the percentage of surveyed children at increased risk of childhood disability. To determine the prevalence of disability among children, the first phase needs to be followed up by a second phase in which children identified as being at increased risk of childhood disability in the first phase are examined by medical and psychological professionals (UNICEF and University of Wisconsin 2008; Durkin et al. 1994).

5. For more information, see the website of Sightsavers International, West Sussex, United Kingdom, http://www.sightsavers.org (accessed January 2010).

## References

Adelman, S. W., D. O. Gilligan, and K. Lehrer. 2008. *How Effective Are Food for Education Programs? A Critical Assessment of the Evidence from Developing Countries.* Food Policy Review 9. Washington, DC: International Food Policy Research Institute.

Ainsworth, M., K. Beegle, and G. Koda. 2001. *The Impact of Adult Mortality on Primary School Enrollment in North-Western Tanzania.* Geneva: UNAIDS.

Alaimo, K., C. M. Olson, and E. A. Frongillo. 2001. "Low Family Income and Food Insufficiency in Relation to Overweight in U.S. Children." *Archives of Pediatrics and Adolescent Medicine* 155 (10): 1161–67.

Alderman, H., J. R. Behrman, and J. Hoddinott. 2005. "Nutrition, Malnutrition, and Economic Growth." In *Health and Economic Growth: Findings and Policy Implications*, ed. G. López-Casanovas, B. Rivera, and L. Currais, 169–94. Cambridge, MA: MIT Press.

Alderman, H., J. Konde-Lule, I. Sebuliba, D. Bundy, and A. Hall. 2006. "Effect on Weight Gain of Routinely Giving Albendazole to Preschool Children during Child Health Days in Uganda: Cluster Randomised Controlled Trial." *British Medical Journal* 333 (7559): 122–24.

American Counseling Association. 2006. *Effectiveness of School Counseling.* Alexandria, VA: American Counseling Association.

Andang'o, P. E., S. J. Osendarp, R. Ayah, C. E. West, D. L. Mwaniki, C. A. de Wolf, R. Kraaijenhagen, F. J. Kok, and H. Verhoef. 2007. "Efficacy of Iron-Fortified Whole Maize Flour on Iron Status of Schoolchildren in Kenya: A Randomised Controlled Trial." *Lancet* 369 (9575): 1799–806.

Anderson, K. G., A. M. Beutel, and B. Maughan-Brown. 2007. "HIV Risk Perceptions and First Sexual Intercourse among Youth in Cape Town, South Africa." *International Family Planning Perspectives* 33 (3): 98–105.

Andersson, M., P. Thankachan, S. Muthayya, R. B. Goud, A. V. Kurpad, R. F. Hurrell, and M. B. Zimmermann. 2008. "Dual Fortification of Salt with Iodine and Iron: A Randomized, Double-Blind, Controlled Trial of Micronized Ferric Pyrophosphate and Encapsulated Ferrous Fumarate in Southern India." *American Journal of Clinical Nutrition* 88 (5): 1378–87.

Arnold, C. 2004. "Positioning ECCD in the 21st Century." *Coordinators Notebook* 28: 1–34.

Ash, D. M., S. R. Tatala, E. A. Frongillo, Jr., G. D. Ndossi, and M. C. Latham. 2003. "Randomized Efficacy Trial of a Micronutrient-Fortified Beverage in Primary

School Children in Tanzania." *The American Journal of Clinical Nutrition* 77 (4): 891–98.

Awasthi, S., R. Peto, V. K. Pande, R. H. Fletcher, S. Read, and D. A. P. Bundy. 2008. "Effects of Deworming on Malnourished Preschool Children in India: An Open-Labelled, Cluster-Randomized Trial." *PLoS Neglected Tropical Diseases* 2 (4): e223.

Bachmann, M. O., and F. L. R. Booysen. 2004. "Relationships between HIV/AIDS, Income, and Expenditure over Time in Deprived South African Households." *AIDS Care* 16: 817–26.

Baltussen, R., J. Naus, and H. Limburg. 2009. "Cost-Effectiveness of Screening and Correcting Refractive Errors in Schoolchildren in Africa, Asia, America, and Europe." *Health Policy* 89 (2): 201–15.

Beaglehole, R., H. Benzian, J. Crail, and J. Mackay. 2009. *The Oral Health Atlas: Mapping a Neglected Global Health Issue.* Geneva: FDI World Dental Education; Brighton, U.K.: Myriad Editions.

Behrman, J. R., and J. Hoddinott. 2005. "Programme Evaluation with Unobserved Heterogeneity and Selective Implementation: The Mexican PROGRESA Impact on Child Nutrition." *Oxford Bulletin on Economics and Statistics* 67 (4): 547–69.

Belot, M., and J. James. 2009. "Healthy School Meals and Educational Outcomes." ISER Working Paper 2009-01, Institute for Social and Economic Research, Essex, U.K.

Bleakley, H. 2007. "Disease and Development: Evidence from Hookworm Eradication in the American South." *Quarterly Journal of Economics* 122 (1): 73–117.

Bleichrodt, N., and M. P. Born. 1994. "A Meta-Analysis of Research on Iodine and Its Relationship to Cognitive Development." In *The Damaged Brain of Iodine Deficiency*, ed. J. B. Stanbury, 195–200. New York: Cognizant Communication.

Bloom, B. R., C. M. Michaud, J. R. La Montagne, and L. Simonsen. 2006. "Priorities for Global Research and Development Interventions." In *Disease Control Priorities in Developing Countries*, 2nd ed., ed. D. Jamison, J. G. Breman, A. R. Measham, G. Alleyne, M. Claeson, D. Evans, P. Jha, A. Mills, and P. Musgrove, 103–18. New York: World Bank and Oxford University Press.

Brooker, S. 2009. *Malaria Control in Schools: A Toolkit on Effective Education Sector Responses to Malaria in Africa.* Washington, DC: World Bank; London: Partnership for Child Development.

Brooker, S., S. Clarke, R. W. Snow, and D. A. P. Bundy. 2008. "Malaria in African Schoolchildren: Options for Control." *Transactions of the Royal Society of Tropical Medicine and Hygiene* 102: 304–5.

Brooker, S., H. Guyatt, J. Omumbo, R. Shretta, L. J. Drake, and J. Ouma. 2000. "Situation Analysis of Malaria in School-Aged Children in Kenya: What Can Be Done?" *Parasitology Today* 16 (5): 183–86.

Browne, G., A. Gafni, J. Roberts, C. Byrne, and B. Majumdar. 2004. "Effective/ Efficient Mental Health Programs for School-Age Children: A Synthesis of Reviews." *Social Science and Medicine* 58 (7): 1367–84.

Bundy D. A. P., D. Aduda, A. Woolnough, L. Drake, and S. Manda. 2009a. *Courage and Hope: Stories from Teachers Living with HIV in Sub-Saharan Africa.* Washington, DC: World Bank.

Bundy, D. A. P., C. Burbano, M. Grosh, A. Gelli, M. Jukes, and L. Drake. 2009b. *Rethinking School Feeding: Social Safety Nets, Child Development, and the Education Sector.* Washington, DC: World Bank.

Bundy, D. A. P., A. Hall, G. F. Medley, and L. Savioli. 1992. "Evaluating Measures to Control Intestinal Parasitic Infections." *World Health Statistics Quarterly* 45 (2–3): 168–79.

Bundy, D. A. P., S. Lwin, J. S. Osika, J. McLaughlin, and C. O. Pannenborg. 2000. "What Should Schools Do about Malaria?" *Parasitology Today* 16 (5): 181–82.

Bundy, D. A. P., S. Shaeffer, M. Jukes, K. Beegle, A. Gillespie, L. Drake, S.-H. F. Lee, A.-M. Hoffmann, J. Jones, A. Mitchell, C. Wright, D. Barcelona, B. Camara, C. Golmar, L. Savioli, T. Takeuchi, and M. Sembene. 2006. "School-Based Health and Nutrition Programs." In *Disease Control Priorities in Developing Countries*, 2nd ed., ed. D. Jamison, J. G. Breman, A. R. Measham, G. Alleyne, M. Claeson, D. Evans, P. Jha, A. Mills, and P. Musgrove, 1091–108. New York: World Bank and Oxford University Press.

Cairncross, S. 2004. "The Health Impact of Sanitation." Presentation to the Rural Water and Sanitation Thematic Group, World Bank, Washington, DC.

Campbell, C., E. Waters, S. O'Meara, and C. Summerbell. 2001. "Interventions for Preventing Obesity in Childhood: A Systematic Review." *Obesity Reviews* 2 (3): 149–57.

Carlson, A. S. 2008. "Optometry in Ethiopia." *South African Optometrist* 67 (1): 42–44.

Carneiro, P., and J. Heckman. 2003. "Human Capital Policy." NBER Working Paper 9495, National Bureau of Economic Research, Cambridge, MA.

Casey, P. H., P. M. Simpson, J. M. Gossett, M. L. Bogle, C. M. Champagne, C. Connell, D. Harsha, B. McCabe-Sellers, J. M. Robbins, J. E. Stuff, and J. Weber. 2006. "The Association of Child and Household Food Insecurity with Childhood Overweight Status." *Pediatrics* 118 (5): e1406–13.

Chandler, A. M., S. P. Walker, K. Connolly, and S. M. Grantham-McGregor. 1995. "School Breakfast Improves Verbal Fluency in Undernourished Jamaican Children." *Journal of Nutrition* 125 (4): 894–900.

Clark, S., M. Poulin, and H. P. Kohler. 2009. "Marital Aspirations, Sexual Behaviors, and HIV/AIDS in Rural Malawi." *Journal of Marriage and Family* 71 (2): 396–416.

Clarke, S. E., S. Brooker, J. K. Njagi, E. Njau, B. Estambale, E. Muchiri, and P. Magnussein. 2004. "Malaria Morbidity among School Children Living in Two Areas of Contrasting Transmission in Western Kenya." *American Journal of Tropical Medicine and Hygiene* 71 (6): 732–38.

Clarke, D., and Bundy, D. A. P. 2004. "The EFA Fast-Track Initiative: Responding to the Challenge of HIV and AIDS to the Education Sector." Education for All–Fast Track Initiative Secretariat, Washington, DC.

———. 2008. "The EFA Fast Track Initiative: An Assessment of the Responsiveness of Endorsed Education Sector Plans to HIV and AIDS." ED/UNP/HIV/2009/IATT/1, UNAIDS Inter-Agency Task Team on Education, Geneva.

Clarke, S. E., M. C. Jukes, J. K. Njagi, L. Khasakhala, B. Cundill, J. Otido, C. Crudder, B. B. Estambale, and S. Brooker. 2008. "Effect of Intermittent Preventive Treatment of Malaria on Health and Education in Schoolchildren: A Cluster-Randomised, Double-Blind, Placebo-Controlled Trial." *Lancet* 372 (9633): 127–38.

Coitinho, D., C. Monteiro, and B. Popkin. 2002. "What Brazil Is Doing to Promote Healthy Diets and Active Lifestyles." *Public Health Nutrition* 5 (1A): 263–67.

Curtis, V., and S. Cairncross. 2003. "Effect of Washing Hands with Soap on Diarrhoea Risk in the Community: A Systematic Review." *Lancet Infectious Diseases* 3 (5): 275–81.

Curtis, V., J. Cardosi, and B. Scott. 2000. "The Handwashing Handbook: A Guide for Developing a Hygiene Promotion Program to Increase Handwashing with Soap." World Bank, Washington, DC.

Datar, A., and R. Sturm. 2006. "Childhood Overweight and Elementary School Outcomes." *International Journal of Obesity* 30 (9): 1449–60.

Datar, A., R. Sturm, and J. L. Magnabosco. 2004. "Childhood Overweight and Academic Performance: National Study of Kindergartners and First-Graders." *Obesity Research* 12 (1): 58–68.

Davidson, J., and A. McFarlane. 2006. "The Extent and Impact of Mental Health Problems after Disaster." *Journal of Clinical Psychiatry* 67 (suppl. 12): 9–14.

Davison, K. K., and C. T. Lawson. 2006. "Do Attributes in the Physical Environment Influence Children's Physical Activity? A Review of the Literature." *International Journal of Behavioral Nutrition and Physical Activity* 3: 19.

Department of Education of the Philippines, Health and Nutrition Center. 2008. *National Oral Health Survey among the Public School Population in the Philippines.* Manila: Department of Education.

de Walque, D., J. S. Nakiyingi-Miiro, J. Busingye, and J. A. Whitworth. 2005. "Changing Association between Schooling Levels and HIV-1 Infection over 11 Years in a Rural Population Cohort in Southwest Uganda." *Tropical Medicine and International Health* 10 (10): 993–1001.

Dietz, W. 1998. "Health Consequences of Obesity in Youth: Childhood Predictors of Adult Disease." *Pediatrics* 101 (suppl.): 518–25.

Dobbins, M., D. Lockett, I. Michel, J. Beyers, L. Feldman, J. Vohra, and S. Micucci. 2001. *The Effectiveness of School-Based Interventions in Promoting Physical Activity and Fitness among Children and Youth: A Systematic Review.* Hamilton, ON: McMaster University.

Donnelly, J. E., J. L. Greene, C. A. Gibson, B. K. Smith, R. A. Washburn, D. K. Sullivan, K. DuBose, M. S. Mayo, K. H. Schmelzle, J. J. Ryan, D. J. Jacobsen, and S. L. Williams. 2009. "Physical Activity across the Curriculum (PAAC): A Randomized Controlled Trial to Promote Physical Activity and Diminish Overweight and Obesity in Elementary School Children." *Preventive Medicine* 49 (4): 336–41.

Douali, M. G., and J. D. Silver. 2004. "Self-Optimised Vision Correction with Adaptive Spectacle Lenses in Developing Countries." *Ophthalmic and Physiological Optics* 24 (3): 234–41.

Dupas, P. 2006. "Relative Risks and the Market for Sex: Teenagers, Sugar Daddies, and HIV in Kenya." Dartmouth College, Hanover, New Hampshire.

Durkin, M. S., L. L. Davidson, P. Desai, Z. M. Hassan, N. Khan, P. E. Shrout, M. J. Thorburn, W. Wang, and S. S. Zaman. 1994. "Validity of the Ten Questions Screen for Childhood Disability: Results from Population-Based Studies in Bangladesh, Jamaica, and Pakistan." *Epidemiology* 5 (3): 283–89.

Eapen, V., L. Al-Gazali, S. Bin-Othman, and A. Abou-Saleh. 1998. "Mental Health Problems among Schoolchildren in United Arab Emirates: Prevalence and Risk Factors." *Journal of the American Academy of Child and Adolescent Psychiatry* 37 (8): 880–86.

Eilander, A., T. Gera, H. S. Sachdev, C. Transler, H. C. M. van der Knaap, F. J. Kok, and S. J. M. Osendarp. 2010. "Multiple Micronutrient Supplementation for Improving Cognitive Performance in Children: Systematic Review of Randomized Controlled Trials." *American Journal of Clinical Nutrition* 91 (1): 115–30.

Esrey, S. A., J. B. Potash, L. Roberts, and C. Shiff. 1991. "Effects of Improved Water Supply and Sanitation on Ascariasis, Diarrhoea, Dracunculiasis, Hookworm Infection, Schistosomiasis, and Trachoma." *Bulletin of the World Health Organization* 69 (5): 609–21.

Fernald, L., C. C. Ani, and S. Grantham-McGregor. 1997. "Does School Breakfast Benefit Children's Educational Performance?" *African Health* 19 (6):19–20.

Fernandes, M. 2008. "The Effect of Soft Drink Availability in Elementary Schools on Consumption." *Journal of the American Dietetic Association* 108 (9): 1445–52.

Fernando, D., D. de Silva, R. Carter, K. N. Mendis, and R. Wickremasinghe. 2006. "A Randomised, Double-Blind, Placebo-Controlled, Clinical Trial of the Impact of Malaria Prevention on the Educational Attainment of Schoolchildren." *American Journal of Tropical Medicine and Hygiene* 74 (3): 386–93.

Ferreira, I., K. van der Horst, W. Wendel-Vos, S. Kremers, F. J. van Lenthe, and J. Brug. 2007. "Environmental Correlates of Physical Activity in Youth: A Review and Update." *Obesity Reviews* 8 (2): 129–54.

Fewtrell, L., and J. Colford. 2004. *Water, Sanitation, and Hygiene: Interventions and Diarrhea—A Review*. Washington, DC: World Bank.

Filmer, D. 2008. "Disability, Poverty, and Schooling in Developing Countries: Results from 14 Household Surveys." *World Bank Economic Review* 22 (1): 141–63.

Freedman, D. S., W. H. Dietz, S. R. Srinivasan, and G. S. Berenson. 2009. "Risk Factors and Adult Body Mass Index among Overweight Children: The Bogalusa Heart Study." *Pediatrics* 123 (3): 750–57.

Fylkesnes, K., R. M. Musonda, M. Sichone, Z. Ndhlovu, F. Tembo, and M. Monze. 2001. "Declining HIV Prevalence and Risk Behaviours in Zambia: Evidence from Surveillance and Population-Based Surveys." *AIDS* 15 (7): 907–16.

Gallant, M., and E. Maticka-Tyndale. 2004. "School-Based HIV Prevention Programmes for African Youth." *Social Science and Medicine* 58: 1337–51.

Geerligs, P. D., B. J. Brabin, and T. A. Eggelte. 2003. "Analysis of the Effects of Malaria Chemoprophylaxis in Children on Haematological Responses, Morbidity, and Mortality." *Bulletin of the World Health Organization* 81 (3): 205–16.

Glewwe, P., A. Park, and M. Zhao. 2006. "The Impact of Eyeglasses on the Academic Performance of Primary School Students: Evidence from a Randomized Trial in Rural China." Conference Paper 6644, Center for International Food and Agricultural Policy, University of Minnesota, St. Paul.

Global Campaign for Education. 2004. "Learning to Survive: How Education for All Would Save Millions of Young People from HIV/AIDS." Global Campaign for Education Secretariat, Johannesburg, South Africa.

Gordon, R. C., M. C. Rose, S. A. Skeaff, A. R. Gray, K. M. Morgan, and T. Ruffman. 2009. "Iodine Supplementation Improves Cognition in Mildly Iodine-Deficient Children." *American Journal of Clinical Nutrition* 90 (5): 1264–71.

Gordon-Larsen, P., M. C. Nelson, P. Page, and B. M. Popkin. 2006. "Inequality in the Built Environment Underlies Key Health Disparities in Physical Activity and Obesity." *Pediatrics* 117 (2): 417–24.

Gordon-Larsen, P., M. C. Nelson, and B. M. Popkin. 2004. "Longitudinal Physical Activity and Sedentary Behavior Trends: Adolescence to Adulthood." *American Journal of Preventive Medicine* 27 (4): 277–83.

Gortmaker, S., K. Peterson, J. Weicha, A. Sobol, S. Dixit, M. Fox, and N. Laird. 1999. "Reducing Obesity via a School-Based Interdisciplinary Intervention among Youth: Planet Health." *Archives of Pediatrics and Adolescent Medicine* 153 (4): 409–18.

Grantham-McGregor, S. M., Y. Bun Cheung, S. Cueto, P. Glewwe, L. Richer, B. Strupp, and the International Child Development Steering Group. 2007. "Developmental Potential in the First 5 Years for Children in Developing Countries." *Lancet* 369 (9555): 60–70.

Grantham-McGregor, S. M., S. Chang, and S. P. Walker. 1998. "Evaluation of School Feeding Programmes: Some Jamaican Examples." *American Journal of Clinical Nutrition* 67 (4): 785s–89s.

Grantham-McGregor, S. M., C. A. Powell, S. P. Walker, and J. H. Himes. 1991. "Nutritional Supplementation, Psychosocial Stimulation, and Mental Development of Stunted Children: The Jamaican Study." *Lancet* 338 (8758): 1–5.

Grassly, N. C., K. Desai, E. Pegurri, A. Sikazwe, I. Malambo, C. Siamatowe, and D. A. P. Bundy. 2003. "The Economic Impact of HIV/AIDS on the Education Sector in Zambia." *AIDS* 17 (7): 1039–44.

Green, J., F. Howes, E. Waters, E. Maher, and F. Oberklaid. 2005. "Promoting the Social and Emotional Health of Primary School-Aged Children: Reviewing the Evidence Base for School-Based Interventions." *International Journal of Mental Health Promotion* 7 (3): 30–36.

Gregson, S., T. Zhuwau, R. M. Anderson, and S. K. Chandiwana. 1998. "Is There Evidence for Behaviour Change in Response to AIDS in Rural Zimbabwe?" *Social Science and Medicine* 46 (3): 321–30.

Grigorenko, E. L., R. J. Sternberg, M. Jukes, K. Alcock, J. Lambo, D. Ngorosho, C. Nokes, and D. A. P. Bundy. 2006. "Effects of Antiparasitic Treatment on Dynamically and Statically Tested Cognitive Skills over Time." *Journal of Applied Developmental Psychology* 27 (6): 499–526.

Gupta, N., and M. Mahy. 2003. "Sexual Initiation among Adolescent Girls and Boys: Trends and Differentials in Sub-Saharan Africa." *Archives of Sexual Behavior* 32 (1): 41–53.

Guyatt, H. L., and R. W. Snow. 2001. "The Epidemiology and Burden of *Plasmodium falciparum*–related Anemia among Pregnant Women in Sub-Saharan Africa." *American Journal of Hygiene and Tropical Medicine* 64 (1–2): 36–44.

Hall, A., E. Bobrow, S. Brooker, M. Jukes, K. Nokes, J. Lambo, H. Guyatt, S. Moulin, J. de Graft Johnson, M. Mukaka, N. Roschnik, M. Sacko, A. Zacher, B. Mahumane, C. Kihamia, L. Mwanri, S. Tatala, N. Lwambo, J. Siza, L. N. B.

Khanh, H. H. Khoi, and N. D. Toan. 2001. "Anaemia in Schoolchildren in Eight Countries in Africa and Asia." *Public Health Nutrition* 4 (3): 749–56.

Hallett, T. B., J. J. C. Lewis, B. A. Lopman, C. A. Nyamukapa, P. Mushati, M. Wambe, G. P. Garnett, and S. Gregson. 2007. "Age at First Sex and HIV Infection in Rural Zimbabwe." *Studies in Family Planning* 38 (1):1–10.

Hargreaves, J. R., C. P. Bonell, L. A. Morison, J. C. Kim, G. Phetla, J. D. H. Porter, C. Watts, and P. M. Pronyk. 2007. "Explaining Continued High HIV Prevalence in South Africa: Socioeconomic Factors, HIV Incidence, and Sexual Behaviour Change among a Rural Cohort, 2001–2004." *AIDS* 21 (suppl. 7): S39–48.

Hargreaves, J. R., L. A. Morison, J. C. Kim, C. P. Bonell, J. D. H. Porter, C. Watts, J. Busza, G. Phetla, and P. M. Pronyk. 2008. "The Association between School Attendance, HIV Infection, and Sexual Behaviour among Young People in Rural South Africa." *Journal of Epidemiology and Community Health* 62 (2): 113–19.

Harvey, B., J. Stuart, and T. Swan. 2000. "Evaluation of a Drama-in-Education Programme to Increase AIDS Awareness in South African High Schools: A Randomized Community Intervention Trial." *International Journal of STD and AIDS* 11 (2): 105–11.

Hoddinott, J., J. A. Maluccio, J. R. Behrman, R. Flores, and R. Martorell. 2008. "Effect of a Nutrition Intervention during Early Childhood on Economic Productivity in Guatemalan Adults." *Lancet* 371 (9610): 411–16.

Holding, P. A., and R. W. Snow. 2001. "Impact of *Plasmodium falciparum* Malaria on Performance and Learning: Review of the Evidence." *American Journal of Tropical Medicine and Hygiene* 64 (1–2): 68–75.

Holdsworth, M., A. Gartner, E. Landais, B. Maire, and F. Delpeuch. 2004. "Perceptions of Healthy and Desirable Body Size in Urban Senegalese Women." *International Journal of Obesity* 28 (12): 1561–68.

Hopkins, G. L., D. McBride, H. H. Marshak, K. Freier, J. V. J. Stevens, W. Kannenberg, J. B. R. Weaver, S. L. Sargent Weaver, P. N. Landless, and J. Duffy. 2007. "Developing Healthy Kids in Healthy Communities: Eight Evidence-Based Strategies for Preventing High-Risk Behaviour." *Medical Journal of Australia* 186 (10 suppl.): S70–S73.

Hotez, P. J., D. A. P. Bundy, K. Beegle, S. Brooker, L. Drake, N. de Silva, A. Montresor, D. Engels, M. Jukes, L. Chitsulo, J. Chow, R. Laxminarayan, C. Michaud, J. Bethony, R. Correa-Oliveira, X. Shuhua, A. Fenwick, and L. Savioli. 2006. "Helminth Infections: Soil-Transmitted Helminth Infections and Schistosomiasis." In *Disease Control Priorities in Developing Countries*, 2nd ed., ed. D. Jamison, J. G. Breman, A. R. Measham, G. Alleyne, M. Claeson, D. Evans, P. Jha, A. Mills, and P. Musgrove, 462–82. New York: World Bank and Oxford University Press.

IASC (Inter-Agency Standing Committee). 2007. "IASC Guidelines on Mental Health and Psychosocial Support in Emergency Settings." IASC, Geneva.

Jacoby, E., S. Cueto, and E. Pollitt. 1996. "Benefits of a School Breakfast Programme among Andean Children in Huaraz, Peru." *Food and Nutrition Bulletin* 17 (1): 54–64.

Jamison, D., J. Breman, A. Measham, G. Alleyne, M. Claeson, D. Evans, P. Jha, A. Mills, and P. Musgrove. 2006. *Disease Control Priorities in Developing Countries.* 2nd ed. New York: World Bank and Oxford University Press.

Jones, H., and B. Reed. 2005. "Water and Sanitation for Disabled People and Other Vulnerable Groups: Designing Services to Improve Accessibility." Water, Engineering, and Development Centre, Loughborough University of Technology, Loughborough, U.K.

Jukes, M. C. H., B. Cheng, and E. Miguel. Forthcoming. "The Effect of Iron Supplementation on Attention and Cognitive Development in Indian Preschool Children."

Jukes, M. C. H., L. J. Drake, and D. A. P. Bundy. 2008. *School Health, Nutrition and Education for All: Leveling the Playing Field.* Cambridge, MA: CABI Publishing.

Jukes, M. C. H., M. Pinder, E. L. Grigorenko, H. B. Smith, G. Walraven, E. M. Bariau, R. J. Sternberg, L. J. Drake, P. Milligan, Y. B. Cheung, B. M. Greenwood, and D. A. P. Bundy. 2006. "Long-Term Impact of Malaria Chemoprophylaxis on Cognitive Abilities and Educational Attainment: Follow-up of a Controlled Trial." *PLoS Clinical Trials* 1 (4): e19.

Jukes, M. C. H., C. A. Nokes, K. J. Alcock, J. K. Lambo, C. Kihamia, N. Ngorosho, A. Mbise, W. Lorri, E. Yona, L. Mwanri, A. D. Baddeley, A. Hall, D. A. P. Bundy, and the Partnership for Child Development. 2002. "Heavy Schistosomiasis Associated with Poor Short-Term Memory and Slower Reaction Times in Tanzanian School Children." *Tropical Medicine and International Health* 7 (2): 104–17.

Kay, E., and D. Locker. 1998. "A Systematic Review of the Effectiveness of Health Promotion Aimed at Improving Oral Health." *Community Dental Health* 15 (3): 132–44.

Kelly, M. J. 2000. "Planning for Education in the Context of HIV/AIDS." International Institute for Educational Planning, UNESCO, Paris.

Kemper, H. C. G., G. B. Post, and W. van Mechelen. 1999. "Lifestyle and Obesity in Adolescence and Young Adulthood: Results from the Amsterdam Growth and Health Longitudinal Study (AGAHLS)." *International Journal of Obesity* 23 (suppl. 3): S34–S40.

Kihara, M., J. A. Carter, and C. R. Newton. 2006. "The Effect of *Plasmodium falciparum* on Cognition: A Systematic Review." *Tropical Medicine and International Health* 11 (4): 386–97.

Kirby, D., B. A. Laris, and L. Rolleri. 2006. *Sex and HIV Education Programs for Youth: Their Impact and Important Characteristics.* Scotts Valley, CA: ETR Associates.

Klepp, K. I., S. S. Ndeki, M. T. Leshabari, P. J. Hannan, and B. A. Lyimo. 1997. "AIDS Education in Tanzania: Promoting Risk Reduction among Primary Schoolchildren." *American Journal of Public Health* 87 (12): 1931–36.

Kobiané, J.-F., and M. Bougma. 2009. *RGPH-2006: Analyse des résultats définitifs: Thème 4: Education: Instruction – alphabétisation – scolarisation* [Analytical report on theme 4: education: teaching, literacy training and schooling]. Ouagadougou, Burkina Faso: Institut National de la Statistique et de la Démographie.

Kohl, H. W. III, and K. E. Hobbs. 1998. "Development of Physical Activity Behaviors among Children and Adolescents." *Pediatrics* 101 (3 suppl.): 549–54.

Kristjansson, E., V. Robinson, M. Petticrew, B. MacDonald, J. Krasevec, L. Janzen, T. Greenhalgh, G. A. Wells, J. MacGowan, A. P. Farmer, B. Shea, A. Mayhew, P. Tugwell, and V. Welch. 2007. "School Feeding for Improving the Physical and Psychosocial Health of Disadvantaged Elementary School Children." *Cochrane Database of Systematic Reviews* 1.

Kruger, H. S., T. Puoane, M. Senekal, and M. T. van der Merwe. 2005. "Obesity in South Africa: Challenges for Government and Health Professionals." *Public Health Nutrition* 8: 491–500.

Kuhn, L., M. Steinberg, and C. Matthews. 1994. "Participation of the School Community in AIDS Education: An Evaluation of a High School Programme in South Africa." *AIDS Care* 6 (2): 161–71.

Lagarde, E., M. Carael, J. R. Glynn, L. Kanhonou, S. C. Abega, M. Kahindo, R. Musonda, B. Auvert, A. Buvé, and the Study Group on the Heterogeneity of HIV Epidemics in African Cities. 2001. "Educational Level Is Associated with Condom Use within Non-spousal Partnerships in Four Cities of Sub-Saharan Africa." *AIDS* 15 (11): 1399–408.

Lalloo, D. G., P. Olukoya, and P. Olliaro. 2006. "Malaria in Adolescence: Burden of Disease, Consequences, and Opportunities for Intervention." *Lancet Infectious Diseases* 6 (12): 780–93.

Lipton, R. B., M. Drum, D. Burnet, B. Rich, A. Cooper, E. Baumann, and W. Hagopian. 2005. "Obesity at the Onset of Diabetes in an Ethnically Diverse Population of Children: What Does It Mean for Epidemiologists and Clinicians?" *Pediatrics* 115 (5): e553–e60.

Lloyd, C., R. Joyce, J. Hurry, and M. Ashton. 2000. "The Effectiveness of Primary School Drug Education." *Drugs: Education, Prevention, and Policy* 7 (2): 109–26.

Lobstein, T., L. Baur, and R. Uauy. 2004. "Obesity in Children and Young People: A Crisis in Public Health." *Obesity Reviews* 5 (suppl. 1): 4–85.

Loeb, M. E., and A. E. Eide. 2004. *Living Conditions among People with Activity Limitations in Malawi: A National Representative Study*. Oslo: SINTEF Health Research.

Lozoff, B. 2007. "Iron Deficiency and Child Development." *Food and Nutrition Bulletin* 28 (4 suppl.): S560–S71.

Luby, S., M. Agboatwalla, D. Feikin, J. Painter, W. Billhimer, A. Altaf, and R. M. Hoekstra. 2005. "Effect of Handwashing on Child Health: A Randomised Controlled Trial." *Lancet* 366 (9481): 225–33.

Lugoe, W. L., K. I. Klepp, and A. Skutle. 1996. "Sexual Debut and Predictors of Condom Use among Secondary School Students in Arusha, Tanzania." *AIDS Care* 8 (4): 443–52.

Lurie, M., P. Pronyk, E. de Moor, A. Heyer, G. de Bruyn, H. Struthers, J. McIntyre, G. Gray, E. Marinda, K. Klipstein-Grobusch, and N. Martinson. 2008. "Sexual Behavior and Reproductive Health among HIV-Infected Patients in Urban and Rural South Africa." *Journal of Acquired Immune Deficiency Syndromes* 47 (4): 484–93.

MacKenzie, G. E., S. Dannhauser, and W. Spijkerman. 2006. "Refractive Outcomes of the November 2005 Deployment of the AdSpec in Ghana." Optometric Science Research Group, University of Johannesburg, South Africa.

Magnani, R. J., A. M. Karim, L. A. Weiss, K. C. Bond, M. Lemba, and G. T. Morgan. 2002. "Reproductive Health Risk and Protective Factors among Youth in Lusaka, Zambia." *Journal of Adolescent Health* 30 (1): 76–86.

Mahar, M. T., S. K. Murphy, D. A. Rowe, J. Golden, A. T. Shields, and T. D. Raedeke. 2006. "Effects of a Classroom-Based Program on Physical Activity and On-Task Behavior." *Medicine and Science in Sports and Exercise* 38 (12): 2086–94.

Maharaj, P. 2005. "Patterns of Condom Use: Perspectives of Men in KwaZulu-Natal, South Africa." *Development Southern Africa* 22 (2): 187–97.

Martorell, R., J. R. Behrman, R. Flores, and A. D. Stein. 2005. "Rationale for a Follow-up Study Focusing on Economic Productivity." *Food and Nutrition Bulletin* 26 (2 suppl. 1): S5–S14.

Martorell, R., B. L. Horta, L. S. Adair, A. D. Stein, L. Richter, C. H. D. Fall, S. K. Bhargava, et al. 2009. "Weight Gain in the First Two Years of Life Is an Important Predictor of Schooling Outcomes in Pooled Analyses from Five Birth Cohorts from Low- and Middle-Income Countries." *Journal of Nutrition* 140 (2): 348–54.

Math, S. B., S. Tandon, S. C. Girimaji, V. Benegal, U. Kumar, A. Hama, K. Jangam, and D. Nagaraja. 2008. "Psychological Impact of the Tsunami on Children and Adolescents from the Andaman and Nicobar Islands." *Primary Care Companion to the Journal of Clinical Psychiatry* 10 (1): 31–37.

Mathenge, W., J. Nkurikiye, H. Limburg, and H. Kuper. 2007. "Rapid Assessment of Avoidable Blindness in Western Rwanda: Blindness in a Postconflict Setting." *PLoS Medicine* 4 (7): e217.

Maticka-Tyndale, E., J. Wildish, and M. Gichuru. 2007. "Quasi-Experimental Evaluation of a National Primary School HIV Intervention in Kenya." *Evaluation and Program Planning* 30 (2): 172–86.

McKay, H., L. Sinisterra, A. McKay, H. Gomez, and P. Lloreda. 1978. "Improving Cognitive Ability in Chronically Deprived Children." *Science* 200 (4339): 270–78.

Meekers, D., and G. Ahmed. 2000. "Contemporary Patterns of Adolescent Sexuality in Urban Botswana." *Journal of Biosocial Science* 32 (4): 467–85.

Mendez, M. A., and L. S. Adair. 1999. "Severity and Timing of Stunting in the First Two Years of Life Affect Performance on Cognitive Tests in Late Childhood." *Journal of Nutrition* 129 (8): 1555–62.

Mete, C., ed. 2008. *Economic Implications of Chronic Illness and Disability in Eastern Europe and the Former Soviet Union.* Washington, DC: World Bank.

Micronutrient Initiative. 2009a. "Investing in the Future: A United Call to Action on Vitamin and Mineral Deficiencies; Global Report 2009." Micronutrient Initiative, Ottawa.

———. 2009b. "Solution in a Pinch." Micronutrient Initiative, Ottawa.

Midford, R., S. Lenton, and L. Hancock. 2000. "A Critical Review and Analysis: Cannabis Education in Schools." New South Wales Department of Education and Training, Sydney, Australia.

Miguel, E., and M. Kremer. 2004. "Worms: Identifying Impacts on Education and Health in the Presence of Treatment Externalities." *Econometrica* 72 (1): 159–217.

Monse, B., R. Heinrich-Weltzien, H. Benzian, C. Holmgren, and W. H. van Palenstein Helderman. 2010. "PUFA: An Index of Clinical Consequences of Untreated Dental Caries." *Community Dentistry and Oral Epidemiology* 38 (1): 77–82.

Monteiro, C. A., W. L. Conde, and B. M. Popkin. 2004. "The Burden of Disease from Undernutrition and Overnutrition in Countries Undergoing Rapid Nutrition Transition: A View from Brazil." *American Journal of Public Health* 94 (3): 433–34.

Montresor, A., D. W. T. Crompton, T. W. Gyorkos, and L. Savioli. 2002. *Helminth Control in School-Age Children: A Guide for Managers of Control Programmes.* Geneva: WHO.

Moretti, D., M. B. Zimmermann, S. Muthayya, P. Thankachan, T. C. Lee, A. V. Kurpad, and R. F. Hurrell. 2006. "Extruded Rice Fortified with Micronized Ground Ferric Pyrophosphate Reduces Iron Deficiency in Indian

Schoolchildren: A Double-Blind Randomized Controlled Trial." *American Journal of Clinical Nutrition* 84 (4): 822–29.

Must, A., J. Spadano, E. Coakley, A. Field, G. Colditz, and W. Dietz. 1999. "The Disease Burden Associated with Overweight and Obesity." *Journal of the American Medical Association* 282 (16): 1523–29.

National Drug Research Institute. 2002. "The Prevention of Substance Use, Risk, and Harm in Australia: A Review of the Evidence." Commonwealth Department of Health and Ageing, Canberra.

Nga, T. T., P. Winichagoon, M. A. Dijkhuizen, N. C. Khna, E. Wasantwisut, H. Furr, and F. T. Wieringa. 2009. "Multi-micronutrient-Fortified Biscuits Decreased Prevalence of Anemia and Improved Micronutrient Status and Effectiveness of Deworming in Rural Vietnamese Schoolchildren." *Journal of Nutrition* 139 (5): 1013–21.

NHS (National Health Service) Information Centre. 2008. "General Ophthalmic Services: Workforce Statistics for England and Wales, 31 December 2007." NHS, London.

Noor, A. M., V. C. Kirui, S. Brooker, and R. W. Snow. 2009. "The Use of Insecticide-Treated Nets by Age: Implications for Universal Coverage in Africa." *BMC Public Health* 9: 369.

Nores, M., and W. S. Barnett. 2009. "Benefits of Early Childhood Interventions across the World: (Under) Investing in the Very Young." *Economics of Education Review* 29 (2): 271–82.

OECD (Organisation for Economic Co-operation and Development). 2004. "Keeping School Safe in Earthquakes." OECD, Paris. http://www.oecdbook shop.org/oecd/display.asp?sf1=indentifiers&st1=952004021E1.

OECD (Organisation for Economic Co-operation and Development) and World Bank. 2007. "Reaching the Unreached: Childhood Disability Screening Concept Paper and Global Strategy Proposal." OECD, Paris, and World Bank, Washington, DC.

Ogden, C., M. Carroll, and K. Flegal. 2008. "High Body Mass Index for Age among U.S. Children and Adolescents, 2003–2006." *Journal of the American Medical Association* 299 (20): 2442–43.

Osei, A. K., R. F. Houser, S. Bulusu, and D. H. Hamer. 2008. "Acceptability of Micronutrient Fortified School Meals by Schoolchildren in Rural Himalayan Villages of India." *Journal of Food Science* 73 (7): 8354–58.

Pasha, O., J. Del Rosso, M. Mukaka, and D. Marsh. 2003. "The Effect of Providing Fansidar (Sulfadoxine-Pyrimethamine) in Schools on Mortality in School-Age Children in Malawi." *Lancet* 361 (9357): 577–78.

Peters, L. W., G. Kok, G. T. Ten Dam, G. J. Buijs, and T. G. Paulussen. 2009. "Effective Elements of School Health Promotion across Behavioral Domains: A Systematic Review of Reviews." *BMC Public Health* 9: 182.

Pollitt, E. 1997. "Iron Deficiency and Educational Deficiency." *Nutrition Reviews* 55 (4): 133–41.

Pollitt, E., S. Cueto, and E. R. Jacoby. 1998. "Fasting and Cognition in Well- and Undernourished Schoolchildren: A Review of Three Experimental Studies." *American Journal of Clinical Nutrition* 67 (4): 779s–84s.

Popkin, B. 2006. "Global Nutrition Dynamics: The World Is Shifting Rapidly toward a Diet Linked with Noncommunicable Diseases." *American Journal of Clinical Nutrition* 84 (2): 289–98.

———. 2009. "What Can Public Health Nutritionists Do to Curb the Epidemic of Nutrition-Related Noncommunicable Disease?" *Nutrition Reviews* 67 (May Suppl. 1): S79–S82.

Popkin, B., W. Conde, N. Hou, and C. Monteiro. 2006. "Is There a Lag Globally in Overweight Trends for Children Compared with Adults?" *Obesity* 14 (10): 1846–53.

Prata, N., F. Vahidnia, and A. Fraser. 2005. "Gender and Relationship Differences in Condom Use among 15–24-Year-Olds in Angola." *International Family Planning Perspectives* 31 (4): 192–99.

Pridmore, P. 2008. "Access to Conventional Schooling for Children and Young People Affected by HIV and AIDS in Sub-Saharan Africa: A Cross-National Review of Recent Research Evidence." SOFIE, Institute of Education, University of London.

Rabie, T., and V. Curtis. 2006. "Handwashing and Risk of Respiratory Infections: A Quantitative Systematic Review." *Tropical Medicine and International Health* 11 (3): 258–67.

Rand Corporation. 2005. *Early Childhood Interventions: Proven Results, Future Promise.* Arlington, VA: Rand.

Republic of Kenya. 2005. *Kenya Education Sector Support Programme, 2005–2010.* Ministry of Education Science and Technology, Nairobi.

Resnikoff, S., D. Pascolini, S. P. Mariotti, and G. P. Pokharel. 2008. "Global Magnitude of Visual Impairment Caused by Uncorrected Refractive Errors in 2004." *Bulletin of the World Health Organization* 86 (1): 63–70.

Risley, C. L., and D. A. P. Bundy. 2007. "Estimating the Impact of HIV&AIDS on the Supply of Basic Education." Paper presented at the second meeting of the World Bank/UNAIDS Economics Reference Group, Geneva, November 8–9.

Robson, S., and K. B. Sylvester. 2007. "Orphaned and Vulnerable Children in Zambia: The Impact of the HIV/AIDS Epidemic on Basic Education for Children at Risk." *Educational Research* 49 (3): 259–72.

Rolnick, A., and R. Grunewald. 2007. "Early Intervention on a Large Scale." *Education Week* 26 (17): 32–36.

Romero, A. J. 2005. "Low-Income Neighborhood Barriers and Resources for Adolescents' Physical Activity." *Journal of Adolescent Health* 36 (3): 253–59.

Rose, D., and N. Bodor. 2006. "Household Food Insecurity and Overweight Status in Young Schoolchildren: Results from the Early Childhood Longitudinal Study." *Pediatrics* 117 (2): 464–73.

Saaddine, J. B., A. Fagot-Campagna, D. Rolka, K. M. Narayan, L. Geiss, M. Eberhardt, and K. M. Flegal. 2002. "Distribution of HbA(1c) Levels for Children and Young Adults in the U.S.: Third National Health and Nutrition Examination Survey." *Diabetes Care* 25 (8): 1326–30.

Sahota, P., M. Rudolf, R. Dixey, A. Hill, J. Barth, and J. Cade. 2001. "Randomised Control Trial of a Primary School–Based Intervention to Reduce Risk Factors for Obesity." *British Medical Journal* 323 (7320): 1–5.

Sallis, J. F., T. L. Conway, J. J. Prochaska, T. L. McKenzie, S. J. Marshall, and M. Brown. 2001. "The Association of School Environments with Youth Physical Activity." *American Journal of Public Health* 91 (4): 618–20.

Sallis, J., J. Prochaska, and T. Wendell. 2000. "A Review of Correlates of Physical Activity of Children and Adolescents." *Medicine and Science in Sports and Exercise* 32 (5): 963–75.

Sandøy, I. F., C. Michelo, S. Siziya, and K. Fylkesnes. 2007. "Associations between Sexual Behaviour Change in Young People and Decline in HIV Prevalence in Zambia." *BMC Public Health* 7: 60.

Sazawal, S., R. R. Black, M. Ramsan, H. M. Chwaya, R. J. Stoltzfus, A. Dutta, U. Dhingra, I. Kabole, S. Deb, M. K. Othman, and F. M. Kabole. 2006. "Effects of Routine Prophylactic Supplementation with Iron and Folic Acid on Admission to Hospital and Mortality in Preschool Children in a High Malaria Transmission Setting: Community-Based, Randomised, Placebo-Controlled Trial." *Lancet* 367 (9505): 133–43.

Schweinhart, L. J., J. Montie, Z. Xiang, W. S. Barnett, C. R. Belfield, and M. Nores. 2005. "Lifetime Effects: The HighScope Perry Preschool Study through Age 40." Monographs of the HighScope Educational Research Foundation 14, HighScope Press, Ypsilanti, MI.

Seshadri, S., and T. Gopaldas. 1989. "Impact of Iron Supplementation on Cognitive Functions in Preschool and School-Aged Children: The Indian Experience." *American Journal of Clinical Nutrition* 50 (3 suppl.): 675–86.

Sharma, M. 2006. "School-Based Interventions for Childhood and Adolescent Obesity." *Obesity Reviews* 7 (3): 261–69.

Shuey, D. A., B. B. Babishangire, S. Omiat, and H. Bangarukayo. 1999. "Increased Sexual Abstinence among In-School Adolescents as a Result of School Health Education in Soroti District, Uganda." *Health Education Research* 14 (3): 411–19.

Siervo, M., P. Grey, O. A. Nyan, and A. M. Prentice. 2006. "A Pilot Study on Body Image, Attractiveness, and Body Size in Gambians Living in an Urban Community." *Eating and Weight Disorders* 11 (2):100–9.

Simeon, D. T., and S. M. Grantham-McGregor. 1989. "Effects of Missing Breakfast on the Cognitive Functions of School Children of Differing Nutritional Status." *American Journal of Clinical Nutrition* 49 (4): 646–53.

Simeon, D. T., S. M. Grantham-McGregor, J. E. Callender, and M. S. Wong. 1995. "Treatment of *Trichuris trichiura* Infections Improves Growth, Spelling Scores, and School Attendance in Some Children." *Journal of Nutrition* 125 (7): 1875–83.

Singh, A. S., C. Mulder, W. R. Twisk, W. van Mechelen, and M. J. Chinapaw. 2008. "Tracking of Childhood Overweight into Adulthood: A Systematic Review of the Literature." *Obesity Reviews* 9 (5): 474–88.

Smith, K., E. Weissberg, and T. G. Travison. 2010. "Alternative Methods of Refraction: A Comparison of Three Techniques." *Optometry and Vision Science* 87 (3): E176–E82.

Snow, R. W., M. H. Craig, C. R. J. C. Newton, and R. W. Steketee. 2003. "The Public Health Burden of *Plasmodium falciparum* Malaria in Africa: Deriving the Numbers." Working Paper 11, Disease Control Priorities Project, Fogarty International Center, National Institutes of Health, Bethesda, MD.

Snow, R. W., and K. Marsh. 2002. "The Consequences of Reducing *Plasmodium falciparum* Transmission in Africa." *Advances in Parasitology* 52: 235–64.

Social and Rural Research Institution of IMRB International. 2005. "A Report on Out-of-School Children." Commissioned by the Ministry of Human Resource Development of India, New Delhi.

Soewondo, S., M. Husaini, and E. Pollitt. 1989. "Effects of Iron Deficiency on Attention and Learning Processes in Preschool Children: Bandung, Indonesia." *American Journal of Clinical Nutrition* 50 (3): 667–74.

Stanton, B. F., X. Li, J. Kahihuata, A. M. Fitzgerald, S. Neumbo, G. Kanduuombe, I. B. Ricardo, J. S. Galbraith, N Terreri, I. Guevara, H. Shipena, J. Strijdom, R. Clemens, and R. F. Zimba. 1998. "Increased Protected Sex and Abstinence among Namibian Youth Following a HIV Risk-Reduction Intervention: A Randomized, Longitudinal Study." *AIDS* 12 (18): 2473–80.

Stephenson, L. 1987. *Impact of Helminth Infection on Human Nutrition*. London: Taylor and Francis.

Stewart-Brown, S. 2006. "What Is the Evidence on School Health Promotion in Improving Health or Preventing Disease and, Specifically, What Is the Effectiveness of the Health Promoting Schools Approach?" WHO Regional Office for Europe, Copenhagen.

Stoltzfus, R. J., J. D. Kvalsvig, H. M. Chwaya, A. Montresor, M. Albonico, J. M. Tielsch, L. Savioli, and E. Pollitt. 2001. "Effects of Iron Supplementation and

Anthelmintic Treatment on Motor and Language Development of Preschool Children in Zanzibar: Double-Blind, Placebo-Controlled Study." *British Medical Journal* 323 (7326): 1389.

Taras, H. 2005. "Nutrition and Student Performance at School." *Journal of School Health* 75 (6): 199–213.

Taras, H., and W. Potts-Datema. 2005. "Obesity and Student Performance at School." *Journal of School Health* 75 (8): 291–95.

Thammasat University. 2003. "Philippine Country Report on School Health Promotion Programme." Thammasat University, Ayyuthaya, Thailand.

Timperio, A., J. Salmon, and K. Ball. 2004. "Evidence-Based Strategies to Promote Physical Activity among Children, Adolescents, and Young Adults: Review and Update." *Journal of Science and Medicine in Sport* 7 (1): 20–29.

Tiwari, B. D., M. M. Godbole, N. Chattopadhyay, A. Mandal, and A. Mithal. 1996. "Learning Disabilities and Poor Motivation to Achieve Due to Prolonged Iodine Deficiency." *American Journal of Clinical Nutrition* 63 (5): 782–86.

Tobler, N., and H. Stratton. 1997. "Effectiveness of School-Based Drug Education Programs: A Meta-analysis of the Research." *Journal of Primary Prevention* 18 (1): 71–128.

Tomlinson, M., L. Swartz, A. Officer, K. Y. Chan, I. Rudan, and S. Saxena. 2009. "Research Priorities for Health of People with Disabilities: An Expert Opinion Exercise." *Lancet* 374 (9704): 1857–62.

Trinitapoli, J. 2009. "Religious Teachings and Influences on the ABCs of HIV Prevention in Malawi." *Social Science and Medicine* 69 (2): 199–209.

Truong, K. D., and R. Sturm. 2005. "Weight Gain Trends across Sociodemographic Groups in the United States." *American Journal of Public Health* 95 (9): 1602–6.

UNAIDS (Joint United Nations Programme on HIV/AIDS). 2008. *Report on the Global AIDS Epidemic 2008*. Geneva: UNAIDS.

UNESCO (United Nations Educational, Scientific and Cultural Organization). 2000. "The Dakar Framework for Action: Education for All—Meeting Our Collective Commitments." Presented at the World Education Forum, Dakar, April 26–28.

———. 2003. *EFA Global Monitoring Report 2003: Gender and Education for All: The Leap to Equality*. Paris: UNESCO.

———. 2007. *UNESCO's Strategy for Responding to HIV/AIDS*. Paris: UNESCO.

———. 2009. *EFA Global Monitoring Report 2009: Overcoming Inequality—Why Governance Matters*. Paris: UNESCO.

———. 2010. *EFA Global Monitoring Report 2010: Reaching the Marginalized*. Paris: UNESCO.

UNICEF (United Nations Children's Fund). 2006. *Africa's Orphaned and Vulnerable Generations: Children Affected by AIDS*. New York: UNICEF.

————. 2008. *Children and AIDS: Third Stocktaking Report*. New York: UNICEF.

————. 2009. *Promoting Quality Education for Orphans and Vulnerable Children: A Sourcebook of Programme Experiences in Eastern and Southern Africa*. New York: UNICEF.

UNICEF (United Nations Children's Fund) and University of Wisconsin. 2008. *Monitoring Child Disability in Developing Countries: Results from the Multiple Indicator Cluster Surveys*. New York: UNICEF.

UNICEF (United Nations Children's Fund) and WHO (World Health Organization). 1994. *World Summit for Children—Mid-Decade Goal: Iodine Deficiency Disorders*. Geneva: UNICEF/WHO Joint Committee on Health Policy.

United Republic of Tanzania Government. 2008. "General Budget Support Annual Review 2008: Final Report." Ministry of Finance and Economic Affairs, Dar es Salaam.

van den Briel, T., C. E. West, N. Bleichrodt, F. J. van de Vijver, E. A. Ategbo, and J. G. Hautvast. 2000. "Improved Iodine Status Is Associated with Improved Mental Performance of Schoolchildren in Benin." *American Journal of Clinical Nutrition* 72 (5): 1179–85.

Vermeersch, C., and M. Kremer. 2004. "Schools Meals, Educational Achievement, and School Competition: Evidence from a Randomized Evaluation." Policy Research Working Paper 2523, World Bank, Washington, DC.

Vir, S. C., N. Singh, A. K. Nigam, and R. Jain. 2008. "Weekly Iron and Folic Acid Supplementation with Counseling Reduces Anemia in Adolescent Girls: A Large-Scale Effectiveness Study in Uttar Pradesh, India." *Food and Nutrition Bulletin* 29 (3): 186–94.

Walker, S. P., S. M. Chang, C. A. Powell, and S. M. Grantham-McGregor. 2005. "Effects of Early Childhood Psychosocial Stimulation and Nutritional Supplementation on Cognition and Education in Growth-Stunted Jamaican Children: Prospective Cohort Study." *Lancet* 366 (9499): 1804–7.

Walker, S. P., T. D. Wachs, J. M. Gardner, B. Lozoff, G. A. Wasserman, E. Pollitt, J. A. Carter, and the International Child Development Steering Group. 2007. "Child Development: Risk Factors for Adverse Outcomes in Developing Countries." *Lancet* 369 (9556): 145–57.

Watanabe, K., R. Flores, J. Fujiwara, and T. H. T. Lien. 2005. "Early Childhood Development Interventions and Cognitive Development of Young Children in Rural Vietnam." *Journal of Nutrition* 135 (8): 1918–25.

Watkins, W. E., and E. Pollitt. 1997. "Stupidity or Worms: Do Intestinal Worms Impair Mental Performance?" *Psychological Bulletin* 121 (2): 171–91.

Wells, J., J. Barlow, and S. Stewart-Brown. 2003. "A Systematic Review of Universal Approaches to Mental Health Promotion in Schools." *Health Education Journal* 103: 197–220.

WFP (World Food Programme). 2006. "Capacity-Building in El Salvador: Annual Performance Report." WFP, Rome.

———. 2007. *Food for Education Works: A Review of WFP FFE Programme Monitoring and Evaluation, 2002–2006.* Rome: WFP.

Whaley, S. E., M. Sigman, C. Neumann, N. Bwibo, D. Guthrie, R. E. Weiss, S. Alber, and S. P. Murphy. 2003. "The Impact of Dietary Intervention on the Cognitive Development of Kenyan Schoolchildren." *Journal of Nutrition* 133 (11): 3965S–71S.

WHO (World Health Organization). 2001. *International Classification of Functioning, Disability, and Health (ICF).* Geneva: WHO.

———. 2007a. "Conclusions and Recommendations of the WHO Consultation on Prevention and Control of Iron Deficiency in Infants and Young Children in Malaria-Endemic Areas." WHO Secretariat on behalf of the participants to the consultation. *Food and Nutrition Bulletin* 28 (4): S621–S27.

———. 2007b. "Oral Health: Action Plan for Promotion and Integrated Disease Prevention." World Health Assembly Resolution WHA60/R17 2007. WHO, Geneva.

———. 2008. *The Global Burden of Disease: 2004 Update.* Geneva: WHO.

———. 2009. "Weekly Iron–Folic Acid Supplementation (WIFS) in Women of Reproductive Age: Its Role in Promoting Optimal Maternal and Child Health." Position Statement, WHO, Geneva.

WHO (World Health Organization), FDI World Dental Federation, International Association for Dental Research, and Chinese Stomatological Association. 2007. "Beijing Declaration: Achieving Dental Health through Fluoride in China and South East Asia." Presented at "Conference on Dental Health through Fluoride in China and South East Asia," Beijing, September 18–19.

World Bank. 2001. *Unlocking the Potential of Youth.* Washington, DC: World Bank.

———. 2002. *Education and HIV/AIDS: A Window of Hope.* Washington, DC: World Bank.

———. 2003a. *Education and HIV/AIDS: A Sourcebook of HIV/AIDS Prevention Programs.* Washington, DC: World Bank.

———.2003b. *School Deworming at a Glance.* Washington, DC: World Bank.

———. 2008. *Education and HIV/AIDS: A Sourcebook of HIV/AIDS Prevention Programs; Volume 2: Education Sector-wide Approaches.* Washington, DC: World Bank.

World Bank, UNICEF (United Nations Children's Fund), and Water and Sanitation Program. 2005. "Toolkit on Hygiene, Sanitation, and Water in Schools." World Bank, Washington, DC. http://www.wsp.org/wsp/sites/wsp .org/files/publications/TOOLKIT.pdf.

World Vision International and the Global Partnership for Disability and Development. 2007. "Education's Missing Millions: Including Disabled Children in Education through EFA-FTI Processes and National Sector Plans." World Vision, London, United Kingdom.

Wouhabe, M. 2007. "Sexual Behaviour, Knowledge, and Awareness of Related Reproductive Health Issues among Single Youth in Ethiopia." *African Journal of Reproductive Health* 11 (1): 14–21.

Yang, X., R. Telama, J. Viikari, and O. Raitakari. 2006. "Risk of Obesity in Relation to Physical Activity Tracking from Youth to Adulthood." *Medicine and Science in Sports and Exercise* 38 (5): 919–25.

Zellner, S. L. 2003. "Condom Use and the Accuracy of AIDS Knowledge in Côte d'Ivoire." *International Family Planning Perspectives* 29 (1): 41–47.

Zimmermann, M. B. 2009. "Iodine Deficiency in Pregnancy and the Effects of Maternal Iodine Supplementation on the Offspring: A Review." *American Journal of Clinical Nutrition* 89 (2): 668S–72S.

Zimmermann, M. B., K. Connolly, M. Bozo, J. Bridson, F. Rohner, and L. Grimci. 2006. "Iodine Supplementation Improves Cognition in Iodine-Deficient Schoolchildren in Albania: A Randomized, Controlled, Double-Blind Study." *American Journal of Clinical Nutrition* 83 (1): 108–14.

Zimmermann, M. B., D. Moretti, N. Chaouki, and T. Torresani. 2003. "Development of a Dried Whole-Blood Spot Thyroglobulin Assay and Its Evaluation as an Indicator of Thyroid Status in Goitrous Children Receiving Iodized Salt." *American Journal of Clinical Nutrition* 77 (6): 1453–58.

# CHAPTER 4

# School Health and Nutrition Programs in Practice

The previous chapter explored education sector responses to some of the most common health and nutrition problems that affect the education of school-age children. The chapter identified the need for maternal and child health (MCH) and early child development (ECD) programs to ensure that children are ready for school. This chapter goes a step further and examines how interventions for school-age children have been incorporated into school health and nutrition programs in practice. There is a considerable diversity of successful options for such programs. The chapter does not aim to provide comprehensive coverage of the options available; instead, it uses selected examples to illustrate certain key issues that should be considered when putting together a school health and nutrition program.

The chapter starts by looking at some of the main issues relevant to program design. Most countries will not be developing a program based on these initial principles, since analysis indicates that almost all countries already have some sort of school health program. Hence a first challenge will be dealing with the change process and building on what already exists. A second design element consideration is the establishment of an effective policy dialogue between the education and health sectors, as well as with other key stakeholders in this intrinsically multisectoral area.

The chapter then explores the issues around the selection of program components, based on cost and effectiveness, describing four specific examples of how countries have sought to expand, improve, or extend existing school health and nutrition programs. The chapter concludes with two examples of how school health and nutrition programs have been mainstreamed within education sector plans. Although not intended to be a "how to" section, it is hoped that the references and links to relevant toolkits in the text that follows will assist education sector specialists to develop their own responses.

## Issues in Designing School Health and Nutrition Programs

When designing school health programs, few countries start from nothing. Many school health programs in low-income countries, particularly in Africa, have descended from colonial antecedents that were intended to serve the minority of children who had access to school in urban centers or who attended elite boarding facilities. These programs rely on specific infrastructures and services—such as school visits by health teams, school nurses, and in-school clinics—that are additional to the normal range of health services provided in schools. Efforts to maintain or increase the coverage of such services are, moreover, often beyond the means of most low-income countries. Analysis of an attempted expansion of a school-nurse program in KwaZulu-Natal in South Africa, for example, showed that despite a relatively high investment (a cost per targeted student of $11.50), coverage was inadequate (18 percent of students) and almost no cases of detected ill health resulted in effective referral and treatment (World Bank 2000).

Such programs present specific challenges to change management. On one hand, staffing for a national school health program may be built around this model, so changing the model can present human resource challenges. On the other hand, although such programs are often intrinsically regressive, the parents of the elite children who benefit from the programs are often well placed to resist change. These are not intractable issues, but they will shape the dialogue around any reform process and are as important to address as the issues of content discussed in the rest of this section.

### *Expanding Coverage and Targeting the Poor*

Poverty is a key consideration in the design of school health and nutrition programs. The negative correlation between ill health, malnutrition, and income level is clearly demonstrated in both cross-country comparisons and individual country analyses (de Silva et al. 2003), partly because lower incomes and higher poverty themselves promote disease and inadequate diets. Similarly, children who are not enrolled in school and are targeted by school health and school feeding programs generally come from households with lower income levels (Filmer and Pritchett 1999). Furthermore, the educational impact of disease and poor nutrition is greatest for the poorest children. These factors suggest that there will increasingly be a return to school health services that are pro-poor and specifically linked to achieving the goals of Education for All (EFA). Thus expanded coverage is critical for the effectiveness of school health and nutrition programs.

The case for overcoming barriers to coverage is strong. Traditional medical practice, for example, emphasizes treatment after individual diagnosis. But analysis of health interventions that are integrated into more inclusive school health and nutrition programs, such as deworming and micronutrient supplements, suggests that mass approaches are preferable—on technical, economic, and equity grounds—to approaches that require diagnostic screening (Hotez et al. 2006). Furthermore, it can be argued that by avoiding the need to access health service facilities, mass approaches serve the goal of equity because such access is positively and significantly associated with income. Poorer populations (which experience more ill health) are systematically overlooked by intervention programs that operate through diagnoses at health facilities. Similar considerations suggest that health education programs will be equitable only if they are universal, since they offer the greatest benefit to those populations who experience a higher incidence of ill health—populations that are also poorer, have less education, and less access to health services.

### Defining Sectoral Roles

It is apparent that there are many ways to approach the delivery of school health and nutrition, but diverse experiences suggest that these interventions share some common features. In particular, a review of existing programs highlights certain consistent roles played by government and nongovernmental agencies and other partners and stakeholders (see table 4.1).

In nearly every program, the Ministry of Education is the lead implementing agency, reflecting both the goal of school health and nutrition programs to improve educational achievement and the fact that the

**Table 4.1 Comparison of the Roles Played by Government Agencies, Partners, and Stakeholders in School Health and Nutrition Programs**

| Partner | Roles | Comments |
|---|---|---|
| Ministry of Education | • Lead implementing agency<br>• Lead financial resource<br>• Education sector policy | • Health and nutrition of schoolchildren is a priority for EFA<br>• Education policy defines school environment, curriculum, duties of teachers<br>• Education system has a pervasive infrastructure for reaching teachers and school-age children |
| Ministry of Health | • Lead technical agency<br>• Health sector policy | • Health of school-age children has lower priority than clinical services and infant health<br>• Health policy defines role of teachers in service delivery and how health materials are procured |
| Other public sector agencies (for example, ministries of welfare, social affairs, local government, agriculture) | • Support education and health systems<br>• Fund holders | • Ministries of local government are often fund holders for teachers and schools, as well as for clinics and health agents<br>• Ministries of welfare and social affairs provide mechanisms for the provision of social funds |
| Private sector (for example, health services, pharmaceuticals, publications) | • Specialist service delivery<br>• Materials provision | • Major role in drug procurement and production of training materials<br>• Specialist roles in health diagnostics |
| Civil society (for example, NGOs, FBOs, PTAs) | • Training and supervision<br>• Local resource provision | • At the local level, serve as gatekeepers and fund holders; may also target implementation<br>• Offer additional resource streams, particularly through INGOs |
| Teacher associations | • Define teachers' roles<br>• Partners in implementation | • School health programs demand an expanded role for teachers |
| Local community (for example, children, teachers, parents) | • Define acceptability of curriculum and teachers' roles<br>• Supplement resources | • Gatekeepers for both the content of health education (especially moral and sexual content) and the role of non-health agents (especially teachers) in health service delivery. Pupils are active participants in all aspects of the process at the school level.<br>• Communities supplement program finances at the margins |

*Source:* Jukes, Drake, and Bundy 2008.

*Note:* FBO = faith-based organization; INGO = international nongovernmental organization; NGO = nongovernmental organization; PTA = parent-teacher association.

education system often provides the most complete existing infrastructure for reaching school-age children. But the education sector must share this responsibility with the Ministry of Health, particularly since the latter has the ultimate responsibility for the health of all children, including school-children. It is also apparent that program success is dependent on the effective participation and support of numerous other stakeholders, especially the beneficiaries and their parents or guardians.

Analysis suggests that universal coverage is most easily achieved through public sector interventions. In fact, there are several characteristics of school health and nutrition programs that make a compelling case for public sector intervention. First, there may be treatment externalities where external benefits accrue to people other than the treated individuals. This is clearly the case for communicable disease interventions, especially against worm infections. For example, a deworming program in Kenya found a reduction in worm loads among children who did not take part in the deworming program, but lived near schools that did (Miguel and Kremer 2004).

Second, some forms of intervention (for example, vector control, health education campaigns, epidemiological surveillance, and interventions with strong externalities) are almost pure public goods; that is, no one can be excluded from using the goods or services that they deliver. Thus the private sector is unlikely to compete to deliver these goods. Finally, there is typically little private demand for general preventive measures, such as information on the value of washing hands with soap. This is not an argument against a private sector role in service delivery, but the facts suggest that private sector demand is likely to be greater among middle-income populations and areas where demand has been created by public sector actions.

To explore these issues further, a widely accepted consensus framework was used to explore how different sectors have contributed to programs in practice. The consensus framework uses the acronym FRESH (Focusing Resources on Effective School Health) and is described in detail in chapter 5, but the essence of the framework is that the following four core components should be made available together in all schools:

- *Policy:* health- and nutrition-related school policies that provide a nondiscriminatory, safe, and secure environment.
- *School environment:* access to safe water and the provision of separate sanitation facilities for girls and boys.

- *Education:* skills-based education that addresses health, nutrition, and hygiene issues and promotes positive behaviors.
- *Services:* simple, safe, and familiar health and nutrition services that can be delivered cost-effectively in schools (for example, deworming, micronutrient supplements, and snacks to avoid hunger), together with increased access to youth-friendly clinics.

Adoption of this framework does not imply that these core components and strategies are the only important elements of a school health and nutrition program, but that implementing all four components in all schools will provide a sound foundation for any pro-poor program.

While there are strong arguments for public programs, the private sector approach to health and nutrition programs has proven sustainable over nearly two decades in urban Indonesia. However, such an approach may require a technical infrastructure and local market base that are lacking in predominantly rural low-income countries.

The private sector approach to health and nutrition programs is modeled on a program initiated in Japan in 1948, which relied on private sector technicians working independently at first, but later formalized within the Japan Association of Parasite Control, which conducted stool examinations and then treated infected individuals for a per capita fee equivalent to approximately $0.74 in 2004 dollars. With growing prosperity, Japan later implemented a sophisticated, comprehensive school health program based on the 1958 School Health Act, but retained the parasite control element of the program because of its remarkable cost-effectiveness. The prevalence of roundworm infection in the population fell from a high of 73 percent in 1949 to less than 0.01 percent by 1985. At its peak, the private sector program conducted some 12 million examinations annually, implying a turnover of nearly $9 million in 2009 prices.

### Delivery Costs and the Use of the School as a Platform

One of the key arguments for using the school as a platform for health delivery is the potential savings offered by the school system, rather than the health system, as the delivery mechanism. From this perspective, schools are seen as providing a pre-existing mechanism, so costs are marginal, but also a system that aims to be sustainable and pervasive, reach disadvantaged children, and promote social equity. Schools do not replace the health system, which remains the main formal conduit for public

**Table 4.2    Examples of Delivery Costs for a Single Mass Deworming Treatment**

| Strategy | Drug | Country | Delivery cost per treatment $ | % of total |
|---|---|---|---|---|
| Mobile team to community | Albendazole | Montserrat | 0.51 | 67 |
| | Albendazole | Bangladesh | — | 42 |
| | Levamisole | Nigeria | 0.32 | 81 |
| | Praziquantel | Tanzania | 0.21 | 24 |
| School-based | Albendazole | Ghana | 0.04 | 17 |
| | Albendazole | Tanzania | 0.03 | 13 |
| Out-of-school children | Praziquantel | Egypt, Arab Rep. | 0.16–0.21 | 40–47 |

*Source:* Guyatt 2003.
*Note:* — = not available.

health delivery and referrals. However, under specific circumstances, the school system can provide a useful complement to traditional health system delivery mechanisms. For example, table 4.2 analyzes the cost of providing deworming treatment to schoolchildren through different delivery mechanisms in six different countries, illustrating the cost savings of using a school-based approach (Guyatt 2003).

In the 1980s and early 1990s most programs were "vertical" in nature; they involved mobile health teams that visited communities and gave treatment to everyone or just to infected residents. The per capita cost of delivering these drugs ranged from $0.21 to $0.51. Note that this was the cost of only delivering treatment and did not include the price of the drug itself. By contrast, the per capita cost of delivering school-based programs is as little as $0.03 to $0.04. This method is more than 10 times less expensive than the more costly mobile treatment teams.

### Prioritizing Interventions on the Basis of Cost and Need

Decisions about which interventions to include in a school health and nutrition program are based partly on matching local needs to the costs of the responses. Table 4.3 illustrates the range of costs, standardized over one year, for providing some common school-based interventions to students. This table illustrates two important points. First, some of the most widely needed interventions can be provided at remarkably low cost. Second, there is significant diversity in the cost of interventions, with correspondingly wide differences in the cost of meeting different needs.

Eritrea used cost data and national epidemiological data to review which health conditions could be meaningfully addressed through schools, based on the budget available (see box 4.1). The first matrix was used to define the interventions that would be made available in schools by teachers, with supervision by the community health service. Epidemiological data showed that iron supplementation was required only in a coastal zone and deworming only in a highland zone, so these interventions were geographically targeted on this basis. The second matrix used a list of interventions that were best addressed by referral to

**Table 4.3    Annual Per Capita Costs of School-Based Health and Nutrition Interventions Delivered by Teachers**

| Condition | Intervention | Annual per capita cost ($) |
|---|---|---|
| Intestinal worms | Albendazole or mebendazole | 0.03–0.20 |
| Schistosomiasis | Praziquantel | 0.20–0.71 |
| Vitamin A deficiency | Vitamin A supplementation | 0.04 |
| Iodine deficiency | Iodine supplementation | 0.30–0.40 |
| Iron deficiency and anemia | Iron folate supplementation | 0.10 |
| Refractive vision errors | Spectacles | 2.50–3.50 |
| Clinically diagnosed conditions | Physical examination | 11.50 |
| Hunger | School feeding | 15–50[a] |

*Source:* Partnership for Child Development 1999; Galloway et al. 2009; Bundy et al. 2009.
a. Costs are standardized for 1,000 kcal for 180 days.

---

**Box 4.1**

## Identifying Priority Interventions in Eritrea

The first step taken in developing a strategic plan for health and nutrition programs in Eritrea was to review the different health conditions affecting schoolchildren in the country and consider how these conditions could be addressed using the four components of the FRESH framework. This exercise enabled policy makers to identify the conditions affecting Eritrean children that could effectively be addressed through school-based health and nutrition services.

Once the relevant conditions were identified, decision-making matrices were constructed to enable policy makers to consider the need, benefit, cost, and feasibility of different services (see tables B4.1a and B4.1b below).

*(continued next page)*

**Box 4.1** *(continued)*

The results of the situation analysis, together with the knowledge and experience of members of the Ministries of Health and Education, were then used to determine which health services would be delivered in different parts of the country.

**Table B4.1a    Decision-Making Matrix for Conditions That Can Be Treated by Teachers in Schools**

| Condition | Need[a] | Scale of benefit | | Per capita cost ($) | Feasibility of universal access[b] |
|---|---|---|---|---|---|
| | | *Education* | *Health* | | |
| Bilharzia | +++[c] | +++ | +++ | 0.80 | +++ |
| Anemia | +++[c] | +++ | +++ | 1.20 | +++ |
| Vitamin A supplementation | +++ | + | +++ | 0.30 | +++ |
| Skin infections | + | + | + | 3.00 | ++ |
| First aid | ++ | ++ | ++ | 0.50 | ++ |

*Source:* Jukes, Drake, and Bundy 2008.
*Notes:* +++ = high; ++ = moderate; + = low.
a. Evidence from situation analysis and Ministry of Health experience.
b. Experience elsewhere.
c. In certain areas.

**Table B4.1b    Decision-Making Matrix for Conditions Where Teachers Can Refer Children to Local Health Services**

| Condition | Need[a] | Scale of benefit | | Per capita cost ($) | Feasibility of universal access[b] |
|---|---|---|---|---|---|
| | | *Education* | *Health* | | |
| Dental decay | ++ | + | +++ | 30.00 | + |
| Refractive error | +++ | +++ | ++ | 5.00 | ++ |
| Eye infections | +++ | ++ | +++ | 3.00 | ++ |
| Hearing impairment | ++ | +++ | + | 200.00 | + |
| Ear infections | ++ | +++ | +++ | 3.00 | ++ |
| Malnutrition | ++ | +++ | +++ | 30.00 | ++ |

*Source:* Jukes, Drake, and Bundy 2008.
*Note:* +++ = high; ++ = moderate; + = low.
a. Evidence from situation analysis and Ministry of Health experience.
b. Experience elsewhere.

health services; for these conditions, teachers were trained to undertake a basic screening and referral role. Based on these decisions on scale, content, and cost, Eritrea successfully launched a national program that an evaluation later showed was able to reach even the most isolated schools and poorest children.

## Examples of Programs in Practice

This chapter has so far looked at the key issues in making choices about what to include in school health and nutrition programs. The starting point for this discussion was the recognition that nearly all countries already have existing programs. These programs are, however, of variable effectiveness and often do not reach the children most in need. It should be no surprise, then, that an examination of what countries are actually doing in this field is improving programs that are already in place.

The following two sections explore what countries have done in practice. First, the text explores four examples of countries that have ramped up existing programs to achieve new objectives, with the examples chosen to help illustrate the importance of carefully matching the choice of intervention to objectives. Second, the text turns to two countries with fairly mature school health and nutrition programs that have sought to embed those programs within the overall goals and processes of the education sector, a process sometimes called mainstreaming.

### Expanding and Refining Existing Programs

The following examples from Kenya, the Philippines, Sri Lanka, and Guyana show how these countries have defined new objectives for existing school health and nutrition programs and then responded by rolling out new program components. In Kenya, the government launched and implemented a national deworming program (see box 4.2); in the Philippines, the government rolled out a combined deworming, toothbrushing, and hand washing program; in Sri Lanka, the government modified its program to become more responsive to regional objectives; and in Guyana, the government extended its school feeding program to cover the most difficult-to-reach children.

### The Philippines' Fit for School Program*

**Objectives and context.** Important health issues for schoolchildren in the Philippines include hygiene-related infectious diseases (for example, diarrhea, acute respiratory infections, pneumonia), worm infections (which affect more than 66 percent of schoolchildren; Belizario et al. 2009), and oral health (80–90 percent of schoolchildren have dental decay and more than 50 percent have dental infections; Department of Education 2008). All of these diseases have a negative impact on the

---

* This section was contributed by Bella Monse and Habib Benzia.

physical and mental development of children, as well as their quality of life, productivity, and ability to learn (see chapter 3 for discussions of each of these conditions). The overall objective of the Fit for School (FFS) Program is "to improve child health and development by institutionalization of an Essential Health Care Programme consisting of three simple, evidence-based interventions: hand washing, deworming, and toothbrushing" (Fit for School 2009, 3).

Child health falls under the remit of the Department of Health in the Philippines. The Department of Education is responsible for school health personnel, but does not have a budget for medical supplies. Decentralization and devolution of responsibilities has resulted in provincial governments playing an increasing role in both health and education. FFS started as a local community program in one province of Mindanao and was scaled up to become a national flagship program that is now implemented in 25 provinces and benefits 1 million children.

**Box 4.2**

## Kenya's National Deworming Program*

Until recently, deworming programs in Kenya had been small in scale and fragmented. But in 2009, the country's National School Health Policy and Guidelines adopted school-based deworming and the Kenyan government took on the chal-

*"Treatment shall be administered to all school-age children, including those out of school, based on the prevalence and intensity of worms and bilharzias in the area."*

Kenya School Health Policy and Guidelines

lenging task of implementing a national school-based deworming program. By collating and mapping existing data (from more than 1,300 previous helminth-related surveys), it was possible to identify the areas at greatest risk and thereby target those children most at risk, rather than deworm every schoolchild in Kenya.

The geographic mapping of surveys, combined with climate-based transmission limitation maps, demonstrated that mass school-based deworming was warranted in 45 districts.[a] These districts were clustered in three geographic regions of the country, which also correlated with areas of high population

(continued next page)

**Box 4.2** *(continued)*

density. By utilizing mapping data, it was possible to target deworming at only one-third of all primary schools in the country, and still reach the majority of children at risk.

In a training program that cascaded from the national to the school level, more than 1,000 district- and division-level personnel, together with 16,000 teachers around the country, were taught to deliver deworming drugs safely and effectively. Drugs were

> *"Kenya is investing 1 million dollars to scale up sustained deworming programs through our national school health program. In 2009, 3 million children in the most 'at-risk' areas of the country will be treated."*
>
> Raila Odinga, prime minister of Kenya

also distributed via the training cascade, which maximized operational efficiency. Community sensitization campaigns were undertaken at national and local levels to ensure that parents, teachers, and children were educated about deworming, its safety, and the potential side effects of treating those with heavy worm infections. The program was a huge success, and in the first phase, all 45 districts were successfully covered, with more than 3.6 million Kenyan children (72 percent of those identified as at risk) in more than 8,200 schools dewormed.

Kenya's experience shows conclusively that school-based deworming programs are not only feasible, but also extremely cost-effective. The Kenyan program cost only $0.36 per child; this figure reflects all program costs, including training, logistics, deworming drugs, monitoring, and printed materials. As demonstrated in table B4.2, the deworming program benefited from external financial support and technical assistance from development partners, including Deworm the World. The approach is to leverage government investment and provide targeted technical and logistical support. With high-level government commitment, the program is also sustainable.

In Kenya, this model of a school-based deworming program appears to be succeeding, as the government has committed to funding the program for a second year. Recent mapping activities in new districts for both soil-transmitted helminths (STHs) and schistosomiasis have identified more

**Table B4.2    Cost per Child of the Deworming Program in Kenya**

| Funder | Kenyan shillings | U.S. dollars |
|---|---|---|
| Kenyan government | 20 | 0.28 |
| Development partners | 6 | 0.08 |
| Total | 26 | 0.36 |

*Source:* Author.

*(continued next page)*

**Box 4.2** *(continued)*

at-risk children in need of treatment. In 2010, the program aims to cover more than 100 districts and treat more than 4 million children for STHs with mebendazole. It also aims to provide treatment for schistosomiasis to more than 150,000 children in several hundred schools in the most acutely affected areas of the country.

**Map B4.2     STH Prevalence in Kenya**

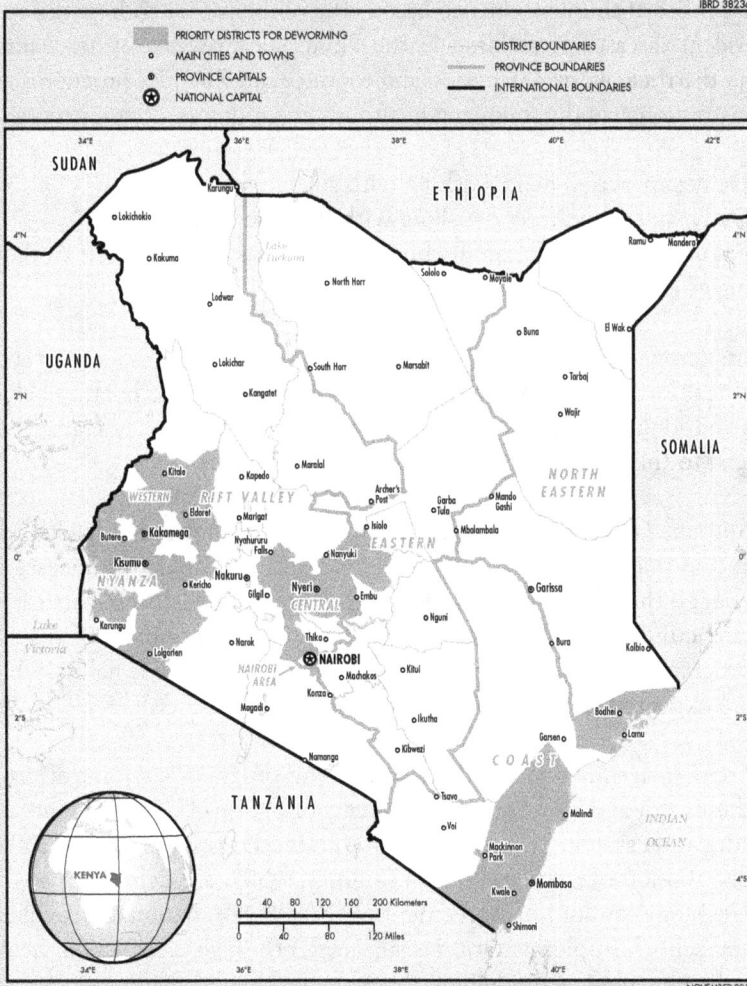

*Source:* Brooker, Clements, and Bundy 2006.
a. According to WHO guidelines, which recommend mass deworming where prevalence is above 20 percent. A color version of the map appears at the end of the book.

* Contributed by Karen Levy, Alissa Fishbane, and Ruth Dixon.

There are agreements among the stakeholders to implement the program in 50 percent of all provinces of the Philippines by 2012 (Monse et al. 2010). The program has been supported by the German development agencies GTZ and InWent.

**Program components.** The innovative cornerstone of the FFS program is the use of existing school structures to implement a package of preventive health strategies (the Essential Health Care Programme). These strategies consist of simple, evidence-based interventions that address the most prevalent diseases of children in the Philippines: respiratory tract infections, diarrhea, worm infections, and tooth decay. The FFS program seeks to institutionalize the following health interventions as school activities:

- Daily supervised hand washing with soap.
- Daily supervised toothbrushing with fluoride toothpaste.
- Biannual deworming of all children by means of supervised swallowing of an albendazole tablet.

Implemented in schools by teachers, this package introduces preventive health and behavioral measures aimed at sustainable healthy behaviors and long-term health improvements. The following key features are crucial to the success of the program:

- *Sustained behavioral change.* Current evidence shows that health education may increase children's knowledge but does not necessarily change their behavior. While health education has been part of the curriculum in the Philippines for decades, the emphasis of the FFS program is on tangible action and the creation of routine habits, which are expected to be sustained throughout life.

- *Local ownership and local leadership.* The program is a joint effort of the health and education departments of provincial governments, the education system, parents, and communities. It is supported by a clear distribution of roles and responsibilities, which are defined in a written Memorandum of Agreement at three levels: national, provincial, and school. Implementation is supported through clear school health policies, technical guidelines, manuals, and practical support (see the end of this section). Implementation of the hygiene measures is the responsibility of the education system, while parents and the community are responsible for improving schools' access to water and the construction of washing facilities in schools. The budget for materials and supplies ($0.50 per child per year for soap, toothpaste, and a toothbrush) is provided by the health department of the provincial government. The Philippine NGO Fit for School provides technical support and capacity development.

- *Overcoming institutional barriers.* The FFS program established intersectoral collaboration by bridging the traditional barriers between the health and education sectors, particularly between education and health professionals. FFS empowers non-healthcare professionals (that is, teachers, children, parents, and politicians) to promote health and prevent disease using existing facilities (primary schools), as well as engaging healthcare professionals to conduct capacity building, referrals, and monitoring and evaluation. Although the FFS program is implemented by the education sector, responsibility for financing and procuring the required consumables (soap, toothpaste, toothbrushes, and deworming tablets) lies with the health sector of the provincial governments.

- *Applying international policies and recommendations.* The program builds on international recommendations by using schools as an ideal setting for health interventions—an appropriate, low-cost, and realistic strategy. In addition, it applies the principles of health promotion outlined in the Ottawa Charter (WHO 1986). Finally, FFS is patterned on the multipartner framework of FRESH (see chapter 5). These policies provide guidance and a common platform for the program, inviting additional stakeholders to join and avoiding program overlap.

**Results and challenges.** Since the launch of the FFS program in 2008, national school health policies have mandated all teachers to implement daily health activities as part of their duties and instructed all school principals to ensure that hand-washing facilities are available in all public elementary schools. All 3,850 participating schools have improved their access to water and hand-washing facilities. All of these schools have also implemented the skills-based health education component. One million schoolchildren now wash their hands and brush their teeth daily and are dewormed twice a year. The 25 provinces implementing the program have created a budget line and allocated funds for the procurement of FFS materials—some provinces for selected areas, other provinces for their entire territories.

Research on students engaged in daily fluoride toothbrushing in public elementary schools in the Philippines has shown a 40 percent reduction in dental decay and a 60 percent reduction in the progression of decay into the pulp of teeth. A comprehensive health outcome study is currently under way to assess the impact of the program. According to international literature, the following benefits are expected from current coverage of hand washing and biannual deworming: a 42–47 percent reduction in diarrheal incidence, a 30 percent reduction in respiratory infections, and a 30 percent reduction in heavy-load worm infections (Savioli, Bundy, and Tomkins 1992; Curtis and Cairncross 2003). These impacts should also reduce absenteeism and contribute to better education outcomes.

The FFS program provides a starting point for broader infrastructure improvements in schools and communities. Hand-washing programs need access to water, which is not available in nearly half of public elementary schools in the Philippines. Department of Education Order 65/2009 has stimulated demand for hand washing, resulting in greater political support for ensuring access to water and the installation of washing facilities at schools. The program has demonstrated scalability, expanding from 1 to 25 provinces in two years, and is presently aiming to reach 6 million schoolchildren (half of all primary students in the country) by 2012.

Additional resources on the Fit for School Program can be accessed at the NGO's website: http://www.fitforschool.ph. Manuals, documentation, and brochures from the program can be downloaded from the site at http://fitforschool.ph/index.php?option=com_docman&Itemid=118.

### The Sri Lanka School Health Promotion Program*

**Objectives and context.** The 25-year history of school health and nutrition interventions in Sri Lanka has contributed to a steady reduction in communicable diseases (especially worms and malaria), as well as malnutrition among schoolchildren. However, uneven economic development and long-running civil conflict have left a legacy of mixed challenges for such interventions in Sri Lanka.

In 2005, the health and education sectors undertook a situation analysis to determine the health and nutrition status of schoolchildren throughout the country, then related this status to education outcomes. The analysis showed that malnutrition and communicable diseases remain prevalent in some rural and conflict-affected areas, and were associated with underachievement in education. Meanwhile, there are growing

---

* This section was contributed by Lesley Drake, Roshini Ebenezer, and Nilanthi de Silva.

concerns in urban centers about increases in noncommunicable diseases, such as diabetes and obesity. It was concluded that to address these challenges, Sri Lanka required a strategic intervention that, on one hand, would combat communicable diseases in certain parts of the country, while on the other, would prioritize noncommunicable diseases in urban centers.

In response to this need, the government of Sri Lanka launched the School Health Promotion Program (SHPP) in 2007. The program aimed to strengthen existing school health programs by implementing the concept of the "Sri Lanka Health Promoting School." Underlying this concept was the realization that children needed to be empowered with the skills and resources to prevent disease and help them maintain their mental and physical health, while improving their educational outcomes. The new program was specifically designed to enable better coordination and more strategic implementation of school health initiatives.

In line with the FRESH framework, a five-pronged strategy was selected to implement "health-promoting schools":

1. Development of policies and partnerships among all stakeholders to promote the health of the school community.
2. Ensuring a safe, healthy environment, both physical and psychosocial, to facilitate learning.
3. Provision of skills-based health education for schoolchildren.
4. Ensuring that schoolchildren have access to health services.
5. Empowering schoolchildren to be change agents to improve the health of their families and communities.

In light of the need for better coordination of school health and nutrition programs, as well as for strategic programming tools, SHPP implemented a monitoring and evaluation framework designed to facilitate the coordination, implementation, and progress of SHPP objectives. Indicators for the program have been integrated into the broader education sector monitoring and evaluation (M&E) framework and are included on the Technical Support Unit checklist conducted by the Finance Commission.

**Program components.** SHPP is the result of a strong partnership between the Sri Lankan Ministry of Education and Ministry of Health and is coordinated by their respective units: the School Health and Nutrition Unit of the education sector and the Family Health Bureau (FHB) of health sector. This partnership has enabled the successful implementation and oversight of school health programs in Sri Lanka. A joint steering committee consisting of representatives of the health and education ministries, including the two school health units, meets regularly to oversee policy and planning for the implementation of SHPP. In addition, a national policy framework laid the groundwork for creating school health focal points at the provincial and district levels of the health and education administrative structures, as well as creating a School Health Committee within each school. The latter works to engage students in achieving the objectives of a Health Promoting School.

In accordance with the implementation plan, major SHPP activities include provision of water and sanitation facilities to ensure a safe and healthy environment; continuation and expansion of the national school feeding program; and, where appropriate, provision of micronutrient supplementation and deworming treatment. School medical inspections are carried out annually with the aim of connecting every schoolchild in the country with health services.

The health education curriculum is being revised to use a skills-based approach to empower children with the knowledge required for healthy living. There is also an effort under way to train teachers and other school staff to teach the new curriculum. In addition, there is an effort to establish school health clubs and promote community participation in school health activities, thus promoting the health of entire communities through the schools.

**Results and challenges.** Sri Lanka's targeted school health program operates in the large majority of its 9,800 schools. Teachers up to and including grade 9 have been trained to deliver the comprehensive school health education program, and multiple health resources have been developed and distributed to 8,000 schools. These resources are currently undergoing translation to enable dissemination in Tamil areas of the country as well.

The availability of basic education through an extensive school system, combined with a well-developed public health infrastructure, helped ensure the success of the program. The school feeding program serves more than 80 percent of schoolchildren in grades 1–5, with higher coverage in the most vulnerable and malnourished areas. Annual school medical inspections—a critical targeting component of the school health program—also cover almost 83 percent of schools in the country. School water and sanitation facilities, which were below minimum recommended standards in almost 2,000 schools, are now part of an ongoing government program designed to ensure all schools have adequate facilities within the next five years; 715 priority schools were reached in 2009.

### School health and school feeding in Guyana*

**Objectives and context.** The community-based school feeding program (SFP) in Guyana is a component of the national education sector plan that was developed through Education for All–Fast Track Initiative (EFA-FTI) and funded by the FTI Catalytic Fund. The primary objectives of the program are to build community participation in local primary schools, increase attendance, and improve school performance and nutritional status. SFP targets 4 of the 11 regions that make up Guyana. These are the remotest regions, which present unique challenges for the provision of services. Guyana's population is just under 1 million, and the hinterland population—which is mostly AmerIndian—is dispersed. There are significant differences in access to and quality of education and health services between this population and the urban population of Georgetown.

Before designing a community-based approach to school feeding, Guyana evaluated past school feeding programs. The evaluation provided evidence that centralized provision of food was not effective. Inconsistent supply, sporadic and high-cost delivery, and problems with preparing a powdered milk formula did not create incentives or lead to the results expected of the program—namely, increased attendance, better nutrition, and enhanced educational performance.

Considering the geography of the hinterland regions, it was impractical to import foodstuffs from the capital. Given high poverty levels in the targeted areas, the community-based approach could potentially offer new economic opportunities for farmers, local merchants, and parents seeking employment as cooks or food preparers. Schools could serve as local, ready markets for agricultural products.

**Program components.** The community-based SFP is designed to operate with parental and community participation. Villages are provided comprehensive training at the start of the program by a multisectoral team led by the Ministry of Education. This training covers how to set up a community-based school feeding program in a village, as well as how to write a proposal to receive funding for the program. The training consists of a general orientation to the program, plus training in finance (that is, basic

---

* This section was contributed by Angela Demas.

bookkeeping), project management, proposal writing, food and nutrition, food preparation and certification, and facilities standards. Villages decide on or elect community members who will serve as the treasurer and cooking staff of their respective programs.

On a rolling basis, communities develop their own school feeding proposals using a template provided during training. Budgets are based on the school population,[1] so villages plan accordingly. A proposal demonstrates a school's commitment to implementing its own community-based SFP and is the basis for grant awards. The standard template facilitates preparation of the proposal and its review, which confirms the number of eligible pupils and the budget ceiling for the school grant. Proposals are evaluated by the National School Feeding Steering Committee, and applicants are awarded both investment and operational funds to carry out their programs.

**Results and challenges.** As of November 2009, Guyana's community-based SFP was benefiting 84 out of 138 primary schools in the interior regions of the country, reaching more than 14,000 children who receive a daily meal when they attend school.

Three key factors of program success are: (i) program design based on a thorough assessment of past school feeding experiences and international best practice; (ii) a detailed operational manual to support implementation of feeding programs with easy-to-use forms and procedures; and (iii) essential preparation activities that include training in local communities; communications and public relations; and positive collaboration with other agencies, ministries, and programs.

Community ownership of SFP has been a significant factor in success of the program and empowers parents and communities to further support their children's nutritional health and education. The mere presence of an SFP in a village functions as an accountability mechanism—parents tend to follow up more with teachers and administrators to make sure their children are receiving a good education in schools where SFPs are operational.

The program has led to a number of additional positive impacts. It has been reported that families whose children attend a school with a community-based SFP tend to have better diet diversity at home. Parents add vegetables to their diets and use recipes provided by school cooks. The mid-term impact evaluation also showed some evidence that treatment communities fared better than comparison communities during the recent food price crisis and economic downturn. Community-based SFPs may be a buffer that protects these communities, which may be less dependent on importing supplies from the capital.

The biggest challenge of such programs is building local sustainability after grant funds are completed. Certain government funds have been earmarked for this goal; however, these monies could benefit other high-poverty areas outside of the four hinterland regions supported under the EFA-FTI grant that do not have school feeding programs. A number of steps are being taken to address the sustainability of the community-based SFPs, such as

- Encouraging new schools coming into the program to plan their investment purchases to provide for sustainability. This task could include the purchase of seeds for school plots, chickens, or other items that continue to produce food resources after a one-time investment.
- Building a small travel budget into the funding allocation of partner ministries to enable the provision of follow-up support to communities.
- In schools where a kitchen is not possible, recommending the purchase of a locally produced nutritional snack.
- Using school kitchen facilities for income-generating purposes after hours and re-investing the earnings into the community-based SFP (for example, catering for events or selling food to the community).

Most of the schools that have not yet been reached by the school medical inspections program (some 17 percent of all schools) are in the most remote areas of the country, where the need is greatest. This reality reflects the common issue of mobile health teams: costs rise in proportion to remoteness. Reaching the most needy (the last 10 percent) of schoolchildren is thus a major resource challenge. Since schools are already present in remote areas, one solution being explored is to give greater emphasis to school-based service delivery.

The second challenge of the new program is implementing its monitoring and evaluation system, which requires clear channels of information management and information sharing between the various stakeholders. The complexities of the administrative apparatus in Sri Lanka pose a challenge to systematizing this process between the Ministry of Health and Ministry of Education. Monitoring and evaluation also require training staff at each level of the program to collect, enter, and analyze data for effective policy making.

## Including the Components of School Health and Nutrition Programs in a Sectorwide Education Approach

Historically, education sector management plans have rarely included school health and nutrition programs. More often than not, a school health unit is a part of a government's health services. This situation is changing, however, as educations sector planners now recognize the relevance of school health and nutrition to education goals and begin to take responsibility for implementing school health and nutrition (SHN) programs. The challenge for the education planner is where to locate these programs in the education service administration and how to include them in education sector plans. This challenge is exacerbated by the fact that certain aspects of the programs are often new and unfamiliar to the education sector, such as procuring drugs and food, and require different channels of funding. One solution is to embed the various components of SHN programs within an overall sectorwide approach, which can permit access to pooled funding from multiple sectors. This subsection examines the current use of this approach by Kenya and its planned use by Indonesia.

### The Kenya education SWAp approach*

**Objectives and context.** The Kenya Education Sector Support Programme (KESSP) is a government-owned education sector development plan that supports EFA and the Millennium Development Goals (MDGs). Most donors working in the education sector in Kenya have agreed to harmonize their support for the national education sector plan, and the government has committed to using a common mechanism for its implementation, as well as local institutions and procedures, in a sectorwide approach (SWAp). Financing is from four main sources: (i) the government of Kenya, (ii) the Catalytic Fund of EFA-FTI, (iii) other, off-budget bilateral support, and (iv) pooled funding (see figure 4.1).

KESSP has 23 "investment programs" (IPs) that cover a wide range of education subcomponents. Three of these IPs form the "school health platform": (i) school health, nutrition, and meals; (ii) HIV/AIDS; and (iii) school infrastructure.

The government supports the school health program to help mitigate the impact of poor health and nutrition on education, as well as combat the growing negative impact of the HIV/AIDS epidemic on the Kenyan

---

* This section was contributed by Andy Tembon and Michael Mills.

**Figure 4.1    Funding Sources for KESSP**

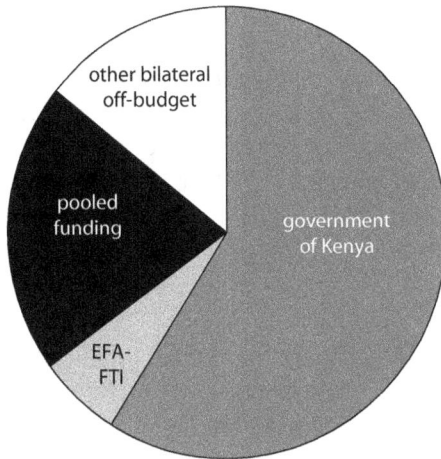

other bilateral
off-budget

pooled
funding

government
of Kenya

EFA-
FTI

*Source:* Author.

education system. According to the school health policy recently adopted by the Ministry of Public Health and Sanitation and the Ministry of Education, school health aims to "enhance the quality of health in school communities by creating a healthy and child-friendly environment for teaching and learning" (Republic of Kenya 2009, 15). The three component investment programs of the school health platform incorporate the activities detailed below.

### The School Health, Nutrition, and Meals Investment Program
*School feeding.* The government has been implementing a home-grown school feeding program since the beginning of 2009. It reaches 538,457 schoolchildren in 1,711 schools. The aim of the program is to ensure that children enroll, attend school regularly, and learn and perform well academically. The program brings together the objectives of school feeding and agricultural development of the local community (that is, support of local food production and increased access to markets), thereby improving the economic development of the areas in which the program is implemented. In this multisectoral intervention, the Ministry of Agriculture works with community farmers to help them improve production; their crops are then purchased by the home-grown school feeding program. In addition to education benefits, the program contributes to food security and poverty reduction.

These latter goals are particularly important in food-insecure areas, which are the target of the program.

*Deworming.* An estimated 5 million children are affected by parasitic worms in Kenya. In response to the educational benefits afforded by deworming, the School Health and Nutrition Programme of the Ministry of Education has implemented a National Deworming Programme in partnership with the Ministry of Public Health and Sanitation and the Eastern and Southern Africa Centre of International Parasite Control at the Kenya Medical Research Institute–Eastern and Southern Africa Centre of International Parasite Control (KEMRI-ESACIPAC). Key support is provided by Deworm the World, the KEMRI–Wellcome Trust, the Partnership for Child Development, Innovation for Poverty Action, Feed the Children, and the Japan International Cooperation Agency (JICA). The first phase of the National Deworming Programme was officially launched in April 2009. By the end of this phase, more than 3.6 million children had been dewormed.

*Prevention of malaria.* While there is no national, school-based malaria treatment program for schoolchildren in Kenya, school health policy has been revised to incorporate malaria prevention education in schools. As of this writing, it is planned that the school health program will be expanded after dissemination of the results of a national survey being carried out by the Ministry of Public Health and Sanitation. New program elements will include (i) distribution of bed nets through schools (via integration with the deworming program) and (ii) intermittent preventive treatment (IPT). A randomized trial of IPT has demonstrated the practicality and cost-effectiveness of this approach, which results in a reduction in anemia and an increase in cognition among schoolchildren.

*Hygiene and maintenance of sanitation facilities.* To support the infrastructure investment program, health education on the importance of hygiene, clean water, and the maintenance of sanitation facilities is included in the curriculum of science subjects in grades 1 through 8. Training on these topics has been conducted using a cascade approach from the central to district to school level.

*Health education.* The existing school curriculum already includes topics on HIV prevention, life skills, malaria prevention, and general hygiene. Secondary school subjects such as biology and home science also include aspects of life skills, HIV prevention, malaria prevention, and hygiene. Life skills were, however, introduced as an additional stand-alone subject in the curriculum in January 2008.

**The School Infrastructure Investment Program.** The Ministry of Education uses this program to ensure a safe and sanitary school environment, as well as to improve access to primary education. The program involves the construction and maintenance of classrooms, toilets, and hand-washing stations in schools. It also encompasses a growing program to ensure access for students and staff with disabilities. The program includes new schools and facilities, as well as the upgrading of existing schools and facilities. With respect to upgrading, schools are requested to send proposals detailing their hardware needs to the Ministry of Education; if the need is confirmed by provincial education teams, resources are sent directly to the school, which implements the work following the standard design of the Ministry of Education.

**The HIV/AIDS Investment Program.** In Kenya, education is now recognized as a priority sector in the multisectoral response to HIV/AIDS. With its allocation from KESSP, the Ministry of Education in recent years has increased its activities in response to the HIV/AIDS epidemic and has sought to mainstream these activities throughout the sector. The 2008–09 pooled funds from KESSP were spent on four components: HIV prevention, HIV response at the workplace, management of this response, and care and support of orphans and vulnerable children enrolled in primary schools. The Ministry of Education has implemented these activities through its AIDS Control Unit (ACU).

**Results and challenges.** KESSP is an important mechanism for applying education sector funding to nontraditional activities. Since this funding is considered on an annual basis, it also allows for a greater degree of flexibility than does more traditional budgeting.

Much of the budget allocated from KESSP to the school health, nutrition, and meals investment program goes to the school feeding component. This weighting reflects the reality that the per capita costs of school feeding are an order of magnitude greater than the intrinsically low costs of the health service elements (deworming and malaria prevention) or the marginal costs of adding health topics to an existing curriculum. Since budget amounts are often equated with importance, the program team needs to make the continued case for adequate technical resources in order to implement the less expensive, but highly cost-effective health components.

A common school health platform was created to avoid fragmentation of the school health components within the Ministry of Education. However, the existence of three investment programs to address common issues presents a coordination challenge among the numerous actors at the headquarters level, including the ACU, school meals unit, school health and nutrition unit, and water and sanitation unit.

A key element of the interministerial program is the formal requirement that the Ministries of Education and of Public Health and Sanitation coordinate and collaborate in the implementation of school health, following a designation of responsibilities set out in formal policy documents. Since each ministry has a school health unit, there is the potential for tension, overlap, and duplication that requires vigilance and responsiveness from both institutions.

At present, some program activities implemented for the health of schoolchildren remain outside of KESSP and the joint interministerial program. These activities include immunizations for measles, poliomyelitis (polio), and tetanus toxoid, together with elimination campaigns for trachoma and chiggers, all of which are implemented in schools by the Ministry of Health and Sanitation.

### Strengthening school health in Indonesia*

**Objectives and context.** The education sector in Indonesia is the fourth largest in the world, with more than 40 million students, 2.6 million teachers, and more than 200,000 schools. About 686,000 primary schoolchildren (142,000 boys and 544,000 girls) are out of school in the country. Despite progress in the transition from primary to junior secondary school, only about 55 percent of children from low-income families are enrolled in junior secondary schools. Efforts to help children enroll in and complete the basic education cycle remain a high priority for the education sector.

Providing a healthy environment for children and overcoming health and nutrition (that is, hunger) barriers to school enrollment and participation are important for reaching the country's education goals. For example, a recent review and analysis (Del Rosso and Arlianti 2009) shows that many of the diseases afflicting children in young childhood (0–5 years) persist during school-age years in Indonesia, especially among younger children. Reported prevalence of nonspecific diarrhea and

---

* This section was contributed by Joy Del Rosso and Rina Arlianti.

typhoid and acute respiratory infection (ARI) is of particular concern. Although malaria is not a universal problem in the country, up to 70 percent of schoolchildren are affected in one province.

The WHO, moreover, has identified Indonesia as a country where worm infections represent a public health problem, estimating that more than 17 million people are at risk of infection, with very few reached for treatment. Much more progress is needed to improve access to clean drinking water and sanitation in the country.

Together with childhood diseases, chronic undernutrition is associated with lower school performance in Indonesia. National-level data show that rates of stunting among children in the country range from roughly 20 percent to more than 50 percent, depending on the province. In the overwhelming majority of provinces, more than one-third of school-age children are stunted. Micronutrient deficiency data show that anemia affects about half the school-age population, with 21 percent of districts reporting that household consumption rates of iodized salt are less than 50 percent of adequate levels.

Finally, the problems of child undernutrition and overweight children (and adults) co-exist in the country. Excess weight gain is now well understood to be an important factor in the development of noncommunicable diseases (for example, diabetes, high blood pressure, heart disease, stroke, and several major cancers), which are currently among the major causes of death in Indonesia.

Although national policies on school health have been in place in Indonesia since the 1950s, a specific school health program, the *Usaha Kesehatan Sekolah* (UKS), was launched in 1984 to address multiple health issues. The program is based on a memorandum of understanding (MOU) among four ministries: the Ministry of National Education, Ministry of Health, Ministry of Religious Affairs, and Ministry of Home Affairs. The purpose of UKS is to improve both the quality of education and student learning achievement by increasing healthy life skills among students; creating a healthy school environment; and improving knowledge, changing student attitudes, and maintaining health by preventing and curing diseases. This goal is reflected in three program pillars: health education, health services at schools, and a healthy school environment.

At the school level, the headmaster and one or more UKS teachers (*guru*) are appointed to oversee UKS activities. Each school is expected to collaborate with health center staff to implement certain program activities. The Ministry of National Education (MONE) primarily sets standards, provides guidelines, and establishes expectations for UKS. As a national program implemented within a decentralized system, UKS activities in one district may look very different from activities in another. At the province and district levels, the resources devoted to UKS are dependent on the commitment of local legislative and decision-making bodies.

**Program components.** The draft minimum level of services (*Standar Pelayanan Minimal,* or SPM) for schools include a clean water supply and adequate sanitation facilities (that is, hand washing facilities and toilets). Several efforts are under way under the auspices of different donor institutions, the Ministry of Health, and MONE to improve the water and sanitation environment in schools, with a network being established to help coordinate implementation.

The School Immunization Program (*Bulan Imunisasi Anak Sekolah,* or BIAS) represents perhaps the most consistent and effective provision of school-linked health services in the country. Introduced in 1998 to provide tetanus and diphtheria boosters, the program was been integrated into the existing UKS structure. Responsibility for BIAS lies with health workers who work directly with individual schools.

At the central government level, UKS in 2009 began to support the improvement of school canteens through both block grants to schools and training activities. Schools must already have functioning canteens to apply for funds, since no infrastructure is provided by the program. In addition to grants, MONE provides technical assistance and training to these same schools in how to create safer and healthier school canteens. Food safety test kits and healthy school canteen educational materials have been distributed to schools participating in the initiative.

In addition to UKS, the School Operational Assistance Program (*Bantuan Operasional Sekolah,* or BOS) disburses block grants to schools across the country on a per student basis. Operational since 2005, BOS is the centerpiece of donor and development partner support for the national school system. BOS supports the government's efforts to improve access to quality education by students at all income levels, with funds available for extracurricular activities that contribute to students' physical health.

**Results and challenges.** The central government is now creating a new basic education development framework, System Improvement through Sector Wide Approaches (SISWA), in conjunction with its medium-term education sector plan (2010–14). SISWA covers key strategies and programs for improving access to and the quality of basic education and is intended to provide a coherent policy framework for donor support. One of its key areas of focus is helping districts by providing them more and better information on how to improve education.

Of note, school child health and nutrition are beginning to be discussed as part of these efforts to improve the quality and equity of basic education. Standards for minimum services in basic education now include expectations of a clean water supply, hand-washing facilities, and appropriate and adequate toilet facilities at all schools. The considerable commitment of the government and its development partners to improving the quality and effectiveness of basic education in Indonesia is providing a platform for redirecting and increasing investments in school health and nutrition. Their work seeks to accomplish the following:

- Target SHN interventions to areas where education outcomes are low and poor health conditions and nutrition status and/or hunger are high
- Strengthen collaboration within the education sector and between the education and health ministries; this collaboration is most essential at the local and school level, but is also important at higher levels
- Take advantage of the returns from certain low-cost SHN interventions by identifying and implementing district-level approaches to remediation (for example, providing mass delivery of deworming medicine, iron supplementation, and treatment and prevention of malaria), where appropriate
- Identify and develop a set of "packages" or "models" that take into account the three main geographic contexts of Indonesia—urban, rural, and island or coastal—as well as the type of school (for example, boarding school)
- Continue and expand on current efforts to ensure clean water and adequate sanitation in all schools
- Improve the quality of health education through behavior-focused communications; health, hygiene, nutrition, and other education is required to promote practices such as the use of clean water, hand washing, and other healthy behaviors among schoolchildren
- Develop a separate model (or models) for stemming the tide of the overweight and obese children; although not directly related to education, the seriousness of the increase in overweight in children in Indonesia suggests that strategies to promote appropriate nutrition and physical activity practices should be an element of SHN

## Conclusion: School Health and Nutrition Programs in Practice

This chapter has explored the lessons that can be learned from the implementation of school health and nutrition programs in practice. In high- and middle-income countries, school health and nutrition programs are near universal. This is also true of low-income countries, where there is a growing movement away from small, complex, and medicalized programs that principally benefit elite urban or boarding schools toward a focus on a few key interventions aligned with the goals of Education for All. Among the examples reviewed in the previous pages are programs that have demonstrated both sustainability and scalability.

**For most countries the challenge is to optimize existing programs.** Most countries are not starting from scratch. They already have a school health and nutrition program—which often includes a school feeding component—that needs to be modified to address new priorities and needs. In most cases the aim is to expand the geographical coverage of an existing program so that it reaches poor and marginalized children. Among the things that countries have done to achieve this goal are the following:

- Change an existing program from being primarily health-system based to an education sector model that uses the network of schools as an extensive delivery platform (for example, Sri Lanka).
- Complement an existing urban school health program with a new rural model to reach new areas of the country (for example, Guyana).
- Supplement an existing comprehensive model that has yet to go to scale with a simplified model that can rapidly be rolled out nationally (for example, the Philippines).

**The political economy is crucial to the success of multisectoral programs.** The diverse experiences of school health and school feeding programs suggest that certain policy elements are common contributors to success:

- *A focus on education outcomes.* Making an explicit link between school health and nutrition programs, on one hand, and education sector priorities (especially EFA goals and gender equity), on the other, helps ensure the commitment of the education sector to program implementation.

- *Development of a formal multisectoral policy and a memorandum of understanding between the health and education sectors.* Education sector actions in the health sphere require the explicit agreement of the health sector. Potential tensions can be resolved by agreeing on sectoral responsibilities at the outset, usually via a formal policy implemented through a memorandum of understanding. Failure of the two sectors to enter into dialogue can effectively stop programs, while consensus can result in programs rapidly going to scale.

- *Initiation of a process of wide information dissemination and consultation, especially with local communities.* There are multiple stakeholders, implementers, enablers, and gatekeepers in a school health and nutrition program. A process of consultation will establish ownership and identify obstacles before they constrain progress. The consultative process should involve at least community-based organizations (CBOs), NGOs, faith-based organizations (FBOs), the local community, pupils, and teacher associations. Parents want to be reassured that the education sector has the support of the health sector when implementing health interventions.

**Simple programs that build on existing platforms are more likely to go to scale and reach the schoolchildren most in need.** This is an area in which the best frequently drives out the good, resulting in programs that are too complex to go to scale. The key goals are to

- *Use existing infrastructure as much as possible.* Building on existing curriculum opportunities and teacher networks will accelerate implementation and reduce costs. Programs that rely on the development of new delivery systems—such as mobile school health teams or a cadre of school nurses—are expensive and complicated to take to scale. Such programs also almost inevitably fail to reach the neediest, since costs rise in proportion to the remoteness of targeted beneficiaries.

- *Build programs around simple, safe, and familiar health and nutrition interventions.* Success in rapidly reaching all schools is crucially dependent on stakeholder acceptance, which is more likely if the interventions are already sanctioned by local and international agencies and in common use in targeted communities.

**Most programs rely on the public sector, but there can be an important role for civil society and the private sector.** There are compelling arguments for public investment in school health and nutrition programs, such as their contribution to economic growth, high rates of return, and large externalities. The majority of interventions are identifiably public goods. Conversely, there is evidence of market failure that precludes private provision of programs. Although public resources may play the major role, contributions from other sectors can be important. NGOs have proven particularly effective in supporting school health and school feeding programs, particularly at the local level. While market failure has precluded the private sector from effectively implementing entire programs, there are examples (for example, Japan, the Republic of Korea, and Indonesia) of successful contributions by private actors, particularly in dense urban populations and middle-income countries.

**Targeting often lies at the heart of practical success.** Targeting reduces costs, facilitates management, and may optimize outcomes. The deworming program in Kenya, for example, reached more than 70 percent of needy children by operating in less than one-third of the country. The school feeding program in Guyana reached its entire target population by working in 4 of the 11 regions of the country. In Sri Lanka, a deliberate decision to precede the School Health Promotion Program with a national mapping exercise led to a matching of program components to local needs—the difference was perhaps most starkly demonstrated in nutrition, with malnutrition the target in the north and obesity the target in the capital.

**School health and nutrition programs can be effectively mainstreamed into the education sector.** Education sector planners are increasingly recognizing the relevance of school health and nutrition to their education goals and beginning to take responsibility for implementing these programs. Increasingly planners are locating these programs in education service administrations and including them in education sector plans. Since the funding channels for certain aspects of the programs are often unfamiliar to the education sector, such as funding for the procurement of drugs and food, one solution is to embed the various components of SHN programs within an overall sectorwide approach. This approach has the added advantage of allowing access to pooled funding from multiple sectors, potentially including the health sector.

## Note

1. The unit cost per child per day is G$175 (US$0.87) for 180 school days in a year, or G$31,500 (US$156.60) per year.

## References

Belizario, V. Y. J., W. U. de Leon, Y. F. Lumampao, M. B. Anastacio, and C. M. Tai. 2009. "Sentinel Surveillance of Soil-Transmitted Helminthiasis in Selected

Local Government Units in the Philippines." *Asia Pacific Journal of Public Health* 21 (1): 26–42.

Brooker, S., A. C. A. Clements, and D. A. P. Bundy. 2006. "Global Epidemiology, Ecology, and Control of Soil-Transmitted Helminth Infections." *Advances in Parasitology* 62: 221–61.

Bundy, D. A. P., C. Burbano, M. Grosh, A. Gelli, M. Jukes, and L. Drake. 2009. *Rethinking School Feeding: Social Safety Nets, Child Development, and the Education Sector.* Washington, DC: World Bank.

Curtis, V., and S. Cairncross. 2003. "Effect of Washing Hands with Soap on Diarrhoea Risk in the Community: A Systematic Review." *Lancet Infectious Diseases* 3 (5): 275–81.

Del Rosso, J. M., and R. Arlianti. 2009. "Investing in School Health and Nutrition in Indonesia." World Bank, Jakarta.

Department of Education of the Philippines, Health and Nutrition Center. 2008. *National Oral Health Survey among the Public School Population in the Philippines.* Manila: Department of Education.

de Silva, N., S. Brooker, P. J. Hotez, A. Montresor, D. Engels, and L. Savioli. 2003. "Soil-Transmitted Helminth Infections: Updating the Global Picture." *Trends in Parasitology* 19 (12): 547–51.

Filmer, D., and L. Pritchett. 1999. "The Effect of Household Wealth on Educational Attainment: Evidence from 35 Countries." *Population and Development Review* 25 (1): 85–120.

Fit for School. 2009. "Project Information Brief." Department of Education, Manila.

Galloway, R., E. Kristjansson, A. Gelli, U. Meir, F. Espejo, and D. A. P. Bundy. 2009. "School Feeding: Outcomes and Costs." *Food and Nutrition Bulletin* 30 (2): 171–82.

Guyatt, H. 2003. "The Cost of Delivering and Sustaining a Control Programme for Schistosomiasis and Soil-Transmitted Helminthiasis." *Acta Tropica* 86 (2–3): 267–74.

Hotez, P. J., D. A. P. Bundy, K. Beegle, S. Brooker, L. Drake, N. de Silva, A. Montresor, D. Engels, M. Jukes, L. Chitsulo, J. Chow, R. Laxminarayan, C. Michaud, J. Bethony, R. Correa-Oliveira, X. Shuhua, A. Fenwick, and L. Savioli. 2006. "Helminth Infections: Soil-Transmitted Helminth Infections and Schistosomiasis." In *Disease Control Priorities in Developing Countries*, 2nd ed., ed. D. Jamison, J. G. Breman, A. R. Measham, G. Alleyne, M. Claeson, D. Evans, P. Jha, A. Mills, and P. Musgrove, 467–82. New York: World Bank and Oxford University Press.

Jukes, M. C. H., L. J. Drake, and D. A. P. Bundy. 2008. *School Health, Nutrition and Education for All: Leveling the Playing Field.* Cambridge, MA: CABI Publishing.

Miguel, E., and M. Kremer. 2004. "Worms: Identifying Impacts on Education and Health in the Presence of Treatment Externalities." *Econometrica* 72 (1): 159–217.

Monse, B., E. Naliponguit, V. Belizario, H. Benzian, and W. van Palenstein Helderman. 2010. "Essential Health Care Package for Children: The 'Fit for School' Programme in the Philippines." *International Dental Journal* 60 (2): 85–93.

Partnership for Child Development. 1999. "The Cost of Large-Scale School Health Programmes Which Deliver Anthelminthics to Children in Ghana and Tanzania." *Acta Tropica* 73 (2): 183–204.

Republic of Kenya. 2009. *National School Health Policy*. Ministry of Public Health and Sanitation and Ministry of Education, Nairobi.

Savioli, L., D. Bundy, and A. Tomkins. 1992. "Intestinal Parasitic Infections: A Soluble Public Health Problem." *Transactions of the Royal Society of Tropical Medicine and Hygiene* 86 (4): 353–54.

World Bank. 1986. *Ottawa Charter*. Geneva: WHO.

———. 2000. "The FRESH Framework: A Toolkit for Task Managers." Human Development Network, World Bank, Washington, DC.

WHO (World Health Organization). 1986. "Ottawa Charter for Health Promotion." Presented at the First International Conference on Health Promotion, Ottawa, November 21.

# CHAPTER 5

# Partnerships to Develop Consensus and Share Knowledge

Few educators have learned about school health and nutrition programs as part of their training, and few education planning manuals go beyond broad references to these programs. Yet these are not simple programs to manage and implement, not least because they deal with unfamiliar topics that span sectors beyond education. It is perhaps no coincidence that the development of this technical area has been accompanied by more than the usual number of support partnerships and networks.

This chapter introduces some of these partnerships and provides some guidance on how to access information about them. The partnerships listed here have sustained engagement over time or, if relatively new, have rapidly developed a wide base of support. These partnerships include governments, civil society, the private sector, and development partners—most often, a mix of all of these.

To try and assist the navigation of these opportunities, the partnerships are grouped by their primary function. There is, however, considerable overlap; many of the partnerships could justify inclusion in several of the arbitrarily assigned categories. The partnerships are categorized as (i) those that support design and implementation issues for school health and nutrition issues generally; (ii) those that focus on HIV/AIDS and education specifically; (iii) those that seek to share knowledge among countries, usually through a regional network; and (iv) those that directly support national programs. The text then describes the objectives, activities, and examples of results and challenges of each partnership.

## Design and Implementation Issues for School Health and Nutrition Programs

These partnerships have provided guidance on the overall design of school health and nutrition programs. The Focusing Resources on Effective School Health (FRESH) partnership was launched in 2000 as part of the World Education Forum in Dakar, Senegal. It was never intended to do more that provide general guidance and has survived in this role. The World Health Organization (WHO) was the lead agency in school health during the 1990s, with its Global School Health Program and a series of excellent technical guidance notes that focused on school health to promote health. This program has now morphed into Health Promoting Schools, with the specific aim of promoting education. The Child Friendly Schools of the United Nations Children's Fund (UNICEF) use the FRESH framework as a guiding principle, but go beyond it to provide much more detailed inputs for an effective, child-centered approach. Finally, the most recent partnership, the Multi-Agency Initiative for Monitoring and Evaluation, arose in 2009 in response to demand for clearer guidance on how the education sector should monitor and evaluate school health programs.

### Focusing Resources on Effective School Health (FRESH)*

**Objectives.** FRESH is one of the earliest and longest-lived partnerships in the area of school health and nutrition, established during the 1990s at a time when there was a proliferation of new agency initiatives that sought to promote school health. The aim of this partnership was to demystify school health to governments and encourage harmonization of the actions of development partners. The "Focusing Resources on Effective School Health (FRESH)" framework (World Bank 2000) was developed jointly by the United Nations Educational, Scientific and Cultural Organization (UNESCO), the WHO, UNICEF, Education International, and the World Bank. The framework was launched in 2000

---

* This section was contributed by Lesley Drake, Anna Maria Hoffmann, and Kwok-Cho Tang.

and conveyed the message that good school health and nutrition is a key component of efforts to achieve Education for All (EFA). Since then, UNESCO has adopted FRESH as one of its flagship programs in support of EFA; other agencies, including the World Food Programme (WFP), the Partnership for Child Development (PCD), and Save the Children USA, have since joined the partnership.

***Description.*** The FRESH framework is based on good practices recognized by all partners and provides a consensus approach to the effective implementation of health and nutrition services within schools. The framework calls for all of the following four core components to be made available together in all schools:

- *Policy*: health- and nutrition-related school policies that provide a nondiscriminatory, safe, and secure environment.
- *School environment*: access to safe water and the provision of separate sanitation facilities for girls and boys.
- *Education*: skills-based education that addresses health, nutrition, and hygiene issues and promotes positive behaviors.
- *Services*: simple, safe, and familiar health and nutrition services that can be delivered cost-effectively in schools (such as deworming, micronutrient supplements, and snacks to avoid hunger), together with increased access to youth-friendly clinics.

Adoption of this framework does not imply that these core components and strategies are the only important elements of a school health and nutrition program, but that implementing all four components in all schools will provide a sound initial basis for any such pro-poor program. Furthermore, these components can be implemented effectively only if supported by strategic partnerships between (i) the health and education sectors, especially teachers and health workers; (ii) schools and their respective communities; and (iii) pupils and others responsible for program implementation.

The common focus of the FRESH framework has encouraged concerted action by participating agencies. It has also provided a common platform on which to build agency-specific programs, such as the Health Promoting School initiative of the WHO and the Child Friendly School of UNICEF. But perhaps the most important consequence of FRESH has been to offer a common "point of entry" for new efforts to improve health in schools.

*Results.* The FRESH framework provides strategic guidance on the design of programs to improve the education, health, and nutrition of school-age children. There is, however, considerable variation in the practical design of actual programs, reflecting differences in local needs and capacity. In a majority of cases, school health and nutrition programs are delivered and funded by the public education sector, with a formal role for the health sector in their design and supervision. In some countries, it was considered too difficult to immediately incorporate school health into existing education systems. As a result, more or less separate and time-bound school health and nutrition programs were established to initiate the process, responsibility for which will be progressively handed over to the education sector.

While this public sector "mainstream" model has proven to be the most popular approach to school health, it is not the only successful approach. In some cases, the public sector has identified appropriate options and developed operational manuals, then used a social fund to provide direct support to communities and schools. These funds select and implement the most relevant actions locally, often with the assistance of nongovernmental organizations (NGOs). In some middle-income countries the move toward a demand-led approach has gone even further, with NGOs providing a private sector service that is dependent on the contributions of parents and/or guardians.

Table 5.1 gives examples of several low- and middle-income countries that have been selected to illustrate the diversity of school health programming. Their programs show how the four core components of FRESH are being supported through both direct public sector and funded private sector interventions.

For more information on FRESH, visit the initiative's website: http://www.freshschools.org.

### Health Promoting Schools and the WHO-Led "Call to Action"*

In 1995, the WHO facilitated a process that led to the establishment of the Global School Health Initiative. This initiative advanced a comprehensive and integrated methodology for school health that has become widely known as Health Promoting Schools (HPS). Both the initiative and HPS methodology were built on the pioneering work and experience of many other programs (described elsewhere in this chapter), including the

---

* This section was contributed by Kwok-Cho Tang.

**Table 5.1  How FRESH Is Used in Low- and Middle-Income Countries**

| Approach | Social fund: Public sector support for community intervention | Private sector: Community payment for NGO-implemented intervention | Public sector: Public sector supported and implemented | Program approach: Parastatal support for public sector intervention |
|---|---|---|---|---|
| Country example | Tajikistan | Indonesia | Guinea, Ghana, and Tanzania | Madagascar |
| Policy | The Ministry of Labor and Social Protection of Tajikistan, together with the Ministries of Education and Health, have developed a Memorandum of Understanding that sets out health policies for the education sector. The program channels resources through PTAs, which identify and assist needy children. A training program, delivered by NGOs, prepares PTA members to develop proposals of up to US$5,000 for their school that support activities selected from a menu of items. | The NGO Yayasan Kusuma Buana has a formal agreement with the education department of Jakarta and three other major cities to train teachers, perform diagnostic tests, and provide medicines and materials. The NGO offers pap smear tests and referral services to teachers. Unit costs are low because parasite diagnosis is conducted via mass screening in a central laboratory (with approximately 2,500 diagnoses per day), and medicines are obtained at preferential rates from two commercial partners. | In all three countries, the respective Ministry of Education (or in Ghana, its executive body, the Ghana Education Service) implements the program under the guidance of the Ministry of Health, based on a formal policy agreement. In Tanzania the Ministries of Community Development and Local Government are also parties to the agreement. Existing in-service teacher training and supply-line infrastructures are used to prepare teachers and supply the necessary materials. | The community nutrition program SEECALINE II provides training and support to the Ministry of Education, based on a formally agreed health policy for the education sector. In all schools in the 43 poorest districts (which make up 44 percent of all districts), the program prepares teachers and provides materials. In addition, the program also provides PTAs with access to a social fund to support construction of facilities. Each PTA can request up to US$500, with a 20 percent community contribution based on a parental contribution of US$0.16 per year. |

*(continued next page)*

**Table 5.1  How FRESH Is Used in Low- and Middle-Income Countries** (continued)

| Approach | Social fund: Public sector support for community intervention | Private sector: Community payment for NGO-implemented intervention | Public sector: Public sector supported and implemented | Program approach: Parastatal support for public sector intervention |
|---|---|---|---|---|
| Environment | Provision of sanitation facilities, potable water, sports facilities. | Not included in program. | Separate sanitation facilities for girls and boys in all new schools; access to potable water in all schools. | Access to potable water and hand washing facilities in all schools; where requested by PTAs, construction of latrines, wells, fences, and sports facilities. |
| Health education | Training of teachers in health promotion. | Nutrition and hygiene education as part of the curriculum. | Health, hygiene, and nutrition education as part of the formal curriculum. | A formal health education curriculum, supported by community information, education, and communication. |
| Health services | Training of teachers to provide first aid, micronutrients, and deworming; provision of food preparation facilities. | Stool examination by laboratory; deworming by teachers as necessary twice a year; iron folate provided by teachers twice a year (for 3 months each time). | Deworming (for both schistosomiasis and intestinal worms) provided by teachers twice a year; in Guinea, this is followed by iron folate supplementation. | Twice yearly deworming and iron folate supplementation (for 3 months) delivered by teachers; tests kits to confirm iodization of local sources of salt; where requested by PTAs, provision of food preparation facilities. |

| Outcomes | The program targets the 100,000 neediest children in all 200 schools in the 6 poorest districts of Tajikistan, at an approximate per capita cost of US$1.00 per year. | The program has been in existence for 17 years and currently reaches 627 schools and 161,000 students, at a cost to parents of US$0.10 per year. | In three years, the Guinea program has reached 600 schools and 350,000 students, the Ghana program has reached 577 schools and 83,000 students (at a cost of US$0.54 per child treated), and the Tanzania program has reached 353 schools and 113,000 students (at a cost of US$0.89 per child treated). | In three years, the program has trained 14,000 teachers in 4,585 schools and reached 430,000 students at an estimated cost of US$0.78 to US$1.08 per capita per year. |

*Source:* Jukes, Drake, and Bundy 2008.
*Note:* PTA = parent-teacher association.

European Network of HPS, which was established in 1992. Since the launch of the initiative, programs to migrate, adapt, and advance HPS methodology have been implemented in all six WHO regions, and HPS Networks have been established within and between countries.

In 2007, the WHO and the Pan-Canadian Joint Consortium for School Health (JCSH) co-hosted a Technical Meeting on Building School Partnerships for Health, Education Achievements, and Development (Vancouver, June 5–8, 2007), with the participation of education and health experts from about 30 countries and a number of United Nations agencies. The meeting built on earlier work to develop strategies that would enable schools to respond more effectively to current and emerging health concerns and development challenges. The meeting statement and the "Call for Action" appended to it reflected collective concerns and ideas on effective school approaches and strategies for promoting health, education, and development (see box 5.1 for an excerpt from the full text of the meeting statement).

For more information on the methodology of Health Promoting Schools, visit the WHO website at http://www.who.int/school_youth_health/gshi/.

Many other organizations are also active in the area of school health, including

- ARC (Arab Resource Collective), Lebanon, which has expertise in children affected by conflict, inclusive education, adolescents' health, early childhood care and development (http://www.mawared.org).
- Child-to-Child Trust, United Kingdom, which has expertise in health education and promotion in schools, early childhood care and development, children in communities affected by HIV/AIDS, adolescent reproductive and sexual health, inclusive education, children in difficult circumstances (http://www.child-to-child.org).
- HAS (Health Action Schools) at Aga Khan University Institute for Educational Development, Pakistan, which has expertise in health promotion in schools (http://www.aku.edu.pk/ied/academics/has/index.shtml).

### Child Friendly Schools*

**Objectives.** Child Friendly Schools is a broad concept through which UNICEF promotes quality education in development planning as well as emergency situations. The approach is an attempt to translate into education

---

* This section was contributed by Anna Maria Hoffmann.

**Box 5.1**

# Excerpt from Statement of Technical Meeting on Building School Partnerships for Health, Education Achievements, and Development (Vancouver, 2007)

### Schools Make a Difference: Evidence of Progress

Every child has the human right to education, health, and security. The central role of schools is teaching and learning, but they are also a unique community resource to promote health and development for children, families, and teachers. Education, health, and other sectors must work together as partners to develop the full potential of young people, mitigating the impact of social and economic disadvantage. There has been significant progress in achieving improved health and educational outcomes over the past decade through school-based health, education, and development initiatives. The consensus on the core components of an effective school program—policy, skills-based health education, a supportive social and physical environment, community partnerships, and health services—derives from decades of experience of implementing school health initiatives. Different countries and international organizations use different terms, although all are based on the same fundamental evidence and principles.

The relationship between school enrollment and participation and improved health outcomes is well established, especially for girls. Since 2000, there has been sustained, albeit inconsistent, progress in achieving higher rates of school participation in all parts of the world.

The strong association between good health and academic achievement and school completion is now well understood. School health and education programs contribute to the achievement of Education for All and the Millennium Development Goals (MDGs).

Better evidence has led to improved school programs that have helped local communities and countries promote healthy lifestyles and environments and combat communicable diseases, such as diarrhea, worm infections, and sexually transmitted diseases, including HIV. School programs have been important agents for change in addressing risk factors for noncommunicable diseases, such as unhealthy eating and tobacco consumption, as well as improving mental health and reducing alcohol and illicit drug use, violence, and injuries.

Effective practice has included approaches that combine traditional health education with more comprehensive, whole-school approaches that create a supportive physical, social, and learning environment and bring together the combined resources of parents, local communities, and organizations.

*(continued next page)*

**Box 5.1** *(continued)*

School health promotion strategies are now better tailored to meet the needs of specific regions and health issues.

**Meeting Current and Emerging Challenges**

Much progress has been made, but much remains to be done. Five key challenges have been identified as important in maintaining progress across all regions and countries:

- Building evidence and experience
- Strengthening implementation processes
- Alleviating social and economic disadvantage
- Harnessing media influence
- Improving partnerships among different sectors and organizations

**A Call for Action**

Achieving the potential offered by schools requires leadership at national, community, and school levels, reflected in a genuine commitment to investing in education and the health of school students and their teachers.

The participants in this Meeting call for leadership by local school communities, governments, and international organizations in five broad areas of action to attain education, health, and development goals over the next decade:

- Invest in education to achieve the highest possible levels of enrollment, participation, and school achievement. This will bring health, social, and economic development benefits at all levels of society.
- Build school infrastructure to create a stimulating, socially supportive, hygienic, and safe environment that fosters high-quality learning, social development, and healthy choices for students, parents, and teachers.
- Invest in capacity to support professional development programs [that] will build the capabilities of teachers and health professionals to plan, implement, and evaluate school health initiatives. This includes support for the effective use of traditional media as well as new media, and increasing access to those technologies; and full use of existing databases, as well as the collection and use of disaggregated social and economic data on health and education achievements for planning [and] reporting on progress and research.
- Implement what we know to be effective through investment in the dissemination of good practice throughout the education and health sectors; by adaptation

*(continued next page)*

**Box 5.1** *(continued)*

of successful programs to the local context, culture, and political conditions; and by achieving the collaboration required for implementation.

• Harmonize action among partners for sustainable partnerships by improving the communication of ideas and the benefits of school health programs across the health and education sectors; by supporting a variety of communities of practice that are relevant to the local needs and priorities of schools; and by developing and strengthening networks to exchange information and knowledge, especially in low-income countries and among United Nations organizations.

*Source:* Tang et al. 2009.

system responses the four core principles of the Convention on the Rights of the Child (CRC):

- Nondiscrimination
- The best interests of the child
- The right to life, survival, and development
- Respect for the views of the child

The 20th anniversary of the CRC in 2009 is a reminder that children should be placed at the heart of human development. The overall goal of a Child Friendly School (CFS) is to ensure that education systems worldwide respect the rights of their children by helping lower the numbers who die of preventable causes, do not attend school, attend a school that cannot offer them an education of good quality, are left abandoned when their parents succumb to AIDS, or are subject to violence, exploitation, and abuse against which they are unable to protect themselves.

To address the myriad problems affecting the lives of the world's children, which threaten progress toward achieving EFA goals and the MDGs, approaches are needed that focus on the whole child and make use of interventions from sectors other than education. The CFS responds to these challenges by promoting child-friendly learning and by teaching within enabling, protective educational environments that also provide access to services.

***Description.*** A CFS is a school or learning space that is protective and enabling, with inclusive and participatory policies and essential facilities, such as safe water and sanitation. It is a school that promotes children's fullest potential through relevant child-centered, participatory, and skills-building learning content and teaching methods. It is also increasingly a center for the delivery of a broad range of essential services. In this respect, the CFS is also a health-promoting school. It contributes to promoting children's physical, mental, and social health by proposing multiple, coordinated, and concrete interventions at the school level in line with the FRESH framework. It particularly calls for the following:

- School principals to ensure inclusive and participatory school policies that both protect children and staff against any form of violence or discrimination and establish respectful codes of conduct and security precautions, such as first aid and regular safety drills.
- School administrators to ensure and maintain safe and sustainable school infrastructure, including safe water, sanitation, the prudent location of schools relative to areas at high risk of disasters, and the use of safe materials and design in school construction.
- Teachers to ensure the teaching of relevant life skills with respect to reducing children's health-related and other risks.
- Local health, nutrition, social, and psychosocial service providers to establish relevant responses to health threats and ensure that all available services are used.
- The community at large to ensure a supportive social context that allows children to transform their life skills into positive behaviors.

Systemic interventions to promote children's physical health and emotional well-being hold out the promise of large-scale change and better coordination of external support. However, such interventions require time before their impact on children can be seen. When children are facing direct threats, such as those posed by HIV/AIDS, or when countries are impacted by a disaster, civil conflict, or a complex emergency, rapid action needs to be combined with strategic planning and coordinated implementation. In these situations, it is crucial to support school-based initiatives that are integral to systemic interventions, but designed to produce major improvements in the health and well-being of children in a relatively short time span.

Such initiatives should also increase the chances of countries to achieve the MDGs. The basic components of FRESH provide a simple quality framework for rapidly making schools a healthier place, one where children can learn better and parents and communities can be assured of the safety and care of their children. Because schools hold large numbers of children at any given time, they are ideal places to provide and promote such essential services for children as deworming, vaccinations, and feeding initiatives—services that in turn help increase the effectiveness of the education provided.

***Results.*** The benefits of coordinating multiple targeted school strategies (for example, combining the curriculum with policies on healthy, safe, and protective learning environments, as well as delivering community health and social services) are now reflected in UNICEF's education strategy. The strategy commits UNICEF to supporting countries to fulfill the education rights of children through national standards that make all schools effective, efficient, safe, and supportive of the provision of multiple services.

By the end of 2008, 61 of 147 reporting countries had adopted CFS standards, up from 43 of 132 reporting countries in 2005. In order to strengthen governments' capacity to plan for, scale up, and mainstream CFS models into national education plans and policies, UNICEF rolled out a training program for six regions (covering 64 countries) in 2009, which will continue operations in 2010.

For more information on CFSs, visit http://www.unicef.org/lifeskills/index_7260.html.

### Multiagency Initiative for Monitoring and Evaluation*
***Objectives.*** A common concern voiced by policy makers, program managers, and donors is the difficulty of ensuring effective monitoring and evaluation (M&E) of school health and nutrition programs (Tang et al. 2009). This problem stems from a number of causes, especially a lack of familiarity with health metrics among education planners and lack of consensus on which processes are most important to measure, as well as which indicators are most appropriate for tracking these processes.

A participatory review by the FRESH partners (see the earlier section on this initiative)[1] conducted 38 key informant interviews and examined 125 M&E resources. The review concluded that there was demand for a generic M&E framework in order to build consensus on monitoring and evaluation, as well as to provide guidance to targeted users, including international organizations, national governments, schools, and individual

---

* This section was contributed by Michael Beasley, Mohini Venkatesh, Natalie Roschnik, Anna Maria Hoffmann, Ekua Yankah, Katri Tala, and Kwok-Cho Tang.

programs (Partnership for Child Development and Save the Children USA 2008).

*Process.* A meeting of the FRESH partners hosted by the WHO in 2008 agreed that the M&E framework should be consistent with the principles of the four FRESH components: health-related school policies, school-based delivery of health services, a safe and sanitary school environment, and skills-based health education. An outline of the framework was proposed that featured two main components: (i) a menu of SHN indicators to monitor interventions that address different thematic areas, which could be used by different countries or programs to meet their particular contexts (see box 5.2); (ii) a limited number of summary indicators drawn from this menu (no more than 10 in total), which would enable tracking and comparison of national and programmatic progress.

---

**Box 5.2**

## Thematic Areas for Monitoring and Evaluation

- Disability
- Education (including concerns such as absenteeism, dropout rates, and achievement)
- Conflict and natural disasters
- Physical environment (including sustainable development)
- First aid
- Sexual and reproductive health
- Hygiene, water, and sanitation
- Malaria
- Violence (against children)
- Social and emotional learning (including mental health and psychosocial well-being)
- Nutrition
- Oral health
- Physical activity
- HIV
- Substance abuse (for example, tobacco, alcohol, drugs)
- Vision, hearing, and skin health
- Worms

For each of the thematic areas, the partners recommended that indicators should be (i) limited in number; (ii) targeted to monitor interventions that are likely to have the greatest impact on the particular thematic area; and (iii) designed to monitor processes and outcomes of interventions, rather than their potential contribution to higher-level impacts on health or education, as the latter are dependent on a number of interventions in society and many (for example, the proportion of the adult population completing primary school education or school life expectancy at age 5) are already measured by established surveys and surveillance systems.

***Developing indicators.***  In the year since the FRESH partners made these decisions, different expert groups have been working together to compile indicators for each of the thematic areas. This participatory approach is illustrated here regarding the process used to develop indicators in the thematic area of the education sector's response to HIV.

The development of indicators in this area occurred under the aegis of the UNAIDS Inter-Agency Task Team (IATT) for HIV and Education (see section on this task team in this chapter). The IATT's coordination enabled a wide number of stakeholders to participate in the identification of indicators, which occurred in a three-stage process: (i) an extensive review of existing indicators for the education sector's response to HIV; (ii) an international meeting among technical experts on M&E on education sector responses to HIV in Southern Africa, the Caribbean, and South and Southeast Asia, who shortlisted the indicators using nine criteria (see box 5.3); and (iii) a meeting of the UNAIDS IATT for HIV and Education to confirm the selection of indicators before their dissemination (see table 5.2).

After country and agency feedback, a finalized list of indicators for the education sector response to HIV/AIDS will be included in the generic M&E framework for school health programs in general. This process will enable countries with different capacities in research and evaluation to consider the appropriateness of the proposed indicators.

Similar processes to those described here are being undertaken by other expert groups in other thematic areas. Once thematic indicators are developed as described previously, a limited number of summary indicators will be selected to enable international, national, and programmatic measurement and comparison of the progress of countries and programs toward implementation of the FRESH framework.

For further information, see "Monitoring and Evaluation of School-Based Health and Nutrition Programmes: A Participative Review"

**Box 5.3**

## Nine Criteria for Identifying M&E Indicators for HIV and AIDS Education Responses

1. Is this indicator needed to measure the education sector contribution to the national HIV and AIDS strategy or a key international commitment?
2. Is it clear how data from this indictor will be used by the education sector to manage its response to HIV and AIDS?
3. Is there national or international agreement on this indicator?
4. Is there consensus among technical experts in this thematic area that this indicator should be monitored?
5. Will this indicator measure what it intends to measure? (Valid: it measures what it should measure; reliable: it produces the same or very similar results even if measured by different instruments, procedures, or observers; robust: it is capable of measuring trends over time.)
6. Is the indicator fully defined?
7. Are systems available to allow this indicator to be measured?
8. Does the measurement of this indicator create an additional human and financial resource burden?
9. Has this indicator been used in practice?

*Note:* To be fully defined, an indicator should have a title and definition; purpose and rationale; a method of measurement; a data collection method; a measurement frequency; data disaggregation; guidelines for its interpretation and use; identified strengths, weaknesses and challenges; and sources of further information.

(Partnership for Child Development and Save the Children USA 2008). The review was conducted for the "FRESH Partners Meeting" held at the WHO in Geneva, September 8–9, 2008.

## Design and Implementation Issues for HIV/AIDS and Education Programs

This group of partnerships arose in response to the HIV/AIDS epidemic.[2] As of 2000, it had become clear to many experts that the education sector had a potentially important role to play in responding to HIV because it reaches almost all young people between 5 and 18 years of age, has a specific mandate to support teaching and learning, and is one of the largest public sector employers. This section describes two interagency initiatives supported by UNAIDS and UNESCO—the Inter-Agency Task

**Table 5.2    Indicators for M&E Priority Areas**

| M&E priority area | Recommended indicator | Alternative or improvement to existing indicator |
|---|---|---|
| *Process* | | |
| Policy | Education-relevant sections of the National Composite Policy Index (UNGASS#2). | Could be improved if UNGASS#2 was adjusted to reflect the education sector more fully. |
| Prevention education | Percentage of schools that provided life skills–based HIV education in the past academic year (UNGASS#11). AND Percentage of schools that also provided cosponsored and/or extracurricular life skills-based HIV education in the past academic year. | Because UNGASS#11 is so imprecise, it was suggested that a better indicator would be "knowledge about HIV tested in national school-leaving examinations." |
| Teacher training | Percentage of teachers graduating from training institutions that receive training to teach HIV prevention education and life skills curricula. | |
| Safe environments | Percentage of schools with standards that include components on physical safety, zero tolerance for discrimination, stigma, or any form of sexual harassment and/or abuse. | |
| *Outcomes* | | |
| Student knowledge (intermediate outcome) | Percentage of young people ages 15–24 who both correctly identify ways of preventing the sexual transmission of HIV and who reject major misconceptions about HIV transmission (UNGASS#13). | Indicator could be improved if respondents were asked the sources of their information: friends, media, school, health sector, and so forth. |
| Student behavior (long-term outcome) | Percentage of students (13–15 years) who have ever had sexual intercourse. (UNGASS#15) | |

*Source:* Partnership for Child Development 2009.

Team for Education and HIV and the Global Initiative on Education and HIV&AIDS (EDUCAIDS)—as well as a global initiative led by the largest federation of teachers unions, EFAIDS.

### The Inter-Agency Task Team for HIV and Education*

*Objectives.* Formed in 2002, the UNAIDS IATT for HIV and Education is convened by UNESCO and brings together UNAIDS cosponsors and multilateral organizations, bilateral agencies, private donors, and civil society organizations with the purpose of accelerating a coordinated, harmonized education sector response to HIV and AIDS.

*Description.* The activities undertaken by the UNAIDS IATT seek to strengthen policy and programmatic action in the area of education and HIV and AIDS, enhance coordination in support of the attainment of EFA goals, and contribute to the achievement of the MDGs related to quality primary education, gender equity, and HIV and AIDS. These objectives are entirely consistent with the policies and strategies of IATT members and the various international commitments to which they have subscribed.

*Results.* Core strategic areas of the IATT in recent years include

- Supporting the mainstreaming of HIV and AIDS prevention in education policies, plans, and programs, for example, by ensuring that HIV and AIDS are adequately mainstreamed in the Education for All–Fast Track Initiative (EFA-FTI) endorsement process and by developing practical tools to support the mainstreaming of HIV and AIDS prevention in education plans by development agencies.

- Generating awareness and mobilizing commitment to the education response among stakeholders within and beyond the education sector by advocating the importance of a comprehensive education response to HIV and AIDS. The IATT has accordingly sought to attend important international and regional events, such as those organized by the Association for the Development of Education in Africa (ADEA), international and regional AIDS conferences, and meetings on major education initiatives, such as EFA-FTI.

---

* This section was contributed by Christopher Castle and Justine Sass.

- Examining and strengthening existing tools for the monitoring and evaluation of HIV- and AIDS-related education initiatives. The IATT has pursued this goal by producing a number of publications, including a global survey to assess the readiness of the education sector to respond to the HIV and AIDS pandemic; providing technical support to the *EFA Global Monitoring Report* to address progress on HIV and AIDS issues in a systematic manner; identifying promising program and policy experiences; and mobilizing stakeholder commitment.

- Producing, widely disseminating, and supporting the use of technical resources in key response areas. These resources address such topics as education on HIV and AIDS treatment, girls' education for HIV prevention, and quality education. The documents serve as important references and guidelines for a range of organizations working in and with the education sector. Many of the materials were launched at regional or global events and have been translated into numerous languages.

- Organizing symposia and internal meetings for its members twice a year to encourage discussion of important developments in the education response to HIV and AIDS and to work toward its overall goals.

For more information on the IATT and links to IATT technical products, visit http://www.unesco.org/aids.

### EDUCAIDS*
**Objectives.** The Global Initiative on Education and HIV&AIDS, known as EDUCAIDS, is a UNAIDS initiative led by UNESCO in collaboration with governments, UN partners, and civil society organizations. It has two primary aims: to prevent the spread of HIV through education and to protect the core functions of the education system from the worst effects of the epidemic.

**Description.** Access to education is widely recognized as an effective means for reducing the vulnerability of children and young people to HIV and AIDS. A comprehensive education sector response is the heart of EDUCAIDS activities at the country level. This means a move away from programming for HIV and AIDS on a project-by-project basis toward a holistic, sectorwide review of the impacts and challenges of

---

* This section was contributed by Christophe Cornu.

HIV. Comprehensive education sector responses have five essential components: (i) quality education; (ii) content, curriculum, and learning materials on HIV and AIDS prevention; (iii) educator training and support; (iv) policy, management, and systems; and (v) approaches and illustrative entry points.

In line with the MDGs and EFA goals, UNESCO supports efforts to ensure that all students have relevant and appropriate learning opportunities of good quality. This means education that is rights based, learner centered, gender responsive, inclusive, culturally sensitive, age specific, and scientifically accurate.

*Results.* UNESCO plays an active role in leading and strengthening EDUCAIDS. In 2008 and 2009, together with other partners, it organized capacity-building workshops on comprehensive education sector responses to HIV and AIDS in the Middle East, the Asia Pacific, Sub-Saharan Africa, Eastern Europe, and Central Asia.

UNESCO has developed a number of training materials with key partners that provide guidance on the technical and operational aspects of a comprehensive approach. These materials include

- EDUCAIDS country snapshots for 17 countries
- EDUCAIDS resource packs in all six UN languages, plus Portuguese, consisting of
  - An EDUCAIDS brochure
  - An updated version of the EDUCAIDS Framework for Action
  - Overviews of practical resources for the five components of a comprehensive education sector response to HIV and AIDS
  - 35 Technical Briefs, grouped according to the five components, with important contributions from across UNESCO sectors and external partners

For more information on EDUCAIDS and links to its training materials, visit http://www.unesco.org/aids.

### EFAIDS*

*Objectives.* Launched in January 2006, the EFAIDS Programme is an initiative of Education International (EI). It is coordinated with the support of its partners, the WHO and the EDC (Education Development

---

* This section was contributed by Delphine Sanglan and the staff of the Solidarity and Development Unit, Education International.

Center). The program deals with two main issues: EFA and HIV and AIDS. The rationale of joining EFA and HIV and AIDS under one umbrella is as follows: if Education for All is not achieved and children cannot get to school, they will not receive the education they need to protect themselves from HIV infection. By the same token, if HIV infection is not prevented, there will not be enough teachers in the classrooms to provide quality education. In other words, a lack of education fuels the HIV and AIDS crisis, just as HIV and AIDS can have a hugely negative impact on the education sector. So the response must be to tackle both sides.

*Description.* The three program goals of EFAIDS that relate directly to the Millennium Development Goals are to

- *Prevent new HIV infections among teachers and learners.* This goal is pursued primarily via the training of teachers in HIV and AIDS education. The training is then passed on to wider circles of teachers and learners via a cascade system.
- *Mitigate the negative effect of HIV and AIDS on EFA goals.* The EFAIDS Programme seeks to foster an open environment where risk reduction, testing, treatment, and care can be discussed and addressed. Attaining these goals entails research on teacher supply and demand, as well as policy development (for example, developing a workplace policy on HIV and AIDS), and, crucially, advocacy of proper training, support, treatment, and care of teachers.
- *Increase the number of students completing basic education.* By means of research, advocacy, and raising public awareness, EI member organizations develop partnerships with other civil society organizations and engage their governments and international organizations to advance the EFA agenda, with an emphasis on educational quality.

*Results.* The EFAIDS program is presently implemented by 80 teacher unions affiliated with EI in 48 countries in Africa, Asia, Latin America, and the Caribbean on the basis of the five EFAIDS working areas: research, policy development, advocacy, publicity, and training.[3] Thanks to these five areas, the program has made a positive impact on thousands of teachers and students through a broad range of activities over the past four years, as described below.

- Through the program, EI member organizations have strengthened their role in national policy dialogue on quality education and HIV and AIDS, while at the same time integrating these issues into core union work.

- Thousands of teachers have been trained in HIV and AIDS prevention and education.
- EI member organizations have also increased their respective capacities to lobby their governments to institutionalize training on HIV and AIDS.
- EI member organizations have also pushed their governments to grant free education for all and improve the quality of education by recruiting more teachers, providing ongoing training, and improving school infrastructure.

More recently the program has worked toward the following developments:

- EI member organizations taking part in the EFAIDS program continue to work for a speedy fulfillment of universal access to HIV prevention, treatment, care, and support, paying special attention to the needs of teachers and students living with HIV.
- As a result of the program, teachers' unions are gaining the confidence to tackle HIV and AIDS prevention and integrate it within union structures and activities.
- Not only are teachers' unions working to prevent new infections among teachers and students, they are also rolling out policies and support groups to ensure that teachers living with HIV can continue to work and contribute to the education sector without fear of discrimination.
- The program has been instrumental in helping teachers make meaningful progress toward the provision of quality education. It helps teachers' unions conduct valid research, which in turn contributes both to sound policy development and informs and strengthens advocacy work (that is, the lobbying of governments and other education stakeholders). As a result, the program is contributing to the ultimate goal of quality education for all children.

The year 2010 will be a period of evaluation and reflection on the past five years of the work of EFAIDS. As it moves toward 2015, the program will identify best practices and refine what is required for effective and sustainable interventions on HIV and AIDS education.

For more information on EFAIDS, visit http://www.ei-ie.org/efaids/en/index.php.

## Intergovernmental Regional Networks that Share Knowledge among Countries

Each of these partnerships is a regional response by a group of countries that seek to share knowledge on how best to address the local health and nutrition needs of their schoolchildren. In all three cases—Sub-Saharan Africa, the Caribbean, and Southeast Asia—development partners have played a role in providing technical support and resources. In the cases of the African and Caribbean partnerships, formal country-led networks have been established, typically based in the relevant regional economic communities.

### Accelerate Initiative*

**Objectives.** In 2002, the UNAIDS IATT on Education established a working group to support countries in Sub-Saharan Africa as they "accelerate the education sector response to HIV and AIDS." Although the initiative was started by development partners, it has become owned by technical representatives of the participating countries, who have created networks for sharing information and the exchange of ideas, typically under the auspices of the Regional Economic Communities that compose the African Union. These networks have defined five objectives:

- To promote leadership by the education sector and create sectoral demand for a response to HIV and AIDS.
- To harmonize support among development partners, so as to better assist countries and reduce transaction costs.
- To promote coordination with national AIDS authorities and enhance access to HIV and AIDS funds.
- To share information on HIV and AIDS that has specific relevance to the education sector.
- To strengthen the technical content and implementation of the education sector response to HIV and AIDS.

**Description.** In response to requests from governments, between 2002 and 2007, 76 organizations contributed to 24 subregional or national workshops in Sub-Saharan Africa—one every two months.[4] A set of key

* This section was contributed by Aggrey Kibenge, Amicoleh Mbeye, Malick Sembene, and Balla Camara.

documents on HIV and AIDS and education were developed in English, French, and Portuguese; a total of 250,000 printed copies were distributed to educators to support the training.

During the same period, representatives of the ministries of education of 37 governments participated in these workshops, 26 of which went on to develop and implement plans at the national level and receive resources from their National AIDS Commissions (NACs). The ministries of education participating in the Accelerate Initiative also created information-sharing subregional networks within the Economic Community of West African States, the Economic Community of Central African States, and the East African Community.

*Results.* An evaluation conducted by the member-designated focal points for HIV and AIDS and school health in the ministries of education of the 34 participating countries in Sub-Saharan Africa (see box 5.4) shows that all these countries now have a national HIV and AIDS policy and 76 percent have an education sector-specific HIV and AIDS strategy and plan of action. Some 32 countries manage their programs through a national unit; another 23 have management systems at the subnational level. All participating countries are providing some HIV prevention education at the primary or secondary level, or both; 31 provide this educa-

---

**Box 5.4**

**Countries Participating in the Accelerate Initiative**

| | | |
|---|---|---|
| Benin | Gabon | Niger |
| Botswana | Gambia, The | Nigeria |
| Burkina Faso | Ghana | Rwanda |
| Burundi | Guinea | São Tomé and Príncipe |
| Cameroon | Guinea-Bissau | Senegal |
| Central African Republic | Kenya | Sierra Leone |
| Chad | Liberia | Tanzania |
| Congo, Dem. Rep. | Madagascar | Togo |
| Congo, Rep. | Malawi | Uganda |
| Côte d'Ivoire | Mali | Zambia |
| Eritrea | Mauritania | |
| Ethiopia | Mozambique | |

tion to students before puberty. In addition, 30 countries are providing training to help teachers protect themselves.

The experience of the past five years shows progress toward the goal of acceleration and the program's other main objectives. One area in which progress has been slow is the establishment of effective M&E procedures and the incorporation of appropriate indicators in associated education management information systems. This deficiency in turn makes it difficult to evaluate HIV and AIDS education programs in terms of school-based, child-focused results. Moving forward, the development of effective M&E systems is an important priority, since in their absence investments are likely to be made in initiatives that are thought to be effective, rather than in those that have been shown to be effective. In a recent move, countries in the various regional networks have begun to develop a common education sector M&E framework.

For more information on the Accelerate Initiative, visit its website: http://www.schoolsandhealth.org/Pages/AcceleratingtheEducationSector ResponsetoHIV.aspx. Also see Bundy et al. (2010), *Accelerating the Education Sector Response to HIV*.

### The Caribbean EduCan Response*

**Objectives and context.** Caribbean governments have identified nutrition, infectious diseases (including HIV and AIDS), noncommunicable diseases, and violence as priority areas related to the health and nutrition needs of school-age children in the region. These governments have also recognized that, as elsewhere in the world, some of the major causes of death in the adult population (including diabetes, hypertension, and heart disease) have their roots in behavioral patterns established during childhood and youth. Furthermore, schoolchildren in the emerging middle-income countries of the Caribbean face the burden of obesity, diabetes, and malnutrition. The region also faces the challenge of being the second most HIV-affected region of the world after Sub-Saharan Africa (UNAIDS 2008).

In response to these challenges, education and health sector leaders in the Caribbean are committed to addressing the specific health and nutrition needs of school-age children through a broad school-based health and nutrition program. The program focuses on noncommunicable diseases (NCDs), but also includes HIV prevention and mitigation initiatives. At

---

* This section was contributed by Tara O'Connell, Arlene Husbands, and Jenelle Babb.

the high-level meeting of the Caribbean Community Council on Human and Social Development in June 2006, Caribbean ministers of education and representatives of national AIDS authorities identified a need to appoint a focal point for school health activities within their respective ministries, as well as to create a regional mechanism to share school health information.

The resulting Caribbean Education Sector School Health and HIV/AIDS Coordinator Network (EduCan) was tasked with sharing information and leading capacity building on national education sector responses to school health and HIV/AIDS throughout the Caribbean. EduCan's overall goal is to strengthen the role of the education sector in preventing HIV/AIDS in the region. Operationally speaking, however, in many cases this role has meant coordinating interventions on broader school health and nutrition topics, including NCDs, particularly, but not solely, focused at the curriculum level.

*Program components.* In early 2008, a rapid survey was undertaken by EduCan to inform the development of both regional- and national-level education sector policy and strategy in these thematic areas. The survey aimed to describe the current situation of the education sector response to school health, nutrition, HIV/ AIDS and the associated stigma, as well as provide a baseline for monitoring progress. It also sought to provide data on the allocation and mobilization of resources used in education sector responses across the region.

HIV/AIDS coordinators[5] at the various Caribbean ministries of education (MoEs) answered a questionnaire on health-related school policies, safe and supportive school environments, skills-based health education, school-based health and nutrition services, and support of MoE school-based health and nutrition and HIV/AIDS responses. Of the 14 countries and territories represented in the EduCan Network, 13 countries (Antigua, the Bahamas, Barbados, Belize, Dominica, Grenada, Guyana, Jamaica, Anguilla,[6] St. Kitts and Nevis, St. Lucia, St. Vincent and the Grenadines, and Trinidad and Tobago) responded to the questionnaire.

Overall, the rapid survey found that government leaders of the Caribbean are committed to reaching children and adolescents with information and life skills training that develop the knowledge, attitudes, and values needed to make sound health-related decisions that promote lifelong healthy behaviors. A majority of MoEs had established effective policies and strategies for addressing school health and nutrition, HIV/AIDS, and other infectious diseases. Since common NCDs (for example, obesity and Type 2 diabetes) are emerging areas of concern in the region, greater policy emphasis will be placed on NCDs in the future. At this stage, governments in the region are shifting away from creating the policy environment to implementing strategies.

***Results and challenges.*** Findings from the survey identify areas where a strong school health and HIV/AIDS response led by the education sector is already present in the Caribbean. These responses include the provision of skills-based health education and school-based provision of vaccinations. Survey findings also identify areas that might benefit from further strengthening, such as monitoring the impact of such programs. School feeding is nearly universal in the 13 countries and territories, while micronutrient supplementation remains highly targeted. Anecdotal experience suggests that there may be a need for a greater focus on the quality of food consumed by school-age children. In the context of the region's growing epidemic of common NCDs, this finding creates an opportunity both to consider the coverage of micronutrient supplementation and assess the quality of food provided through school feeding programs, as well as that accessed through food vendors in schools.

There is clear evidence that schools have placed a strong emphasis on ensuring a hygienic and safe environment and providing psychosocial support to students. While there is little data on the availability of exercise facilities in schools, this item is an important factor for consideration, given the emergence of obesity and Type 2 diabetes in school-age children in the region.

A high level of teacher training is generally provided in the countries of the Caribbean, which includes training in life-skills education and the delivery of HIV prevention messages. Teacher training, however, is primarily provided through in-service presentations; it is not a substantive component of preparing pre-service teachers for teaching careers. The questionnaire pointed to the need to ensure that more skilled teachers are equipped with sexuality training.

Overall, questionnaire responses revealed that in all countries of the Caribbean, the education sector response to school health, nutrition, and HIV/AIDS is under way and being further refined to more effectively address health conditions specific to Caribbean school-aged children.

### Sharing Programmatic Practices in the Greater Mekong Subregion of South East Asia*

**Objectives and context.** In the Greater Mekong Subregion (GMSR), the education and health sectors have long recognized that certain school health and nutrition services can help address basic health problems faced by schoolchildren. More recently, life skills modules and HIV prevention education have begun to be introduced with the aim of promoting positive and healthy behaviors. The current low levels of HIV infection in the GMSR make a focus on prevention all the more timely. As a result, delivering comprehensive, scaled, systematic, and sustainable school health and nutrition programs based on the FRESH framework—programs that include HIV prevention—are becoming increasingly common in the subregion.

In 2007, representatives of school health programs from six nations in the region (Cambodia, Lao People's Democratic Republic, Myanmar, Thailand, Vietnam, and the Yunnan Province of China) participated in a workshop on "Strengthening the Education Sector Response to School Health, Nutrition, and HIV/AIDS Programs." An exercise facilitated by the country teams identified and documented examples of promising practices in contemporary school health and nutrition programs in the subregion. Notable programs were described by representatives of the governments and civil society organizations among the six participating country teams. The programs varied in focus, content, and process, but when compared across the subregion, a number of similarities emerged.

**Best practice program components and their results.** This section summarizes the best practices in school health and nutrition programs identified by the team at the 2007 workshop, which are categorized under six broad programmatic areas:

**Health-related school policy.** An area of convergence among promising programs in the subregion was a comprehensive, established policy for school health and nutrition that included HIV/AIDS. Practices that were based on well-defined policy at the national, provincial, district, and school levels were generally felt to be more widely supported by health and education staff, parents, and students. Multilevel implementation was also found to foster much wider coverage and encourage sustainability by broadening the response base. Among the promising

---

* This section was contributed by Tara O'Connell, Lesley Drake, Simon Baker, and Emmanuelle Abrioux.

practices in health-related school policy identified in the subregion were Ministry of Education efforts to mainstream HIV/AIDS education in Cambodia, Lao PDR's work in coòrdinating the implementation of school health activities, and Thailand's innovative use of a "Sin Tax" (levied on alcohol and tobacco products) to bring additional resources to its Ministry of Education.

**Safe and supportive school environment.** Programs and activities were found more likely to meet with success when implemented in a supportive and inclusive school environment. The recognition of teachers as key implementers, together with the provision of capacity building in the form of pre- and in-service teacher training, were identified as critical elements in effective implementation of HIV/AIDS programming. Due in part to cultural taboos concerning sexuality, many teachers in the subregion are reportedly reticent and ill-prepared to broach the topic of HIV/AIDS in the classroom. Pre- and in-service training that focuses on teaching techniques in relation to school health and nutrition, including HIV/AIDS, has proven a valuable first step in implementing curricula that address the disease.

In addition, many promising programs also included specific provisions to address the needs of all students, including those with special needs (for example, psychosocial support). Of particular note are the use of scholarships in Cambodia to promote gender balance among teachers and a program of inclusive education for children with special needs in Lao PDR.

**Skills-based health education.**  There is general consensus that promising practice in SHN programming in the subregion involves the inclusion of a life-skills component that includes HIV/AIDS prevention education. Promoting healthy behaviors related to nutrition, sexuality, and a healthy lifestyle in general is crucial. Providing knowledge alone is not enough; young people also need to develop the skills necessary to effect behavioral change. School systems are an established and efficient means of reaching children and adolescents with information as well as training in life skills, enabling children to develop the knowledge, attitudes, and values needed to make sound health-related decisions that promote a healthy lifestyle in general.

Among the promising practices in these areas are prevention education for college students in China; a nationally implemented program that offers both life-skills–based education and educational services to out-of-school youth in Myanmar; and the involvement of students in the development of behavioral change communication materials, information, and education in Vietnam.

**School-based health and nutrition services.** A number of promising practices involve the delivery of health and nutritional services to school-age children. Programs demonstrate how simple, safe, and familiar services, such as deworming and micronutrient supplementation, can be cost-effectively delivered through the existing network of schools to address health issues that are prevalent among a target population. Deworming efforts in a number of countries in the subregion were identified as particularly promising, as were China's efforts at developing educational services for HIV-affected children.

**Partnerships.** Creating and maintaining strong partnerships—between governments and donor agencies, between ministries of education and health, and between schools and communities—has proven vital to successful implementation of school health, nutrition, and HIV/AIDS programming in the GMSR. Partnerships have generally proven most effective when established in the early planning stages of activities, allowing widespread buy-in and participation by all stakeholders in planning and implementation processes. Such partnerships have been found to help drive the collaborative process; promote innovation at community, national, and regional levels; and encourage sustainability through shared responsibility and ownership. One particular feature of partnerships in the subregion has been the empowerment of young people, who play a role in the development of programs, particularly the development of program materials. Such an approach increases young peoples' ownership and buy-in to educational interventions and ensures that programs have greater relevance to their lives.

**Monitoring and evaluation.** Efficient M&E systems are critical for ensuring accountability and transparency of operations. Although such systems are widely recognized as a core component of effective school health and nutrition programming in GMSR countries, they remain a challenge. Practitioners report that the evaluation of SHN programs has been hampered by the lack of an effective plan, including identification of measurable indicators to gauge how well a program meets its intended goals and objectives; a plan to collect and analyze data on these indicators; an understanding of how to utilize these data to measure outcomes; and estimates of the resources needed to support an M&E system.

For more detailed information on promising programs in the GMSR, see the published report, *School Health, Nutrition, and HIV&AIDS Programming* (Bundy et al. 2009b).

## Support for National Programs

This concluding group of partnerships spans a wider range of approaches than those discussed so far. Yet they all share the primary goal of supporting national-level action. The engagement of this group of partnerships is also characterized by being relatively recent, perhaps reflecting a growing trend to move beyond policy to action.

It may be surprising for some readers to see the Education for All–Fast Track Initiative on this list. EFA-FTI is best known as the compact among countries and donors to promote EFA goals. It is included here because the EFA-FTI partnership has shown a strong commitment to supporting school health and nutrition programs—including school feeding and HIV/AIDS education programs—as critical components of country efforts to achieve EFA.

In addition, Save the Children was an early civil society supporter and activist for school health and nutrition and has a particularly distinguished record in working with countries to address malaria in schoolchildren. Deworm the World has made a relatively recent appearance in the field, but has become the global leader in school-based deworming and is one of the few civil society organizations that specifically describes its health intervention as targeting an educational outcome. The World Food Programme–World Bank partnership is a specific agency response to the current financial crisis that seeks to help countries better use their school feeding programs (with school health services, where appropriate) to help children stay in school and weather the social shocks of the crisis.

### *Education for All–Fast Track Initiative\**

EFA-FTI was established in 2002 as a "global compact" between low-income countries and donors to ensure that all children receive a quality primary school education. Donor countries committed to ensuring that no country with a "credible education plan" for achieving Education for All would fall short of meeting the 2015 Millennium Development Goals due to lack of external financing. Since its creation in 2002, EFA-FTI has

---

\* This section was contributed by Koli Banik, Andy Tembon, Tara O'Connell, and Robert Prouty.

grown steadily to become a dynamic global partnership that, as of December 2009, had endorsed the education sector plans of 40 countries, 23 of which are in Sub-Saharan Africa. An additional 10 low-income countries were expected to join the FTI partnership by the end of 2010. To date, EFA-FTI has allocated approximately $1.5 billion from its multi-donor trust fund, the Catalytic Fund (CF), to support the national educa-tion plans of 31 low-income countries.

The main objectives of FTI include (i) helping countries accelerate progress, which requires more effective aid and greater external funding; (ii) assuring improved efficiency and lower transaction costs for donor assistance, given that donors come together to support a single country plan, rather than engaging in fragmented efforts; and (iii) recognizing that progress must be country-driven—that is, more funding at the global level alone is not enough.

The FTI partnership accelerates countries' progress toward EFA goals by supporting credible and sustainable education sector plans that address the key constraints to accelerating EFA. Malnutrition, health problems, and the HIV/AIDS epidemic contribute to these constraints. In the case of the latter, the importance of an effective education sector response to the epidemic is identified in the EFA-FTI Framework (Education for All–Fast Track Initiative 2004, 5), where endorsement of country plans through the FTI review process requires "[a] sector-wide program for education agreed with in-country donors and including a strategy for HIV/AIDS, gender equality, capacity building, monitoring and evaluation."

***FTI funding mechanisms.*** FTI is governed by a partnership of donor and development agencies and managed by a Secretariat. There are two direct funding mechanisms: the Education Program Development Fund (EPDF), which is intended to support the preparation of country educa-tion sector plans (ESPs), and the Catalytic Fund (CF), which is intended to provide support for the implementation of the plans.[7]

For governments that have an endorsed ESP in place, an education project proposal is developed and costed in consultation with the local education donor group and civil society representatives. The goal of this exercise is to prepare a financing framework that identifies all funding sources, including a country's CF request. The local education group (LEG) ensures that school health, nutrition, and HIV/AIDS components (including deworming) are included in the ESP. In cases where an educa-tion plan or project was previously developed without elements of a school health program and is already being funded by the CF, the LEG can request a restructuring of the plan or project to include school health, especially in countries where the rate of disbursement of CF funds is poor. This restructuring will lead to faster implementation for results, with a focus on quicker expenditure related to school health, nutrition, HIV/AIDS.

*FTI and the education sector response to HIV/AIDS.* On two occasions, the UNAIDS IATT on Education and the FTI Secretariat have assessed the HIV/AIDS responsiveness of education sector plans already endorsed by the EFA-FTI Partnership. The first study, completed in October 2004, found that the initial 12 endorsed plans did not adequately address HIV/AIDS, with 5 of the 12 country plans failing to mention HIV/AIDS at all (Clarke and Bundy 2004). As a result of the assessment, recommendations were made to strengthen FTI processes and help countries take school health, nutrition, and HIV/AIDS components into consideration when first elaborating education sector plans , or when the plans are subsequently revised, for example, when applying for a second phase of Catalytic funding.

A second assessment was conducted in 2006 (Clarke and Bundy 2008). It reviewed eight country plans that had been endorsed by FTI following implementation of recommendations from the 2004 review. These country plans paid greater attention to HIV/AIDS and addressed more school health issues than was the case with the plans reviewed by the first assessment. However, considerable variation remained in the quality and depth of plan contents and appraisal processes. These shortfalls could have significant consequences: two of the eight countries assessed were experiencing generalized HIV/AIDS epidemics, but included no HIV/AIDS components in their education sector plans.

A World Bank study has found that at least two-thirds of the countries in Eastern and Western Africa and three in Central Africa exempt orphans and vulnerable children from paying school fees, although implementation of this policy is uneven. Only in some countries did ministries of education keep data on orphans and vulnerable children. Kenya and Malawi have begun to put in place systematic mechanisms that coordinate educational support to orphans and vulnerable children. In Tanzania, consultations between the government, UNICEF, and other stakeholders resulted in the finalization in September 2006 of a fully costed Action Plan (2006–10) to mitigate the effects of HIV/AIDS on the most vulnerable children and reduce their vulnerability (Bundy et al. 2010). The development of these programs was funded by EPDF funds in order to help countries in Sub-Saharan Africa accelerate their education sector responses to HIV/AIDS.

Based on these findings, the FTI Secretariat has encouraged more "upstream" support for inclusion and equity in education plans by (i) providing technical assistance through the EPDF to help countries include school health, nutrition, and HIV/AIDS components in education sector plans (for example, programs for school feeding, HIV/AIDS prevention, gender-specific health, and school health more broadly); and (ii) enhancing the quality of the processes for reviewing the school health content of education sector plans. The Secretariat has also sought more "downstream" support during the implementation of these plans by encouraging greater awareness of school health issues and stronger linkages with nontraditional partners that have specific skills in this area, such as National AIDS Commissions, the health sector, specialist development partners (for example, UNESCO, the United Nations Girls' Education Initiative [UNGEI], UNICEF, the WHO, and the World Bank), and civil society organizations (for example, Save the Children, World Vision, and Deworm the World).

FTI appraisal and endorsement guidelines, the only formal guidance provided to countries for preparation (or appraisal) of educational sector plans, now specifically address inclusion and equity, including school health and HIV/AIDS components. Inclusion and equity issues are also now a routine component of feedback on sector plans by the FTI Secretariat.

***FTI funds support school health and school feeding.*** EPDF and CF funds are being used by countries to include school health and HIV/AIDS components in education sector plans, as well as to provide countries with additional technical assistance and user-friendly guidance on developing policy frameworks, M&E indicators, and implementation strategies (see Bundy et al. 2010). Currently, a school health guidance package, based on school-based deworming as a point of entry, is being tested by the governments of The Gambia, Kenya, Liberia, and Sierra Leone, with support from Deworm the World, the WHO, and the World Bank.

A mainstreaming toolkit for development partners has also been produced by the UNAIDS IATT on Education to help local education donor groups assess the inclusion and mainstreaming of HIV/AIDS responses when considering sector plans for endorsement.

The FTI has supported the development of more than five school feeding programs as part of its policy response. These programs are seen as important mechanisms for impacting the negative effects of the economic crisis on education and addressing social vulnerability. In many FTI countries, families must make basic choices for their child's well-being;

currently, it is increasingly difficult for parents to provide adequate supplies for their children and themselves. School feeding programs can thus increase school enrollment and help keep children in school, as well as enhance educational outcomes. These programs can also contribute to social safety nets and provide a potential point of entry to the community.

School feeding programs exist in all high- and upper-middle-income countries, but they have significant sustainability challenges in low-income countries (Bundy et al. 2009a). According to World Food Programme estimates, these programs are present in 71 of 108 low- and lower-middle-income countries, with countries such as Malawi and Burkina Faso actively seeking to scale up school feeding efforts. In order to help countries make rational decisions about initiating or scaling up school feeding operations, current, evidence-based guidance is needed on the education sector costs and benefits of these programs, as well as on good operational practices.

Between 2002 and 2008, Benin, Cambodia, Djibouti, Haiti, Madagascar, Mali, and Mauritania received FTI funding to implement their national education strategies. All of these countries have a school feeding strategy. Djibouti has a policy to include school feeding facilities in all rural schools. Mauritania received three allocations from the CF, providing sustainable financing for school feeding programs; this support is complemented by funding from other donors. A grant of $14 million was approved in May 2007, of which 14 percent is dedicated to fund school feeding. The government manages the school feeding programs with support from various donor organizations under the umbrella of FTI and the WFP. In 2009, Lao PDR's Education Sector Plan was endorsed by the FTI. The government is now developing a school feeding program that will be funded by an upcoming CF grant. Quantitative assessment of the effects of these programs will take place during the next review of education sector plans—slated for 2010—but it is apparent that governments are increasingly recognizing the relevance of health and nutrition issues for EFA efforts.

### Save the Children USA*

**Objectives.** Save the Children USA is a nonprofit agency that works in more than 50 countries, including the United States, in the operational areas of education, health, food security, child protection, and HIV/AIDS.

---

* This section was contributed by Seunghee F. Lee, Natalie Roschnik, Dan Abbott, and Mohini Venkatesh.

In 1998, the agency allocated funds to pilot school health and nutrition (SHN) programs in three countries: Mali, Malawi, and Mozambique. By the end of the 1999 school year, the program had reached about 100,000 children in approximately 300 schools. Ten years later, similar programs were reaching about 1.5 million school-age children in 19 countries across Africa, Asia, the Middle East, Latin America, and the Caribbean.

***Description.*** The implementation approach of Save the Children USA has been to create model programs through strong partnerships with governments, local organizations, and communities, as well as to conduct advocacy for and support the scaling up of SHN activities. These programs have two main types of objectives: educational (for example, increased attendance rates, reduced dropout rates, and improved reading levels) and health (for example, reduced rates of anemia and decreases in parasite prevalence).

The key strategies of these programs are based on FRESH principles and aim to

- Increase the use of health and nutrition services in schools
- Increase access to water and sanitation facilities in schools
- Promote healthy behaviors through behavior-centered programming and skills-based education, including HIV/AIDS prevention
- Advance school health-related policies in communities and governments at local, regional, national, and international levels

These strategies have been adapted to both local contexts and the resources available for creating appropriate, cost-effective SHN interventions. After 10 years of SHN implementation, Save the Children has successfully increased its reach, serving more children each year and effectively assisting many governments to adopt national SHN programs. In Malawi, the Ministry of the Education's national SHN program is modeled on pilots in the Mangochi and Balaka districts. Save the Children was one of the lead agencies that drafted a national school health and nutrition policy in Nepal, which is now being implemented and supported jointly by that nation's departments of education and child health, and in Burkina Faso, the organization is one of three NGO implementers of the Ministry of Education's SHN program.

***Results.*** The actual results of SHN programs supported by Save the Children have been mixed

- In Bangladesh, children receive deworming tablets every 6 months, together with iron and vitamin A supplementation. The children are less anemic and are doing better in school than they did previously, but parasite rates remain high because of poor hygiene practices, which allow children to become re-infected.
- In both Mali and Malawi, communities have successfully provided water and latrines in schools in the area of intervention, but most of these schools lack the soap needed to ensure effective hand washing.
- The school malaria treatment program in Malawi has improved child survival rates and reduced absenteeism, but changes in drug protocols have resulted in school-based treatments being stopped (see the malaria section in chapter 3).

In all cases where data were collected—typically before and after interventions—there were improvements in educational measures, including attendance, enrollment, and dropout rates, as well as in the results of national standard tests and reading tests.

### Deworm the World: Improving Children's Educational Development through School-Based Deworming*

School-based deworming is now recognized as a significant contribution to the achievement of the Education for All initiative and the education Millennium Development Goals. It is one of the most cost-effective methods of improving attendance and overall schooling outcomes, but of the 400 million school-age children who are infected, the vast majority remain untreated.

In response to this situation, Deworm the World (DtW) was launched by the Education Task Force of the Young Global Leaders of the World Economic Forum at Davos in 2007. DtW coordinates partner actions to identify and remove barriers to the effective implementation of systematic, scaled, and sustainable school-based deworming programs. The coalition now includes more than 50 governmental, technical, and financial partners and is working in more than 26 countries around the world.

In 2009, DtW supported government actions to target more than 20 million children. These same 20 million children will continue to be targeted in 2010, along with an expected 30 million or more. Because these school-based deworming programs can operate at a cost far less

---

* This section was contributed by Lesley Drake, Ruth Dixon, and Alissa Fishbane.

than $0.50 per child per year, this method of improving school participation is achievable for education sectors across the globe.

Additionally, in 2009, the EFA-FTI Secretariat included deworming in its mandate, recognizing that deworming children improves educational results at minimal cost. DtW provides technical guidance and support to deworming programs of education sectors in FTI-endorsed countries. The achievements of DtW and its partners in 2009 have laid the foundations for achieving the WHO goal of treating 75 percent of school-age children at risk of infection by 2015, in pursuit of the goals of EFA and the education MDGs.

For more information on Deworm the World, visit its website at http://www.dewormtheworld.org/.

### The World Food Programme–World Bank School Feeding Partnership*

*Objectives.* Soaring food and fuel prices had already pushed 130 million to 155 million more people into extreme poverty before the financial crisis of 2008. The UN World Food Programme (WFP) estimates that around 66 million children go to school hungry every day in low-income countries. The demand for funds from the World Bank–administered Global Food Crisis Facility shows that school feeding programs are emerging as a common social safety net response to the crisis, as well as an investment in sustaining human capacity development.

In July 2008, the World Bank and the WFP initiated a joint review of school feeding programs, which was published as *Rethinking School Feeding* (Bundy et al. 2009a). A key message of the study is that the transition to sustainable national programs depends on mainstreaming school feeding programs into national policies and plans, especially education sector plans, as well as increasing national financial and institutional implementation capacity. Together with a study undertaken by the WFP, *Learning from Experience* (WFP 2009), the review identified such common characteristics of effective and sustainable school feeding programs as needs-based, cost-effective quality program design and a sustainability strategy.

The August 2009 Group of 8 (G8) Summit focused on food security, resulting in growing interest in linking school feeding programs with local agricultural production. These programs can contribute to increasing local

---

* This section was contributed by Kristie Neeser, Nancy Walters, Andy Chi Tembon, and Lesley Drake.

food production by ensuring stable and predictable demand on the local market and by meeting this demand through local purchases of food.

Based on the abovementioned analyses, the World Bank and the WFP have formed a partnership to

- Mainstream school feeding, including relevant school health activities (for example, deworming and micronutrient fortification), into national development policies, plans, and strategies, with clearly defined development objectives
- Develop national institutional capacity to implement school feeding programs in an effective, cost-efficient, and sustainable manner
- Promote the transition toward nationally owned and resourced school feeding programs over the long term

**Description.** There is a consensus between the World Bank and the World Food Programme that the "new-generation" approach to school feeding described in *Rethinking School Feeding* (Bundy et al. 2009a) is the basis for a mutually beneficial partnership. In many countries, school feeding provides a rapidly deployable social safety net; it is also one of three main approaches to bringing children to school, along with the abolition of school fees and conditional cash transfers.

The appropriateness of school feeding is context specific; hence there is a major role for knowledge management on the part of the World Bank and the WFP. This role means facilitating evidence-based decision making regarding education policy options for school feeding. Although *Rethinking School Feeding* has built consensus on SHN programs, it has also identified areas of uncertainty, especially the cost-effectiveness of different modalities and the relevance of school feeding for nutrition. One key question is how to maximize the benefits of SHN programs for children without such programs becoming a "tax" on the education system, particularly its capacity to meet increased demand for educational services.

**Results.** Bangladesh, Côte d'Ivoire, Ghana, Haiti, Kenya, Lao PDR, Malawi, and Mozambique are participating in the first phase of World Bank–WFP partnership activities, which include technical assistance for

- Policy mapping by the national development agency to define the strategic objectives of a national school feeding program. This process will identify the rationale for the school feeding program; its objectives and targets; and how it relates to other elements of the national development strategy. The mapping will include a country-specific investment case.

- Identifying key stakeholders on the basis of existing national-level partnerships (for example, those that address national nutrition strategies, EFA-FTI, national deworming, neglected tropical disease initiatives) and supporting government efforts to access available resources (for example, through such mechanisms as the FTI funds, the Global Food Crisis Response Programme, and the Rapid Social Response Fund).
- Facilitating a national stakeholder workshop to (i) take stock of current school feeding programs, (ii) map the position of the country in the transition to national sustainability, (iii) assess the status of existing programs against quality standards, and (iv) identify capacity gaps, challenges, and bottlenecks to the transition process.
- Working with the agricultural sector to explore opportunities for local procurement of food, thereby contributing to the sustainability of the school feeding program and promoting local production.
- Supporting needs assessments to design or redesign school feeding programs and develop national action plans that identify milestones, required resources and capacities, and timelines. These plans will also identify the type of capacity building support that a country currently requires to reach sustainability.

To date, detailed analyses of costs and implementation aspects have been prepared in Bangladesh, Ghana, Kenya, Lao PDR, and Malawi, with stakeholder workshops used to develop transition road maps in Ghana and Kenya.

## Conclusions: Partnerships Develop Consensus and Share Knowledge

Perhaps because school health and nutrition programs address issues with which the education sector is unfamiliar and which are intrinsically multisectoral, a large number of technical partnerships have been established. The analysis above suggests that for nations seeking to implement or improve school health and nutrition programs, such partnerships can provide them access to critical information.

Existing partnerships have helped foster a technical consensus on the components that contribute to a quality school health and nutrition program.

This consensus is built on the guiding principles of the FRESH framework launched at the World Education Forum in Dakar in 2000 and is reflected in the areas of policy overlap among Child Friendly Schools, Health Promoting Schools, and other major initiatives. Although a bewildering variety of options may seem to exist for school health and nutrition programs, there has been a positive trend of convergence toward consensus on the following four core components:

- *Policy*: health- and nutrition-related school policies that provide a nondiscriminatory, safe, and secure environment.
- *School environment*: access to safe water and the provision of separate sanitation facilities for girls and boys.
- *Education*: skills-based education that addresses health, nutrition, and hygiene issues and promotes positive behaviors.
- *Services*: simple, safe, and familiar health and nutrition services that can be delivered cost-effectively in schools (for example, deworming, micronutrient supplements, and snacks to avoid hunger), together with increased access to youth-friendly clinics.

This consensus does not imply that these core components are the only important elements of a school health and nutrition program. Rather, it means that these components provide a sound initial basis for such a program. The context of a program is important, too. These four components can, moreover, be implemented effectively only if supported by strategic partnerships between (i) the health and education sectors, especially teachers and health workers; (ii) schools and their respective communities; and (iii) pupils and others responsible for program implementation.

**The response to HIV/AIDS by the education sector is still largely separate from other important health and nutrition issues.** While the epidemic undoubtedly warrants special attention, there is a potential that responses to it may lose out on opportunities to become integrated into school health and nutrition programs. There was a strong case at the beginning of the 2000s for a focus on HIV/AIDS, not least because of the lack of clarity within the education sector about what needed to be done and the lack of a defined role for the sector. It was then realized that the sector had much to offer because it reaches almost all young people between 5 and 18 years of age, has a specific mandate to support teaching and learning, and is usually the largest public sector employer. Today the need to act has not diminished and the potential role of the education sector remains just as important, but the focus of HIV/ AIDS programming is now, as in other areas of health and nutrition, on integration (to promote synergy) and mainstreaming responses within the overall policy objectives of the education sector.

**Intergovernmental regional networks are an efficient way of sharing scarce knowledge and skills about a relatively new technical area.** The examples from Africa, the Caribbean, and Southeast Asia described in this chapter indicate that networks have helped in three main ways, enabling countries to

- Build consensus around appropriate local responses, reassuring countries that have made bold steps toward introducing new policies and encouraging catch-up among countries that have moved more slowly
- Take stock of the various experiences of different countries and then use this evidence to fine-tune priorities and approaches
- Share scarce skills with neighboring countries

The Caribbean and African experiences have led to the establishment of formal intergovernmental networks, in both cases based in subregional economic communities where the network can be overseen by existing education (and health) committees at the ministerial level. This governance structure may provide a useful model for other subregions.

**There are growing opportunities for countries to gain direct support for developing and sustaining effective school health and nutrition programs.** A growing number of diverse actors have emerged—including major donors, civil society, the private sector, and UN agencies—that are working directly with countries to provide support in key areas, such as

- Technical assistance in designing or, more usually, redesigning school health and nutrition programs
- Donation of commodities, such as bed nets to avoid malaria and deworming drugs, that reduce the costs of implementation
- Support for policy reforms to mainstream school health and nutrition programs in education sector plans
- Budgetary support to catalyze the rollout of school health and nutrition programs

School health and nutrition is an expanding area of education opera-tions, perhaps reflecting the demand of countries for programs that help keep children in school and provide a social safety net during the current financial crisis.

## Notes

1. The partners that conducted the review included the Child-to-Child Trust, the Education Development Center, Education International, the Food and Agriculture Organization, the International Rescue Committee, Partnership for Child Development, the Roll Back Malaria Partnership, Save the Children USA, Joint United Nations Programme on HIV/AIDS (UNAIDS), UNESCO, UNICEF, the United Nations Office on Drugs and Crime (UNODC), the World Bank, the WFP, and the WHO.

2. Initiatives in the thematic area of HIV/AIDS differ in how they refer to the epidemic. The subsections that follow reflect the specific terminology used by each of the various initiatives.

3. The 48 countries by region are **Africa:** Benin, Botswana, Burkina Faso, Burundi, Côte d'Ivoire, Gabon, Ghana, Guinea, Kenya, Lesotho, Liberia, Malawi, Mali, Namibia, Niger, Rwanda, Senegal, Sierra Leone, South Africa, Swaziland, Tanzania, Uganda, Zambia, and Zimbabwe; **Latin America:** Argentina, Brazil, Colombia, Costa Rica, Dominican Republic, Guatúmala, Honduras, Nicaragua, and the República Bolivariana de Venezuela; **Caribbean:** Antigua and Barbuda, Belize, Suriname, Dominica, Grenada, Haiti, Jamaica, Nevis, St. Lucia, St. Vincent and the Grenadines, and Trinidad and Tobago; and **Asia Pacific:** India, Indonesia, Papua New Guinea, and Nepal.

4. The organizations comprised the 9 UNAIDS cosponsoring agencies, 15 bilat-eral donors, and 52 civil society organizations.

5. This category includes MoE Health and Family Life Education coordinators, as well as education officers and guidance counselors who serve as HIV/AIDS coordinators.

6. Joint British and Dutch Overseas Caribbean Territories.

7. Plans are now under way to simplify these processes, including merging into single funds.

## References

Bundy, D. A. P., C. Burbano, M. Grosh, A. Gelli, M. Jukes, and L. Drake. 2009a. *Rethinking School Feeding: Social Safety Nets, Child Development, and the Education Sector*. Washington, DC: World Bank.

Bundy, D. A. P., T. O'Connell, L. Drake, S. Baker, and E. Abrioux. 2009b. *School Health, Nutrition, and HIV&AIDS Programming: Good Practice in the Greater Mekong Sub-region*. London: Partnership for Child Development.

Bundy, D. A. P., A. Patrikios, C. Mannathoko, S. Manda, and A. Tembon. 2010. *Accelerating the Education Sector Response to HIV: Five Years of Experience from Sub-Saharan Africa*. Washington, DC: World Bank.

Clarke, D., and Bundy, D. A. P. 2004. "The EFA Fast-Track Initiative: Responding to the Challenge of HIV and AIDS to the Education Sector." Education for All–Fast Track Initiative Secretariat, Washington, DC.

———. 2008. "The EFA Fast Track Initiative: An Assessment of the Responsiveness of Endorsed Education Sector Plans to HIV and AIDS." ED/UNP/HIV/2009/IATT/1, UNAIDS Inter-Agency Task Team on Education, Geneva.

Education for All–Fast Track Initiative. 2004. "Framework." EFA-FTI Secretariat, Washington, DC. http://www.educationfasttrack.org/media/library/Framework NOV04.pdf.

Jukes, M. C. H., L. J. Drake, and D. A. P. Bundy. 2008. *School Health, Nutrition and Education for All: Leveling the Playing Field*. Cambridge, MA: CABI Publishing.

Partnership for Child Development. 2009. *Identification of Priority Indicators for the Monitoring and Evaluation of the Education Sector Response to HIV and AIDS: Synthesis Report on the Process*. London: Partnership for Child Development.

Partnership for Child Development and Save the Children USA. 2008. "Monitoring and Evaluation of School-Based Health and Nutrition Programmes: A Participative Review." Review conducted for the FRESH Partners Meeting held at the World Health Organization, Geneva, September 8–9.

Tang, K.-C., D. Nutbeam, C. Aldinger, L. St. Leger, D. A.P. Bundy, A. M. Hoffmann, E. Yankah, D. McCall, G. Buijs, S. Arnaout, S. Morales, F. Robinson, C. Torranin, L. Drake, M. Abolfotouh, C. V. Whitman, S. Meresman, C. Odete, A.-H. Joukhadar, C. Avison, C. Wright, F. Huerta, D. Munodawafa, D. Nyamwaya, and K. Heckert. 2009. "Schools for Health, Education, and Development: A Call for Action." *Health Promotion International* 24 (1): 68–77.

UNAIDS (Joint United Nations Programme on HIV/AIDS). 2008. *Report on the Global AIDS Epidemic 2008*. Geneva: UNAIDS.

WFP (World Food Programme). 2009. *Learning from Experience: Good Practices from 45 Years of School Feeding*. Rome: WFP.

World Bank. 2000. "The Dakar Framework for Action: Education for All—Meeting Our Collective Commitments." Presented at the World Education Forum, Dakar, April 26–28.

# CHAPTER 6

# School Health and Nutrition Programs as a Component of Education for All

There have been major changes in school health and nutrition programming over the past decade. Since 2000, there has been an increasing recognition in middle- and low-income countries that school health and nutrition programs offer important benefits to education and can sometimes serve as a productive social safety net. This recognition has resulted in a movement away from the traditional perception of school health and nutrition programs as primarily a health-promotion tool implemented by the health sector toward a vision of programs that aim to improve educational outcomes. Such programs are largely implemented by the education sector and designed to reach the poorest segments of the population.

These changes have been surprisingly rapid, especially given the apparent inertia in the education sector prior to 2000, and have coincided with national, regional, and global efforts to achieve Education for All (EFA). A causal link seems probable; it may be argued that for many countries, school health and nutrition programs are viewed as part of the spectrum of efforts necessary to achieve universal primary completion, alongside fee abolition, expansion of the teaching force, and other interventions that fall within the more traditional role of the education sector.

A second part of this change is the recognition that school health and nutrition programs are part of a larger, life-cycle process that supports child development. From a programmatic point of view this might be seen as a sequence of programs throughout the life of a child, each program building on the success of its predecessor. From this perspective, maternal and child health (MCH) programs address the health and nutrition needs of children from fetal development through the age of 2 years (that is, from –9 to 24 months), early child development programs add behavioral stimulation to good health and nutrition until the child goes to school (2 to 6 years), and school-based interventions address health, nutrition, and hunger issues during school age. The education sector has a role to play in each stage of this process—and a notable self-interest in promoting MCH and ECD programs—but the sector's major role is in supporting school-age children.

This final chapter summarizes the main conclusions of the review and identifies challenges and research issues going forward.

## The Education Sector Case for School Health and Nutrition Programs

Based on the arguments developed in this book, three main reasons explain why school health and nutrition (SHN) programs contribute to the achievement of the goals of Education for All. These programs

- *Improve equity in education.* Illness and hunger affect education outcomes and are more common among the poor, meaning that they most compromise the education of poor and disadvantaged children. Treating such conditions brings the greatest educational benefits to these children. These programs are unusual in this respect, since most other education interventions benefit better-off, more able children who have the capacity to take full advantage of educational opportunities. School health and nutrition programs help poor children better realize their potential and take better advantage of the educational opportunities available to them. Such programs have been described as leveling the playing field for poor children.

- *Have substantial impact.* The potential impact of SHN programs is attributable to the high prevalence of certain diseases and the substantial educational benefits of treating them. The major health conditions that impact children's education (for example, iron-deficiency anemia, hunger, worm infections, and malaria) can affect hundreds of millions of children and are highly prevalent among poor schoolchildren. Indeed, some diseases, such as worm infections, have the greatest consequences for this age group.

These conditions can be associated with the loss of 3.75 to 6 IQ points and the equivalent of between 200 million and 524 million years of primary schooling. Treating such diseases can have a large impact on children's education, increasing the time that they spend at school and their ability to learn while there. It also reinforces education efforts, since healthy children are more able to benefit from improvements in education quality. When replicated across the enormous numbers of children suffering from common illnesses, such educational benefits add up to a substantial global impact.

- *Are a cost-effective "quick win."* Many of the major conditions of ill health and poor nutrition that affect education are preventable or treatable using simple, safe, and familiar interventions that can be delivered though schools. Such treatments can be highly cost-effective as education interventions when implemented through the school system. In cost-benefit analyses, they often compare well with other education interventions and have the additional benefit of optimizing the benefits of education that accrue to poor children. Not all interventions are relevant in all contexts, but in the complex set of conditions required for a child to learn well, improved health and nutrition can be one of the simplest and cheapest to achieve.

These three arguments combine to make an education case for ensuring the good health of schoolchildren. The first two arguments—the potential for substantial global impact and the rare opportunity to improve equity in educational opportunities—suggest that SHN programs are an important option in education policy that deserves attention. The third argument—that they can be cost-effective—makes these programs an attractive policy option in the right context. It is important not to overstate the case: such programs are not the solution to global educational challenges, but they can play a useful part in the solution. Arguably no education solution will be complete without them. They therefore warrant consideration as a potentially important component of education sector efforts to achieve the goals of Education for All.

## A Life-Cycle Approach to Child Development and Education

Throughout this book it has been argued that programs for school-age children are part of a continuum of supportive programs, from maternal and child health during fetal development and infancy, through early child development in early childhood, and, finally, school health and nutrition programs as a component of Education for All. The World Bank Education Strategy identifies three key objectives that can help improve the education outcomes of schoolchildren: (i) ensuring that children are ready to learn and enroll on time; (ii) keeping children in school and learning by enhancing attendance and reducing dropout rates; and (iii) improving learning at school by enhancing cognition and educational achievement.

Improvements in health and nutrition can contribute to this strategy, but they need to start early and support the child throughout the development process. Other interventions, such as malaria control and micronutrients, may be viewed as relevant throughout early life and during school age, while still others, such as deworming, are especially important during school age because the infection is most prevalent and intense in this age group. Hunger, too, is often a major constraint on education. In early adolescence, refractive error and the need for vision correction becomes more common, as does the relevance of behavioral interventions related to sexual health. These are broad generalizations and will vary among countries, but they are intended to illustrate the need for a life-cycle approach to child development and education in order to meet the three key objectives of World Bank education strategy.

One implication of the life-cycle approach is that it is in the interest of the education sector to encourage and promote the general sequence of maternal and child health, early child development, and school health and nutrition programs, although the extent of potential involvement by the sector in these programs will vary considerably. MCH is almost exclusively the responsibility of the health sector. By contrast, ECD programs—even in high- and middle-income countries—are most commonly implemented for younger children by civil society organizations and the private sector, often with little involvement of the public sector. In an increasing number of cases, the education sector contributes to ECD programs by taking children into a preschool program one year or, rarely, two years, before statutory enrollment. In contrast, health and nutrition programs during school age are most frequently implemented by the education sector, typically in close collaboration with the health sector. All of these programs may be supported to a greater or lesser extent by social protection mechanisms.

## Health and Nutrition Interventions Can Promote Gender Equity and Equality and Contribute to MDG3

The centrality of gender in education is recognized in the third Millennium Development Goal (MDG3), which specifically addresses the need for gender equality and equity in education. This goal was missed in 2010, and a ramping up of efforts is now needed to achieve both goals by 2015. School health and nutrition programs can play an important role in contributing to the goal of gender equity, not least because some of the most common health conditions affecting education are more prevalent among girls and because gender-based vulnerability and exclusion can place girls at greater risk of ill health, neglect, and hunger.

This book has cited examples of the many different ways in which SHN interventions help address gender imbalances in education. Women and girls are, for physiological reasons, more likely to experience higher rates of iron-deficiency anemia, which have well-documented consequences for cognition. Two of the most common school-based interventions, deworming and iron supplementation, each address anemia directly and therefore offer particular benefits to girls. Iron-fortified food also can also contribute to reducing anemia, with evidence that such school feeding interventions can disproportionately benefit the enrollment of girls. The scale of impact can be large: avoiding malaria infection in early life results in increased participation by girls in education during school age; in The Gambia this difference was the equivalent of an extra year of schooling.

This book has attempted to highlight gender issues wherever possible. In practice, however, many studies need to make a greater effort to ensure disaggregation of data by sex so that the role of SHN programs in addressing gender equity can be better understood. Nevertheless, the evidence suggests that many of the most common SHN interventions have potentially important consequences for gender, and that these programs should be a recognized component of efforts to achieve MDG3 and the EFA gender goals.

## The Unfinished Research Agenda

Although enough is known to begin expanding and/or improving school health and nutrition programs worldwide, particularly in low-income countries, there is a need for further research to specifically clarify which conditions are a good fit for the SHN agenda. It is remarkable, for example, that the educational relevance of conditions as important as disability or as prevalent as toothache has yet to be quantified. There are also areas where research for the purpose of operational guidance could rapidly be translated into meaningful action, as in the examples listed below.

- Malaria has emerged as a very important condition for schoolchildren in terms of anemia and cognition. In many countries in Africa malaria is most prevalent in schoolchildren because of the success of efforts to control infection in other age groups. Yet there is a lack of formal policy guidance on how to address malaria in schools.

- Vision correction is a priority from an education perspective. Yet traditional approaches to dispensing eyeglasses are often ineffective in serving poor children in Sub-Saharan Africa, largely because of the lack of appropriately trained personnel. This area would benefit from a comparative cost analysis of the approaches available to providing vision correction, including formal assessment of the efficacy and safety of self-refracting eyeglasses.

- Cost-benefit studies are needed that compare interventions, especially those that compare traditional health and education interventions. Such studies are needed to assist governments in making rational decisions about the place of SHN programs in national development policy. There is also a need for more comparative cost-benefit analyses of SHN programs versus other education and social safety net interventions, including conditional cash transfers.

## An Evolving Role for Development Partners

The World Education Forum held in Dakar in 2000 started an important dialogue about school health and nutrition, a dialogue that involves countries, development agencies, and civil society organizations. The proliferation of SHN programs over the subsequent decade reflects the engagement of all three partners. But it is hard to escape the conclusion that it is individual countries themselves that have made the greatest changes to their internal policies and thinking in order to promote the cross-sectoral work of effective SHN programs. In general, development partners remain focused either on health or on education; when they address both, they often face challenges in working across administrative boundaries. One administrative change that might help agencies

**Box 6.1**

## A Development Partner Dilemma: No DAC Purpose Codes Exist for School Health Programs

The Development Cooperation Directorate of the Organisation for Economic Co-operation and Development (OECD) has created a financial reporting system to help development partners coordinate their assistance. This Creditor Reporting System is based on a series of single-purpose codes, each of which describes a specific use of financial resources (for example, building schools, training teachers). These Creditor Reporting System purpose codes are supervised by the Development Assistance Committee (DAC) and are commonly described as DAC codes.

There appears to be no DAC code for education sector investments in health. Moreover, the DAC codes for basic health care and basic nutrition are so broad that they do not allow school-based health programming to be highlighted or differentiated. Bilateral donors and other development partners thus have the choice of either supporting school health and then not being able to report that they have done so, or committing resources to other educational components for which there are DAC codes. To quote a representative of one major bilateral donor to education programs in low-income countries: "Not reporting the use of development assistance is not an option for my Minister."

It would seem useful for OECD DAC to generate codes for reporting school health and nutrition activities specifically.

work more easily across sectors would be to create Development Assistance Committee (DAC) purpose codes to report on cross-sectoral SHN programs (see box 6.1).

The absence of a focal point for the cross-sectoral work of education and health bureaucracies has perhaps had an important positive benefit: the creation of partnerships across traditional sectoral boundaries. Instead of having a single coordination point, the SHN area is characterized by an exceptionally large number of partnerships and networks, many of which have proven effective at promoting knowledge sharing and coordination. These networks and partnerships should perhaps receive more direct and specific support from development partners in order to help individual countries help themselves. There is nevertheless a tendency for these initiatives to coalesce around single issues—most notably, HIV/AIDS—which has perhaps contributed to a certain fragmentation of effort, as well as distracting the partners involved from the broader goals of SHN programs. An important next step in the evolution of these partnerships might be for development partners to work toward harmonization and alignment across sectors, a process that is already under way in some country programs.

## A Time for Consolidation

Since 2000, the FRESH framework and the operational guidance of Child Friendly Schools have made clear that school health and nutrition programs that seek to improve education require several elements to achieve successful outcomes. Reviews of country and development partner policies show that, for example, linking good health education with good health services has been widely accepted, promoted, and implemented. However, there has been a tendency for this process to result in the fragmentation of effort, with separate and different administrative structures developing around different health issues. This is perhaps most notable with respect to HIV/AIDS, but is also recognizable in hand washing and vision promotion—two areas that are most often led by the health sector. Similarly, school feeding has often been viewed as an intervention managed separately from school health, a position that no longer fits well with the vision of these programs as components of national education policy.

Within the health sector globally, there is major movement to develop a more systematic approach to health interventions, based on the recognition that good health is dependent on health systems that can address multiple diseases. The new vision of SHN programs is entirely consistent with this view of health delivery, representing a well-proven means of improving the health and education of a subset of the population that is often poorly served by more traditional health systems. Now is the time for the health and education sectors to mainstream and consolidate their joint SHN activities, and for ministries of health and education to agree formally on their respective responsibilities and strengths within national school health programs.

## Safe and Simple Interventions that Reach the Poor

School health and nutrition programs can contribute to achieving the goals of EFA by helping children enroll on time, complete their educations, and realize their cognitive potential to learn. Achieving these goals depends on reaching the children most in need. One strong feature of SHN programs is that they benefit poor, sick, and hungry children far more than better-off children. However, poor children can benefit only if the programs reach them.

While a growing number of countries are targeting their SHN programs at the poor, it is apparent that large-scale programs that reach the needy are much less common than programs that, despite good intentions, extend little beyond elite urban schools. Efforts to provide comprehensive programs can result in programs that are too complex or too demanding to go to scale—the classic challenge of the best driving out the good.

There are good examples of how implementing one or a few simple, yet important, interventions is well within the scope of education systems that work with the health sectors of their respective countries. For example, the Kenya deworming program reached 3.5 million needy children in one year, and the Philippines Fit for School Program is going to scale nationally with deworming, hand washing, and toothbrushing. Programs that aim for simplicity rather than comprehensiveness have a much better record of going to scale and reaching the poor.

This book has described how schools have been used as a platform for delivering familiar, safe, and simple health and nutrition interventions to even hard-to-reach children in low-income countries. The success of such interventions has often been achieved by reducing school health programs to their simple essentials and by targeting delivery at the communities most in need. The watch words for pro-poor school health programs may thus become safe, simple, and scalable.

## Enough Known to Act Now

School health and nutrition program are nearly universal in rich and middle-income countries, where they are often viewed as essential to the longer-term development of children, especially the establishment of life-long healthy behaviors and diet. Low-income countries are also now seeking to implement effective school health and nutrition programs, especially since the Dakar meeting of 2000, but the focus of programs in these countries is rather different. Ill health and hunger remain common, especially among the poor, and have important consequences for education. An increasing number of low-income countries accordingly use their schools as a platform for delivering simple, safe, and cost-effective health and nutrition interventions with the specific aims of achieving the education MDGs and the goals of Education for All.

There are necessary caveats in moving toward wider implementation of SHN programs. The use of schools as a delivery platform should not detract from their primary role of teaching and learning—that is, the delivery of health and nutrition interventions should not function as a tax on the education system which it is trying to help. Similarly, the potentially large increase in demand for education created by SHN interventions must be matched by a concomitant increase in the supply of quality education. In other words, SHN programs should be mainstreamed within a systematic education sector plan. There are good examples of countries that have recognized these issues and rolled out effective programs which have avoided these potential pitfalls.

Enough is known now to recognize the importance of SHN programs as contributors to educational achievement in low-income countries. These programs should be viewed alongside more traditional interventions (for example, school fee abolition, cash transfers, and incentives or subsidies) as important components of the battery of responses that can contribute to increasing participation in education. These interventions may not be relevant everywhere, but in many communities and countries using schools to promote good health and avoid hunger may make a crucial contribution to achieving the goals of Education for All.

# APPENDIX A

# Selected Bibliography of Source Materials and Toolkits

## Programming Approaches

Bundy, D. A. P. 2005. "School Health and Nutrition: Policy and Programs." *Food and Nutrition Bulletin* 26 (2 suppl. 2): S186–92.

Bundy, D. A. P., S. Shaeffer, M. Jukes, K. Beegle, A. Gillespie, L. Drake, S.-H. F. Lee, A.-M. Hoffmann, J. Jones, A. Mitchell, C. Wright, D. Barcelona, B. Camara, C. Golmar, L. Savioli, T. Takeuchi, and M. Sembene. 2006. "School-Based Health and Nutrition Programs." In *Disease Control Priorities in Developing Countries*, 2nd ed., ed. D. Jamison, J. G. Breman, A. R. Measham, G. Alleyne, M. Claeson, D. Evans, P. Jha, A. Mills, and P. Musgrove, 1091–108. New York: World Bank and Oxford University Press.

Bundy, D. A. P., and H. L. Guyatt. 1996. "Schools for Health: Focus on Health, Education, and the School-Age Child." *Parasitology Today* 12 (8): 1–16.

Drake, L. J., C. Maier, M. C. H. Jukes, A. Patrikios, D. A. P. Bundy, A. Gardner, and C. Dolan. 2002. "School-Age Children: Their Health and Nutrition." In *SCN News* 25, ed. A. D. Moreira. Geneva: UN Standing Committee on Nutrition.

Jukes, M. C. H., L. J. Drake, and D. A. P. Bundy. 2008. *School Health, Nutrition and Education for All: Leveling the Playing Field*. Cambridge, MA: CABI Publishing.

Tang, K.-C., D. Nutbeam, C. Aldinger, L. St. Leger, D. A. P. Bundy, A. M. Hoffmann, E. Yankah, D. McCall, G. Buijs, S. Arnaout, S. Morales, F. Robinson, C. Torranin, L. Drake, M. Abolfotouh, C. V. Whitman, S. Meresman, C. Odete,

A.-H. Joukhadar, C. Avison, C. Wright, F. Huerta, D. Munodawafa, D. Nyamwaya, and K. Heckert. 2009. "Schools for Health, Education, and Development: A Call for Action." *Health Promotion International* 24 (1): 68–77.

UNESCO (United Nations Educational, Scientific and Cultural Organization). n.d. "FRESH: Focusing Resources on Effective School Health." http://www .unesco.org/education/fresh.

WHO (World Health Organization). n.d. "WHO Information Series on School Health." WHO, Geneva. http://www.who.int/school_youth_health/resources/ information_series/en/.

World Bank. 2000. "The FRESH Framework: A Toolkit for Task Managers." Human Development Network, World Bank, Washington, DC.

———. 2003. *School Health at a Glance*. Washington, DC: World Bank.

## Early Interventions

Arnold, C. 2004. "Positioning ECCD in the 21st Century." *Coordinators Notebook* 28: 1–34.

Carneiro, P., and J. Heckman. 2003. "Human Capital Policy." NBER Working Paper 9495, National Bureau of Economic Research, Cambridge, MA.

Grantham-McGregor, S. M., Y. Bun Cheung, S. Cueto, P. Glewwe, L. Richer, B. Strupp, and the International Child Development Steering Group. 2007. "Developmental Potential in the First 5 Years for Children in Developing Countries." *Lancet* 369 (9555): 60–70.

Nelson, C. A., M. de Haan, and K. M. Thomas. 2006. *Neuroscience and Cognitive Development: The Role of Experience and the Developing Brain*. New York: John Wiley.

Rand Corporation. 2005. *Early Childhood Interventions: Proven Results, Future Promise*. Arlington, VA: Rand.

Walker, S. P., S. M. Chang, C. A. Powell, and S. M. Grantham-McGregor. 2005. "Effects of Early Childhood Psychosocial Stimulation and Nutritional Supplementation on Cognition and Education in Growth-Stunted Jamaican Children: Prospective Cohort Study." *Lancet* 366 (9499): 1804–7.

Watanabe, K., R. Flores, J. Fujiwara, and T. H. T. Lien. 2005. "Early Childhood Development Interventions and Cognitive Development of Young Children in Rural Vietnam." *Journal of Nutrition* 135 (8): 1918–25.

## Deworming

Bleakley, H. 2007. "Disease and Development: Evidence from Hookworm Eradication in the American South." *Quarterly Journal of Economics* 122 (1): 73–117.

Bundy, D. A. P. 1997. "This Wormy World: Then and Now." *Parasitology Today* 13 (11): 407–8.

Bundy, D. A. P., A. Hall, G. F. Medley, and L. Savioli. 1992. "Evaluating Measures to Control Intestinal Parasitic Infections." *World Health Statistics Quarterly* 45 (2–3): 168–79.

de Silva, N., S. Brooker, P. J. Hotez, A. Montresor, D. Engels, and L. Savioli. 2003. "Soil-Transmitted Helminth Infections: Updating the Global Picture." *Trends in Parasitology* 19 (12): 547–51.

Drake, L. J., and D. A. P. Bundy. 2001. "Multiple Helminth Infections in Children: Impact and Control." *Parasitology* 122 (suppl.): 573–81.

Grigorenko, E. L., R. J. Sternberg, M. Jukes, K. Alcock, J. Lambo, D. Ngorosho, C. Nokes, and D. A. P. Bundy. 2006. "Effects of Antiparasitic Treatment on Dynamically and Statically Tested Cognitive Skills over Time." *Journal of Applied Developmental Psychology* 27 (6): 499–526.

Hotez, P. J., D. A. P. Bundy, K. Beegle, S. Brooker, L. Drake, N. de Silva, A. Montresor, D. Engels, M. Jukes, L. Chitsulo, J. Chow, R. Laxminarayan, C. Michaud, J. Bethony, R. Correa-Oliveira, X. Shuhua, A. Fenwick, and L. Savioli. 2006. "Helminth Infections: Soil-Transmitted Helminth Infections and Schistosomiasis." In *Disease Control Priorities in Developing Countries*, 2nd ed., ed. D. Jamison, J. G. Breman, A. R. Measham, G. Alleyne, M. Claeson, D. Evans, P. Jha, A. Mills, and P. Musgrove, 467–82. New York: World Bank and Oxford University Press.

JPAL (Jameel Poverty Action Lab). 2005. "Education: Meeting the Millennium Development Goals." *Fighting Poverty: What Works* 1: 1–4.

Miguel, E., and M. Kremer. 2004. "Worms: Identifying Impacts on Education and Health in the Presence of Treatment Externalities." *Econometrica* 72 (1): 159–217.

Montresor, A., D. W. T. Crompton, T. W. Gyorkos, and L. Savioli. 2002. *Helminth Control in School-Age Children: A Guide for Managers of Control Programmes.* Geneva: WHO.

Partnership for Child Development. 1999. "The Cost of Large-Scale School Health Programmes Which Deliver Anthelminthics to Children in Ghana and Tanzania." *Acta Tropica* 73 (2): 183–204.

Watkins, W. E., and E. Pollitt. 1997. "Stupidity or Worms: Do Intestinal Worms Impair Mental Performance?" *Psychological Bulletin* 121 (2): 171–91.

World Bank. 2003. *School Deworming at a Glance.* Washington, DC: World Bank.

## School Feeding

Adelman, S. W., D. O. Gilligan, and K. Lehrer. 2008. *How Effective Are Food for Education Programs? A Critical Assessment of the Evidence from Developing*

*Countries.* Food Policy Review 9. Washington, DC: International Food Policy Research Institute.

Alderman, H., D. O. Gilligan, and K. Lehrer. 2008. "The Impact of Alternative Food for Education Programs on School Participation and Education Attainment in Northern Uganda." World Bank, International Food Policy Research Institute, and University of British Columbia.

Bundy, D. A. P., C. Burbano, M. Grosh, A. Gelli, M. Jukes, and L. Drake. 2009. *Rethinking School Feeding: Social Safety Nets, Child Development, and the Education Sector.* Washington, DC: World Bank.

Caldes, N., and A. U. Ahmed. 2004. "Food for Education: A Review of Program Impacts." International Food Policy Research Institute, Washington, DC.

Del Rosso, J. M. 1999. "School Feeding Programs: Improving Effectiveness and Increasing the Benefit to Education; A Guide for Program Managers." Partnership for Child Development, Oxford, U.K.

Gelli, A., N. Al-Shaiba, and F. Espejo. 2009. "The Costs and Cost Efficiency of Providing Food through Schools in Areas of High Food Insecurity." *Food and Nutrition Bulletin* 30 (1): 68–76.

Kristjansson, E., V. Robinson, M. Petticrew, B. MacDonald, J. Krasevec, L. Janzen, T. Greenhalgh, G. A. Wells, J. MacGowan, A. P. Farmer, B. Shea, A. Mayhew, P. Tugwell, and V. Welch. 2007. "School Feeding for Improving the Physical and Psychosocial Health of Disadvantaged Elementary School Children." *Cochrane Database of Systematic Reviews* 1.

WFP (World Food Programme). 2009. "Home-Grown School Feeding: A Framework for Action." WFP, Rome.

## Malaria

Brooker, S. 2009. *Malaria Control in Schools: A Toolkit on Effective Education Sector Responses to Malaria in Africa.* Washington, DC: World Bank; London: Partnership for Child Development.

Brooker, S., S. Clarke, R. W. Snow, and D. A. P. Bundy. 2008. "Malaria in African Schoolchildren: Options for Control." *Transactions of the Royal Society of Tropical Medicine and Hygiene* 102: 304–5.

Bundy, D. A. P., S. Lwin, J. S. Osika, J. McLaughlin, and C. O. Pannenborg. 2000. "What Should Schools Do about Malaria?" *Parasitology Today* 16 (5): 181–82.

Clarke, S. E., M. C. Jukes, J. K. Njagi, L. Khasakhala, B. Cundill, J. Otido, C. Crudder, B. B. Estambale, and S. Brooker. 2008. "Effect of Intermittent Preventive Treatment of Malaria on Health and Education in Schoolchildren: A Cluster-Randomised, Double-Blind, Placebo-Controlled Trial." *Lancet* 372 (9633): 127–38.

Fernando, D., D. de Silva, R. Carter, K. N. Mendis, and R. Wickremasinghe. 2006. "A Randomised, Double-Blind, Placebo-Controlled, Clinical Trial of the Impact of Malaria Prevention on the Educational Attainment of Schoolchildren." *American Journal of Tropical Medicine and Hygiene* 74 (3): 386–93.

## HIV/AIDS

Bundy D. A. P., D. Aduda, A. Woolnough, L. Drake, and S. Manda. 2009. *Courage and Hope: Stories from Teachers Living with HIV in Sub-Saharan Africa.* Washington, DC: World Bank.

Evans, D. K., and E. Miguel. 2007. "Orphans and Schooling in Africa: A Longitudinal Analysis." *Demography* 44 (1): 35–57.

Jukes, M., S. Simmons, M. C. Smith Fawzi, and D. A. P. Bundy. 2008. "Educational Access and HIV Prevention: Making the Case for Education as a Health Priority in Sub-Saharan Africa." Joint Learning Initiative on Children and HIV/AIDS, FXB International, Geneva.

Risley, C. L., and D. A. P. Bundy. 2007. "Estimating the Impact of HIV&AIDS on the Supply of Basic Education." Paper presented at the second meeting of the World Bank/UNAIDS Economics Reference Group, Geneva, November 8–9.

UNESCO (United Nations Educational, Scientific and Cultural Organization). 2008. "EDUCAIDS Overviews of Practical Resources." http://portal.unesco .org/en/ev.php-URL_ID=36412&URL_DO=DO_TOPIC&URL _SECTION=201.html.

UNICEF (United Nations Children's Fund). n.d. "Life Skills." http://www.unicef .org/lifeskills/.

———. 2009. *Promoting Quality Education for Orphans and Vulnerable Children: A Sourcebook of Programme Experiences in Eastern and Southern Africa.* New York: UNICEF.

World Bank. 2002. *Education and HIV/AIDS: A Window of Hope.* Washington, DC: World Bank.

———. 2003. *Education and HIV/AIDS: A Sourcebook of HIV/AIDS Prevention Programs.* Washington, DC: World Bank.

———. 2008. *Education and HIV/AIDS: A Sourcebook of HIV/AIDS Prevention Programs; Volume 2: Education Sector-wide Approaches.* Washington, DC: World Bank.

## Hygiene, Water, and Sanitation

Curtis, V., J. Cardosi, and B. Scott. 2000. "The Handwashing Handbook: A Guide for Developing a Hygiene Promotion Program to Increase Handwashing with Soap." World Bank, Washington, DC.

IRC (International Rescue Committee) International Water and Sanitation Centre. n.d. "WASH in Schools." http://www.schools.watsan.net/.

UNICEF (United Nations Children's Fund). 1998. *A Manual on School Sanitation and Hygiene*. New York: UNICEF.

Water and Sanitation Program. n.d. "Global Scaling Up Handwashing with Soap Project." http://www.wsp.org/index.cfm?page=page_disp&pid=1586.

World Bank, UNICEF (United Nations Children's Fund), and Water and Sanitation Program. 2005. "Toolkit on Hygiene, Sanitation, and Water in Schools." World Bank, Washington, DC. http://www.wsp.org/wsp/sites/wsp.org/files/publications/TOOLKIT.pdf.

## Oral Health

Beaglehole, R., H. Benzian, J. Crail, and J. Mackay. 2009. *The Oral Health Atlas: Mapping a Neglected Global Health Issue*. Geneva: FDI World Dental Education; Brighton, U.K.: Myriad Editions.

Curnow, M. M. T., C. M. Pine, G. Burnside, J. A. Nicholson, R. K. Chesters, and E. A. Huntington. 2002. "A Randomised Controlled Trial of the Efficacy of Supervised Toothbrushing in High-Caries-Risk Children." *Caries Research* 36 (4): 294–300.

Department of Oral Health, College of Dental Sciences, Radboud University. "About BPOC." http://www.globaloralhealth-nijmegen.nl/bpoc_start .html#.

Gooch, B. F., S. O. Griffin, S. K. Gray, W. G. Kohn, R. G. Rozier, M. Siegal, M. Fontana, D. Brunson, N. Carter, D. K. Curtis, K. J. Donly, H. Haering, L. F. Hill, H. P. Hinson, J. Kumar, L. Lampiris, M. Mallatt, D. M. Meyer, W. R. Miller, S. M. Sanzi-Schaedel, R. Simonsen, B. I. Truman, and D. T. Zero. 2009. "Preventing Dental Caries through School-Based Sealant Programs: Updated Recommendations and Reviews of Evidence." *Journal of the American Dental Association* 140 (11): 1356–65.

Kwan, S. Y., P. E. Petersen, C. M. Pine, and A. Borutta. 2005. "Health Promoting Schools: An Opportunity for Oral Health Promotion." *Bulletin of the World Health Organization* 83 (9): 677–85.

Marinho, V. C., J. P. Higgins, S. Logan, and A. Sheiham. 2002. "Fluoride Gels for Preventing Dental Caries in Children and Adolescents." *Cochrane Database of Systematic Reviews* 2.

Monse, B., R. Heinrich-Weltzien, H. Benzian, C. Holmgren, and W. H. van Palenstein Helderman. 2010. "PUFA: An Index of Clinical Consequences of Untreated Dental Caries." *Community Dentistry and Oral Epidemiology* 38 (1): 77–82.

Pine, C. M., M. M. T. Curnow, G. Burnside, J. A. Nicholson, and A. J. Roberts. 2007. "Caries Prevalence Four Years after the End of a Randomised Controlled Trial." *Caries Research* 41 (6): 431–36.

U.S. Centers for Disease Control. n.d. "Oral Health Guidelines." http://www .cdc.gov/OralHealth/guidelines.htm.

WHO (World Health Organization). 2007. "Fact Sheet on Oral Health." Fact Sheet 318. WHO, Geneva. http://www.who.int/mediacentre/factsheets/fs318/ en/index.html.

## Noncommunicable Diseases

Baum, C. L., and W. F. Ford. 2004. "The Wage Effects of Obesity: A Longitudinal Study." *Health Economics* 13 (9): 885–99.

Datar, A., and R. Sturm. 2006. "Childhood Overweight and Elementary School Outcomes." *International Journal of Obesity* 30 (9): 1449–60.

Davison, K. K., and C. T. Lawson. 2006. "Do Attributes in the Physical Environment Influence Children's Physical Activity? A Review of the Literature." *International Journal of Behavioral Nutrition and Physical Activity* 3: 19.

Donnelly, J. E., J. L. Greene, C. A. Gibson, B. K. Smith, R. A. Washburn, D. K. Sullivan, K. DuBose, M. S. Mayo, K. H. Schmelzle, J. J. Ryan, D. J. Jacobsen, and S. L. Williams. 2009. "Physical Activity across the Curriculum (PAAC): A Randomized Controlled Trial to Promote Physical Activity and Diminish Overweight and Obesity in Elementary School Children." *Preventive Medicine* 49 (4): 336–41.

Fernandes, M. 2008. "The Effect of Soft Drink Availability in Elementary Schools on Consumption." *Journal of the American Dietetic Association* 108 (9): 1445–52.

Florence, M. D., M. Asbridge, and P. J. Veugelers. 2008. "Diet Quality and Academic Performance." *Journal of School Health* 78 (4): 209–15.

Popkin, B., W. Conde, N. Hou, and C. Monteiro. 2006. "Is There a Lag Globally in Overweight Trends for Children Compared with Adults?" *Obesity* 14 (10): 1846–53.

# Accelerating Deworming by the Education Sector: Checklist of Good Practice

This checklist is based on the experience of implementing national school-based deworming programs in multiple countries in Africa and Asia during 2009. It reflects numerous dialogues that occurred during workshops and country missions, as well as the major learning points that resulted in the formation of sustainable, successful, low-cost programs.

The checklist is a work in progress and is not intended to be a guide to creating a minimum or ideal package, but rather, to provide an *aide memoire* of issues that have consistently emerged as central to an effective education sector response. The checklist may, however, be considered when preparing an effective school-based deworming program. Each country response will be different and the relevance of the items listed here will vary depending on local needs and circumstances.

The checklist addresses four central issues:

- Education sector policy for deworming
- Education sector management and planning to implement school-based deworming
- Implementation and monitoring of school-based deworming
- Complementary actions to support deworming and maximize success

## Sector Policy Checklist

| Item | Comments |
| --- | --- |
| National deworming strategy<br>• Have adopted by the government<br>• Include education in a multisectoral approach led by the ministry of education (MoE) with key technical support from the ministry of health (MoH) | Demonstrates a government's recognition of the benefits of deworming and its commitment to responding to the problem. The inclusion of the education sector and the health sector recognizes the role of each sector and their collaboration in the response. |
| National education sector deworming *strategy*<br>• Sectorwide<br>• Have adopted by MoE<br>• Incorporate in national sector plan<br>• Budget plans of action<br>• Specifically address targeting | Shows how education sector plans to take ownership of deworming through schools nationally. Costing of the plan of action and including it in the education (and Education for All) plan indicates how the strategy will be implemented. Targeting is a crucial part of the strategy, as it is usually unnecessary to treat all children. It is much more cost-effective to select areas where children are at risk and then treat this population according to World Health Organization (WHO) guidelines. |
| National education sector *policy* for deworming<br>• Sectorwide<br>• Have adopted by MoE<br>• Share with all stakeholders and disseminate widely<br>• Address evidence base, prevalence, worm types, targeting, and treatment guidelines | Addresses sector-specific deworming issues. Establishing policy is the essential first step in an effective sectoral response. Policy will be effective, however, only if it is owned by the relevant stakeholders and is widely known and understood. The policy defines education sector roles, as well as the support of and collaboration with the MoH. Addressing these issues at this stage facilitates better communication and ownership of different aspects of the program. Inclusion of strategic policy related to prevalence, targeting, and strategy will facilitate improved planning for future implementation. |

## Management and Planning Checklist

| Item | Comments |
| --- | --- |
| Strategy for targeting at-risk children<br>• Map existing prevalence data in country, overlaid with any climatic limiters to indicate where worms might be<br>• Identify gaps in data and plan to implement surveys to gather data | Demonstrates commitment to a sustainable, cost-effective program. Targeting at-risk children rather than every child reduces the cost of the program and maximizes its cost benefit. Where technical skills for mapping do not exist in-country, external technical support agencies may be able to provide predictive maps for each species (see http://www.dewormtheworld .org). Where gaps exist, surveys can be carried out at low cost; the WHO can provide advice on how to conduct such surveys (see WHO newsletter, *Action Against Worms*, http://www.who.int/wormcontrol/ newsletter/en/). |
| Use of WHO treatment guidelines and available data<br>• Use maps to determine areas which need treatment<br>• Use education management information system or school survey data to determine number of schools, children, and teachers in areas to be treated<br>• Use WHO guidelines to determine quantities of drugs required to treat identified at-risk children<br>• Procure mebendazole/albendazole/ praziquantal from reputable supplier in appropriate quantities<br>• Identify and follow drug importation procedures; store drugs in appropriate location | |
| Developing training materials and training structure<br>• Create training cascade from master trainers at national level to teachers in individual schools; base training program on number of schools to be treated and administrative breakdown of country<br>• Include quality assurance in training plan and schedule<br>• Make training materials specific to country in terms of both language and cultural references<br>• Include monitoring mechanisms for training materials and actual training | |

## Implementation Checklist

| Item | Comments |
|---|---|
| Drugs distributed according to need<br>• Identify drugs required in each area, district, and school<br>• Repackage and label drugs accordingly<br>• Distribute drugs via training cascade all the way to school level | |
| Teachers trained in all schools implementing deworming program<br>• Implement training cascade: all teachers who will be delivering deworming are trained<br>• Include in training: background on deworming, drug storage, drug administration, potential side effects, monitoring and reporting<br>• Develop strategy to deal with adverse events | |
| Adequate community sensitization must take place<br>• Get high-level politicians and ministers publicly on board with policy<br>• Secure extensive media coverage in appropriate languages and delivery modes: radio, TV, posters, and so forth<br>• Design sensitization campaign to directly address benefits and safety of deworming, expected side effects of drugs, dates and places of deworming, and the fact that children not enrolled in school are welcome to participate<br>• Identify and deal with country-specific issues during community sensitization | Good community sensitization is crucial for the successful implementation and sustainability of a program. Deworming drugs (albendazole and mebendazole) are extremely safe—side effects are experienced due to the effects of the drugs on the worms in people with heavy worm loads, rather than adverse reactions to the drug itself. Having good community sensitization will ensure maximum turnout on the deworming day, the presence of unenrolled children, and prevent hysteria over perceived side effects. |
| Deworming days<br>• Coordinate within districts<br>• Welcome children not enrolled in school to participate | |

*(continued next page)*

| Item | Comments |
|---|---|
| Monitoring and evaluation<br>• Distribute monitoring forms to schools, which record the number of pills received, number of pills utilized, number of children treated, number of drugs returned, number adverse events reported<br>• Put system in place for collation and analysis of monitoring forms | Monitoring and evaluation of the program is important to record how many children were reached in each area and ensure that drugs are misused. It also enables future tailoring of the program and measurement of which areas have had a sustained program. It is possible for small prevalence surveys to be carried out in parallel with the deworming itself, which can help verify and increase the accuracy of mapping and monitor the effects of the program. |

## Complementary Action Checklist

| Check item | Comments |
|---|---|
| Complementary approaches<br>• Have media campaigning specifically address hand washing, wearing shoes, hygiene, and prevention issues<br>• Implement policy to improve toilet facilities in schools and ensure that clean water for hand washing is always available there<br>• Use school feeding to provide additional benefits for children's cognitive abilities and educational achievement<br>• Include worm transmission information in school curriculum | A holistic approach is ideal in order to maximize the benefits of deworming and reduce the risk of reinfection. Combining school-based deworming with education campaigns for "prevention" via schools and their curricula is an additional aspect of the program that should be owned by the education sector. The education sector can also collaborate with other key ministries on school feeding and micronutrient supplementation to improve school participation; alleviate short-term hunger; and increase children's ability to concentrate, learn, and perform specific tasks. Additionally, long-term investments in school hygiene facilities will help reduce worm transmission. |

# Accelerating the HIV/AIDS Response of the Education Sector in Africa: Checklist of Good Practice

This checklist is based on the experience of education sector teams from 37 countries in Africa from November 2002 through June 2006. It reflects the dialogues that occurred during workshops and country missions that formed part of the multiagency effort to "Accelerate the Education Sector Response to HIV/AIDS in Africa," which was led by a working group of the Joint United Nations Programme on HIV/AIDS (UNAIDS) Inter-Agency Task Team (IATT) on Education.

The checklist is not intended to be a guide to creating a minimum or ideal package, but rather, to provide an *aide memoire* of issues that have consistently emerged as central to an effective education sector response. The checklist may, however, be considered when preparing an effective education sector response to HIV and AIDS. Each country response will be different and the relevance of the items listed here will vary depending on local needs and circumstances.

The checklist addresses four central issues:

- Education sector policy for HIV and AIDS
- Education sector management and planning to mitigate the impact of HIV and AIDS

- Prevention of HIV and AIDS by education systems
- Ensuring access to *and completion of* a basic education for orphans and vulnerable children

This checklist is a work in progress. It was developed by a team from the World Bank (Don Bundy, Seunghee Francis Lee, Alexandria Valerio, Stella Manda, and Andy Tembon); UNICEF (Amaya Gillespie and Marcel Ouatara); UNESCO (Bachir Sarr and Christine Panchaud); DFID (David Clarke), and the Partnership for Child Development (Lesley Drake, Anthi Patrikios, and Matthew Jukes).

## Sector Policy Checklist

| Item | Comments |
| --- | --- |
| National HIV and AIDS strategy<br>• Have adopted by the government<br>• Include education in a multisectoral approach | A national strategy demonstrates the government's commitment to responding to HIV and AIDS. The inclusion of the education sector recognizes the role of the sector in the response. |
| National education sector HIV/AIDS *strategy*<br>• Sectorwide (address all subsectors)<br>• Have adopted by MoE<br>• Incorporate into national sector plan<br>• Budget plans of action<br>• Specifically address gender | The education sector strategy shows how sector plans will contribute to the response to HIV and AIDS nationally. Costing the national plan of action and including it in the education (and Education for All) plan indicates how the strategy will be implemented. Gender is a crucial element of the strategy because girls are more vulnerable to infection and are more likely to be excluded from education. |
| National education sector *policy* for HIV/AIDS<br>• Sectorwide (address all subsectors)<br>• Have adopted by MoE<br>• Share with all stakeholders and disseminate widely<br>• Address gender, curriculum content, planning issues, and education needs of orphans and vulnerable children<br>• Include a workplace policy | Education sector policy addresses sector-specific HIV and AIDS issues. Establishing policy is the essential first step in an effective sectoral response. Policy will be effective, however, only if it is owned by the relevant stakeholders, especially teachers' unions, and is widely known and understood. Addressing curriculum at this stage can facilitate dialogue and agreement with the community on sensitive issues that may otherwise slow progress in implementation. HIV and AIDS presents major new issues for the workplace (for example, school and the office). |

*(continued next page)*

| Item | Comments |
| --- | --- |
| Workplace policy<br>• Address stigma and discrimination in recruitment and career advancement in education sector<br>• Address sick leave and absenteeism<br>• Include enforcement of codes of practice, especially with respect to the role of teachers in protecting children<br>• Address care, support, and treatment of staff, as well as access to voluntary counseling and testing (VCT) | Recruitment and career progression are constrained by stigma and discrimination; sick leave policies rarely cope with long-term diseases and encourage undisclosed absenteeism; codes of practice that forbid sexual abuse of pupils are rarely enforced. Teachers need to receive appropriate psychosocial support and ready access to voluntary counseling and testing. The public sector can often learn from the private sector in developing a workplace response. Autonomous tertiary-level institutions should also be encouraged to develop individual HIV and AIDS policies. |

## Management and Planning Checklist

| Item | Comments |
| --- | --- |
| Management of the sector response requires:<br>• An interdepartmental or subsectoral committee<br>• Department focal points for whom HIV and AIDS activities are a specific part of their job descriptions<br>• A secretariat or unit that supports mainstreaming of the government's response and has clear political support<br>• Understanding of new sources of financial support and effective dialogue with the national AIDS authority<br>• Building monitoring and evaluation of the government's response into the education management information system (EMIS) | Mainstreaming an education sector response to HIV and AIDS requires, at least initially, mechanisms for involving all subsectors (the committee) and for implementation (the unit). The keys to success are ensuring that focal points have space in their work program to allocate time to HIV and AIDS; that the implementation unit report to the highest level and is led at the department director level. Through national AIDS authorities, the sector can access new financial resources (for example, the Multi-Country HIV/AIDS Program and the Global Fund to Fight AIDS, Tuberculosis, and Malaria). |
| For short- to medium-term planning, EMIS or school survey data should be used to assess the following at both national and district levels:<br>• HIV- and AIDS-specific indicators<br>• Teacher mortality and attrition data<br>• Teacher attendance data | Even where an effective EMIS is unavailable, school and institutional survey data can be used to assess the impact of HIV and AIDS on the education system. This should relate district-level education data to the geographical pattern of the epidemic, using epidemiological data from the health service. |

*(continued next page)*

| Item | Comments |
|---|---|
| • Attendance by orphans and vulnerable children, or status of nonorphan and vulnerable children<br>• Proportion of children receiving prevention education | |
| For long-term planning:<br>• Develop a computer model projection of the impact of HIV and AIDS on education supply and demand<br>• Assess the implications of changes in supply for teacher recruitment and training<br>• Assess demand implications of changes in the size of the school-age population and the proportion of orphans and vulnerable children<br>• Determine completion rates by orphans and vulnerable children, or of nonorphans and vulnerable children | The effects of the epidemic occur over decades—impacts only slowly become apparent. Long-term planning similarly requires projecting the impact of the diseases over decades, preferably using computer projection models that combine epidemiological and education data. Projections allow for the planning of future teacher supply needs and, where necessary, the reform of teacher training schedules and planning for future demand. |

## Prevention Checklist

| Item | Comments |
|---|---|
| Achieve Education for All (EFA) | Completing a quality basic education is a "social vaccine" against HIV and AIDS. |
| The national curriculum uses a life-skills approach, including:<br>• Formal and nonformal components<br>• Grade- and age-specific content, beginning before the onset of sexual activity<br>• Participatory teaching methods<br>• Bases prevention modules in a carrier subject<br>• Teaching in the context of school health (for example, FRESH)<br>• Community ownership and support | Teaching needs to start before risky behaviors have become established, and content needs to be matched to the developmental stage of the child. Teaching methods that establish knowledge, values, and skills that support positive behaviors should be used. A single carrier subject (for example, social studies) is simpler and avoids spreading messages thinly across subjects (for example, integration or infusion). Failure to involve the community in this sensitive area is one of the major causes of implementation delays. |

*(continued next page)*

| Item | Comments |
|---|---|
| HIV/AIDS prevention requires that teachers develop skills in participatory methods through: <br>• Pre-service training and materials <br>• In-service training and materials <br>• Messages and approaches that help teachers protect themselves | Preventive education is more frequently taught as part of in-service training than pre-service teacher training. Whereas both are necessary, new teachers may be more readily trained in the participatory methods that are required to teach the subject. Teacher training institutions frequently overlook the benefits of helping teachers protect themselves. |
| Complementary approaches: <br>• Peer education <br>• Ministry of education (MoE) has input to community information, education, and communication (IEC) strategies <br>• MoE coordinates with nongovernmental organization (NGO), faith-based organization (FBO), and community-based organization (CBO) prevention and mitigation programs <br>• MoE assists ministry of health (MoH) in promoting youth-friendly clinics for VCT, the treatment of sexually transmitted infections (STIs) and condom distribution | A holistic approach is essential for effective prevention. Peer education can reinforce active learning by youths. IEC strategies ensure consistent messages in the school, home, and community. Building on existing programs speeds up the response. Early and effective treatment of sexually transmitted infections is effective in reducing HIV transmission; youths also need access to voluntary counseling and testing, as well as condoms, to translate learned behaviors into practice. |

## Orphans and Vulnerable Children Checklist

| Item | Comments |
|---|---|
| Eliminate financial barriers to education: <br>• Achieve Education for All <br>• Abolish school fees <br>• Develop a mitigation strategy to avoid informal and illegal levies <br>• Subsidize payment of informal levies | Achieving EFA enhances educational access for all children, including orphans and vulnerable children. School fees in particular may prevent this group from accessing education. Abolition of school fees provides partial relief, but fees are often substituted by levies (for example, for textbooks, parent-teacher associations [PTAs], uniforms), which must be addressed in financing plans for fee abolition. Social funds may offer subsidies through schools and PTAs, or the community may help overcome these barriers. |

(continued next page)

| Item | Comments |
|---|---|
| Help maintain school attendance by<br>• Offering conditional cash (or food) transfers<br>• Providing school health programs to support children (for example, FRESH), including psychosocial counseling | Ensuring that orphans and vulnerable children are able to attend school is only the beginning: this group also requires support to remain in school. One effective method is to offer caregivers cash (or food) transfers that are conditional upon children's attendance. Orphans and vulnerable children may require special care because of their experiences. They may also benefit from school health programs based on the FRESH framework, including psychosocial counseling. |
| Have education sector work with other agencies to provide care, support, and protection:<br>• MoE coordinates with NGOs, FBOs, and CBOs<br>• MoE coordinates with ministries of welfare or social affairs | In practice, civil society and FBOs are most often directly involved in these programs and offer an immediate point of entry. The MoE can ensure that education system programs are complementary with these activities. Long-term care, support, and protection of orphans and vulnerable children are typically the mandate of social programs under ministries of welfare or social affairs. |

Reference materials for supporting the development of key components of an education sector response to HIV and AIDS are available from eservice@worldbank.org or http://www.schoolsandhealth.org.

**Sector policy**
- "An ILO Code of Practice on HIV/AIDS and the World of Work" (ILO 2001)
- Implementing the ILO Code of Practice: An Education and Training Manual (CD format)
- The Namibia Ministry of Education National Policy on HIV/AIDS and Education
- "HIV/AIDS and Education: A Strategic Approach" (DFID et al. 2003).
- *Education and HIV/AIDS: A Window of Hope* (World Bank 2002)

## Management and planning

- *Education and HIV/AIDS: Modeling the Impact of HIV/AIDS on Education Systems—A Training Manual* (World Bank and UNAIDS 2002)
- "Using School Survey Data to Project the Impact of HIV/AIDS on the Education Sector in Mozambique, as a Component of the Planning for the FTI Response" (Valerio and Desai 2002)

## Prevention

- *Education and HIV/AIDS: A Sourcebook of HIV/AIDS Prevention Programs in Schools* (World Bank and Development Co-operation Ireland 2003)
- "UNAIDS Benchmarks for Effective HIV/AIDS Prevention Programmes in Schools" (UNAIDS IATT Working Group 2002)
- "Focusing Resources on Effective School Health: A FRESH Start to Enhancing the Quality and Equity of Education" (UNESCO et al. 2000)
- "Focusing Resources on Effective School Health: A FRESH Approach to Achieving Education for All" (UNESCO et al. 2002)
- "Focusing Resources on Effective School Health: A FRESH Start to Enhancing HIV/AIDS Prevention" (UNICEF et al. 2002)

## Orphans and vulnerable children

- "Education and HIV/AIDS: Ensuring Education Access for Orphans and Vulnerable Children—A Training Module" (World Bank and UNICEF 2002)
- "Children on the Brink 2002: A Joint Report on Orphan Estimates and Program Strategies" (UNICEF and USAID 2002)
- "The Role of Education in Supporting and Caring for Orphans and Other Children made Vulnerable by HIV/AIDS" (UNAIDS IATT Working Group 2003)

## References

DFID (U.K. Department for International Development), Education Development Center, Education International, European Commission, ILO (International Labour Organization), UNESCO (United Nations Educational, Scientific and Cultural Organization), UNAIDS (Joint United Nations Programme on HIV&AIDS), UNDCP (United Nations International Drug Control Programme), UNDP (United Nations Development Programme), UNFPA

(United Nations Population Fund), UNICEF (United Nations Children's Fund), USAID (U.S. Agency for International Development), WHO (World Health Organization), and World Bank. 2003. "HIV/AIDS and Education: A Strategic Approach." IIEP Publications, Paris.

ILO (International Labour Organization). 2001. "An ILO Code of Practice on HIV/AIDS and the World of Work." ILO, Geneva.

UNAIDS (Joint United Nations Programme on HIV&AIDS) IATT (Inter-Agency Task Team for HIV and Education) Working Group. 2002. "UNAIDS Benchmarks for Effective HIV/AIDS Prevention Programmes in Schools." UNAIDS, Geneva.

———. 2004. "The role of education in the protection, care and support of orphans and vulnerable children living in a world with HIV and AIDS." UNAIDS, Geneva.

UNICEF (United Nations Children's Fund), UNESCO (United Nations Educational, Scientific and Cultural Organization), WHO (World Health Organization), and World Bank. 2000. "Focusing Resources on Effective School Health: A FRESH Start to Enhancing the Quality and Equity of Education." World Bank, Washington, DC.

———. 2002. "Focusing Resources on Effective School Health: A FRESH Approach to Achieving Education for All." UNESCO, Paris.

———. 2002. "Focusing Resources on Effective School Health: A FRESH Start to Enhancing HIV/AIDS Prevention." UNESCO, Paris.

UNICEF (United Nations Children's Fund) and UNAIDS (Joint United Nations Programme). 2002. "Children on the Brink 2002: A Joint Report on Orphan Estimates and Program Strategies." TvT Associates, Washington, DC.

Valerio, A., and K. Desai. 2002. "Using School Survey Data to Project the Impact of HIV/AIDS on the Education Sector in Mozambique, as a Component of the Planning for the FTI Response." World Bank, Washington, DC.

World Bank. 2002. *Education and HIV/AIDS: A Window of Hope.* Washington, DC: World Bank.

World Bank. 2003. *Education and HIV/AIDS: A Sourcebook of HIV/AIDS Prevention Programs in Schools.* Washington, DC: World Bank.

World Bank and UNAIDS (Joint United Nations Programme). 2002. *Education and HIV/AIDS: Modeling the Impact of HIV/AIDS on Education Systems—A Training Manual.* Washington, DC: World Bank.

World Bank and UNICEF (United Nations Children's Fund). 2002. "Education and HIV/AIDS: Ensuring Education Access for Orphans and Vulnerable Children—A Training Module." World Bank, Washington, DC.

# School Health and Nutrition Programs by Country in Sub-Saharan Africa, the Greater Mekong Subregion, and the Caribbean

## Sub-Saharan Africa

| Policies and strategies | West Africa | | | | | | | | | | | | | | | Central Africa | | | | | | | East Africa | | | | | | | | | | | |
|---|---|---|---|---|---|---|---|---|---|---|---|---|---|---|---|---|---|---|---|---|---|---|---|---|---|---|---|---|---|---|---|---|---|---|
| | Benin | Burkina Faso | Côte d'Ivoire | Gambia, The | Ghana | Guinea | Guinea-Bissau | Liberia | Mali | Mauritania | Niger | Nigeria | Senegal | Sierra Leone | Togo | Cameroon | Central African Republic | Chad | Congo, Dem. Rep. | Congo, Rep. | Gabon | São Tomé and Príncipe | Burundi | Eritrea | Ethiopia | Kenya | Madagascar | Malawi | Mozambique | Rwanda | Tanzania (mainland) | Uganda | Zambia | Zanzibar |
| National SHN policy | ✓ | ✓ | ✓ | ✓ | ✓ | ✓ | ✓ | NR | ✓ | ✓ | ✓ | ✓ | ✓ | ✓ | NR | ✓ | | ✓ | | | ✓ | | ✓ | ✓ | | | ✓ | ✓ | ✓ | ✓ | ✓ | | ✓ | |
| National HIV and AIDS strategy | ✓ | ✓ | ✓ | ✓ | ✓ | ✓ | ✓ | ✓ | ✓ | ✓ | ✓ | ✓ | ✓ | ✓ | ✓ | ✓ | ✓ | ✓ | ✓ | ✓ | ✓ | ✓ | ✓ | ✓ | ✓ | ✓ | ✓ | ✓ | ✓ | ✓ | ✓ | ✓ | ✓ | ✓ |
| Education sector HIV and AIDS strategy | ✓ | ✓ | ✓ | ✓ | ✓ | ✓ | ✓ | ✓ | ✓ | NR | ✓ | ✓ | ✓ | ✓ | ✓ | ✓ | | ✓ | ✓ | ✓ | NR | ✓ | ✓ | ✓ | ✓ | ✓ | ✓ | ✓ | ✓ | ✓ | ✓ | ✓ | ✓ | ✓ |
| Education sector HIV and AIDS action plan | ✓ | ✓ | ✓ | ✓ | ✓ | ✓ | ✓ | ✓ | ✓ | ✓ | ✓ | ✓ | ✓ | NR | ✓ | ✓ | | ✓ | ✓ | ✓ | ✓ | ✓ | ✓ | ✓ | ✓ | ✓ | ✓ | ✓ | ✓ | ✓ | ✓ | ✓ | NR | ✓ |
| National workplace policy | ✓ | ✓ | ✓ | | ✓ | ✓ | ✓ | NR | | | ✓ | ✓ | ✓ | ✓ | | | | | ✓ | | | | ✓ | | | NR | ✓ | ✓ | ✓ | ✓ | | ✓ | ✓ | |
| Education sector HIV and AIDS policy that includes workplace regulations | NR | NR | | ✓ | ✓ | ✓ | | | NR | NR | | | | | NR | ✓ | | | | | | | | | | NR | | | | | NR | | NR | NR |

*Source:* World Bank 2007.
*Note:* NR = no response.

Table: Planning and management

| Planning and management | West Africa | | | | | | | | | | | | | | | Central Africa | | | | | | | East Africa | | | | | | | | | | | |
|---|---|---|---|---|---|---|---|---|---|---|---|---|---|---|---|---|---|---|---|---|---|---|---|---|---|---|---|---|---|---|---|---|---|---|
| | Benin | Burkina Faso | Côte d'Ivoire | Gambia, The | Ghana | Guinea | Guinea-Bissau | Liberia | Mali | Mauritania | Niger | Nigeria | Senegal | Sierra Leone | Togo | Cameroon | Central African Republic | Chad | Congo, Dem. Rep. | Congo, Rep. | Gabon | São Tomé and Príncipe | Burundi | Eritrea | Ethiopia | Kenya | Madagascar | Malawi | Mozambique | Rwanda | Tanzania (mainland) | Uganda | Zambia | Zanzibar |
| SHN unit in the MoE | ✓ | ✓ | ✓ | ✓ | ✓ | ✓ | ✓ | ✓ | ✓ | ✓ | ✓ | ✓ | ✓ | | | ✓ | ✓ | ✓ | ✓ | | | | ✓ | ✓ | | | ✓ | ✓ | ✓ | ✓ | ✓ | | ✓ | |
| Full-time SHN unit coordinator | ✓ | NR | ✓ | ✓ | ✓ | ✓ | ✓ | NR | ✓ | ✓ | NR | ✓ | ✓ | | | ✓ | ✓ | ✓ | | | | | | ✓ | | | NR | NR | ✓ | ✓ | | | ✓ | |
| HIV and AIDS part of the SHN unit | | ✓ | ✓ | | ✓ | ✓ | ✓ | ✓ | | ✓ | ✓ | | ✓ | | | ✓ | | ✓ | ✓ | | ✓ | ✓ | ✓ | ✓ | | ✓ | | ✓ | ✓ | ✓ | ✓ | | | ✓ |
| Separate HIV and AIDS unit in the MoE | ✓ | | | ✓ | ✓ | | | | ✓ | | | ✓ | | ✓ | ✓ | | ✓ | | | ✓ | | | | | ✓ | | ✓ | | ✓ | | | | ✓ | |
| HIV and AIDS focal point in the MoE | ✓ | ✓ | ✓ | ✓ | ✓ | ✓ | ✓ | ✓ | ✓ | ✓ | ✓ | ✓ | ✓ | ✓ | ✓ | ✓ | ✓ | ✓ | ✓ | ✓ | ✓ | ✓ | ✓ | ✓ | ✓ | ✓ | ✓ | ✓ | ✓ | ✓ | ✓ | ✓ | NR | ✓ |
| Full-time HIV and AIDS focal point | ✓ | ✓ | ✓ | ✓ | ✓ | ✓ | ✓ | ✓ | NR | NR | ✓ | ✓ | | | | | | | | | | | | | | | NR | ✓ | ✓ | ✓ | NR | ✓ | NR | ✓ |

(continued next page)

| Planning and management | West Africa | | | | | | | | | | | | | | | Central Africa | | | | | | | East Africa | | | | | | | | | | | |
|---|---|---|---|---|---|---|---|---|---|---|---|---|---|---|---|---|---|---|---|---|---|---|---|---|---|---|---|---|---|---|---|---|---|---|
| | Benin | Burkina Faso | Côte d'Ivoire | Gambia, The | Ghana | Guinea | Guinea-Bissau | Liberia | Mali | Mauritania | Niger | Nigeria | Senegal | Sierra Leone | Togo | Cameroon | Central African Republic | Chad | Congo, Dem. Rep. | Congo, Rep. | Gabon | São Tomé and Príncipe | Burundi | Eritrea | Ethiopia | Kenya | Madagascar | Malawi | Mozambique | Rwanda | Tanzania (mainland) | Uganda | Zambia | Zanzibar |
| SHN focal points at the subnational level | ✓ | ✓ | ✓ | ✓ | ✓ | ✓ | ✓ | NR | ✓ | ✓ | ✓ | ✓ | ✓ | ✓ | NR | ✓ | | ✓ | ✓ | | NR | NR | | ✓ | | ✓ | NR | ✓ | ✓ | ✓ | ✓ | NR | NR | |
| HIV and AIDS focal points at the subnational level | ✓ | ✓ | ✓ | ✓ | NR | ✓ | NR | NR | ✓ | ✓ | ✓ | ✓ | ✓ | ✓ | ✓ | ✓ | NR | ✓ | ✓ | ✓ | NR | NR | ✓ | ✓ | ✓ | ✓ | ✓ | ✓ | ✓ | ✓ | ✓ | NR | ✓ | ✓ |
| SHN or HIV and AIDS inter-departmental committee within the MoE | ✓ | ✓ | ✓ | ✓ | | ✓ | | | ✓ | ✓ | ✓ | ✓ | ✓ | ✓ | NR | ✓ | ✓ | ✓ | ✓ | ✓ | | ✓ | ✓ | ✓ | ✓ | ✓ | | ✓ | ✓ | ✓ | ✓ | | ✓ | ✓ |
| MoE collects data at least annually on health-related attrition and absences of teachers | ✓ | | ✓ | | ✓ | | | NR | | ✓ | | ✓ | ✓ | | | ✓ | | | | | | | | ✓ | | NR | | | | ✓ | ✓ | ✓ | ✓ | ✓ |

Source: World Bank 2007.
Note: NR = no response.

Skills-based health education including HIV prevention

| | West Africa | | | | | | | | | | | | | | | Central Africa | | | | | | | East Africa | | | | | | | | | | | |
|---|---|---|---|---|---|---|---|---|---|---|---|---|---|---|---|---|---|---|---|---|---|---|---|---|---|---|---|---|---|---|---|---|---|---|
| | Benin | Burkina Faso | Côte d'Ivoire | Gambia, The | Ghana | Guinea | Guinea-Bissau | Liberia | Mali | Mauritania | Niger | Nigeria | Senegal | Sierra Leone | Togo | Cameroon | Central African Republic | Chad | Congo, Dem. Rep. | Congo, Rep. | Gabon | São Tomé and Príncipe | Burundi | Eritrea | Ethiopia | Kenya | Madagascar | Malawi | Mozambique | Rwanda | Tanzania (mainland) | Uganda | Zambia | Zanzibar |
| National health education curriculum | ✓ | ✓ | ✓ | ✓ | ✓ | ✓ | ✓ | NR | | ✓ | | ✓ | ✓ | NR | | ✓ | | ✓ | ✓ | | | ✓ | | ✓ | ✓ | NR | ✓ | | NR | ✓ | ✓ | ✓ | NR | |
| National health education curriculum that is adaptable at subnational level | NR | ✓ | ✓ | NR | ✓ | ✓ | ✓ | NR | | ✓ | | ✓ | ✓ | NR | | ✓ | | ✓ | ✓ | | | ✓ | | ✓ | ✓ | NR | ✓ | | NR | ✓ | ✓ | ✓ | NR | |
| Nutrition education in schools | ✓ | ✓ | ✓ | ✓ | ✓ | ✓ | ✓ | NR | ✓ | ✓ | ✓ | ✓ | ✓ | ✓ | ✓ | ✓ | ✓ | NR | ✓ | ✓ | ✓ | ✓ | ✓ | ✓ | ✓ | ✓ | | ✓ | ✓ | ✓ | ✓ | ✓ | NR | ✓ |
| Hygiene education in schools | ✓ | ✓ | ✓ | ✓ | ✓ | ✓ | ✓ | ✓ | ✓ | ✓ | ✓ | ✓ | ✓ | ✓ | ✓ | ✓ | ✓ | ✓ | ✓ | ✓ | ✓ | ✓ | ✓ | ✓ | ✓ | ✓ | | ✓ | ✓ | ✓ | ✓ | ✓ | NR | ✓ |
| Malaria prevention education in schools | ✓ | ✓ | ✓ | ✓ | ✓ | ✓ | ✓ | ✓ | ✓ | ✓ | ✓ | NR | ✓ | ✓ | ✓ | ✓ | ✓ | ✓ | ✓ | ✓ | ✓ | ✓ | ✓ | ✓ | ✓ | NR | | ✓ | ✓ | ✓ | ✓ | ✓ | NR | ✓ |
| Peer education within the education sector | ✓ | ✓ | ✓ | ✓ | ✓ | ✓ | ✓ | ✓ | ✓ | ✓ | ✓ | ✓ | ✓ | ✓ | ✓ | ✓ | ✓ | ✓ | ✓ | ✓ | | ✓ | ✓ | ✓ | ✓ | ✓ | NR | ✓ | ✓ | ✓ | ✓ | ✓ | ✓ | ✓ |
| Peer education in primary schools | ✓ | ✓ | ✓ | ✓ | ✓ | ✓ | ✓ | NR | ✓ | NR | ✓ | ✓ | ✓ | ✓ | ✓ | ✓ | | ✓ | ✓ | ✓ | ✓ | ✓ | NR | ✓ | ✓ | NR | NR | ✓ | NR | ✓ | ✓ | ✓ | NR | ✓ |
| Peer education in secondary schools | ✓ | ✓ | ✓ | ✓ | ✓ | ✓ | ✓ | NR | ✓ | NR | ✓ | ✓ | ✓ | ✓ | ✓ | ✓ | | ✓ | ✓ | ✓ | ✓ | ✓ | NR | ✓ | ✓ | NR | NR | ✓ | NR | ✓ | ✓ | ✓ | NR | ✓ |

(continued next page)

Skills-based health education including HIV prevention

| Skills-based health education including HIV prevention | West Africa | | | | | | | | | | | | | | | Central Africa | | | | | | | East Africa | | | | | | | | | | | |
|---|---|---|---|---|---|---|---|---|---|---|---|---|---|---|---|---|---|---|---|---|---|---|---|---|---|---|---|---|---|---|---|---|---|---|
| | Benin | Burkina Faso | Côte d'Ivoire | Gambia, The | Ghana | Guinea | Guinea-Bissau | Liberia | Mali | Mauritania | Niger | Nigeria | Senegal | Sierra Leone | Togo | Cameroon | Central African Republic | Chad | Congo, Dem. Rep. | Congo, Rep. | Gabon | São Tomé and Príncipe | Burundi | Eritrea | Ethiopia | Kenya | Madagascar | Malawi | Mozambique | Rwanda | Tanzania (mainland) | Uganda | Zambia | Zanzibar |
| HIV and AIDS prevention education in primary schools | ✓ | | ✓ | ✓ | ✓ | ✓ | ✓ | ✓ | ✓ | ✓ | ✓ | ✓ | ✓ | ✓ | | ✓ | ✓ | ✓ | ✓ | ✓ | ✓ | NR | | ✓ | ✓ | ✓ | ✓ | ✓ | ✓ | ✓ | ✓ | ✓ | ✓ | ✓ |
| HIV and AIDS prevention education in secondary schools | ✓ | ✓ | ✓ | ✓ | ✓ | ✓ | ✓ | ✓ | ✓ | ✓ | ✓ | ✓ | ✓ | ✓ | ✓ | ✓ | ✓ | ✓ | ✓ | ✓ | ✓ | NR | | ✓ | ✓ | ✓ | ✓ | ✓ | ✓ | ✓ | ✓ | ✓ | ✓ | ✓ |
| HIV and AIDS education infused in a carrier subject | ✓ | ✓ | ✓ | ✓ | ✓ | ✓ | ✓ | ✓ | ✓ | ✓ | ✓ | ✓ | ✓ | ✓ | ✓ | ✓ | ✓ | ✓ | ✓ | ✓ | ✓ | NR | | ✓ | ✓ | ✓ | ✓ | ✓ | ✓ | ✓ | ✓ | ✓ | ✓ | ✓ |
| HIV and AIDS taught using a life-skills approach | ✓ | ✓ | ✓ | ✓ | ✓ | ✓ | ✓ | ✓ | ✓ | ✓ | NR | ✓ | ✓ | ✓ | ✓ | ✓ | ✓ | ✓ | ✓ | ✓ | NR | NR | | ✓ | ✓ | ✓ | ✓ | NR | ✓ | ✓ | NR | ✓ | ✓ | ✓ |
| HIV and AIDS prevention education in the informal setting | ✓ | NR | ✓ | NR | ✓ | ✓ | ✓ | NR | NR | ✓ | | ✓ | ✓ | ✓ | NR | | | ✓ | ✓ | ✓ | NR | NR | | ✓ | ✓ | NR | NR | ✓ | NR | ✓ | ✓ | ✓ | NR | NR |
| HIV and AIDS taught using a life-skills approach in the informal setting | NR | | ✓ | ✓ | NR | ✓ | ✓ | NR | ✓ | ✓ | NR | ✓ | ✓ | ✓ | | ✓ | | ✓ | ✓ | ✓ | NR | NR | | ✓ | ✓ | NR | ✓ | ✓ | ✓ | ✓ | NR | ✓ | ✓ | ✓ |

*Source:* World Bank 2007.

*Note:* NR = no response.

274

| Teacher training | West Africa | | | | | | | | | | | | | | | Central Africa | | | | | | | East Africa | | | | | | | | | | | |
|---|---|---|---|---|---|---|---|---|---|---|---|---|---|---|---|---|---|---|---|---|---|---|---|---|---|---|---|---|---|---|---|---|---|---|
| | Benin | Burkina Faso | Côte d'Ivoire | Gambia, The | Ghana | Guinea | Guinea-Bissau | Liberia | Mali | Mauritania | Niger | Nigeria | Senegal | Sierra Leone | Togo | Cameroon | Central African Republic | Chad | Congo, Dem. Rep. | Congo, Rep. | Gabon | São Tomé and Príncipe | Burundi | Eritrea | Ethiopia | Kenya | Madagascar | Malawi | Mozambique | Rwanda | Tanzania (mainland) | Uganda | Zambia | Zanzibar |
| Teachers trained in life-skills education | ✓ | ✓ | ✓ | ✓ | ✓ | ✓ | ✓ | NR | ✓ | | NR | ✓ | | ✓ | ✓ | NR | | ✓ | | ✓ | | ✓ | ✓ | ✓ | ✓ | NR | | ✓ | ✓ | ✓ | ✓ | ✓ | ✓ | ✓ |
| Teachers trained in life-skills education preservice | ✓ | ✓ | ✓ | ✓ | ✓ | ✓ | ✓ | NR | ✓ | | NR | ✓ | ✓ | ✓ | ✓ | NR | | ✓ | | | | ✓ | ✓ | ✓ | ✓ | NR | | ✓ | ✓ | | ✓ | ✓ | ✓ | ✓ |
| Teachers trained in life-skills education in service | ✓ | ✓ | ✓ | ✓ | ✓ | ✓ | ✓ | NR | ✓ | ✓ | NR | ✓ | | ✓ | ✓ | NR | | ✓ | ✓ | ✓ | | ✓ | ✓ | ✓ | ✓ | NR | | ✓ | ✓ | ✓ | ✓ | ✓ | ✓ | ✓ |
| Teachers taught to protect themselves from HIV | ✓ | ✓ | ✓ | ✓ | ✓ | ✓ | ✓ | ✓ | ✓ | ✓ | NR | ✓ | ✓ | ✓ | ✓ | ✓ | ✓ | ✓ | | ✓ | ✓ | ✓ | ✓ | ✓ | ✓ | ✓ | ✓ | ✓ | ✓ | ✓ | ✓ | ✓ | ✓ | ✓ |
| Teachers given HIV and AIDS training | ✓ | ✓ | ✓ | ✓ | ✓ | ✓ | ✓ | ✓ | ✓ | ✓ | NR | ✓ | ✓ | ✓ | ✓ | ✓ | ✓ | ✓ | | ✓ | ✓ | ✓ | ✓ | ✓ | ✓ | ✓ | ✓ | ✓ | ✓ | ✓ | ✓ | ✓ | ✓ | ✓ |
| Teachers given HIV and AIDS training preservice | ✓ | ✓ | ✓ | ✓ | ✓ | ✓ | ✓ | ✓ | NR | ✓ | NR | ✓ | ✓ | ✓ | ✓ | | | ✓ | NR | | | ✓ | ✓ | ✓ | ✓ | NR | ✓ | ✓ | | ✓ | ✓ | ✓ | ✓ | ✓ |
| Teachers given HIV and AIDS training in-service | ✓ | ✓ | ✓ | ✓ | ✓ | ✓ | ✓ | ✓ | NR | ✓ | NR | ✓ | ✓ | ✓ | ✓ | ✓ | ✓ | ✓ | NR | ✓ | ✓ | ✓ | ✓ | ✓ | ✓ | NR | ✓ | ✓ | | ✓ | ✓ | ✓ | ✓ | ✓ |
| Data collection on teachers trained and training materials in learning institutes | ✓ | ✓ | ✓ | ✓ | ✓ | ✓ | ✓ | NR | | ✓ | NR | ✓ | | ✓ | ✓ | NR | | ✓ | | | ✓ | | NR | ✓ | ✓ | NR | ✓ | ✓ | NR | ✓ | ✓ | ✓ | ✓ | ✓ |

Note: NR = no response.

| Health and nutrition services | West Africa | | | | | | | | | | | | | | | Central Africa | | | | | | | East Africa | | | | | | | | | | | |
|---|---|---|---|---|---|---|---|---|---|---|---|---|---|---|---|---|---|---|---|---|---|---|---|---|---|---|---|---|---|---|---|---|---|---|
| | Benin | Burkina Faso | Côte d'Ivoire | Gambia, The | Ghana | Guinea | Guinea-Bissau | Liberia | Mali | Mauritania | Niger | Nigeria | Senegal | Sierra Leone | Togo | Cameroon | Central African Republic | Chad | Congo, Dem. Rep. | Congo, Rep. | Gabon | São Tomé and Príncipe | Burundi | Eritrea | Ethiopia | Kenya | Madagascar | Malawi | Mozambique | Rwanda | Tanzania (mainland) | Uganda | Zambia | Zanzibar |
| Vaccinations for school-age children (SAC) | ✓ | ✓ | ✓ | ✓ | ✓ | ✓ | ✓ | ✓ | ✓ | ✓ | ✓ | ✓ | ✓ | NR | NR | ✓ | ✓ | | | ✓ | | ✓ | ✓ | ✓ | ✓ | NR | ✓ | ✓ | ✓ | ✓ | ✓ | ✓ | ✓ | ✓ |
| School feeding provided for SAC | ✓ | ✓ | ✓ | ✓ | ✓ | ✓ | ✓ | ✓ | ✓ | ✓ | ✓ | ✓ | ✓ | NR | | ✓ | ✓ | ✓ | | ✓ | | ✓ | ✓ | ✓ | ✓ | NR | ✓ | ✓ | ✓ | ✓ | ✓ | ✓ | ✓ | |
| Vitamin A capsules provided for SAC | ✓ | ✓ | ✓ | ✓ | ✓ | ✓ | ✓ | NR | ✓ | NR | ✓ | ✓ | ✓ | NR | ✓ | ✓ | ✓ | ✓ | ✓ | ✓ | | ✓ | ✓ | ✓ | ✓ | ✓ | ✓ | ✓ | ✓ | ✓ | ✓ | NR | ✓ | |
| Iron supplementation program for SAC | ✓ | ✓ | ✓ | ✓ | ✓ | ✓ | ✓ | NR | ✓ | ✓ | ✓ | ✓ | ✓ | NR | ✓ | | ✓ | ✓ | ✓ | ✓ | | ✓ | ✓ | ✓ | ✓ | ✓ | ✓ | ✓ | ✓ | ✓ | ✓ | NR | ✓ | |
| Deworming programme for SAC | ✓ | ✓ | ✓ | ✓ | ✓ | ✓ | ✓ | ✓ | ✓ | ✓ | ✓ | ✓ | ✓ | NR | | ✓ | | ✓ | ✓ | ✓ | | | ✓ | ✓ | ✓ | ✓ | ✓ | ✓ | ✓ | ✓ | ✓ | ✓ | ✓ | |
| Reproductive health services for SAC | ✓ | ✓ | ✓ | ✓ | | ✓ | ✓ | ✓ | ✓ | ✓ | NR | NR | ✓ | ✓ | | ✓ | | ✓ | ✓ | ✓ | | ✓ | ✓ | ✓ | ✓ | ✓ | ✓ | ✓ | ✓ | ✓ | ✓ | ✓ | NR | ✓ |
| Counseling services for teachers | ✓ | ✓ | ✓ | ✓ | | ✓ | ✓ | ✓ | ✓ | NR | NR | ✓ | ✓ | ✓ | NR | ✓ | | | | ✓ | NR | ✓ | ✓ | ✓ | ✓ | | ✓ | ✓ | ✓ | ✓ | ✓ | ✓ | ✓ | ✓ |
| Malaria control services for SAC | ✓ | ✓ | ✓ | NR | | ✓ | NR | NR | NR | ✓ | NR | NR | ✓ | NR | ✓ | ✓ | | | ✓ | ✓ | | ✓ | ✓ | ✓ | ✓ | | ✓ | ✓ | ✓ | ✓ | ✓ | NR | ✓ | ✓ |
| Medical examinations for SAC | ✓ | ✓ | NR | | ✓ | | | NR NR | NR NR | ✓ | ✓ | NR | ✓ | NR | ✓ | ✓ | | | | ✓ | ✓ | | | | ✓ | | ✓ | ✓ | ✓ | ✓ | ✓ | NR NR | NR NR | |
| Hearing and sight examinations for SAC | ✓ | | NR | | ✓ | | | NR NR | NR NR | NR | ✓ | NR ✓ | ✓ | NR | ✓ | | | | | | | ✓ | | ✓ | ✓ | ✓ | NR ✓ | ✓ | ✓ | ✓ | ✓ | NR | ✓ | ✓ |

Source: World Bank 2007.
Note: NR = no response.

| Orphans and vulnerable children (OVCs) | West Africa | | | | | | | | | | | | | | | Central Africa | | | | | | | East Africa | | | | | | | | | | | |
|---|---|---|---|---|---|---|---|---|---|---|---|---|---|---|---|---|---|---|---|---|---|---|---|---|---|---|---|---|---|---|---|---|---|---|
| | Benin | Burkina Faso | Côte d'Ivoire | Gambia, The | Ghana | Guinea | Guinea-Bissau | Liberia | Mali | Mauritania | Niger | Nigeria | Senegal | Sierra Leone | Togo | Cameroon | Central African Republic | Chad | Congo, Dem. Rep. | Congo, Rep. | Gabon | São Tomé and Príncipe | Burundi | Eritrea | Ethiopia | Kenya | Madagascar | Malawi | Mozambique | Rwanda | Tanzania (mainland) | Uganda | Zambia | Zanzibar |
| National policy of free primary school EFA | ✓ | NR | ✓ | ✓ | ✓ | ✓ | ✓ | ✓ | ✓ | ✓ | ✓ | ✓ | ✓ | ✓ | ✓ | ✓ | ✓ | ✓ | | ✓ | ✓ | ✓ | ✓ | ✓ | ✓ | ✓ | ✓ | ✓ | ✓ | ✓ | NR | ✓ | ✓ | ✓ |
| OVCs do not pay school tuition or fees | ✓ | ✓ | ✓ | NR | ✓ | ✓ | NR | ✓ | ✓ | ✓ | NR | ✓ | ✓ | ✓ | ✓ | ✓ | | ✓ | | | ✓ | ✓ | ✓ | ✓ | ✓ | | ✓ | | ✓ | ✓ | ✓ | ✓ | ✓ | NR |
| Programs for conditional cash transfers | | NR | | NR | | NR | ✓ | | | NR | NR | | ✓ | | | | | | | | | | | | | | | NR | | ✓ | | NR | NR | |
| Affirmative action to boost enrollment and attendance of girls | ✓ | ✓ | ✓ | ✓ | | ✓ | ✓ | ✓ | ✓ | ✓ | ✓ | ✓ | ✓ | ✓ | | ✓ | ✓ | ✓ | ✓ | | | | ✓ | ✓ | ✓ | ✓ | ✓ | ✓ | ✓ | ✓ | ✓ | ✓ | ✓ | ✓ |
| MoE keep data on OVCs | ✓ | ✓ | ✓ | NR | ✓ | ✓ | ✓ | ✓ | ✓ | NR | ✓ | ✓ | ✓ | | | | | | | | | | ✓ | | | ✓ | ✓ | ✓ | ✓ | ✓ | ✓ | ✓ | ✓ | |

*Source:* World Bank 2007.
*Note:* NR = no response.

## Greater Mekong Subregion

| Policy and strategies | Bhutan | Cambodia | China, Yunnan Province | Lao PDR | Thailand | Vietnam |
|---|---|---|---|---|---|---|
| National SHN policy | | ✓ | ✓ | ✓ | ✓ | |
| National SHN policy implemented by MoH | NR | | ✓ | ✓ | ✓ | NR |
| National SHN policy implemented by MoE | NR | ✓ | ✓ | ✓ | ✓ | |
| Education sector HIV and AIDS strategy | ✓ | ✓ | | ✓ | ✓ | |
| Education sector HIV and AIDS action plan | ✓ | ✓ | | ✓ | ✓ | |
| National workplace policy | | | ✓ | ✓ | ✓ | ✓ |
| HIV and AIDS issues addressed in national workplace policy | NA | | ✓ | ✓ | ✓ | ✓ |

*Source:* Bundy et al. 2009.
*Note:* NR = no response.

| Planning and management | Bhutan | Cambodia | China, Yunnan Province | Lao PDR | Thailand | Vietnam |
|---|---|---|---|---|---|---|
| SHN unit in the MoE | ✓ | ✓ | ✓ | ✓ | ✓ | ✓ |
| Full-time SHN unit coordinator | ✓ | ✓ | ✓ | | ✓ | ✓ |

*Source:* Bundy et al. 2009.

| School environment | Bhutan | Cambodia | China, Yunnan Province | Lao PDR | Thailand | Vietnam |
|---|---|---|---|---|---|---|
| National policies that require schools to provide safe, potable drinking water | ✓ | ✓ | ✓ | ✓ | ✓ | ✓ |
| National policies that require schools to provide hand washing facilities | | ✓ | | ✓ | ✓ | |
| National policies that require schools to provide separate latrines for boys and girls | | ✓ | ✓ | ✓ | ✓ | ✓ |
| National policies that require schools to provide separate latrines for students and teachers | | ✓ | | | ✓ | |
| Annual sanitation surveys conducted in all schools | | | ✓ | | ✓ | |
| Established school hygiene regimen including scheduled rubbish removal and maintenance of school buildings and facilities | ✓ | | | ✓ | ✓ | ✓ | ✓ |

*Source:* Bundy et al. 2009.

| Skills-based health education including HIV prevention | Bhutan | Cambodia | China, Yunnan Province | Lao PDR | Thailand | Vietnam |
|---|---|---|---|---|---|---|
| National health education curriculum | ✓ | ✓ | ✓ | ✓ | ✓ | ✓ |
| National health education curriculum that is adaptable at subnational level | | ✓ | | | ✓ | |
| Health education taught as separate subject | | | | | ✓ | |
| Nutrition education in primary schools | ✓ | ✓ | ✓ | ✓ | ✓ | ✓ |
| Nutrition education in secondary schools | ✓ | ✓ | ✓ | | ✓ | |
| Hygiene education in primary and secondary schools | ✓ | ✓ | ✓ | ✓ | ✓ | ✓ |
| HIV and AIDS prevention education in schools in any form | ✓ | ✓ | ✓ | ✓ | ✓ | ✓ |
| HIV and AIDS prevention education in primary and secondary schools | | ✓ | ✓ | ✓ | ✓ | ✓ |
| HIV and AIDS prevention education in the informal setting | ✓ | ✓ | ✓ | ✓ | ✓ | ✓ |
| HIV and AIDS education infused in a carrier subject | ✓ | ✓ | ✓ | ✓ | ✓ | ✓ |
| HIV and AIDS taught using a life-skills approach in primary and secondary schools | | ✓ | ✓ | ✓ | ✓ | ✓ |
| HIV and AIDS taught using a life-skills approach in the informal setting | | ✓ | ✓ | ✓ | ✓ | ✓ |

*Source:* Bundy et al. 2009.

| Teacher training | Bhutan | Cambodia | China, Yunnan Province | Lao PDR | Thailand | Vietnam |
|---|---|---|---|---|---|---|
| Teacher training curriculum includes SHN | ✓ | ✓ | ✓ | ✓ | ✓ | |
| Teachers given health education | ✓ | ✓ | ✓ | ✓ | ✓ | ✓ |
| Teachers given health education preservice | ✓ | ✓ | | ✓ | ✓ | |
| Teachers given health education in-service | ✓ | ✓ | ✓ | ✓ | ✓ | ✓ |
| Teachers trained in life-skills education | ✓ | ✓ | ✓ | ✓ | ✓ | ✓ |
| Teachers trained in life-skills education preservice | | ✓ | | ✓ | | NR |
| Teachers trained in life-skills education in-service | ✓ | ✓ | ✓ | ✓ | ✓ | ✓ |
| Teachers taught to protect themselves from HIV | | ✓ | ✓ | ✓ | ✓ | ✓ |
| Teachers taught to protect themselves from HIV preservice | | ✓ | | ✓ | | NR |
| Teachers taught to protect themselves from HIV in-service | | ✓ | ✓ | ✓ | ✓ | ✓ |

*Source:* Bundy et al. 2009.
*Note:* NR = no response.

| Health and nutrition services | Bhutan | Cambodia | China, Yunnan Province | Lao PDR | Thailand | Vietnam |
|---|---|---|---|---|---|---|
| Vaccinations for school-age children (SAC) | ✓ | ✓ | ✓ | ✓ | ✓ | ✓ |
| School feeding provided for SAC | ✓ | ✓ | ✓ | ✓ | ✓ | ✓ |
| Iron supplementation program for SAC | ✓ | ✓ | | ✓ | ✓ | |
| Deworming program for SAC | ✓ | ✓ | ✓ | ✓ | ✓ | ✓ |
| Reproductive health services for SAC | ✓ | ✓ | ✓ | ✓ | ✓ | ✓ |
| Counseling services for teachers | | ✓ | | | ✓ | ✓ |
| Malaria control services for SAC | ✓ | ✓ | ✓ | ✓ | ✓ | ✓ |
| Medical examinations for SAC | ✓ | ✓ | ✓ | ✓ | ✓ | ✓ |
| Hearing and sight examinations for SAC | ✓ | ✓ | ✓ | ✓ | ✓ | ✓ |

*Source:* Bundy et al. 2009.

## Caribbean

| Policy and strategies | Anguilla | Antigua | Bahamas, The | Barbados | Belize | Dominica | Grenada | Guyana | Jamaica | St. Kitts and Nevis | St. Lucia | St. Vincent and the Grenadines | Trinidad and Tobago |
|---|---|---|---|---|---|---|---|---|---|---|---|---|---|
| MoE education sector policy | | | ✓ | ✓ | ✓ | | NR | ✓ | ✓ | | | ✓ | ✓ |
| MoE education sector strategy | | | | ✓ | ✓ | | ✓ | ✓ | ✓ | | NR | ✓ | |
| National SHN policy | | | | ✓ | ✓ | | NR | ✓ | NR | ✓ | | | ✓ |
| National SHN policy implemented by MoH | | | | ✓ | | | NR | ✓ | NR | ✓ | | | |
| National SHN policy implemented by MoE | | | | ✓ | ✓ | | NR | ✓ | NR | | | | ✓ |
| Education sector HIV and AIDS strategy | | | | | ✓ | | ✓ | ✓ | ✓ | | | | ✓ |
| Education sector HIV and AIDS action plan | | ✓ | | | | | ✓ | ✓ | ✓ | | ✓ | ✓ | |
| National workplace policy | | | NR | ✓ | | | ✓ | ✓ | ✓ | ✓ | | NR | ✓ |
| HIV and AIDS issues addressed in national workplace policy | | | NR | NR | | | ✓ | ✓ | ✓ | ✓ | | NR | ✓ |
| Education sector HIV and AIDS policy that includes workplace regulations | NR | ✓ | ✓ | | | | | | | | NR | ✓ | ✓ |

*Source:* O'Connell, Venkatesh, and Bundy 2009.
*Note:* NR = no response.

| Planning and management | Anguilla | Antigua | Bahamas, The | Barbados | Belize | Dominica | Grenada | Guyana | Jamaica | St. Kitts and Nevis | St. Lucia | St. Vincent and the Grenadines | Trinidad and Tobago |
|---|---|---|---|---|---|---|---|---|---|---|---|---|---|
| SHN Unit in the MoE | ✓ | | | ✓ | ✓ | | | ✓ | ✓ | | | | ✓ |
| Full-time SHN unit coordinator | ✓ | | | ✓ | ✓ | | | | ✓ | | | | ✓ |
| Free-standing SHN unit | | | | ✓ | | | | ✓ | NR | | | | ✓ |
| HIV and AIDS part of the SHN unit | ✓ | | | ✓ | ✓ | | | ✓ | | ✓ | | | |
| Separate HIV and AIDS unit in the MoE | | ✓ | ✓ | | | | | | ✓ | | NR | | |
| HIV and AIDS focal point in the MoE | ✓ | ✓ | ✓ | ✓ | ✓ | | ✓ | ✓ | ✓ | ✓ | ✓ | | ✓ |
| Full-time HIV and AIDS focal point | | ✓ | ✓ | ✓ | ✓ | | ✓ | ✓ | ✓ | | ✓ | | ✓ |
| Official job description for focal point | | | | ✓ | ✓ | | ✓ | ✓ | ✓ | | ✓ | | ✓ |
| SHN focal points at the subnational level | | | | ✓ | ✓ | | NR | | NR | ✓ | | NR | NR |
| HIV and AIDS focal points at the subnational level | | | | ✓ | ✓ | | NR | | ✓ | ✓ | | | ✓ |
| SHN or HIV and AIDS interdepartmental committee within the MoE | | ✓ | ✓ | ✓ | | | ✓ | ✓ | ✓ | ✓ | | | ✓ |
| MoE collects data at least annually on health-related attrition and absences of teachers | | | | ✓ | ✓ | ✓ | ✓ | ✓ | NR | ✓ | | | ✓ |

Source: O'Connell, Venkatesh, and Bundy 2009.
Note: NR = no response.

| School environment | Anguilla | Antigua | Bahamas, The | Barbados | Belize | Dominica | Grenada | Guyana | Jamaica | St. Kitts and Nevis | St. Lucia | St. Vincent and the Grenadines | Trinidad and Tobago |
|---|---|---|---|---|---|---|---|---|---|---|---|---|---|
| National policies that promotes a safe, child-friendly school environment | ✓ | ✓ | ✓ | ✓ | ✓ | ✓ | ✓ | ✓ | NR | | | ✓ | ✓ |
| National policies that require schools to provide psychosocial support for students | ✓ | ✓ | ✓ | ✓ | ✓ | ✓ | ✓ | ✓ | NR | | | ✓ | ✓ |
| National policies that require schools to provide safe, potable drinking water | ✓ | ✓ | ✓ | ✓ | ✓ | ✓ | NR | ✓ | NR | | | | ✓ |
| National policies that require schools to provide hand washing facilities | ✓ | ✓ | ✓ | ✓ | ✓ | ✓ | NR | ✓ | NR | | | | ✓ |
| National policies that require schools to provide separate latrines for boys and girls | ✓ | ✓ | ✓ | ✓ | ✓ | ✓ | ✓ | ✓ | NR | | ✓ | | ✓ |
| National policies that require schools to provide separate latrines for students and teachers | ✓ | ✓ | ✓ | ✓ | ✓ | ✓ | ✓ | ✓ | NR | | ✓ | | ✓ |
| Annual sanitation surveys conducted in all schools | ✓ | | ✓ | ✓ | ✓ | | ✓ | | NR | | | ✓ | |
| Established school hygiene regimen including scheduled rubbish removal | ✓ | ✓ | ✓ | ✓ | ✓ | ✓ | ✓ | ✓ | ✓ | ✓ | ✓ | ✓ | ✓ |
| Established school hygiene regimen including maintenance of school buildings and facilities | ✓ | ✓ | ✓ | NR | ✓ | ✓ | ✓ | ✓ | ✓ | ✓ | ✓ | ✓ | ✓ |

Source: O'Connell, Venkatesh, and Bundy 2009.
Note: NR = no response.

| Skills-based health education including HIV prevention | Anguilla | Antigua | Bahamas, The | Barbados | Belize | Dominica | Grenada | Guyana | Jamaica | St. Kitts and Nevis | St. Lucia | St. Vincent and the Grenadines | Trinidad and Tobago |
|---|---|---|---|---|---|---|---|---|---|---|---|---|---|
| National health education curriculum | ✓ | ✓ | ✓ | ✓ | ✓ | ✓ | ✓ | ✓ | ✓ | ✓ | | ✓ | ✓ |
| National health education curriculum that is adaptable at subnational level | ✓ | NR | ✓ | NR | ✓ | ✓ | NR | ✓ | NR | ✓ | | ✓ | ✓ |
| Health education taught as separate subject | ✓ | ✓ | ✓ | ✓ | ✓ | ✓ | ✓ | ✓ | ✓ | ✓ | ✓ | ✓ | ✓ |
| Nutrition education in primary schools | ✓ | ✓ | ✓ | ✓ | ✓ | ✓ | ✓ | ✓ | ✓ | ✓ | ✓ | ✓ | ✓ |
| Nutrition education in secondary schools | ✓ | ✓ | ✓ | ✓ | NR | ✓ | ✓ | ✓ | NR | ✓ | ✓ | ✓ | ✓ |
| Hygiene education in primary and secondary schools | ✓ | ✓ | ✓ | ✓ | ✓ | ✓ | ✓ | ✓ | ✓ | ✓ | ✓ | ✓ | ✓ |
| Dengue prevention education in schools | | ✓ | ✓ | ✓ | ✓ | | ✓ | ✓ | NR | | ✓ | ✓ | ✓ |
| Peer education within the education sector | | ✓ | ✓ | ✓ | ✓ | ✓ | ✓ | ✓ | ✓ | ✓ | ✓ | ✓ | ✓ |
| Peer education in primary schools | | | NR | NR | NR | | | ✓ | NR | ✓ | ✓ | | |
| Peer education in secondary schools | | ✓ | ✓ | ✓ | ✓ | ✓ | ✓ | ✓ | ✓ | ✓ | ✓ | ✓ | ✓ |
| HIV and AIDS prevention education in schools in any form | ✓ | ✓ | ✓ | ✓ | ✓ | ✓ | ✓ | ✓ | ✓ | ✓ | ✓ | ✓ | ✓ |
| HIV and AIDS prevention education in primary and secondary schools | ✓ | ✓ | ✓ | ✓ | NR | NR | NR | ✓ | ✓ | ✓ | ✓ | ✓ | ✓ |
| HIV and AIDS prevention education in the informal setting | ✓ | | ✓ | ✓ | NR | NR | NR | ✓ | ✓ | ✓ | ✓ | ✓ | ✓ |
| HIV and AIDS education infused in a carrier subject | | ✓ | ✓ | ✓ | ✓ | ✓ | ✓ | ✓ | ✓ | ✓ | ✓ | ✓ | ✓ |
| HIV and AIDS taught using a life-skills approach in primary and secondary schools | ✓ | ✓ | ✓ | ✓ | ✓ | ✓ | ✓ | ✓ | ✓ | ✓ | ✓ | | ✓ |
| HIV and AIDS taught using a life-skills approach in the informal setting | | | | ✓ | ✓ | NR | NR | | | ✓ | ✓ | NR | ✓ |

Source: O'Connell, Venkatesh, and Bundy 2009.
Note: NR = no response.

| Teacher training | Anguilla | Antigua | Bahamas, The | Barbados | Belize | Dominica | Grenada | Guyana | Jamaica | St. Kitts and Nevis | St. Lucia | St. Vincent and the Grenadines | Trinidad and Tobago |
|---|---|---|---|---|---|---|---|---|---|---|---|---|---|
| Teacher training curriculum includes SHN | | ✓ | ✓ | NR | ✓ | ✓ | ✓ | ✓ | ✓ | ✓ | ✓ | ✓ | ✓ |
| Teachers given health education | | ✓ | ✓ | NR | ✓ | ✓ | ✓ | ✓ | ✓ | ✓ | | ✓ | ✓ |
| Teachers given health education preservice | | ✓ | ✓ | NR | ✓ | NR | ✓ | ✓ | NR | | | ✓ | ✓ |
| Teachers given health education in-service | | ✓ | ✓ | NR | ✓ | ✓ | ✓ | ✓ | NR | ✓ | | ✓ | ✓ |
| Teachers trained in life-skills education | ✓ | ✓ | ✓ | ✓ | ✓ | ✓ | ✓ | ✓ | ✓ | ✓ | ✓ | ✓ | ✓ |
| Teachers trained in life-skills education preservice | | ✓ | | NR | ✓ | NR | NR | ✓ | NR | | | ✓ | |
| Teachers trained in life-skills education in-service | | ✓ | | NR | ✓ | ✓ | ✓ | ✓ | ✓ | ✓ | ✓ | ✓ | ✓ |
| Teachers taught to protect themselves from HIV | ✓ | ✓ | ✓ | ✓ | ✓ | ✓ | ✓ | ✓ | ✓ | ✓ | ✓ | ✓ | ✓ |
| Teachers taught to protect themselves from HIV preservice | ✓ | ✓ | | ✓ | ✓ | NR | NR | ✓ | ✓ | | | ✓ | |
| Teachers taught to protect themselves from HIV in-service | NR | ✓ | ✓ | ✓ | ✓ | ✓ | ✓ | ✓ | ✓ | ✓ | ✓ | ✓ | ✓ |
| Teachers given HIV and AIDS training | ✓ | ✓ | ✓ | ✓ | ✓ | ✓ | ✓ | ✓ | ✓ | ✓ | ✓ | ✓ | ✓ |
| Teachers given HIV and AIDS training preservice | NR | ✓ | | ✓ | ✓ | NR | NR | ✓ | ✓ | | | ✓ | |
| Teachers given HIV and AIDS training in-service | ✓ | ✓ | ✓ | ✓ | ✓ | ✓ | ✓ | ✓ | ✓ | ✓ | ✓ | ✓ | ✓ |
| Teaching training materials for the primary level | ✓ | ✓ | ✓ | ✓ | ✓ | NR | ✓ | ✓ | ✓ | ✓ | ✓ | | ✓ |
| Teaching training materials for the secondary level | ✓ | ✓ | ✓ | ✓ | ✓ | NR | ✓ | ✓ | ✓ | ✓ | NR | ✓ | ✓ |
| Data collection on teachers trained and training materials in learning institutes | | ✓ | | ✓ | ✓ | | ✓ | ✓ | NR | | ✓ | ✓ | ✓ |

Source: O'Connell, Venkatesh, and Bundy 2009.
Note: NR = no response.

| Health and nutrition services | Anguilla | Antigua | Bahamas, The | Barbados | Belize | Dominica | Grenada | Guyana | Jamaica | St. Kitts and Nevis | St. Lucia | St. Vincent and the Grenadines | Trinidad and Tobago |
|---|---|---|---|---|---|---|---|---|---|---|---|---|---|
| Vaccinations for school-age children (SAC) | ✓ | ✓ | ✓ | ✓ | ✓ | ✓ | ✓ | ✓ | ✓ | ✓ | ✓ | ✓ | ✓ |
| School feeding provided for SAC | | ✓ | ✓ | ✓ | ✓ | ✓ | ✓ | ✓ | ✓ | ✓ | ✓ | ✓ | ✓ |
| Vitamin A capsules provided for SAC | | | | | ✓ | NR | NR | | NR | | | ✓ | |
| Iron supplementation program for SAC | | | | ✓ | ✓ | NR | ✓ | | NR | | | ✓ | |
| Deworming program for SAC | ✓ | | | ✓ | ✓ | ✓ | NR | ✓ | NR | ✓ | | ✓ | ✓ |
| Reproductive health services for SAC | ✓ | ✓ | ✓ | ✓ | ✓ | ✓ | ✓ | ✓ | ✓ | ✓ | ✓ | ✓ | |
| Counseling services for teachers | ✓ | ✓ | ✓ | ✓ | ✓ | ✓ | ✓ | ✓ | NR | ✓ | ✓ | ✓ | ✓ |
| Dengue prevention services for SAC | ✓ | | ✓ | ✓ | ✓ | ✓ | ✓ | ✓ | NR | ✓ | NR | ✓ | ✓ |
| Medical examinations for SAC | ✓ | | ✓ | ✓ | ✓ | | NR | | ✓ | ✓ | ✓ | ✓ | ✓ |
| Hearing and sight examinations for SAC | ✓ | | ✓ | ✓ | ✓ | ✓ | ✓ | ✓ | ✓ | ✓ | ✓ | ✓ | ✓ |

*Source:* O'Connell, Venkatesh, and Bundy 2009.
*Note:* NR = no response.

| Support to MoE SHN and HIV responses | Anguilla | Antigua | Bahamas, The | Barbados | Belize | Dominica | Grenada | Guyana | Jamaica | St. Kitts and Nevis | St. Lucia | St. Vincent and the Grenadines | Trinidad and Tobago |
|---|---|---|---|---|---|---|---|---|---|---|---|---|---|
| NGOs contracted by MoE to support HIV education | | | | ✓ | ✓ | | ✓ | ✓ | ✓ | | | ✓ | ✓ |
| Private sector working with MoE to support HIV education | | ✓ | ✓ | ✓ | ✓ | | ✓ | | | ✓ | ✓ | ✓ | |
| Receipt of Fast Track Initiative (FTI) funding | | | NR | | | | NR | ✓ | NR | | | | NR |

*Source:* O'Connell, Venkatesh, and Bundy 2009.
*Note:* NR = no response.

## References

Bundy, D. A. P., T. E. O'Connell, E. Abrioux, S. Baker, and L. J. Drake. 2009. "School Health, Nutrition, and HIV/AIDS Programming: Promising Practice in the Greater Mekong Sub-Region." World Bank, Washington, DC.

O'Connell, T. E., M. Venkatesh, and D. A. P. Bundy. 2009. "Strengthening the Education Sector Response to School Health, Nutrition, and HIV/AIDS in the Caribbean Region: A Rapid Survey of 13 Countries." World Bank, Washington, DC.

World Bank. 2007. "Accelerating the Education Sector Response to HIV/AIDS in Sub-Saharan Africa: A Rapid Situation Analysis of 34 Countries." Prepared for the Networks of African Ministry of Education HIV/AIDS Focal Points 2nd Annual Meeting, Nairobi, Kenya, November.

# Index

Boxes, figures, maps, notes, and tables are indicated by *b*, *f*, *m*, *n*, and *t*, respectively.

**Map 1.1    Poverty: Percentage of Population Living in Households with Per Capita Consumption or Income below the Poverty Line**

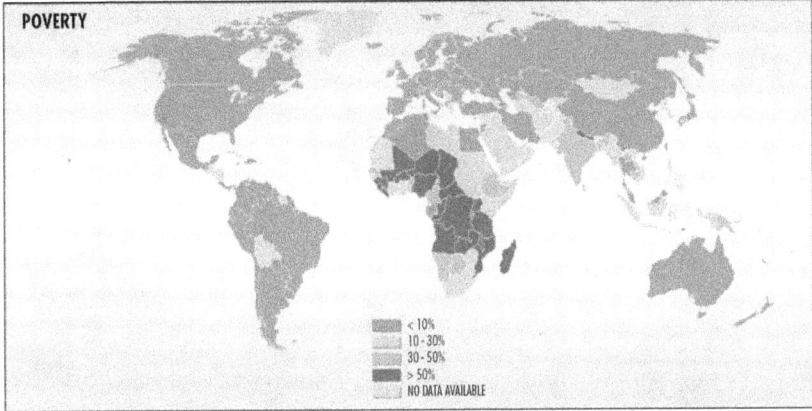

POVERTY

< 10%
10 - 30%
30 - 50%
> 50%
NO DATA AVAILABLE

*Source:* Bundy et al. 2009.
*Note:* The poverty line estimates use purchasing power parity exchange rates for latest available year.

**Map 1.2    Hunger: Percentage of Population below the Minimum Level of Dietary Energy Consumption, 2002–05**

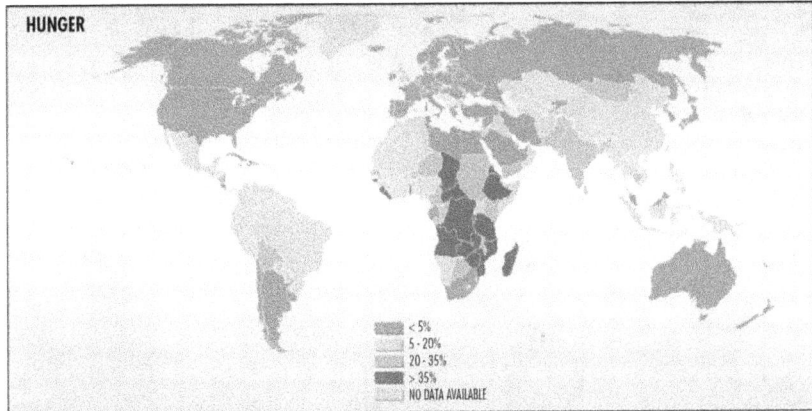

HUNGER

< 5%
5 - 20%
20 - 35%
> 35%
NO DATA AVAILABLE

*Source:* Bundy et al. 2009.
*Note:* The proportion of the population below the minimum level of dietary energy consumption, referred to as the prevalence of undernourishment, is the percentage of the population that is undernourished or food deprived. Figures are from latest available year. Standards derived from an FAO/WHO/UNU Expert Consultation (FAO, WHO, and UN University 2004).

## Map 1.3  Primary School Completion Rate, 2000–06

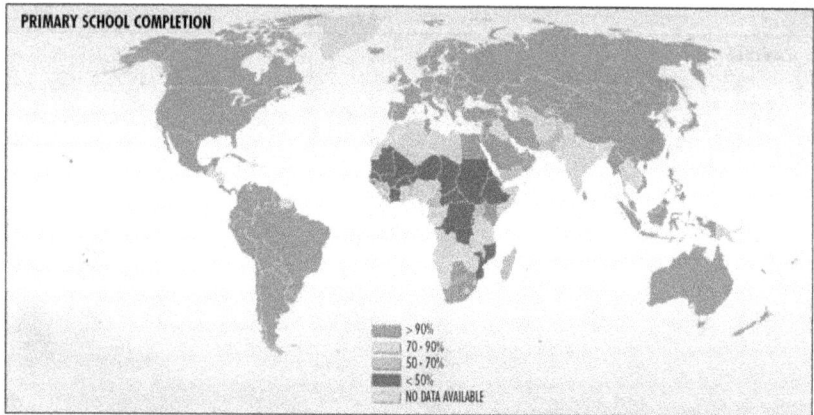

PRIMARY SCHOOL COMPLETION

> 90%
70 - 90%
50 - 70%
< 50%
NO DATA AVAILABLE

Source: Bundy et al. 2009.
Note: Primary completion rate is the total number of students in grade 6 (excluding repeaters) divided by the total number of children of grade age. Figures are from latest available year. All data are from the UNESCO Institute for Statistics except for Australia, Canada, China, Japan, New Zealand, Sweden, Thailand, and the United Kingdom, which are from national data.

## Map 1.4  School Feeding: Country Programs, 2006–08

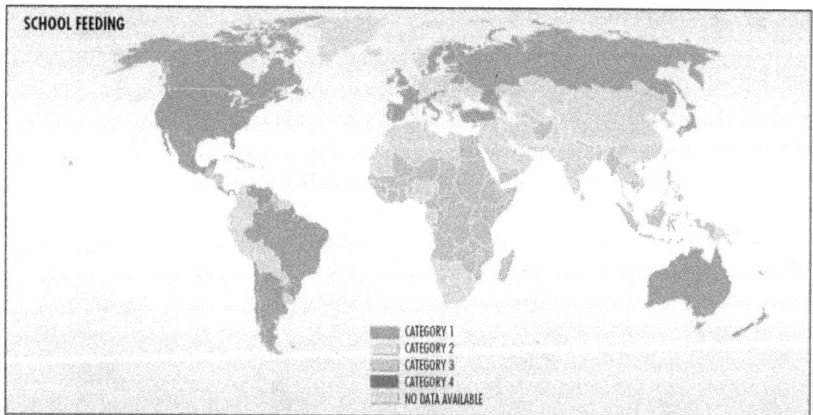

SCHOOL FEEDING

CATEGORY 1
CATEGORY 2
CATEGORY 3
CATEGORY 4
NO DATA AVAILABLE

Source: Bundy et al. 2009.
Note: Category 1 = countries where school feeding is available in most schools, sometimes or always; category 2 = countries where school feeding is available in some way and at some scale; category 3 = countries where school feeding is available primarily in the most food-insecure regions; category 4 = countries where there is no school feeding. The sources are World Food Programme data for low-income and lower-middle-income countries and national data for the remaining countries. Because this is a work in progress, comments and any further information on school feeding programs are welcomed.

## Map B4.2　STH Prevalence in Kenya

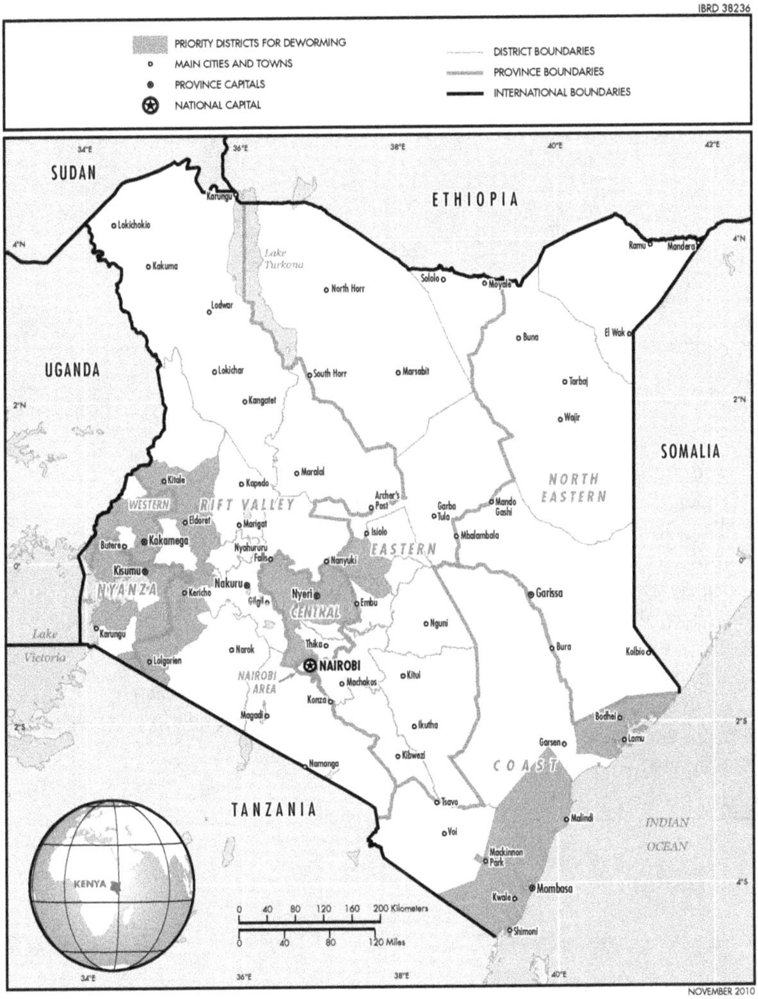

Source: Brooker, Clements, and Bundy 2006.

www.ingramcontent.com/pod-product-compliance
Lightning Source LLC
Chambersburg PA
CBHW050458270326
41927CB00009B/1804